Four Hundred Years
of Shakespeare
in Europe

Four Hundred Years of Shakespeare in Europe

Edited by
A. Luis Pujante and
Ton Hoenselaars

With a Foreword by Stanley Wells

Newark: University of Delaware Press
London: Associated University Presses

© 2003 by Rosemont Publishing & Printing Corp.

All rights reserved. Authorization to photocopy items for internal or personal use, or the internal or personal use of specific clients, is granted by the copyright owner, provided that a base fee of $10.00, plus eight cents per page, per copy is paid directly to the Copyright Clearance Center, 222 Rosewood Drive, Danvers, Massachusetts 01923. [0-87413-812-4/03 $10.00 + 8¢ pp, pc.]

Other than as indicated in the foregoing, this book may not be reproduced, in whole or in part, in any form (except as permitted by Sections 107 and 108 of the U.S. Copyright Law, and except for brief quotes appearing in reviews in the public press.

Associated University Presses
2010 Eastpark Boulevard
Cranbury, NJ 08512

Associated University Presses
Unit 304
The Chandlery
50 Westminster Bridge Road
London SE1 7QY, England

Associated University Presses
P.O. Box 338, Port Credit
Mississauga, Ontario
Canada L5G 4L8

The paper used in this publication meets the requirements of the American National Standard for Permanence of Paper for Printed Library Materials Z39.48-1984.

Library of Congress Cataloging-in-Publication Data

Four hundred years of Shakespeare in Europe / edited by A. Luis Pujante and Ton Hoenselaars ; with a foreword by Stanley Wells.
    p. cm.
  Includes bibliographical references and index.
  ISBN 0-87413-812-4 (alk. paper)
  1. Shakespeare, William, 1564–1616—Appreciation—Europe. 2. Shakespeare, William, 1564–1616—Stage history—Europe. 3. Shakespeare, William, 1564–1616—Translations—History and criticism. 4. Shakespeare, William, 1564–1616—Influence. I. Pujante, Angel-Luis. II. Hoenselaars, A. J., 1956–
PR2971.E85 F68   2003
822.3'3—dc21   2002014506

PRINTED IN THE UNITED STATES OF AMERICA

Contents

Foreword STANLEY WELLS	7

Part I: Introductions

Shakespeare and Europe: An Introduction TON HOENSELAARS and A. LUIS PUJANTE	15
Constructing Shakespeares in Europe BALZ ENGLER	26

Part II: Appropriations

Shakespeare as a Character on the Spanish Stage: A Metaphysics of Bardic Presence KEITH GREGOR	43
Enter Shakespeare: The Contexts of Early Polish Appropriations MARTA GIBIŃSKA	54
Route 66: The Political Performance of Shakespeare's Sonnet 66 in Germany and Elsewhere MANFRED PFISTER	70
Shakespearean Fascist: A. K. Chesterton and the Politics of Cultural Despair G. D. WHITE	89
Shakespeare: Man of the Millennium BOIKA SOKOLOVA	98

Part III: Translations

More Alternative Shakespeares DIRK DELABASTITA	113
Telling What Is Told: Original, Translation, and the Third Text—Shakespeare's Sonnets in Czech MARTIN HILSKÝ	134
Royal and Bourgeois Translators: Two Late-Nineteenth- Century Portuguese Readings of *The Merchant of Venice* FILOMENA MESQUITA	145

Part IV: Productions

Shakespeare and the Cold War 163
  DENNIS KENNEDY

Spanish Productions of *Hamlet* in the Twentieth Century 180
  RAFAEL PORTILLO and MERCEDES SALVADOR

Apocalyptic Beginnings at the End of the Millennium:
Stefan Bachmann's *Troilus and Cressida* 196
  SYLVIA ZYSSET

Shakespeare's History Plays in Belgium: Taken Apart and
Reconstructed as "Grand Narrative" 211
  JOZEF DE VOS

Shakespeare on the French Stage: A Historical Survey 223
  ISABELLE SCHWARTZ-GASTINE

Bibliography: Shakespeare in European Culture 241
  TON HOENSELAARS

Contributors 260
Index 265

Foreword

Stanley Wells

THE 1990S WERE, AS TON HOENSELAARS AND A. LUIS PUJANTE outline in their introduction to this volume, which prints papers delivered in Spain at the end of that decade, a time of unprecedented activity in the study of the interaction between Shakespeare and Europe (and, it must be added, of the playwright's impact on the rest of the world as well). These years saw, too, an exceptional quantity of original work deriving from Shakespeare, as is witnessed by the appearance within five years (noted by Martin Hilský) of four different new translations of the Sonnets into Czech. The reasons for this activity are complex. They include the greater involvement of Britain in the European community, developments in the theory of translation study, the general increase in ease of communication, the resurgence of the Shakespeare film industry supplemented by the international availability of films on video, and, somewhat paradoxically, the increasing dominance of the English language as a medium of international communication. Those for whom English is not a native language have, perhaps, become more aware of their own linguistic heritage as they see it challenged from the West. And the fact that non-Anglophone Shakespeare scholars are, as the contents of this volume show, more willing and able to publish in English than many of them once were, gives English speakers less excuse for ignoring their contributions.

Encouraged but not excused by their geographical insularity, the English are, as some of us have acknowledged while not doing enough about it, notoriously lazy in the acquisition of foreign languages, shamed by the multilingualism of many of their overseas colleagues. This has been our loss: the study of Shakespeare's impact in countries and in languages other than those in which they originated can, as the essays printed here show, be a two-way process, blessing those who give as well as those who receive. Anyone who studies Shakespeare, a writer who during at least the last two centuries has increasingly permeated European consciousness, can only benefit from knowing more about his reception outside England and the U.S.

Though translation has long been "the Cinderella of Shakespeare studies," as Dirk Delabastita remarks in his trenchant, challenging, and somewhat chastening essay, it can (as he shows) result both in genuinely creative writing and in illuminating exploration of the text translated. Study of translated versions of the plays and (as Manfred Pfister brilliantly shows in his essay on the sociological and political uses to which Sonnet 66, largely ignored by native critics, has been put) the poems can illuminate the societies for which they were performed as well as telling us something about the range of meanings that the works can stimulate. Anyone who has read Pfister's essay will hear new overtones on every re-reading of "Tired with all these, for restful death I cry." And Martin Hilský, also writing on translations of sonnets, draws our attention to the "third text," that created by the reader in the space between the original texts and their linguistic transmutation.

Linguistic translation is not, of course, simply a matter of replacing the words and syntax in which the works were written with equivalents from the language into which they are translated. Both the culture of the recipient language and the social circumstances of the translator may influence the translation, as is clear from Filomena Mesquita's comparison of translations into Portuguese of *The Merchant of Venice*, one by King D. Luís of Portugal, the other by one of his subjects. But theatrical performance far more clearly demonstrates the susceptibility of plays to cultural translation. In the postwar period especially but by no means exclusively they have often been appropriated for political purposes, as Dennis Kennedy, who has done so much to awaken Anglo-American scholars to the interest and importance of studying European stagings of Shakespeare, makes clear.

It is largely because Shakespeare is a dramatist, writing in the knowledge that artists other than himself would make their contribution to the creative process, that his writings have proved so acceptable to cultures different in both place and in time from those for which they were conceived. Textually indeterminate and susceptible to wide ranges of interpretation though they are even in English, they change, sometimes drastically, in the process of translated performance. This has been so ever since Shakespeare's lifetime, when traveling players on the Continent gave heavily adapted versions of some of his plays, occasionally in English but more often in translation, in performances that are unlikely to have acknowledged his authorship. As we may read in several of the essays printed here, transmission of the texts in the eighteenth and nineteenth centuries often occurred at second or third hand, with translators in, for instance, Poland and Spain working from versions such as those of the ubiquitous Frenchman Jean-François Ducis, who spoke no English and himself translated and adapted, often drastically, from other men's translations. Lacking a single point of origin, derivative plays bear witness to the absorption of Shakespeare into the bloodstream of European civilization. A result is, as Balz Engler points out, that Shakespeare takes on the status of a maker, sometimes a transmitter, of myths, in plays relating no more directly to their ancestral texts than his own plays do to Homer, Ovid, or Boccaccio.

Engler's essay leaves us in no doubt that much remains to be done, and suggests some of the paths that future work might take. But the task is of its very nature unending; scholars will never be able to keep up with the European products of Shakespeare's creativity. In the mean time, this admirable volume both fills gaps and opens up new areas for research.

Four Hundred Years
of Shakespeare
in Europe

Part I
Introductions

Shakespeare and Europe: An Introduction

Ton Hoenselaars and A. Luis Pujante

MOST OF THE ARTICLES COLLECTED IN THIS VOLUME WERE ORIGInally presented as papers at a conference entitled *Four Hundred Years of Shakespeare in Europe*, which was organized by the University of Murcia (Spain) from 18–20 November 1999. The conference testified to a widely felt need to assess the cultural impact of Shakespeare on European culture from the Elizabethan period to the present, and to explore the possibility of a more permanent organization for further research into this area.

The Murcia conference was not an isolated venture. It took its cue from earlier conferences on related topics. In April 1990 Dirk Delabastita and Lieven D'hulst hosted the *European Shakespeares* conference at the University of Antwerp's Higher Institute for Translators and Interpreters. Concentrating on the romantic translation-as-appropriation of Shakespeare, the conference moved beyond the cases of French and German Shakespeare that had long received a privileged and isolated treatment, thus aiming, as the organizers put it in the introduction to their *European Shakespeares*, "to contribute to the study of Shakespeare translations on a truly European scale."[1] The Antwerp conference—with distinguished speakers including Werner Habicht, Yuri Levin, Theo Hermans, Kristian Smidt, and Péter Dávidházi—was certainly successful in its primary objective. Nevertheless, the organizers ended their assessment of the project on a critical note. Since translation studies had left behind the normative view of translation as one of linguistic transcoding and had instead come to recognize translation as a complex process of cultural transfer, Delabastita and D'hulst considered that one could only speak of a truly European initiative if a form of exchange were developed with Britain. This, they felt, was not yet sufficiently the case. As a result, *European Shakespeares* presented itself "not just as a supplement to recent Shakespeare studies, but in a way as a critical comment on its British insularity."[2]

A year after the Antwerp conference, with its predominantly historical focus, there followed the *Shakespeare in the New Europe* conference held in Sofia, Bulgaria, in 1993. The Sofia conference explicitly responded to the momentous events of 1989, when the razing of the Berlin Wall marked the disintegration of communist Eastern Europe into nation-states. The reunification of Germany soon followed, all at a time when Western Europe, laboring to secure an economic power base and promoting a supranational ideal of cosmopolitanism, was preparing to transform itself into the European Union by 1992. Given the exchange program between Sheffield and the Bulgarian academe, the Sofia conference had a strong British impulse behind it. As a result, its abundant proceedings—including papers by Jonathan Bate, Alexander Shurbanov, Boika Sokolova, Terence Hawkes, Michael Hattaway, Richard Burt, and Mark Sokolyanski—represented a variegated picture of the impact on Shakespearean scholarship and theatrical practice made by the commotion across Europe and beyond.[3] As Peter Holland put it, in a review that recognized *Shakespeare in the New Europe* as "one of the most exciting volumes in Shakespeare performance criticism to have appeared in many years":

> Analysis of Shakespeare production is too often Anglophone-centred and, within that, dominated by the work of the Royal Shakespeare Company. *Shakespeare in the New Europe* is a brilliant and powerful collection attesting to the world elsewhere, the rich cultures in which Shakespeare speaks, in which, indeed, he is the uniquely necessary voice, often speaking with many times the eloquence he currently attains in English.[4]

Given these fateful initiatives during the early 1990s, it seemed only natural that a Europe-oriented Shakespeare discussion should be planned for the third conference of the European Society of English Studies (ESSE), held in Glasgow, Scotland, in 1994. The resulting roundtable discussion was the initiative of Mariangela Tempera of the University of Ferrara, Italy.[5] It was at the Glasgow panel that most of those present first learned of Balz Engler's challenging initiative at Basel University, which included the production of a critical bilingual edition of Shakespeare, and the project now known as "Shakespeare in European Culture," or Sh:in:E. Conducting international research into the cultural history of Shakespeare, the project does not primarily concentrate on Shakespeare in individual national cultures. Instead, it focuses on the fate of Shakespeare as different European cultures come into contact with one another. It concentrates on forms of interaction that may be marked by processes of repression and destruction, as well as tolerance and emulation. In the ambitious Basel project, therefore, Shakespeare really functions as a *tertium comparationis*. He functions as a means of establishing whether there is "a European culture" in the first place, and his work, "especially in the shape of the classic dramatic texts," the organisers believe, "facilitates the comparison of ... geographically and historically different articulations." The twin question that a detailed and broad cultural analysis of Shakespeare must answer is whether one may indeed speak of "a European culture that goes beyond the common roots (re-constructed in the Renaissance) of Greek and Roman antiquity," or whether we should, perhaps, acknowledge that precisely "the diversity of cultures, like that of languages [is] characteristic of the notion of Europe."[6]

Though not primarily designed as a contribution to the rising wave of Europe-oriented Shakespeare studies, Dennis Kennedy's *Foreign Shakespeare* did much to encourage the unmistakable trend. Kennedy set out to complement the Anglocentric approach to Shakespeare in theater studies with a new perspective, namely that of a Shakespeare "performed outside of the English-speaking theatre," a Shakespeare performed "without his language."[7] Its relevance to the Shakespeare in Europe momentum, however, was almost a coincidence. As Kennedy himself acknowledges in the preface to *Foreign Shakespeare*:

> In objecting to Anglo-centric approaches to Shakespeare, the volume ... runs the risk of merely substituting European ones. To a certain extent this is inevitable, since most Shakespeare productions outside of English still occur in Europe, and European theatres have led the way in redefining performance models.[8]

It was in the wake of these developments that the Murcia conference sought to appraise the entire European heritage of Shakespeare from the earliest times until the end of the second millennium, and to consider future options. However, as A. Luis Pujante, the initiator of the Murcia conference, was to emphasize:

> [L]et us remind ourselves that the history of Shakespeare in Europe is also part of the history of European culture. Despite obvious differences, the various European countries share much more than they sometimes believe or are led to believe; if culturally they have a great deal in common, the work to do on Shakespeare in Europe will have to be done in common. Only in this way can safe comparisons be made and solid

conclusions drawn. And this must be done in a climate of professional coordination and cooperation, not in a spirit of retrospective competitiveness. To the best of my knowledge, such an enterprise has not been attempted so far, at least not in a comprehensive way. . . . [I]t will take time, but this should not deter those interested: at no other period has there been a better chance for Europeans to get to know each other and work together, and never before have research and information been made more accessible.[9]

Pujante's ideal met with full acclaim at the Murcia conference on *Four Hundred Years of Shakespeare in Europe*. The members of the conference unanimously agreed that the various initiatives that had sprung up in the course of the 1990s called for a new form of collaborative research into the European making and reception of Shakespeare, especially in non-English-speaking contexts. A new European research network would encourage research into specific national contexts, but also on various regional levels, thus advancing an exchange of information from archival collections and the development of appropriate methodologies that should increasingly permit a more accurate assessment of the constitutive role of Shakespeare in European culture as a whole. It was also agreed that, though centered around a specific Continent with a variegated and, also in global terms, certainly not always unproblematic past, the envisaged European research network for Shakespeare studies should not be exclusive in any way. Instead, it should continually invite new forms of interaction and exchange with other areas and fields, inside Europe and beyond.

As the bibliography that accompanies this volume amply illustrates, there has been no shortage of academic attention for Shakespeare in Britain or on the European Continent. A quick glance at the available material, however, reveals that from the British perspective, the Continent still seems rather isolated. In a similar way, though, the various individual national initiatives on the Continent seem rarely to collaborate. We may have indispensable studies like Jonathan Bate's *Shakespearean Constitutions*, Michael Dobson's *Making of the National Poet*, Péter Dávidházi's *The Romantic Cult of Shakespeare*, Wilhelm Hortmann's *Shakespeare on the German Stage*, or Zdeněk Stříbrný's valuable contribution to the Oxford Shakespeare Topics series, entitled *Shakespeare and Eastern Europe*, but there is as yet no equivalent to Michael Bristol's *Shakespeare's America / America's Shakespeare*.[10] A number of publications devote attention to specific national manifestations of Shakespeare, like the *Shakespeare Yearbook* (general editor, Holger

Klein), with volumes devoted to France, Hungary, Italy, and Japan. These are very valuable indeed, but one welcomes initiatives that explore cultural issues on a larger scale, like Minoru Fujita and Leonard Pronko's *Shakespeare East and West*, the University of Delaware Press series devoted to International Studies in Shakespeare and His Contemporaries (which occasionally adopts a supranational perspective), or the *Shakespeare Bulletin*'s annual winter issue devoted to international theater.[11]

One of the hazards involved in propagating new, collaborative Shakespearean research along the lines sketched above is the charge of Eurocentrism. However, the scholars involved in the project hold the view that Eurocentrism must never be the ideology of the group's researchers. At best, Eurocentrism features on the list of themes for research. Team members acknowledge that there is no continent whose history—be it Greek, Roman, or Medieval—has fed more conspicuously into the production of Shakespeare's own work than Europe. They also, however, recognize the excessive degree to which, in later centuries, the ideology of European nations was associated with the image of Shakespeare, as, together, they achieved their politico-cultural expansion. The "Shakespeare in European Culture" initiative is brought into focus between the impact of Classical, Medieval, and Renaissance culture on the one hand, and, the variegated history of Shakespearean appropriation and dissemination in England, the British Isles, and continental Europe on the other. It nearly goes without saying that it is first and foremost a supranational type of expertise that may best appraise and chart this phenomenon. The broader the range of researchers and the more comparative their approach, the more successful this joint research network will be. In a responsible academic community, there would, as in the case of *Foreign Shakespeare*, prove to be "no such thing as a 'European value system' for Shakespeare."[12] Instead, this community would combine an interest in Shakespearean reception with a vigorous exchange of values and methods.

In his introductory contribution on "Constructing Shakespeares in Europe," Balz Engler conceptualizes the breadth and variety of what he calls the "re-production" of Shakespeare in Europe. He does so by proposing a research framework that is comprised of three types and three stages. Engler identifies three main fields in which this re-production may take place: scholarship, the theater, and "common culture." He further distinguishes the following possible phases: beyond the rules, beyond criticism, and beyond the text. Engler looks to the future and points to some areas—like

"Shakespeare in education" and "Shakespeare the man"—that, he believes, should receive more attention in the study of Shakespeare in European culture.

Keith Gregor shows how Spain has greatly contributed to the image of Shakespeare as a "man of the theater," and did so even before his plays had been performed or heard of in that country. Gregor sheds original new light on the Bard's presence in Spain as a stage character and a cultural icon, tracing the historical development from *Shakespeare enamorado* [Shakespeare in love, 1828] and *Guillermo Shakespeare* [William Shakespeare, 1853]—respectively based on a French play and a French novel—via Manuel Tamayo y Baus's *Un drama nuevo* [A new play] of 1867 (successful both in Spain, France, Italy, Germany, and the U.S.), to Jaime Salom's *El otro William* [The other William, 1998].

Marta Gibińska, too, devotes attention to the early reception of Shakespeare. In Poland this took place through adaptations in the theater—as Shakespeare was not read there until the second half of the nineteenth century—and was bound up with Enlightenment culture as well as contemporary politics, including the political collapse of the country. In her paper, Gibińska, among other things, draws attention to the individual Polish voices in the eighteenth century who, rather uncommonly, did not join the familiar neoclassical opposition to Shakespeare. She further discusses the early German influence in Shakespeare's favor (Lessing, Goethe), the active role played by directors of Polish theaters (Bogusławski, Kamiński), and the later influence of Schlegel promoting a more "organic" and authentic Shakespeare.

In his contribution to the section on appropriations, Manfred Pfister illustrates how Shakespeare's Sonnet 66 has been looked upon with indifference by Anglo-American critics, whereas its voice of protest has found favor in a number of European countries during the twentieth century. Though it does not seem to have been used critically by dissidents in Mussolini's Italy, Franco's Spain, or Salazar's Portugal, this sonnet has been frequently appropriated in Germany and Eastern European countries, particularly when these were "tongue-tied by authority," as Manfred Pfister shows in his well-documented survey. Drawing on critical writings and manifold translations, as well as theatrical productions and musical settings (including one by Dimitri Shostakovich), Pfister traces the fortunes of a Shakespearean sonnet whose surprising political potential has long spoken across geographical and historical barriers.

As Graham White indicates, the political appropriation of Shakespeare in Europe may also adopt a rather grim appearance. Although the Fascists were never in power in Britain, British Fascism shared with its continental counterparts a denunciation of the cultural decay that followed the First World War and an effort to bring about a process of regeneration. Graham White writes about the case of A. K. Chesterton, theater critic of the *Stratford Herald* and editor of the *Shakespeare Review* in the late 1920s, and internationally known as an ideologue of the far right, who championed Shakespeare as a cultural regenerator. Chesterton celebrated Shakespeare as a philosopher and as a bearer of eternal truths against the values of contemporary democracy. As White shows, through this idealization of Shakespeare's work as a transcendent category, Shakespeare could become "the inspiration for a monstrous English nationalism" that shared many features with the various European Fascisms rampant in the 1930s.

The choice of Shakespeare as "Personality of the Millennium" by listeners of BBC Radio 4 in 1998 leads Boika Sokolova to explore the importance of the Bard in Eastern Europe during the second half of the twentieth century. Sokolova shows how the openness and inconclusiveness of Shakespeare's plays is particularly well revealed in significant stagings of *Hamlet* in the former Communist countries (Grotowski, Dresen and Hamburger, Daniel, Lubomiv, Cernescu and Tsankov). Contrary to official cultural orthodoxy in these countries at the time, she argues, the Shakespearean theatre provided "a privately darkened emotional space" that made political dissent possible.

The section on translation is spearheaded by Dirk Delabastita. In his wide-ranging paper, Delabastita introduces an impressive diagram of metatextual relationships to map the variety of Shakespearean translation, and proceeds to point out what has been called "scandals of translation." Delabastita identifies "translation" as the Cinderella of Shakespeare studies. Although a small number of English-speaking scholars have in the past occupied themselves with this unique form of Shakespearean appropriation, most of their colleagues seem to have ignored the fact that translation ought to be acknowledged as a very real instance of "alternative" Shakespeare, denoting a field that holds unmistakable academic interest. This explains why, for example, the translating and editing of Shakespeare have never been systematically studied jointly, even when they share an obvious common ground. Delabastita continues to express the hope that one day we may be able to bridge the existing gap between two academic disciplines whose collaboration could only prove mutually illuminating.

Martin Hilský's contribution is best appreciated within the context of the four translations of Shakespeare's Sonnets into Czech, which appeared within a period of only five years during the 1990s. On the basis of this remarkable occurrence, Hilský, himself one of the five translators, examines the cultural, political, poetic, and linguistic implications of translating the Sonnets. Among other things, he shows how the plurality of translations affects our perception of literary texts; how in bilingual editions the meaning of the original is not reflected, but refracted; and how the interaction of the two texts side by side creates a "third [unprinted] text," which is "written" by the reader when reading or comparing the two printed ones. One of Hilský's conclusions is that translating Shakespeare is a way to be faithful to one's own culture.

Jorge Luis Borges has observed that a literary translator can translate *against* another. The case studied by Filomena Mesquita illustrates this remark perfectly. In effect, King D. Luís of Portugal's translation of *The Merchant of Venice* (1879) was followed by Bulhão Pato's translation of the same play in 1881. As Mesquita shows, Pato's version may be read as a direct response to the king's, notably one that transcended the linguistic boundaries: a "bourgeois" (republican) translation against a "royal" one, with all the literary, cultural, and political attitudes involved. Some of the linguistic choices provided by the two translations still prove culturally and ideologically revealing.

In the section devoted to stagings of Shakespeare, Dennis Kennedy concentrates on the years from 1945 until the mid-sixties, and illustrates how Western and Central European productions of Shakespeare were characterized by an attempt to recover and reconstruct values that were considered under threat or lost. However, discussing a range of postwar productions of *Richard II* in France and Italy, productions of *Hamlet* in Germany, and analyzing the theatrical appropriation of Shakespeare as a "cold warrior," Kennedy shows how the original humanism and ideology of these European productions eventually yielded to Shakespeare as "another product for marketing and display."

Rafael Portillo and Mercedes Salvador show that *Hamlet* is the Shakespearean play most frequently translated into Spanish, but not his most frequently staged play in Spain. Their survey of twentieth-century Spanish productions of *Hamlet* reveals how some productions used modern dress in this play for the first time (Santacana's in 1928), betrayed the influence of Francoist religious orthodoxy by making Hamlet a Roman Catholic (Luca de Tena's in 1949), broke away from the traditional stereotype of a doubting Hamlet (Tamayo's in 1961), or were presented as leading cultural events under the Socialist government (Plaza's in 1989). Given the play's high sensitivity to social and cultural developments, Portillo and Salvador predict an all-female Spanish *Hamlet* in the near future.

Sylvia Zysset examines the distinctive qualities of Stefan Bachmann's 1998 production of *Troilus and Cressida*—performed at both Salzburg (Austria) and Basel (Switzerland)—against the cultural background in which the performances took place. She points to the open and human attitude of the company director, who, far from using the actor as a pawn, respected his or her work as creative. Zysset discusses the reception of the performances by audience and critics in two centers as different as Salzburg and Basel, considering both the specific circumstances and the general expectations of German-speaking audiences, as contrasted with those in the Anglo-American world. Zysset's detailed account of the production shows how its blatantly contemporary elements were particularly apt in communicating the idea of the "Apocalypse" at the end of the twentieth century.

As the Flemish translator and adaptor Tom Lanoye has remarked, outside Britain the names Richmond and Kent are first associated with well-known cigarette brands. This may suggest that Shakespeare's histories travel badly. In his contribution to the section on Shakespeare staged, Jozef de Vos explains how Flemish producer Luk Perceval, in collaboration with Lanoye, presented Shakespeare's two tetralogies rewritten as an explicitly ahistorical trilogy, a postmodern reinterpretation in which the spectator had "no sense of witnessing a series of events from English history." In effect, what their 1997–98 production (entitled *Ten Oorlog* [Into battle]) proposed was to create "an impression of seven hundred years of humanity." De Vos discusses the change of costume, atmosphere, and acting styles from a vague past evoking the Middle Ages of Richard II to a contemporary cynical and violent society in the third part, as well as the way the text adapted itself gradually to these changes and even incorporated French, English, and American slang. Could Shakespeare get more "foreign"?

The final contribution to this volume illustrates how the Shakespeare industry has always had an important branch in France, particularly on the French stage. At present, as Isabelle Schwartz-Gastine notes, Shakespearean stagings in France actually outnumber productions of plays from the French classic repertoire. In her comprehensive historical survey, Schwartz-Gastine explains how this miraculous rise has come to pass, from the curious eighteenth-century adaptations of Jean-François Ducis to the contemporary experimentation by Antoine Vitez and Patrice Chéreau. Schwartz-

Gastine underlines significant details of the various productions in the past three centuries, but also pays attention to the type of French translation or adaptation used, as well as the social, cultural, and political contexts within which these stagings have taken place. One of her conclusions is that the present-day Shakespeare industry in France should, after all these years, perhaps, come to be recognized primarily as an independent manifestation of the native French cultural scene, liberated from a dependence on current English Shakespeare as a model or source of inspiration for its practice.

The Murcia conference of 1999 was prepared in the conviction that the political circumstances were different from those surrounding the Sofia conference, which took place just after the European map had been redrawn largely as a result of the collapse of the Soviet Empire. In the months leading up to the Murcia conference, the organizers were aware of a different historical narrative, aware of a process by which the European nations seemed to be rapidly proliferating while supranational and transnational organizations, notably the European Community, were being strengthened.[13] The question of cultural identity was being posed in a particularly fascinating way: there seemed to be a pan-European desire to define smaller cultural communities within political structures that were looking more like federations. The problem was particularly interesting, given the ambivalent position of the U.K., which, while undergoing a kind of "balkanization" itself (a process now known as devolution) was unable to launch itself into the European mainstream.

In some ways, it was felt, the history of "Shakespeare" intermeshed with these lines of cultural development. Shakespeare had been "appropriated" by a number of national cultures, while at the same time he had always been regarded as a European figure, an instrument for the definition of cultural and aesthetic change (at the time of the development of romanticism, for example), as the author of texts upon which political agendas might be inscribed, in the academy or in the theater, as a quarry for a pan-European lexis or collection of myths. The effect has been to "decenter" English Shakespeare: it was no longer necessary to regard translations or foreign Shakespeare performances as adaptations or fallings off from the native stock. Shakespeare seemed to constitute a cultural myth as potent as the myths of Greek and Roman culture, and the Bible—whose impact on his own work is beyond doubt—and as worthy of serious study. Against this background, the Murcia conference was devised as a moment at which to speak of new kinds of synthesis, new perspectives, new tools and materials for the examination of translation practice and theory, the history of performance and criticism, and the writing of cultural history. It is hoped that the newly established network for research into European Shakespeares will profit from these insights.

Notes

1. Dirk Delabastita and Lieven D'hulst, eds. *European Shakespeares: Translating Shakespeare in the Romantic Age* (Amsterdam: John Benjamins, 1993), 12.
2. Ibid., 21.
3. Michael Hattaway, Boika Sokolova, and Derek Roper, eds. *Shakespeare in the New Europe* (Sheffield: Sheffield Academic Press, 1994).
4. Peter Holland, "Shakespeare in the New Europe," *The European English Messenger* 6, no. 2 (1997), 75–77. The "velvet revolution" of 1989 also featured as the background to Marta Gibińska and Jerzy Limon's project around *Hamlet East-West*, with an international conference held in Gdańsk in September 1996. Its proceedings have been published as *Hamlet East-West*, edited by Marta Gibińska and Jerzy Limon (Gdańsk: Theatrum Gedanense Foundation, 1998).
5. The panel included: Christiane Bimberg (University of Dortmund), Balz Engler (University of Basel),Ton Hoenselaars (Utrecht University), Patricia Kennan (University of Parma), John McRae (University of Nottingham), Filomena Mesquita (University of Coimbra), Barbara Puschmann-Nalenz (University of Bochum), Alexander Shurbanov and Boika Sokolova (University of Sofia), Mariangela Tempera (University of Ferrara, chair).
6. The source of the quotations in the text is the project's website at Basel University: <www.unibas.ch/shine>.
7. Dennis Kennedy, ed. *Foreign Shakespeare: Contemporary Performance* (Cambridge: Cambridge University Press, 1993), xvii; and "Introduction: Shakespeare without His Language," 1–20.
8. Ibid., xvii–xviii.
9. A. Luis Pujante, "Spanish and European Shakespeares," *Folio* 6, no. 2 (1999), 18–38, 38.
10. Jonathan Bate, *Shakespearean Constitutions: Politics, Theatre, Criticism, 1730–1830* (Oxford: Clarendon Press, 1989); Michael Dobson, *The Making of the National Poet: Shakespeare, Adaptation, and Authorship, 1660–1769* (Oxford: Clarendon Press, 1992); Péter Dávidházi, *The Romantic Cult of Shakespeare: Literary Reception in an Anthropological Perspective* (London: Macmillan, 1998); Wilhelm Hortmann, *Shakespeare on the German Stage: The Twentieth Century* (Cambridge: Cambridge University Press, 1998); Zdeněk Stříbrný, *Shakespeare and Eastern Europe* (Oxford: Oxford University Press, 2000); and Michael D. Bristol, *Shakespeare's America/America's Shakespeare* (London: Routledge, 1990).
11. One regrets the passing of the Japanese translation journal *Shakespeare Worldwide*, and welcomes current attempts in Europe to resuscitate it.
12. Kennedy, *Foreign Shakespeare*, xviii.
13. The organizing committee of the Murcia conference consisted of Manfred Draudt (University of Vienna), Michael Hattaway (Sheffield University), Ton Hoenselaars (Utrecht University), A. Luis Pujante (Murcia University), and Alexander Shurbanov (Sofia University).

Constructing Shakespeares in Europe

Balz Engler

IN 1758 A COLLECTION OF PLAYS APPEARED IN BASEL, ENTITLED *NEUE Probstücke der englischen Schaubühne, aus der Ursprache übersetzet von einem Liebhaber des guten Geschmacks* [New specimen plays from the English stage, translated from the original by a devotee of good taste].[1] It offered translations into German of nine English tragedies, largely from the post-Restoration canon. In the second of the three volumes is *Romeo and Juliet*, in David Garrick's adaptation, the first translation of a Shakespeare play into German blank verse.

The editor and translator of the collection was Simon Grynäus (1725–99).[2] He had studied theology, traveled in England, and at the time of publication (1753–61) worked as an assistant to the Protestant parson of Strasbourg.[3] His list of more than fifty publications consists mainly of translations, many of them from English, among them Milton's *Paradise Regained* (1752), Young's *Satires* (1755 and 1756), and Thomson's *The Seasons* (1768), as well as a number of religious writings.[4]

His translation of *Romeo and Juliet* is obviously the one that is of most interest here. I need not discuss its quality (as his output indicates, Grynäus translated rather quickly).[5] Rather, I will note that the play appears in a collection of mainly eighteenth-century plays associated with middle-class culture. *Romeo and Juliet*, a play without kings and queens, with a setting among rival families of equal position and a conflict between social convention and love, is perhaps the Shakespearean tragedy most appropriate to a collection of this kind.

But why did Grynäus include it at all? In his preface he explains: "So far I have included only one play by Shakespeare in this collection, in order to find out whether a translation of his plays, complete and as literal as possible, would be welcome."[6] In other words, Grynäus was testing the waters for a complete translation of Shakespeare's plays, one that was as literal as possible, and one that would also take into account his verse. Grynäus made his test very cautiously; he used Garrick's adaptation to contemporary tastes rather than the originals. Obviously it was too early; Grynäus did not translate another Shakespeare play into German blank verse. Instead, Christoph Martin Wieland's prose translation of twenty-two plays began to appear four years later (in 1762) with a Zurich publisher, under the auspices of the critic Johann Jakob Bodmer.

This episode may serve to remind us of a time when Shakespeare's position was still uncertain; when the way he was to be presented had to be carefully adapted to the readiness of people to accept certain of his features; when the texts as originally published would as much harm Shakespeare's fame as help it.

In the following pages I shall propose a framework in which European Shakespeare reception may be conceptualized.[7] After a brief discussion of concepts, I shall sketch three types and three phases of reception. These will serve as a basis for suggesting directions in which, in my opinion, the study of Shakespeare reception in Europe should be moving.

If we are to look at "four hundred years of Shakespeare in Europe," the very notion involves concepts of increasing difficulty; and there is an additional term that needs to be mentioned in this context: *reception*. Only the first of these four may be undisputed. *Four hundred years*: It was on September 21, 1599, that Thomas Platter recorded seeing *Julius Caesar* in London, an important record of a contemporary Shakespeare performance, and one by a Continental—a European?—observer.[8] I should note, perhaps, considering the status that Shakespeare would later acquire, that the name of the author is not even mentioned.

But even this date may be questioned. Depending on one's perspective, it may be tempting to take as a starting point the first critical opinion on Shakespeare ever published outside England, which seems to have been in the preface to Antonio Conti's tragedy *Il Cesare,* published circa 1726—"Sasper è il Cornelio degl'Inglesi" [Shakespeare is the Corneille of the English].[9]

Shakespeare is a more difficult concept. Does the term refer to a person, to a set of printed texts, to a cultural icon, to a theatrical tradition, or to a combination of all of these? I take the position that it should definitely refer to all of these, and should additionally take into account the way they are related to each other. In recent decades, the focus of criticism may have been on the printed texts and on theatrical tradition, but this need not be so.

Reception is a useful term because it suggests less passivity on our part than *influence*—perhaps the kind of politeness we show to an honored guest. It also suggests less violence than the notion of *appropriation*, which suggests kidnaping rather than welcoming, as it is clearly meant to do in the title of Brian Vickers's controversial study.[10]

But do all these concepts describe what is actually going on? They are based on the notion of an encounter with something fixed and well-defined. But "Shakespeare" only comes into being when performed, whether on the page, on the stage, or elsewhere. Instead of influence, reception, or appropriation, I would therefore prefer *production*, and, in the case of something that has a tradition, *re-production*.

Europe is perhaps the most difficult term. It cannot simply be defined in terms of square miles. Like the concept of "Shakespeare," it is something constantly re-produced. This is most obvious, perhaps, when we consider its borders. The concept of its eastern border being in the Ural Mountains was introduced by a Russian geographer in the eighteenth century in order to make Russia a European country.[11] And in the west the border still seems to be uncertain. In England, people still cross the English Channel to get to what they think of as "Europe." And to what extent should our use of the concept take into account the way it has changed over time? To what extent should it be taken into account as a political projection, as something we are helping to create by talking about it?[12] The legacy of nationalism both resists a definition of Europe and is a characteristic part of it, especially in literary study, which was often employed as a handmaiden in the founding of nations.

Linking the four terms, *Four centuries—Shakespeare—reception—Europe*, no matter what definitions one uses, produces an area so vast, so various, so ill-defined, and so important at this particular historical moment, that the task of giving an account of it is daunting. But people have tried.

Surveys are bound to be selective, superficial, or reductive. I should like to mention a few representative examples of studies that cover more than one country: J. G. Robertson, in his account of 1910, does not include Britain and juxtaposes only France and Germany.[13] Augustus Ralli, in his two-volume *History of Shakespeare Criticism* (1932) covering the period from the beginnings to 1925, organizes his evaluative summaries into chapters devoted to three countries: twenty-one to England (conveniently including the U.S. as well), six to France, and eleven to Germany.[14] In his groundbreaking anthology *Shakespeare in Europe* of 1963, Oswald

LeWinter offers us critical texts by writers from various Continental nations, including Russia. From the perspective of somebody born in Europe but living in the United States, he takes the existence of Europe as an entity for granted.[15] Klaus Peter Steiger's entertaining short account, *Die Geschichte der Shakespeare-Rezeption* [The history of Shakespeare reception], published in 1987, concentrates on episodes mainly from English and German history, but including two pages on Voltaire's rejection of Shakespeare ("Monsieur de Voltaire *vs.* Billy the Kid").[16]

Often such surveys have been the effort of collectives and have been restricted to specific areas or periods. I am thinking in particular of Delabastita and D'hulst's *European Shakespeares: Translating Shakespeare in the Romantic Age*, Bauer's *Das Shakespeare-Bild in Europa zwischen Aufklärung und Romantik*, or—a book that brilliantly catches a specific moment—Hattaway, Sokolova, and Roper's *Shakespeare in the New Europe*.[17]

Where these accounts cover a longer historical period they usually offer a genealogy, rooted in Shakespeare's works in English and dividing into national limbs and branches. In Robertson's account, for example, France and Germany are seen as dependent on England, the Romance countries, Poland and Russia as dependent on France, and Scandinavia on Germany—the Balkans, also complex in this case, are left out. But there is evidence that already at an early stage there were what one might call European correspondences across these lines. Voltaire's comparison of Shakespeare with Corneille, for example, almost literally repeats what Conti had said before in Italian;[18] and Johann Jakob Bodmer, who was influential in German Shakespeare reception, may have taken his idiosyncratic spelling *Sasper* from the same Italian source. And in case you are, in good European fashion, getting suspicious, it is an English not an Italian critic who has made these claims.[19]

There is also a fascinating moment in the round table at the end of *European Shakespeares,* where Michael Windross comments on the "almost monotonous regularity about the way Shakespeare entered the various national literatures." He suggests that this may have happened within other literary trends, as part of the Enlightenment interest in historical writing: "We have heard how translators of Shakespeare frequently relied on existent translations as their source. It was not, then, Shakespeare the poet who attracted them."[20] Although the answer fails to persuade me (can an interest in historical fiction have had such wide-ranging effects?), the observation is useful because it suggests that various European national cultures may have been ready to welcome Shakespeare at the same time and for the same reasons.

What can we learn from this brief survey? Obviously the task has proved too large for those who have tried to tackle it; the only hope is a network of the kind we are establishing here.

I shall therefore try to sketch a framework for what remains to be done. It offers for discussion three types of re-production and three phases of history. In his book *What Was Shakespeare: Renaissance Plays and Changing Critical Practice*, Edward Pechter distinguishes "various social practices by which we produce Shakespeare."[21] He names three institutions:

> Unlike Homer, Dante, Wordsworth, and other classics whose works thrive almost exclusively in university classrooms and in the writing of university professors, Shakespeare is still vital beyond the institutions of academic criticism and pedagogy. The major difference is the existence of a healthy theatrical tradition.... To make matters more complicated, there are versions of Shakespeare outside both the academy and the theater—in the streets, so to speak.... Shakespeare still has a substantial authority in the popular culture of the English-speaking world.[22]

Pechter's analysis clearly shows the perspective of the American professor.

Boldly claiming homogeneity for Europe, I should probably define the three institutions slightly differently. In particular I should assign a less prominent role to the university, and acknowledge the problems with simply calling *popular* all culture not associated with high-cultural institutions. I should want to reckon with a common culture existing beside and complementing education and the theater, associated with quality newspapers, radio programs, galleries, literature and its lonely readers, but also with media like cartoons and the cinema.

In these three areas, scholarship, the theater, and common culture—areas for which I would claim equal importance—we have been served in different ways.

As I have indicated, we do have histories of Shakespeare criticism. We do not have, however, studies of how Shakespeare has been taught—of how he has been re-produced—in schools and universities. Even in individual nations little work has been done in this field. I am aware of Ruth Freifrau von Ledebur's work on Germany after 1945, and Patricia Shaw's "Estudio y docencia de Shakespeare en la universidad española" [The study and the teaching of Shakespeare in Spanish universities].[23] This lack is, of course, due to a widespread lack of interest in the history of pedagogy. This may, however, be changing.[24]

The study of Shakespeare production in the theater is a well-established field, and there are impressive accounts of national histories, most recently Wilhelm Hortmann's *Shakespeare on the German Stage: The Twentieth Century*.[25] There are few accounts, however, that do not limit themselves to a single country. Among them, I am thinking of David Daniell's *"Coriolanus" in Europe*, but especially of Dennis Kennedy's *Foreign Shakespeare* and *Looking at Shakespeare*. They remind us of how much remains to be done.[26]

What we do not have is a history of Shakespeare re-production as part of what I have called common culture. There are single studies that are of considerable interest, particularly Brown and Fearon's classic on England *Amazing Monument: A Short History of the Shakespeare Industry* (which finds it difficult to take its topic seriously), Gary Taylor's notorious *Reinventing Shakespeare,* and, more recently, Barbara Hodgdon's *The Shakespeare Trade: Performances and Appropriations.*[27] The beginnings of Shakespeare re-production in this area are best served by Michèle Willems's *La genèse du mythe shakepearien* [The making of the Shakespeare myth].[28]

This takes me to the three phases I would like to distinguish. They are as schematic as the three types of re-production. In particular, they need not be contemporaneous in different parts of the world; in Europe, however—I have already referred to Michael Windross's comments—they seem to be relatively synchronous. I should provisionally like to label these phases: *beyond the rules, beyond criticism,* and *beyond the text.* I have deliberately chosen these tags so as not to suggest that one of them must be over for the other to begin; the moments of co-existence and conflict between them may often be the most interesting. I should like to comment on each of these in turn.

Shakespeare beyond the rules. The early history of European Shakespeare re-production in the eighteenth century, as we all know, was closely associated with the attempt to adapt or displace rule poetics. As this was an aristocratic poetics based on hierarchies, using Shakespeare to do so was also a political move.[29] Shakespeare, the son of the Stratford glover, appeared as a bourgeois hero, a great autonomous individual. Rule poetics was gradually replaced by a poetics of genius.

It is important to note here that it was not primarily the texts of

Shakespeare's works that were crucial, but rather what their author stood for. The definitive shape of the texts was still being established, and in any case they were often unknown yet. As Péter Dávidházi has reminded us, in many cases Shakespeare began to be revered as a cultural hero *before* his works were even available.[30]

There is an important European complication to this, which I have to introduce here as an aside. The version of the early history of Shakespeare reception I learned is the following: In the eighteenth century, the dead hand of all-powerful French classicist rule poetics lay on European writing and stifled all poetic innovation. Writers and critics were looking for a way to free themselves from its grip, and it was Shakespeare who helped them to loosen it. In this version, Voltaire is the villain—as he also appears in Steiger's *Geschichte der Shakespeare-Rezeption*—especially in his "Appel à toutes les nations de l'Europe" [Appeal to all nations of Europe] of 1761.

Not surprisingly, I learned this version in a German-speaking school and as a student of German—and it clearly shows an anti-French tendency.[31] Also unsurprisingly, such accounts are not appreciated in France. In a slightly intemperate manner, José Lambert has observed:

> Paradoxically, as Germany was quick to claim for itself a key role in promoting the genius of Shakespeare, moreover exploiting it in its anti-French policies, France continued to serve as an agent in establishing a new theatrical paradigm, which often seemed to be incompatible with French traditions. In fact, throughout Europe French commentaries were used as an introduction to Shakespeare, and the French translations often served as a model.[32]

Indeed, it can be shown that an educated German public (as people elsewhere) first got to know Shakespeare via the French translations of English periodicals like *The Spectator*, and that Voltaire's early promotion of Shakespeare (especially his translation of Hamlet's "To be or not to be" soliloquy) was crucial in this. That he later came to think that things had gone too far and needed to be stopped is a different matter.[33]

The national, even nationalist, dimension of Shakespeare re-production is certainly characteristic of Europe, having to do with the association of language and nation and the need to translate his works. But Shakespeare himself invited such national perspectives by writing plays on the history of his own nation at the beginning of a European age of nation states. In Germany this went as far, of course, as some extremists wanting a complete appropriation of him; the best account is that by Michelsen.[34]

But let me finish this aside. *Beyond the rules:* I note in conclusion that beginnings tend to have long-lasting effects: When cultural phenomena become visible as such, they acquire a definite shape that later re-productions will always imitate, vary, or react against, but which will not disappear.

The second phase, which I have labeled *beyond criticism*, begins with the triumph of the poetics of genius—with the romantic enthronement of Shakespeare as the creator per se. Once Shakespeare had acquired the status of a classic, it was no longer the critic who judged Shakespeare but Shakespeare who judged the critic. Shakespeare is celebrated as the creator of lifelike individuals, constructed like he himself as an author, which offer us patterns of identification. This produces a type of criticism that concentrates on the motives of Shakespearean figures. Some of the greatest Shakespeare criticism, notably Bradley's *Shakespearean Tragedy,* are part of this tradition. Critics who accept the premises of character criticism will view stage performance as irrelevant (like Bradley), or be hostile to it, because it distracts the critics from their task of reading the figures' minds.[35] The most striking example of such hostility is probably Charles Lamb on *King Lear* in his "On the Tragedies of Shakespeare" of 1811.[36] This is also the phase in which Shakespeare's text becomes sacred, and textual criticism tries to establish the one single, authentic, inspired text. Greg's *The Shakespeare First Folio* of 1955 is a monument to this.[37] In many respects this phase is still with us. Harold Bloom's strident apotheosis in *Shakespeare: The Invention of the Human,* published in 1999, ascribes the shape of Western humanity, *tout court,* to Shakespeare: "Shakespeare will go on explaining us, in part because he invented us."[38]

Finally, Shakespeare *beyond the text.* In this phase there is a new critical interest in theatrical production, as first impressively documented in Granville-Barker's *Prefaces to Shakespeare.*[39] It begins cautiously by unfolding the theatrical implications of the text, but also takes for granted that there is more than one possible version of doing a play. In this phase, the idea of the single text begins to dissolve. It begins to be accepted that there may be more than one Shakespearean text, for example, due to revision. And quite practically, various critical texts, all claiming authority for themselves, exist beside each other—not only for marketing reasons. The same trend leads to critics beginning to be interested in foreign Shakespeare and in translations, even to theaters doing productions in more than one language, like Karin Beyer's Düsseldorf production of *A Midsummer Night's Dream* (premiere 31 October 1995). The text, and with it language, is losing its central role. As with the popular ballad, various versions exist beside each other, which recognizably share certain figures and their constellations, certain stories, and certain motives. To put it provocatively, Shakespeare has acquired a position similar to the one poetry used to have in an oral society.[40]

By way of a conclusion, I should like to turn to what research is to be done in the area of European Shakespeare reception. Obviously, in all three types of re-production I have mentioned, much work remains to be done, especially if the European dimension is to be taken as seriously as it deserves. In particular, the history of Shakespeare in education should receive more attention than it has in the past. But I should like to concentrate on an area in which the last type and the last phase of re-production meet: common culture beyond the text. Here I see the following areas in particular where useful new work is to be done in and for Europe.

We should extend the study of how Shakespeare has been constructed beyond the beginnings (where we are relatively well served) into the nineteenth and twentieth centuries; and we should study how this has been done in various countries. The aims in doing so will be different from those of Samuel Schoenbaum, who has taught us so much about the history of Shakespeare in his classic *Shakespeare's Lives*. He describes his book "as a novel species of Shakespearian biography, with the protagonist gradually emerging from the mists of ignorance and misconception, to be seen through a succession of different eyes and from constantly shifting vantage points."[41] Instead of *mists* we should speak of *myths*, and not consider them in terms of ignorance and misconception but of constituting what Shakespeare has meant at different times in different places.

We should then be interested in not only Shakespeare the man but also the figures of his plays—as the protagonists in novels and plays, as the object of reverence in sacred places like Stratford and Verona, as the subjects of painting and sculpture, and the like. We should be interested in Shakespeare as the hero of cartoons and films. *Shakespeare in Love,* significantly, uses elements of *Romeo and Juliet* in constructing its hero. The film suggests that biography leads to art; we, as an audience, know that it is the other way round.

We may even show renewed interest in an area that has been

much neglected, even despised, in authorship theories. But we would do so not because we are looking for truth and authenticity, but because we want to know why and how people came to form such strong opinions about this problem. From a European perspective, it may be good to know that there have been, as far as I can see, not only English, but also Irish, French, and Italian candidates, but no German ones.[42]

We can also take the relative stability produced by the second phase I have posited and use it for the comparison of cultures. Patricia Shaw has observed that in Spain the most popular Shakespeare plays were (in this order) *Hamlet* and *Macbeth*, *Romeo and Juliet*, *Othello*, *Julius Caesar* and *The Taming of the Shrew*, *The Merchant of Venice*, and *King Lear*.[43] It may be difficult to determine the respective places of plays in such a popularity contest, but the results would certainly look different in different countries. Why?

Translation is usually studied in terms of a comparison between the work in the source and in the target language. But this is not the only possibility. If we compare translations into various languages with each other, using Shakespeare's English text as a *tertium comparationis*, as it were, we can learn about how different cultures and languages cope with specific issues. One area that lends itself specifically to this kind of study is metaphor, which has interested us in the Basel *Shakespeare in Europe* project. Also, preparing bilingual critical editions at Basel, we have also become aware of how different cultures need different kinds of explanation—an area that offers itself for more detailed study.

Finally, the presence of Shakespeare's works in the discourse of various cultures casts light both on the history of Shakespeare reproduction and the respective cultures. Some figures, allusions, and quotations may be present in most European languages, often without people being aware of their origins. Hamlet's "To be or not to be" is a case in point. Ultimately, Voltaire is probably responsible for this; but how, for example, could it become one of Hitler's favorite phrases, albeit with quite a different meaning? Preliminary research on *Hamlet* in Basel has shown that not only have different quotations become proverbial in different countries, but the same quotations may also be used in different ways.

Much work, then, remains to be done, work of different kinds, work illuminating widely different areas, but work also that will help us to understand what Shakespeare was at different times in different places—his various authenticities, as it were. This issue may be of special urgency in Europe at this particular moment, but it is vital to cultures in all parts of the world.

Notes

1. Simon Grynäus, *Neue Probstücke der englischen Schaubühne, aus der Ursprache übersetzet von einem Liebhaber des guten Geschmacks* (Basel: J. J. Schorndorff, 1758). The collection contains mainly tragedies. In volume 1: Edward Young, *The Revenge* (1721), Joseph Addison, *Cato* (1713), Edward Young, *Busiris* (1719). In volume 2: John Dryden and Nathaniel Lee, *Oedipus* (1678), Thomas Otway, *The Orphan* (1680), William Shakespeare, *Romeo and Juliet* (Garrick adaptation, 1748). In volume 3: William Congreve, *The Mourning Bride* (1697), William Mason, *Elfrida: A Dramatic Poem* (1752), Nicholas Rowe, *The Fair Penitent* (1703).

2. He was a distant relative of the Renaissance scholar of the same name. See Hans Küry, *Simon Grynäus von Basel 1725–1799, der erste deutsche Uebersetzer von Shakespeares Romeo und Julia* (Riehen/Basel: Schudel, 1935).

3. Later he was deacon in the parish of St. Peter in Basel.

4. Küry offers a list of these (*Simon Grynäus*, 15–17).

5. As a reviewer wrote on Grynäus's Shakespeare translation: the lines are "sometimes so stumbling, the euphony and the caesuras so much missing, in brief, so—Swiss, that we should much prefer harmonious prose to such verse" [bisweilen so holpricht, die Harmonie und der Abschnitt so verabsäumt, kurz, so schweizerisch, dass wir eine wohlklingende Prose diesen Versen weit vorziehen würden]. Review in *Bibliothek der schönen Wissenschaften* 6 (1758), 60ff (quoted by Küry, *Simon Grynäus*, 67).

6. Küry, *Simon Grynäus*, 11. "Ich habe nur ein einziges Stück von dem Shakespeare dieser Sammlung bisher beygefüget, um zu erfahren, ob man es für gut halte, desselben Stücke allso ganz, und so viel als möglich buchstäblich in das Deutsche zu übertragen."

7. In doing exploratory work for this essay, I have found A. Luis Pujante's work particularly useful. See A. Luis Pujante, "Spanish and European Shakespeares: Some Considerations," in *Actas del XXI Congreso Internacional AEDEAN*, ed. F. Toda Iglesia et al. (Sevilla: Secretariado Publicaciones de la Universidad de Sevilla, 1999), 17–33. Reprinted in *Folio* (Shakespeare Society of the Low Countries), 6, no. 2 (1999), 17–38.

8. On the Platter family, see Emmanuel Le Roy Ladurie, *Le Siècle des Platter, 1499–1628*, 2 vols. (Paris: Fayard, 1995–2000).

9. Antonio Conti, *Il Cesare* (Faenza: G.A. Archi, 1726), 54–55.

10. Brian Vickers, *Appropriating Shakespeare: Contemporary Critical Quarrels* (New Haven: Yale University Press, 1993).

11. Eric J. Hobsbawm, "Welchen Sinn hat Europa?" *Die Zeit*, 4 October 1996, 40.

12. Another issue: Speaking of European Shakespeare reception, where does the United States come in? To what extent should it be considered as a product of Europe, to what extent has Europe been shaped as a counter-image to the United States in recent years? The scope of my paper does not allow me to discuss this question.

13. J. G. Robertson, "Shakespeare on the Continent," in *The Cambridge His-*

tory of English Literature, ed. A. W. Ward and A. R. Waller, vol. 5, part 1 (Cambridge: Cambridge University Press, 1910), 282–308.

14. Augustus Ralli, *A History of Shakespeare Criticism*, 2 vols. (London: Oxford University Press, 1932).

15. This is how we have to read the first sentence of his introduction: "The history of Shakespeare criticism on the Continent is the history of the development of European consciousness since the sixteenth century." See Oswald LeWinter, ed., *Shakespeare in Europe* (Cleveland: World Publishing Company, 1963), 15.

16. Klaus Peter Steiger, *Die Geschichte der Shakespeare-Rezeption* (Stuttgart: Kohlhammer, 1987), 75–77.

17. Dirk Delabastita and Lieven D'hulst, eds., *European Shakespeares: Translating Shakespeare in the Romantic Age* (Amsterdam: John Benjamins, 1993); Roger Bauer, ed., *Das Shakespeare-Bild in Europa zwischen Aufklärung und Romantik* (Bern: Peter Lang, 1988); and Michael Hattaway, Boika Sokolova, and Derek Roper, eds., *Shakespeare in the New Europe* (Sheffield: Sheffield Academic Press, 1994).

18. "Sasper è il Cornelio degl'Inglesi, ma molto più irregolare del Cornelio, sebbene al pari di lui pregno di grandi idee, e di nobili sentimenti" [Shakespeare is the Corneille of the English, much less regular than Corneille, even though equal to him where grand ideas and noble emotions are concerned]. See Antonio Conti, *Il Cesare* (Faenza: G.A. Archi, 1726), 54–55. Voltaire, in his eighteenth "Lettre philosophique": "Shakespeare, qui passoit pour le Corneille des Anglais, fleurissoit à peu près dans le temps de Lope de Vega: il créa le théâtre" [Shakespeare, who may be considered as the Corneille of the English, flourished at the time of Lope de Vega: he created the theater]. Quoted by Gaby Petrone Fresco, *Shakespeare's Reception in 18th Century Italy: The Case of Hamlet*, Europäische Hochschulschriften, Series XVIII:70 (Bern: Peter Lang, 1993), 52.

19. Robertson, "Shakespeare on the Continent," 1923.

20. Frank Peeters, "Round Table," in *European Shakespeares,* edited by Delabastita and D'hulst, 238.

21. Edward Pechter, *What Was Shakespeare? Renaissance Plays and Changing Critical Practice* (Ithaca, NY: Cornell University Press, 1995), 2.

22. Ibid., 2.

23. Ruth Freifrau von Ledebur, *Deutsche Shakespeare-Rezeption seit 1945* (Frankfurt am Main: Akademische Verlagsgesellschaft, 1974); and Patricia Shaw, "Estudio y docencia de Shakespeare en la universidad española" [The study and teaching of Shakespeare in Spanish Universities] in *Shakespeare en España: Crítica, traducciones y representaciones*, edited by José Manuel González (Alicante/Zaragoza: Universidad de Alicante/Libros Pórtico, 1993), 95–117.

24. See Balz Engler and Renate Haas, eds., *European English Studies: Towards the History of a Discipline* (Leicester: The English Association for ESSE, 2000).

25. Wilhelm Hortmann, *Shakespeare on the German Stage: The Twentieth Century* (Cambridge: Cambridge University Press, 1998).

26. David Daniell, *"Coriolanus" in Europe* (London: Athlone Press, 1980); Dennis Kennedy, ed., *Foreign Shakespeare: Contemporary Performance* (Cambridge: Cambridge University Press, 1993); and Dennis Kennedy, *Looking at Shakespeare: A Visual History of Twentieth-Century Performance* (Cambridge: Cambridge University Press, 1993).

27. Ivor Brown and George Fearon, *Amazing Monument: A Short History of the Shakespeare Industry* (London: Heinemann, 1939); Gary Taylor, *Reinventing Shakespeare: A Cultural History from the Restoration to the Present* (London: Ho-

garth Press, 1990); and Barbara Hodgdon, *The Shakespeare Trade: Performances and Appropriations* (Philadelphia: University of Pennsylvania Press, 1998).

28. Michèle Willems, *La genèse du mythe shakespearien, 1660–1780* (Paris: Presses Universitaires de France, 1979).

29. This point is explicitly made by Voltaire: Corneille "was uneven like Shakespeare and full of genius like him; but Corneille's genius compared with Shakespeare's is as a lord with respect to a man of the people born with the same intelligence" [était inégale comme Shakespeare, et plein de génie comme lui; mais le génie de Corneille était à celui de Shakespeare ce qu'un seigneur est à l'égard d'un homme du peuple né avec le même esprit que lui]. See Voltaire, "Observation sur le *Jules César* de Shakespeare," in *Voltaire, La mort de César*, edited by A. M. Rousseau (Paris: Société d'Edition d'Enseignement Supérieur, 1964), 192.

30. Péter Dávidházi, *The Romantic Cult of Shakespeare: Literary Reception in an Anthropological Perspective* (London: Macmillan, 1998).

31. Jonathan Bate has written on the political implications of romantic Shakespeare reception in "The Politics of Romantic Shakespeare Criticism: Germany, England, France," *European Romantic Review* 1, no. 1 (1990), 1–26.

32. "Le paradoxe est que, si l'Allemagne se donne vite un rôle-clef dans la propagation du génie shakespearien, en l'exploitant d'ailleurs dans sa politique anti-française, la France elle-même va continuer à fonctionner comme médiatrice dans l'établissement d'un nouveau paradigme théâtral qui paraît souvent incompatible avec les traditions françaises. En effet, l'Europe entière utilisera certains commentaires français pour s'initier à Shakespeare, et les traductions françaises servent souvent de modèle." See José Lambert, "Shakespeare en France au tournant du XVIIIe siècle: Un dossier européen," in *European Shakespeares,* edited by Delabastita and D'hulst, 25–44, 30.

33. See Kenneth E. Larson, "Introduction: Traditions and New Directions in the Study of French and German Shakespeare Reception," *Michigan Germanic Studies* 15, no. 2 (1989), 103–13; and Arnold Miller, "Voltaire's Treason: The Translation of Hamlet's Soliloquy," *Michigan Germanic Review* 15, no. 2 (1989), 136–59.

34. Peter Michelsen, "Review of Lawrence Marsden Price, *Die Aufnahme englischer Literatur in Deutschland, 1500–1800*, Bern: Francke, 1961," *Göttingische Gelehrte Anzeigen* 220 (1968), 239–82.

35. A. C. Bradley, *Shakespearean Tragedy* (London: Macmillan, 1904).

36. Charles Lamb, "On the Tragedies of Shakespeare" (1811), in *Shakespeare Criticism: A Selection, 1623–1840*, edited by D. Nichol Smith (London: Oxford University Press, 1916), 190–212.

37. W. W. Greg, *The Shakespeare First Folio: Its Bibliographical and Textual History* (Oxford: Clarendon Press, 1955). This urge to define a single text is not, by the way, restricted to the English-speaking world; a similar tendency may be observed with the Schlegel-Tieck version in the German-speaking world.

38. Harold Bloom, *Shakespeare: The Invention of the Human* (London: Fourth Estate, 1999), xvii. We should note, perhaps, the constructivist twist here: It is not only Shakespeare's universal genius, but also the re-production of his works that has made us what we are.

39. Harley Granville-Barker, *Prefaces to Shakespeare* (London: Sigdwick and Jackson, 1927; reprint, London: Batsford, 1927–1947).

40. See Balz Engler, "Shakespeare's Passports," *International Shakespeare: The Tragedies*, edited by Patricia Kennan and Mariangela Tempera (Bologna: CLUEB, 1996), 11–16.

41. Samuel Schoenbaum, *Shakespeare's Lives* (Oxford: Oxford University Press, 1993), x.

42. See on these issues John Michell, *Who Wrote Shakespeare?* (London: Thames and Hudson, 1996); Schoenbaum, *Shakespeare's Lives*, 441; and Ina Schabert, ed., *Shakespeare-Handbuch* (Stuttgart: Alfred Kröner, 1992), 199. The Italians John Florio and his father Michelangelo Florio were proposed as candidates for authorship, as was the Frenchman Jacques Pierre, and the Irishman Patrick O'Toole.

43. The source of this claim is Eduardo Juliá, *Shakespeare en España* (Madrid: Tipografía de la Revista de Archivos, Bibliotecas y Museos, 1918), 96. Juliá refers to the late nineteenth and early twentieth centuries, and restricts himself to translations. The situation in the theater may well have been different. [See, in this respect, Rafael Portillo and Mercedes Salvador, "Spanish Productions of *Hamlet* in the Twentieth Century," in this volume. Eds.]

Part II
Appropriations

Shakespeare as a Character on the Spanish Stage: A Metaphysics of Bardic Presence

Keith Gregor

> The actor is the iconic sign *par excellence*: a real human being who has become a sign for a human being.
> —Martin Esslin, *The Field of Drama*

IN A WELL-KNOWN AND MUCH-CITED ESSAY, THE FRENCH PHILOSOpher Jacques Derrida explored the effects of what he described as a break or rupture in the concept of structure. The "event" that signaled this rupture was the exposure of the vacuity of the notion of a "center" or invariable presence at the heart of the discourses of the human sciences in which the concept of structure was paramount. The history of the latter, according to Derrida, is to be conceived as nothing more than

> a series of substitutions of center for center, as a linked chain of determinations of the center. Successively, and in a regulated fashion, the center received different forms or names. The history of metaphysics, like the history of the West, is the history of these metaphors and metonymies. Its matrix . . . is the determination of Being as *presence* in all senses of this word.[1]

With the erasure of the center, the self-repeating pillar of structure and its interpretation, the stage seemed set for a transcendence of what Derrida polemically called "man and humanism, the name of man being the name of that being who, throughout the history of metaphysics or ontotheology [. . .] has dreamed of full presence, the reassuring foundation, the origin and the end of play."[2]

Though it is always a dangerous activity to apply Derridean analyses to particular instances, a possible early symptom of the process the philosopher had in mind can be found in the evanescence in literary and, more specifically, Shakespeare studies of the all-pervasive figure of the author and a (post-romantic) insistence on the necessarily orphaned, impersonal nature of his work. The process in Shakespeare's case was, according to Richard Wilson, marked by the emergence of a modernist aesthetic that "began to revel . . . in the presumption that, as Mark Twain rejoiced, the playwright *'hadn't any history to record.* There is no getting around that deadly fact.'" In the very period when the positivist literary history of scholars like Sir Sidney Lee and E. K. Chambers was helping to establish Shakespeare as the best-known and most-documented of all Elizabethans, "a collective amnesia insisted that none of this counted, because, as [Henry] James averred, 'There should really, to clear the matter up, be no such Person. . . . There *is* no such Person.'"[3] As Wilson also goes on to contend, however, the more or less wilful Bardicide of writers like Twain, Henry James, Charles Dickens, and Matthew Arnold—or that of the historicism represented by G. Wilson Knight and E. M. W. Tillyard and their transatlantic successors, rallying to the Derridean cry "There is nothing outside the text"—is far from having supplanted the resilient notion of a Shakespearean "presence" in, behind, and beyond the texts attributed to him. The "Death of the Author" celebrated by Roland Barthes and the champions of a new New Critical "cultural poetics" has not entirely erased the figure of the Bard conceived, if not exactly in numinal terms as an invisible presence immune to material analysis—the "origin and owner of meaning" hallowed by nineteenth-century literary biography—then one conceived in cultural materialist terms as "a cultural construct determined by the representational practices of a particular historical era."[4] These "representational practices" do not of course exclude, and indeed are dominated by, the theater. And in this respect, Spanish theater presents an intriguing and illustrative example.

Despite its initial indebtedness to French adaptations of his work, Spain has played an extremely active role in fashioning an image of Shakespeare that is entirely consonant with his image in other European nations as a "man of the theater." The image is largely romantic and authorial—Shakespeare as the *creator* of great dramas—though, from a very early date, has been bolstered by what could be called an *iconic* presentation of the man "himself"— Shakespeare as the *character* of other people's dramas. Thus, the 1998 movie *Shakespeare in Love*, hugely successful in Spain as elsewhere, was predated by nearly two centuries by *Shakespeare enamorado* [Shakespeare in love, 1828], a play brought to the Spanish stage by Ventura de la Vega. Like so many of Spain's early Shakespeares, Vega's model was almost entirely French: the *Shakespeare amoureux* [Shakespeare in love] dreamt up by Alexandre

Duval.[5] Duval's original had actually been staged in Barcelona in 1810, but De la Vega can be credited with the first Spanish-language approximation to the character of this still largely unperformed English playwright. And this indeed is the most striking feature of *Shakespeare enamorado:* not what Alfonso Par has termed the "infantile and insipid" plot of the jealous—though decorously unmarried—dramatist's love for Enriqueta, the nubile actress in his newly penned play *Richard III*, but the mere fact that the comedy marked the baptism of Shakespeare as a much-loved *character* on the Spanish stage and that it did so long before the vast majority of Shakespeare's plays had been performed or even heard of.[6] Even more surprisingly, perhaps, rather than whet audience's appetites for "real" plays by the "real," meaning biographical, playwright, the most immediate effect of *Shakespeare enamorado* was to generate demand for a stream of revivals of the *same play*, with distinguished actors like Carlos Latorre, Julián Romea, and José Tamayo falling over each other to get the main part.

How can we explain the success of Duval's and De la Vega's character in Spain? In his path-breaking study *Shakespeare en la literatura española* [Shakespeare in Spanish literature], Alfonso Par—who did more than anyone else in the early part of the present century to found a genuine "school" of Spanish Shakespeare criticism—points to the nascent romanticism of a nation keen to break all ties with an outmoded classical tradition and to feel the winds of philosophical and aesthetic change blowing in across the Pyrenees. Citing approvingly the words of the anonymous contributor to a December 1825 edition of the *Diario Mercantil de Cádiz*, for whom Shakespeare possessed "the art of drawing a character in two brushstrokes," and though disparaging the "prissy sentimentality and falsification of character" in Duval's piece, Par notes the proximity of the premiere of *Shakespeare enamorado* to director and translator José María Carnerero's 1825 version of the Frenchman Ducis's version of *Hamlet*.[7] Just three years separate the two plays, the inference being that the appearance of the archetypal Romantic character Hamlet is somehow at the basis of the subsequent transmogrification of his author, Shakespeare, into an as yet imperfect and roughly drawn dramatis persona, "Shakespeare."

Though Par is not primarily concerned with biography, it is surely no coincidence that the first half of the nineteenth century marks the first serious attempts in Spain to set the record straight concerning the life and times of the English playwright. Just as Spain had largely inherited French tastes when it came to the dramatic representation of Shakespeare's works, so its image of the man behind the theatrical mask had been severely distorted by a welter of secondhand opinions, hearsay, and (more often than not) plain ignorance. Typical of late eighteenth-century approaches to "the life" is the prologue by "Inarco Celenio" to Moratín's translation of *Hamlet*, where in addition to citing such well-worn commonplaces as Shakespeare's humble education and marriage to an older woman, his deer-poaching, flight from Stratford, and early career as playhouse ostler, the author allows himself such licences as the assertion that Shakespeare "played the part of the dead man in *Hamlet* to perfection—a tribute, surely, to his want of skill in the art of declamation."[8] With the dawning of the Romantic age, and despite a residually neoclassical or simply *moral* contempt for Shakespearean dramatic rule-bending, critics like Juan Federico Muntadas, whose dissertation entitled *Discourse on Shakespeare and Calderón* (1849) was one in a long series of studies to point up the similarities and differences between the characters of Shakespeare and the Spanish Golden Age playwright,[9] and later Luis Carreras, whose 1866 article called "Shakespeare" included a plastercast portrait of the dramatist, went some way to putting a personality and, in the case of Carreras, a face to the name of the English author.[10]

It is around this period, the mid-nineteenth century, that Spanish theatergoers' interest in the man himself and the culture he stood for was rewarded with two further theatrical portraits, one derivative, the other entirely original. *Guillermo Shakespeare* (1853), written and produced by—as well as starring—Enrique Zumel, is based on a Spanish translation of the French novel by Clemence Robert, a Hugoesque fantasy that casts Shakespeare as the virtuous and handsome brother of the scheming and loathsome Caliban-figure Medianoche, or "Midnight," torn by his affections for the daughter of the earl of Southampton, the haughty Isabel, and the simple, selfless actress Ariela.[11] Here already we spot a difference with respect to Duval's comedy since Shakespeare, it transpires, is married to Ana, the daughter of a puritan Attarway, in whose hut in the forest of Worcester Shakespeare had been living as a poacher. In further contrast to Duval's piece, the ending of *Guillermo Shakespeare* is irremediably tragic, with Ariela being poisoned by Midnight, the guilty Isabel retiring to a convent, and Shakespeare being escorted home to Worcester by Susana, the daughter borne him by Ana. Zumel, after Robert, thus mingles intertextual fiction (as well as the obvious references to *The Tempest*, there are clear textual borrowings from *Othello*) with scraps of biographical "fact," while in a prologue-scene to the play itself, he demonstrates his (not entirely informed) interest in the world of the Elizabethan theater by conjuring up a meeting in Ariela's rooms between Shakespeare, Christopher Marlowe, Robert Greene, Thomas Middleton, and the impresario Johnsson who, just to give the lie to Moratín's anecdote, is deeply impressed by Shakespeare's declamatory skills and takes him on as an actor.

The rather unsuccessful *Guillermo Shakespeare* (it was to run for four nights only) was overshadowed in 1867 by the immensely popular and wholly original *Un drama nuevo* [A new play] by Manuel Tamayo y Baus.[12] The title of the play alludes to the imaginary tragedy of jealousy by an unnamed writer, in which Count Octavio, goaded on by the manipulative and envious Landolfo, discovers and determines to avenge the infidelity of his young wife Beatriz with Manfredo who, to add insult to injury, has lived as friend, ward, and virtual son to Octavio. Despite his initial reservations, Shakespeare, who in Tamayo's work is the established playwright and director of the "mature" years, agrees to let the company fool Yorick play the main role, only to discover that the "fictional" plot of the new play

Jesús Tordesillas (right) as Shakespeare in the 1946 Spanish film *Un drama nuevo*, based on the 1867 homonymous play by Manuel Tamayo y Baus. (Courtesy of the Filmoteca Española, Madrid).

bears an uncanny resemblance to the "real" nature of the relationship between the ageing Yorick, his wife Alicia, and her Platonic lover Edmundo. In a fatherly gesture of understanding and good old-fashioned Christian charity, Shakespeare takes the young lovers under his wing and vows to find a solution to their dilemma: "If I could only do this one good deed, I would gladly forego *Othello* and *Macbeth*, and all those foolish things" (88). Act 1 ends with the still-ignorant Yorick, goaded on by the manipulative and envious Walton (for whom the Octavio role was originally intended) reciting his pivotal "Tremble, unfaithful wife!" speech to a guilt-ridden Alicia who can only exclaim "Forgive me!" before swooning.

Shakespeare's self-appointed role as protector of Alicia and Edmundo leads in Act 2 to Yorick's suspicion that his wife's lover is none other than his old friend the playwright. In an Othello-like fit of madness, Yorick threatens his wife with physical violence, only to be stopped by the timely intervention of Shakespeare, who, "with imposing serenity" (111), calmly but authoritatively conducts Alicia to the safety of her room, leaving the deranged Yorick to muse:

> What is this? Has life's reality become a wondrous comedy, whose end's uncertain? Am I the victim of the dark machinations of witches, elves or demons? . . . Shakespeare! . . . Ay, there's no doubt . . . Nay, nay, it's impossible! What suffering it is to live in perpetual darkness! The light, eternal God, the light! And he's gone with her! They're together! . . . Damnation! I'll force them apart! (112)

Yorick's threat is defused by the entrance of Walton, who has promised to reveal the true identity of Alicia's lover. Yorick's Calderón-like meditation on the fragile boundaries between dream and reality, life and the theater, now switches to the equally orthodox defense of the code of honor, of the husband's duty to avenge his wife's *dis*honor. At this point Shakespeare reappears with Alicia and Edmundo, chides Walton for his deceit, and laughingly waves aside Yorick's hysterical accusations. The act ends with Yorick weeping inconsolably in Shakespeare's arms, and Alicia and Edmundo vowing to flee the following day.

First and last, however, comes the play-within-a-play of the vengeance of Count Octavio, the "wondrous comedy" alluded to by Yorick standing as both metaphor and tragic resolution of "life's reality" as it affects the play's main characters. Yorick's success as the wounded count is the final straw for Walton, who, piqued with envy, seizes the real letter Edmundo had written off-stage for Alicia plotting their escape and, as the devious confidant Landolfo, delivers it on-stage to Yorick in the role of Octavio, leaving Shakespeare clutching the unwritten stage prop and spitting revenge: "The serpent has deceived the lion! Let the lion crush the serpent!" (134). Octavio/Yorick reads the letter and slays the unfortunate Manfredo/Edmundo, and Beatriz/Alicia's very real scream brings author, prompter, actors, and stagehands scurrying on to the stage, together with Shakespeare, who is left to deliver the play's "epilogue":

> Ladies and gentlemen, there you have it! *(Addressing the audience, breathless and deeply moved.)* The play you are watching cannot be completed. Yorick, his reason blinded by enthusiasm, has wounded the actor playing Manfredo. Nor is this the only misfortune heaven has sent us. The famous actor Walton has also passed away. He has just been found in the street with a rapier wound to the heart. In his right hand he was clutching a sword. He must have been slain by his adversary in a face-to-face quarrel. Pray for the dead. Ah, and pray for their killers too! (143–44)

Glossing Shakespeare's final words, the play's most recent editor, Alberto Sánchez, has written that they "echo the sentiments of the devout Christian Tamayo," opposed as he was to these "'*affaires d'honneur*,' seeking prayers not just for the dead but for the 'killers' too, the transgressors of both moral and canon law and henceforth victims of a tortured conscience" (144, n.82). One cannot help recalling that other conscience-torn hero, Hamlet, guiltily subordinating the thirst for immediate revenge to respect for the praying Claudius. As Jonathan Bate has argued, there is a peculiarly Elizabethan residue to the word "conscience" of the notion of consciousness or self-awareness. It is the latter, rather than simply Hamlet's *conscience*, which distinguishes him from the traditional revenger:

> When alone on stage, reflecting on his own situation, he seems to embody the very nature of human *being*; it is consciousness that forms his sense of self, his "character," and in so doing makes it agonizingly difficult for him to perform the action that is demanded of him.[13]

Tamayo's Shakespeare goes one better than Shakespeare's Hamlet in immediately obeying his impulse to revenge: the lion crushes the serpent, but in so doing, becomes in Tamayo's Christian mind-set the "victim" of a tortured conscience or, in Bate's terms, of acute self-knowledge that henceforth seals his (self-)identity as character or, to put it differently, his character as a human *being*.

It was indeed in such overtly Romantic and Schiller-inspired terms that Tamayo himself, in his address to the Spanish Royal Academy, *La verdad considerada como fuente de belleza en la literatura dramática* [Truth conceived as the source of beauty in dramatic literature], that eight years earlier had assessed the impact of Shakespeare's work:

> Recall the world animated in the sphere of art by the presiding genius *(numen)* of Shakespeare. Therein we find the infinite variety of Nature, each character distinguished from the rest by a physiognomy of his own; therein the human being with neither mutilation nor amendment, prompting both pity and admiration; therein the innermost impulses of the will, the most impenetrable operations of consciousness, the deepest abysses of the mind and heart; therein Lady Macbeth, Juliet, Desdemona, Shylock, Richard III, Macbeth, Othello, Romeo, Hamlet, Lear, seemingly brought to life by an authentic soul; therein a portraiture of humanity itself in all its stages, at its most imposing and expressive; and this is why the name of Shakespeare extends to every corner of the globe.[14]

To this litany of Shakespearean worthies, Tamayo would add the name of Shakespeare himself, sealing once and for all the presence of the Bard on the Spanish stage as both presiding authorial genius and, in *Un drama nuevo*, as director and unwitting protagonist of an unnamed author's "wondrous tragedy."

In its deliberate staginess, its blurring of the boundaries between art and fiction and, above all, its modernistic immersion of the author in a plot over which he has no control, *Un drama nuevo* marks the end of Spanish drama's love affair with Romanticism, while inaugurating a new stage of literary self-consciousness which would reach a high-point at the turn of the century in the work of dramatists such as Ramón María del Valle-Inclán and novelists such as Miguel de Unamuno. Shakespearean stage presence has waned somewhat in the present century while, ironically, his status as playwright has grown enormously, actually outscoring, in the last few years, the number of productions of plays by Spain's Golden Age authors, Tirso de Molina, Pedro Calderón de la Barca, and Félix Lope de Vega. Shakespearean translation and criticism has grown apace, presaging, as one critic has recently remarked, a "promising tomorrow," but in the meantime consolidating Shakespeare's place "at the forefront" of modern Spanish culture.[15] This position of primacy has not precluded, and undoubtedly stimulated, theatrical attempts at belittling Shakespeare's claim to the authorship of his own work. A case in point is Jaime Salom's recently produced *El otro William* [The other William], an anti-Stratfordian fantasy in which William Stanley, earl of Derby, is presented as the real writer of the plays, while Shakespeare is depicted as the rascally, opportunistic actor presented by numerous polemicists in the ongoing authorship debate in Britain and the United States.[16]

Paradoxically, of course, rather than belittle the Shakespearean claim to greatness, such fantasies as Salom's show just how firmly Shakespeare is rooted at the "forefront" of Spain's theatrical culture. It is, after all, a measure of the foreign author's integration in the host culture that the latter can afford to cast in doubt, albeit in a lighthearted way, the former's status as author of the works attributed to him. In the case of Salom's Shakespeare, the Bardic presence is underwritten by his successive apparitions throughout the nineteenth century as fully fledged character on the Spanish romantic stage. Rather than spell the end of Shakespeare's place at the center of that stage, "The *Other* William" thus merely displaces and *reconstructs* the *same* William in *another* guise.

Like Zumel writing over a century earlier, Salom uses the gaps in Shakespeare's biography to fashion a new and (artistically at least) "coherent" image of the English actor and playwright. As one Spanish critic has put it, the "mystery" of a popular and successful playwright who "neither signed nor claimed a single one of his plays, left not a single letter, who declines to sue those who accuse him of plagiarism, who allows himself to be manipulated with impunity" is taken as sufficient grounds to convert him into a fictional character.[17] But as Spanish stage history so amply demonstrates, the character largely predates the very emergence of the mystery, Shakespeare's presence as character on the Spanish stage being established well before biographers discovered the elusiveness of their object and, when they did, being equipped with a consciousness that defied the positivist bases of their enquiries. Bardic presence in the Spanish theater has come in many shapes and sizes, but its value as cultural icon is without doubt the legacy of Tamayo. The rest is metaphysics.

Notes

The epigraph is from Martin Esslin, *The Field of Drama: How the Signs of Drama Create Meaning on Stage and Screen* (London: Methuen, 1987), 56.

1. Jacques Derrida, "Structure, Sign and Play in the Discourse of the Human Sciences," in *Writing and Difference*, translated by Alan Bass (London: Routledge and Kegan Paul, 1981), 279.
2. Derrida, "Structure, Sign and Play," 292.

3. Richard Wilson, *Will Power: Essays on Shakespearean Authority* (Hemel Hempstead: Harvester Wheatsheaf, 1993), 5.

4. Ibid., 18.

5. On France's "cultural hegemony" over its neighbors in the contemporary arena of Shakespearean translation, see José Lambert, "Shakespeare en France au tournant du XVIIIe siècle: Un dossier européen," in *European Shakespeares: Translating Shakespeare in the Romantic Age*, edited by Dirk Delbastita and Lieven D'hulst (Amsterdam: John Benjamins, 1993), 25–44.

6. The critique of the play is voiced by Alfonso Par, *Representaciones shakespearianas en España*, 2 vols. (Barcelona: Biblioteca Balmes, 1936); *Tomo I: Época galoclásica; época romántica*, 74. (The translation in the text and all subsequent translations are my own.) The number of different plays by Shakespeare performed in Spain prior to the premiere of De la Vega's translation is restricted to just four, all of them tragedies: *Hamlet, Macbeth, Romeo and Juliet*, and, most widely, *Othello. Othello* just happens to be the play Shakespeare is currently working on in Duval's comedy, which is presumably sufficient to explain his jealousy.

7. Alfonso Par, *Shakespeare en la literatura española, juicios de los literatos españoles, con noticias curiosas sobre algunos de ellos y sobre sucesos literarios famosos*, 2 vols. (Madrid and Barcelona: Biblioteca Balmes, 1935), I (*Galoclasicismo; romanticismo*), 215–16. Par's critique of the "sentimentality" of Duval's play is matched elsewhere by his enumeration of the litany of what he conceives as French-classical excesses in the Carnerero translation: the *"heavens, manes, hymens*, melancholies, natural, simple sentiments, etc., generally amplified, because he is unable to condense in a single hendecasyllable the lapidary sentences of the original" (*Representaciones shakespearianas en España*, 1: 72). The critique of both plays is, one suspects, based more on their *Frenchness* than on their respective artistic merits.

8. In the unpaginated prologue to Leandro Fernández de Moratín, *Hamlet, Tragedia de Guillermo Shakespeare, traducida e ilustrada con la vida del autor y notas críticas por Inarco Celenio* (Madrid: Oficina de Vallapando, 1798). Inarco Celenio was actually a pseudonym of Moratín. For an assessment of these and other considerations of Shakespeare's career by Celenio/Moratín, see Blanca López Román, "Biografías españolas de Shakespeare," in *Shakespeare en España: Crítica, traducciones y representaciones*, edited by José Manuel González (Alicante/Zaragossa: Universidad de Alicante/Libros Pórtico, 1993), 137–57, 138–40.

9. "Shakespeare, the profound thinker, vague, fantastic, concise, full of spleen, emphasizes his own character, while describing the court of Queen Elizabeth; Calderón, gently melancholic, gallant, passionate, pompous in his expression, is the interpreter of the sumptuous court of Philip IV." See *Discurso sobre Shakespeare y Calderón* (Madrid: Impr. de La Publicidad, 1849), 13–14.

10. Luis Carreras, "Shakespeare," *El museo universal* (1866), 141.

11. Enrique Zumel, *Guillermo Shakespeare: Drama en cuatro actos precedido de un prólogo, y en verso, original de D. Enrique Zumel* (Granada: Impr. y Librería José María Zamora, 1853).

12. *Un drama nuevo*, edited by Alberto Sánchez (Madrid: Ediciones Cátedra, 1979). All references are to this edition of the play. Performed in Spain throughout the nineteenth and early twentieth centuries, and adapted for the Spanish cinema in 1946 (see photograph on page 4), *Un drama nuevo* was also familiar to audiences in France, Germany, Italy, and, perhaps more remarkably, in the United States, where it was produced under the title *Yorick* in 1874. The play has been published

in English as *A New Drama*, translated by John D. Fitzgerald and Tacher H. Guild (New York: Publications of the Hispanic Society of America, 1915), and in German as *Das Neue Drama*, translated by Otto Goldschmidt (Berlin: R. Boll, 1887).

13. Jonathan Bate, *The Genius of Shakespeare* (London: Picador, 1997), 257.

14. Cited by Alberto Sánchez, Introduction, *Un drama nuevo*, 39.

15. José Manuel González, "Vicisitudes y desventuras del Shakespeare español," in *Shakespeare en España*, edited by González, 38.

16. Jaime Salom, *El otro William. Un hombre en la puerta* (Madrid: Editorial Fundamentos, 1998). In his introduction to the play, Salom rehearses some of the arguments of "the great problem" that has vexed scholars since the nineteenth century:

> If we refer to a knowledge of music, the plastic arts, heraldry, hunting, horseriding, fencing, law, astrology, occult sciences, natural history, travelogues, military and naval strategy, court life, religion, language or vocabulary so conscientiously contained in his monumental work, is it not in complete and unyielding opposition to what is known of the biographical details of Shakespeare of Stradtford [*sic*]? (20)

Salom rightly decries the "irrational and unconvincing mysticism" of certain strands of Bardolatry, but unfortunately produces no rational or convincing arguments to back the case of Stanley as the author of the plays, save for the attribution of "many scholars" (21).

17. José Antonio Zabalbeascoa, "Shakespeare, personaje de ficción," *Héroe y antihéroe en la literatura inglesa. Actas del V Congreso de AEDEAN* (Madrid: Editorial Alhambra, 1983), 391–401, 391. Zabalbeascoa uses this argument as the basis of his discussion of Tamayo's *Un drama nuevo* and Edward Bond's *Bingo*, but fails to address the more pressing point as to why Shakespeare should emerge so early as a fictional character in Spain and not in his native England, or why Tamayo's portrait is "favorable" [*sic*] and Bond's is not.

Enter Shakespeare:
The Contexts of Early Polish Appropriations

Marta Gibińska

THE EARLIEST POLISH APPROPRIATIONS OF SHAKESPEARE TOOK PLACE in Polish theaters at the end of the eighteenth century. The texts of the earliest Polish "Shakespeare plays" were based on the adaptations of Jean-François Ducis and F. L. Schröder. They were not accompanied by translations of Shakespeare's plays, single or the whole canon; Shakespeare was not read in Poland until the second half of the nineteenth century. So the contexts for early Polish interpretations of Shakespeare are to be found to a large extent in Europe. Before consulting those contexts, it is imperative to discuss two aspects of the direct Polish context (both, of course, inextricably connected): the Enlightenment and the political collapse of the country. I shall begin with the latter because it may be gauged by dates against which the fate of early Shakespearean adaptations, productions, and criticism in Poland may be followed.

In 1772 the three powers surrounding Poland—Russia, Prussia, and Austria—took the first step towards the annexation of Polish territories. Two further partitions followed twenty years later, in 1793 and 1795. Until 1807 Warsaw, the capital of the Polish kingdom, was a Prussian provincial town, and Cracow, the old historic metropolis, was Austrian. The years 1807–13 brought a partial re-creation of the Polish state under the aegis of Napoleon. His fall and the Congress of Vienna brought an end to the Duchy of Warsaw. In 1815 Warsaw became the capital of the Polish Kingdom, an integral part of the Russian empire. Cracow was returned to Austria. This state of affairs lasted until 1830, when the first serious national uprising shook the peace established in Vienna, raised the consciousness of the national tragedy among Poles, and brought into effect stricter political measures taken against Polish language and culture in all three occupied territories. The years preceding the November Uprising of 1830 saw the beginning of Polish romanticism—the uprising became a sort of catalyst that brought its flowering.

The time of the "early Polish Shakespeare" covers the end of the 1790s to 1830; so, in the political context, we may speak of Shakespeare's presence in the Polish theater only after Poland lost its independence. However, the context of the Enlightenment moves us significantly back in years—to at least 1764. Without taking account of this, much of what happens later cannot be fully understood.

The beginning of the Polish Enlightenment coincides with the inauguration of the reign of the last Polish king, Stanisław August Poniatowski. As a highly educated, enlightened monarch, Stanisław August promoted the activities of the Reform Party in Poland, whose chief aim in the 1760s was to improve the school system and to bring to life new institutions that would in future produce the intellectual elite of the country, a whole new generation of enlightened intelligentsia who were to play a key role in furthering education, learning, arts, and, last but not least, a feeling of political responsibility for the fate of the country and of the nation. At the same time the educational effort underwent a vigorous growth, as the king and his court sponsored the nation's cultural life in an unprecedented manner. This sponsorship meant much more than just money: the enlightened monarch set a fashion for new interests in literature, theater, learned debates, and journalism. Addison's *Spectator* was emulated by the *Monitor,* published regularly in the years 1765–1785 under the protection of the king and the Reform Party. The best poets and writers of the day published in it, imitating the form of Addison's essays and often repeating his ideas. Shakespeare figured large in an anonymous essay on the history of theater and drama in 1765. A year later a long essay repeated much of Dr. Johnson's *Preface* to his edition of Shakespeare's plays, under the title "On the Illusion and the Imagination." This is definitely the first notable mentioning of Shakespeare in Poland. The importance of this essay lies in its basic opposition to the strictures of French neoclassicism, the mainstream along which education in literature was shaped in Poland, and the rules by which drama and theater were to be judged for many years to come. Generally speaking, the Polish Enlightenment had very clear and close ties with French culture and thinking, which were taken to be superior to other European traditions. The English language and English cultural heritage were practically unknown, certainly not spread at schools and universities. The French neoclassical theories about drama made the unities into a dogma that underlay all expectations of a "well-made" tragedy or comedy. It is, therefore, most interesting to see that regarding Shakespeare the English opinion is consulted. Dr.

Johnson's broad-minded, intelligent, and imaginative reading of Shakespeare seems to be the first doorway through which Shakespeare was able to enter onto the Polish cultural stage. The king himself knew English quite well, visited London in the 1750s, and, in his memoirs (written around 1775), left a famous remark showing that the French influence was not indomitable:

> I have brought with me a vivid memory of all the elegant rules about the unity of place, action, and time, which being strictly adhered to have given the French dramatic writers a conviction of their superiority over the English; but I have to owe that the more I came to know Shakespeare's plays, the less was I ready to believe in that assumed superiority.[1]

It is not difficult to see the affinity of these words to Dr. Johnson's famous comparison of Shakespeare's works to "a forest, in which oaks extend their branches, and pines tower in the air" as contrasted with "the work of a correct and regular writer" that is like "a garden accurately formed and diligently planted."[2] The king, it is important to remember, could only see the Shakespeare who had been created by the eighteenth-century literary and theatrical tastes and practice. In the 1750s London theaters were no longer producing Tate's or Davenant's Shakespeare. Garrick's revival of *Macbeth* in 1744 opened a new perspective on Shakespeare's tragedy, one that revealed the "gold and diamonds in inexhaustible plenty," though purified from the "mass of meaner minerals" (to quote Dr. Johnson again) according to the current tastes; and these still refused too violent a shaking of the accepted decorum, while expecting an impressive spectacle that allowed changes of place because they provided an opportunity to impress the audience with settings. The "gold and diamonds" of Shakespeare's language and poetry got explored for character and action alike.

However, England did not figure in the usual educational trips of young Polish noblemen. We may of course assume that the king was not the only Pole who traveled to London, and probably not the only enlightened spectator to draw such conclusions about Shakespeare. The articles in the *Monitor* point to some knowledge of the language and current events in England. But there is no continuation—political controversies and debates centering on the pros and cons of the national versus European cultural modes of Polish life monopolized contemporary writing. Conservative Sarmatian values were opposed to the fashionable French ways and brought about a paradoxical interchange of elements between the two sides: in effect, the newly emerging model of the enlightened Pole combined neoclassical (read French) education and modern political (meaning, more democratic) views with a loving attention to Polish traditions. This did not leave much room for the news from England. Countess Isabella Czartoryska (*née* Fleming), who practiced unashamed Bardolatry, was rather an exception in Poland. She visited England several times, went to Stratford, and bought Shakespeare souvenirs to place in a special museum called the Gothic House, built in the English park that she founded on her estate in 1784. Her exalted but solitary example confirms the opinion that Shakespeare as an English bard was at the time known to few Poles. The slowly growing critical and literary consciousness of the equally slowly growing group of Polish intelligentsia was educated on traditions of imagination, illusion, and literary art other than the English. The group standing behind the *Monitor* in the 1760s tried to broaden the field. Some more efforts were made in the seventies and eighties, but they were too dependent on the authority of the French sources. Prince Czartoryski, for example, recommended a translation of a French compendium of theory and history of literature and fine arts for the students of the famous new School for Cadets (Szkoła Rycerska). The young adepts of the school, including the future "father of the Polish theater" Wojciech Bogusławski and the future most eminent neoclassical writer and critic Jan Ursyn Niemcewicz, learned from their handbook that Shakespeare's tragedies were "a collection of low dialogues and of sentences high and beautiful, at the same time admirable, and simple and despicable.... The beauties there are very rare and hence we can hardly find [read] any completely estimable work."[3] The handbook in question is *Essai sur l'histoire des sciences, des belles lettres et des arts* [Essay on the history of sciences, belles-lettres, and arts] by Félix Juvenel de Carlencas, which appeared in Lyon in 1740, and which was translated and recommended for the use of the school in the 1760s. However, Czartoryski himself must have had doubts about the opinion of the learned Frenchman. In 1771 he wrote a famous preface to a play entitled *Panna na wydaniu* [A girl to be married], in which he repeated the views on art of Jean Baptiste Dubos, who in 1719 published *Réflexions critiques sur la poésie et la peinture* [Critical reflections on poetry and painting]. Czartoryski added his own opinion that modified the French views to a considerable extent. Namely, he tried to show the relationship between Shakespeare's poetic imagination and a very special English character and temper, which in turn was the result of English history, one that differed from the history of other European countries. It was in the historical differences that Czartoryski found the source of Shakespeare's indifference to the poetic rules of the ancients so well adapted by the French. In his eyes, Shakespeare suffered from a lack of education, but due to the rarest of talents with which nature had endowed him, he was able to understand man to the deepest layers of his conscience and to present the whole truth of man and his feelings in the most unusual and unexpected words. Almost twenty years later, Ignacy Bykowski, an author of many tragedies and novels—a second-rate writer moving in the shadow of the best writers and poets, who frequented Czartoryska's salon—published an essay entitled "Poeci angielscy" [English poets] in 1790, in which he enthusiastically wrote about Shakespeare, "Until today the genius of English poetry is like a shadowy tree planted by nature, which throws carelessly some twigs here and there, but in itself grows with great power," while Shakespeare's "sweet irregularity pleases much better than modern wisdom."[4] But this is more or less all that may be found in Polish criticism of the time. The thread that begins with the early essays published in the *Monitor* in the 1760s breaks here, not to be taken up for quite a while. In 1793 Voltaire's *Lettres philosophiques* are published in a Polish translation. In critical thinking about Shakespeare, theater, tragedy, and comedy, the French now dominate without question.

France was not the only foreign context for the developing Polish cultural life of the last twenty-five years of the eighteenth century. The neighbor much closer to Poland and much more vigorously developing its Shakespeare was Germany. Dates once again may help us to see certain parallels and connections. Gotthold Ephraim Lessing wrote his *Hamburgische Dramaturgie* in 1767–1769 in an attempt to create the first national theater in cooperation with Johann Friedrich Loewen. The project failed for commercial reasons, but Lessing's reviews and essays testify to a positive criticism of Shakespeare's art, especially his critique of the mistaken notions of the French, particularly in polemics against Voltaire's views and plays but also in opposition to Corneille. In 1765 Stanisław August established a regular theatrical group in Warsaw subsidized from the royal pocket, though retaining the character of private business. The idea was closer to the Hamburg enterprise than to the then popular aristocratic theaters proliferating at German courts. The king and the Warsaw elite aimed at establishing a cultural institution that would be instrumental in the ambitious global reform of the conservative, provincial, and unenlightened country. For some time the theater kept a French and an Italian group of actors, but the idea was to develop the Polish group and to introduce a steady Polish repertoire. Polish plays were encouraged, even though at the beginning they were no more than rather poor adaptations of French and Italian plays. The prevailing model was a didactic comedy of manners. The crisis came only in 1772 with the first partition of Poland. After some ups and downs, a courtier of the king's bought the rights to the theatrical business and built a new home for the theater in 1779. The new building became known from the start as the National Theater, and it functioned as such until 1833. Its repertoire was far from strictly national (though it did play a very important role as a national institution in backing political reforms and opposition against the infiltration of the Russian and Prussian political influence in the 1790s), and the theater itself did not function in the way that Lessing, some ten years earlier, imagined a national theater should. Operas, ballets, and foreign plays, often presented by foreign troupes, were the staple diet. But the result was that the National Theater in Warsaw imported trends and fashions, especially from Germany. In 1781 a German troupe performed *Hamlet*, almost certainly in Schröder's version.

The competition of foreign troupes and the rage for opera and ballet made Polish actors set off for the provinces. Before the century came to an end, many Polish towns, both east and west, enjoyed the presence of regular theater groups who managed to obtain their own theaters, in rented buildings adapted or those built expressly as theaters. In 1789 an old Franciscan church in Lemberg became the town's theater. Cracow has boasted its own theater since 1799, and in Vilna the theater got its quarters in one of the palaces in 1796. The troupes moved around a lot, and there were many irregular but frequent events in numerous small towns or manor houses across the country—especially in the eastern lands. The towns with their own theater building also enjoyed visits by foreign troupes, most often Austrian and German, bringing with them adaptations of Shakespeare, but also introducing a taste for the Gothic and the sentimental, usually cooked together in a drama of terror and sensibility, and presented in impressive settings whenever possible. And in Germany, more or less at the same time, we see the influence of Heinrich Wilhelm von Gerstenberg's *Briefe über Merkwürdigkeiten der Literatur* [Letters on literary curiosities, 1766–1770) promoting Shakespeare as a great poet to read. This was made possible by the efforts of Christoph Martin Wieland, who in the years 1762–1766 managed to translate and publish twenty-two plays by Shakespeare.[5] They were probably more widely read than any other drama at that time in Germany.[6] Wieland's translation was also used by German theaters as the material for adaptations. So when Goethe in all confidence exclaimed in 1771 "Und ich ruf Natur! Natur! nichts so Natur als Shakespeares Menschen!" [And I call on nature! Nature! Nothing is so much in nature as Shakespeare's people] ("Zum Shakespears Tag") and called Shakespeare a genius who competed with Prometheus, he was referring to Shakespeare read rather than staged. And although during his long life Goethe spent many years working for the theater in Weimar (1775–1817), his essay "Shakespeare und kein Ende" [Endless Shakespeare]—written over a two-year period, with part one completed in 1813 and part 2 in 1815—discusses Shakespeare the poet as the greatest of the great, whose art can be best appreciated when read aloud rather than acted: "There is no higher or purer pleasure than to sit with closed eye and hear a naturally expressive voice recite, not declaim, a play of Shakespeare's."[7] Part two discusses Shakespeare in the theater, and here Goethe praises Schröder for his adaptations arguing against the unnaturalness of Shakespeare's theater, in fact arguing against the nonillusory theater. But understandably enough: his theater, as well as his experience of theater in a more general sense, was of the kind that tried to build verisimilitude on the stage; which lived on the idea that the stage can and indeed should create an illusion of reality (no matter whether that illusion was limited to the unities or whether it was Gothic beyond belief). One can almost hear the anger in his voice when he damns all those who think that not an iota should be cut from Shakespeare's work when staged; he seems to finish on a note of supremely egoistic *Schadenfreude* when he concludes that such practice would drive Shakespeare from the stage: "which for that matter would be no great misfortune; for then the reader, whether he be solitary or sociable, will be able to get so much the purer pleasure out of him."[8] Critics understand these remarks as an attempt at self-justification of his own dramatic art. It is, however instructive to see in the opinion of Goethe the symptomatic dictate of current theatrical practice as well as aesthetics. Shakespeare was an absolute genius on the level of private reading, but did not make sense as a playwright because he could not be squeezed into the theatrical practice of the time, into the theater that produced drama rather than tragedy.[9] An excellent illustration of my point here are Goethe's remarks about Schröder's *King Lear*.

I have lingered over Goethe because I find in his views the reflection of the difficulties with the reception of Shakespeare symptomatic of European attitudes at the time. The idea that Shakespeare's plays are more suitable to private reading will be repeated by many a great critic for many years to come all over Europe, England included (to think only of Coleridge). On the other hand there is great enthusiasm for Shakespeare in the theater—but Shakespeare inevitably cut and adapted to the kind of theater that existed. Lucky Germany could enjoy Shakespeare both in reading and on the stage; the Poles were limited to the theater. So inevitably the first entrance of Shakespeare onto the Polish stage was in the shape of Schröder and Ducis.

For Goethe was right: the European theater could only deal with Shakespeare cut to measure. On the one hand, this was dictated by the aesthetics of melodrama (Gothic terror and the soft movements of delicate hearts mingled with the neoclassical ideas of poetic justice, which boiled down to an all-satisfying happy ending of sorts). On the other hand, the taste for great spectacle did not agree with long speeches that consumed time that was really needed for the spectacular stage representations; also, increasingly, the acting of emotions was preferred to speaking emotions (or speaking of emotions). Above all, the drama preferred an action with a momentum, a movement in time at a pace that would keep the audience in suspense; slow meditation did not fit here.

Polish theater at the very beginning of its history was blessed with outstanding artists whose efforts ensured its continuity, although political events would argue to the contrary: the protracted fall of Poland and its dismembered existence in various political configurations in the early nineteenth century made Poles change their citizenship sometimes several times in their lives. The authorities of Russia, Prussia, and Austria in varying ways made the life of the National Theater in Warsaw and of the smaller private theaters in Vilna, Lemberg, or Cracow extremely difficult. Yet the theater not only persisted; it developed. Much of this we owe to Wojciech Bogusławski. His career is checkered: he directed the National Theater in the years 1783–1785, then moved to Vilna 1785–1789. He then returned again to Warsaw for five important seasons (1790–1794). Shortly before the final partition he escaped to Lemberg, where he spent another five years, until 1799, when he returned to Warsaw and stayed firmly as the director of the National Theater until 1814. He was known for his popular tastes and for playing up to the audience; yet it would be unjust to say that he did this only to keep the box office in balance. The truth is that his conception of theater was one that grew out of the tradition of early Enlightenment in Poland: the theater had to appeal to a wide audience because its aim was to educate and offer cultured entertainment. For this attitude he was much criticized towards the end of his third directorship. As a man who was throughout an artist of the contemporary theater he was very much like Schröder: a director, an actor, and a playwright in one person. And it was Schröder's adaptations of *Hamlet* that fitted him best when he reached out for Shakespeare to show the tragedy in Polish. He adapted the play, or, perhaps, composed his own adaptation with the stage in mind, without much attention paid to Shakespeare. Jerzy Got has meticulously examined Bogusławski's sources: he used a German theatrical manuscript that in itself was a compilation of the second and third adaptations of Schröder as well as the translation by Schlegel.[10] He was working in Lemberg at the time. The famous first night took place on April 8, 1798 and brought much enthusiasm from the audience. Bogusławski himself described the success in his *Memoirs*. He noted that mad Ophelia made a particular impact on the audience. At this point it is perhaps instructive to remember that Schröder improving Franz Heufeld's version helped himself with direct knowledge of the English text and brought into his adaptation things that Heufeld did not include. Among other things, he reintroduced the mad Ophelia scenes. He did it with the aim of enhancing the melodramatic effect rather than with the idealistic need to be faithful to Shakespeare: the obscenities were inevitably cut. Bogusławski's Ophelia made a great impression with her madness, but nobody's delicate feelings were offended, whereas everybody's taste for the thrill of terror was elegantly satisfied.

Hamlet was not the first Shakespearean adaptation shown in Lemberg. In 1796, the audiences were shown a play called *The Tombs of Verona*. It was a Polish translation of a French melodrama based on *Romeo and Juliet* and written by Louis Mercier. The translator, Bishop Józef Kossakowski, did his best to ensure the sentimental pathos and pity that could then evolve towards the unexpected happiness of the lovers. The play, however, had more to offer than this. The production, prepared by Bogusławski, testified to the fashionable grand spectacle in his theater as well as to his employment of Gothic scenery—especially in the last act, which had an impressive setting of underground tombs or dungeons painted by one of the better theater artists of the day. That Gothic setting was filled with numerous fencing parties, while Romeo, pale and suffering, would lean against a column, gazing at Juliet's body. Mercier's adaptation, however, is a play that treats the original material very loosely and obviously strives to achieve a properly moralistic effect. The preserved manuscript announces that *The Tombs of Verona* is a "drama in 5 Acts translated from the French." Shakespeare's name is not even mentioned. So it is the 1798 *Hamlet* that is traditionally believed to be the first Polish premiere of a Shakespearean play—the plays were staged in Vienna, Berlin, or Hamburg.

When Bogusławski got the directorship of the National Theater for the third time, he brought with him the experience of the Lemberg years, which was to shape much of his repertoire. He never forgot the ideals of the national character of the theater in Warsaw. After the third partition, the name National Theater did not exist officially. But in 1807 he brought the name back to official use and it stayed—also in official documents—until the end of the November Uprising (1830). In 1810 the Grand Duke of the Duchy of Warsaw, Frederic August, signed a document that granted the National Theater the official patronage of the government. The body called the Government Directorate took responsibility for everything that concerned the activities of the theater. The irony of history is striking: this institution lasted until 1915, independent of all the political changes. Until 1815, the Government Directorate acted mainly on paper, and the director of the National Theater practically had the decisive voice in everything that was done. However, after 1815, when the new order in Europe was firmly established, the role of the director diminished; the choice of plays was largely in the hands of the government, and the pressure of censorship intensified. On the other hand, the governmental character of the institution of the theater in Warsaw guaranteed its survival.[11]

Before the Government Directorate was established, and before the pressures against his directorship and art increased, Bogusławski's theater introduced Shakespeare to the Warsaw audiences. *Hamlet* was shown in 1799. The same year witnessed the Warsaw premiere of *The Tombs of Verona*. In 1801 and in 1804 *Othello* was staged, and *King Lear* in 1805 (though probably there had been a production in 1803). All these plays were, of course, translations of Schröder's and Ducis's adaptations. Their literary merit was poor, but the productions did their best to bring out an impressive and emotional spectacle on the stage.

However, to discuss Shakespeare's presence in the Polish theater of the time only in connection with Bogusławski and the Warsaw Theater would not do justice to what was going on in Poland. Besides Bogusławski another important figure must be mentioned: Jan Nepomucen Kamiński, who, like his more famous colleague, was a theater director, translator, actor, and playwright all in one person. Kamiński was responsible for the vigorous growth of theatrical life east of Warsaw. His early quarters were based in the small provincial town of Kamieniec in far-away Podolia, though later he worked for the theaters in Lemberg and Vilna as well. He was very familiar with what was going on in European theaters, especially in the German theater with which he kept steady contact, by traveling there himself and by inviting German troupes to Poland. He encouraged psychological, expressive, and exalted acting, which he learned from German actors, but combined it with care to render beauty and grace. He also laid great stress on the individuality and unique style of particular actors. During his directorship in Lemberg he developed a company of actors who had a huge influence on the future fate of the acting style in Poland. This was linked to early Shakespearean roles. He had access to Shakespearean adaptations currently used everywhere, and he made ample use of them. According to Andrzej Żurowski, the extant theatrical manuscripts of Kamiński's Shakespearean adaptations (*King Lear* and *Macbeth*) testify to his great sense of the stage. Kamiński's translations were many and varied.[12] His adaptations of Shakespeare appeared in the company of plays by Kotzebue, Zschokke, Pixérécourt, Molière, Calderón, and Schiller. He catered to the eclectic taste of his audiences and was far less fettered by neoclassical constraints or criticism than Bogusławski, especially in his Warsaw years after 1800. Kamiński's translation of *Hamlet* was printed in 1805, in a small provincial town under a protectorate of an eccentric nobleman. Kamiński knew Bogusławski's first production of 1798, but for his theater he decided to follow Schröder's third version. He published it with an epigraph from Schiller's *Robbers*, thus firmly placing his Shakespeare in the contemporary German context, and in the context of the drama of action and spectacle. The translation was obviously made in haste, and many stylistic blunders make it laughable for a twentieth-century reader. However, Kamiński did not try to embellish and smooth the language of characters, and often, almost against all expectations, the Polish translation of the German translation does manage to offer a glimmer of a Shakespearean kind. Apart from *Hamlet*, Kamiński put on *King Lear* in Vilna 1815, and again in Lemberg 1816. The preserved theatrical manuscript of 1828 documents his constant work on the tragedy: he tried to straighten the story line so that the sensational and the horrible could be given enough stress in performance. His *Macbeth* (after Schröder) appeared in Kamieniec in 1805, in Lemberg in 1809, and in Cracow in 1818. Again, a preserved copy of the theatrical manuscript testifies to Kamiński's taste and art taking Shakespeare's tragedy in the direction of a well-formed Gothic drama. The manuscript, like the other preserved copies of theatrical renderings, show the increasing tendency of translating horror into the spectacle, often leaving actors with the minimum of words, expecting them to enact rather than verbalize great emotions. Kamiński also had his own version of *Othello* (probably after Schröder), again most likely prepared around 1805. He showed this *Othello* on the stage in Lemberg in 1817. The Warsaw productions of *Othello* were based on the adaptation by Ducis.

This short review of the theatrical practices of the two main translators, adaptors, and directors of Shakespeare in Poland shows without doubt the aesthetics that followed the main theatrical tastes in German theaters. But if Kamiński, operating away from Warsaw, was much freer in following the Gothic and sentimental taste in the spectacle, Bogusławski found himself under strong criticism from the reviewers who had monopolized the Warsaw press ever since 1802. The reviewers did not share the public taste, and quite openly set out to teach audiences to be more discerning. This discernment was dictated by a renewed attack from the neoclassicists. The reviewers were both great authorities of the previous century (and of the previous epoch, which in many ways came to an end in 1795) and their younger followers brought up on the by then conservative lines of the pride of Polish neoclassicism—the great schools founded some forty years earlier. Shakespeare adaptations got critical censure in the same measure as other dramas: for example, the reviewer of *Othello* (in *Gazeta Warszawska*, 1804) deplores the scene in which Othello kills Desdemona because it brings horror and repulsion instead of feelings of tender pity and grief. One would have thought that it is the production that is being blamed, but no, it is the play. It becomes obvious when the critic takes Voltaire's *Zaïre* as an instructive example of a proper tragedy. The same stale thinking was continued eight years later in a review of *Hamlet* (in *Gazeta Warszawska*, 1812). The reviewer mocks the play and the hero: "Such a great philosopher as Hamlet is very much afraid of apparitions and ghosts, and sees them ever so often." In both instances the opinions exclude the more interesting context of German thinking about Shakespeare; the reviewers demonstrate views almost opposite to Lessing's, not because they come to write fifty years later but because they have put the clock back fifty years or more. One remembers Lessing's argument about the futility of Voltaire's plays in raising pity or addressing imagination in comparison to Shakespeare's power.[13] It is a pity that Polish Shakespeare followed the German context only in the theater and not in critical thinking as well. The Polish reviewers were totally unsympathetic to the developing theatrical aesthetics, and they not only criticized the current productions but also demanded changes in the repertoire. The reason for the unprecedented neoclassical attack seems to lie partly in the political situation: in Warsaw under the Prussian rule things German were politically incorrect, while things French were most welcome, first, because the reviewers were educated on French writers, and second, because the French were naturally seen as the only allies against the German oppressor; Napoleon's march across Europe brought "freedom" to the Duchy of Warsaw. For a long time Napoleon was perceived as a liberator. French culture and literature settled then before 1830 as the strongest influence on Polish literati, however with the clock turned back: Voltaire and his *Lettres Philosophiques,* translated into Polish in 1793, were to dictate the taste and the critical thinking of the conservative elite for quite some time. The programmatic essay published by a group of Warsaw critics in 1801 stated that the only way to perfect Polish theater was to follow the path taken by the French tragedy about 150 years earlier. Polish actors should give up all those "German dramas" and turn towards "regular" plays, meaning "written according to the rules in France discovered and tested."[14] German dramas do not disappear, as Shakespeare's presence on the Polish stages testifies, but the French repertoire does increase in the first decade of the nineteenth century. Among other things, Bogusławski left the National Theater because he did not want or could not cope with the increasing pressure of the neoclassical critics. His successor, Ludwik Osiński, was a different man. The most eminent critics and writers, who in 1814 gathered in an organization called the Society of Xs (since all reviews were signed "x"), backed up Osiński, who tried to change the character of the productions and to educate both actors and audiences. The Xs were extremely consistent in following their ideals, and, as is the case with extreme positions, were the great losers in the end (they symbolically broke their pens in 1819). They fired their guns not without reason: much of what was shown in the theater was less than mediocre in taste and had no artistic value. The Xs showed much courage in opposing popular habits, especially when they criticized the public for applauding each time the words "Poland" and "fatherland" fell from the stage, irrespective of the merit of the play. Such audiences, they stated, precisely because they were unable to react to the true value of the play, were responsible for preventing any real progress on the stage. Thus one has to give them their due insofar as they were fighting against everything that was a matter of easy habit and imitation in the theater. But when they attacked Bogusławski for following Molière and Shakespeare ("who also played up to the crowd") they had clearly put themselves in a position that was increasingly difficult to defend. Their efforts brought visible effects in increasing the number of good classical plays on the stage, made actors work on their techniques of speaking verse, and generally improved the level of acting in Warsaw. They were also responsible for introducing a number of important national tragedies that achieved great recognition and, to the present part, are of the great achievements of Polish neoclassical drama. However, that peak of Polish neoclassicism ended by 1819. The program was too conservative and too much at odds with the rising currents to stay. Charles Nodier's *Phantome*, mounted in Warsaw in 1821, was played on thirty occasions before 1830. Soon the Vilna Theater showed it as well. The ghosts came back with a vengeance—the Vilna theater, which in the 1820s had excellent actors and a very modern repertoire, was the place where the best Polish romantic poets and playwrights, Adam Mickiewicz and Juliusz Słowacki, got their first experience of what theater was about. The imagination, much maligned, pushed into the margins of popular tastes in the Gothic horrors, eventually triumphed via preromantic drama, which included Shakespeare. His presence, like that of the imagination in the theater, was cut and adapted. As a playwright who himself catered to the tastes of his audiences, he presumably would not object. He practiced theater, and so cut and adapted himself. His early entrance in Poland is one that should not disquiet anybody: he came with actors, in a company of the best of them. And any traveler knows that the route from England to Poland across the continent must wind its way through Germany.

And through Germany, indeed, it came many times. The last context I would like to bring in here is August Wilhelm Schlegel and his great step in propagating the new romantic reception of the works of Shakespeare. His famous lectures *Über dramatische Kunst und Literatur* [On dramatic art and literature, 1809–1811] had a great and immediate impact on European discussions at the center of which was Shakespeare.[15] The impact of the new debates did not omit Poland and is first traceable in a most unexpected place: at Warsaw University, in the series of lectures given over a few years by Ludwik Osiński—the same Osiński who took over the National Theater and worked hand in hand with the conservative Xs. He began the lectures in 1818 and continued for quite a few years. The subject was comparative literature; one full lecture was about Shakespeare; during other lectures, as on Racine, he would bring in Shakespeare for comparison. What did Osiński, the very symbol of conservatism and not a very popular professor, have to say about Shakespeare? Well, it was endless praise: "a man endowed with genius; in spite of a lack of patterns to imitate in the surrounding wilderness, he was able to shine with his own power and was for over two-hundred years to amaze England. English theater begins with him and none of the later writers diminished his fame."[16] "Who better than he knew the mystery of the human heart? Who was able to penetrate more deeply its mysteries?" Shakespeare's poetry reaches levels higher than any other art could reach. And Osiński finds proof in the "so rightly beloved monologue of Hamlet" or in the fearful scenes of *Othello* and *King Lear*. The great power of Shakespeare is the greatness of his ideas and the universal character of the problems and questions contained in his plays. Osiński even dares to criticize Voltaire, who was mistaken in mocking Shakespeare's art, forgetting that a writer so much valued by his own nation could not achieve this fame without true merits. When Osiński criticized Shakespeare, it was not for Ophelia's madness or the Witches in *Macbeth*, not even for the Porter scene, but for the freedom the great playwright took with time and the infelicities of style—"the style of Shakespeare is most dangerous," he said. The great and important conclusion of Osiński was that Shakespeare's work was an organic whole and must not be changed. "I strongly protest against all adaptations which lose the logic, the wisdom and the beauty of Shakespearean tragedies. Both the French and the Germans gave Europe a disabled Shakespeare. He must be brought back to good health as soon as possible," ended Osiński emphatically. (His lectures were published together with his other writings in 1861.) One of his students, the writer K. W. Wójcicki, commented on Osiński's metamorphosis from a sworn classicist to an admirer of Shakespeare: "in the first years he treated Shakespeare, Schiller and Goethe lightly, while his highest authority was La Harpe and Boileau . . . but he slowly changed his opinion and judgement: Schlegel took the place of La Harpe, and the great poets of Germany and Albion found their place in his lectures."[17] The romantic reception of Shakespeare in Poland began not only in the theater: paradoxically, a great conservative classicist was to proclaim publicly a re-evaluation of Shakespeare that testified not only to the great important context next door, German thought, but also to its spreading and penetration of the very bastion of conservatism—the university. In his dramatic plea for the whole of Shakespeare Osiński put his finger on the greatest problem with Shakespeare in Poland—so far no whole and organic Polish Shakespeare had appeared. This problem would still be valid for the romantic reception: Shakespeare would be known in fragments, German (mostly) but also French translations would be used. The trauma after the 1830 uprising delayed Poles' direct engagement with the English language and the English texts of Shakespeare.

NOTES

1. Stanisław Helsztyński, "Szekspir w Polsce," in Annex to *William Szekspir, Tragedie*, edited by Helsztyński, R. Jabekowska, and A. Staniewska (Warsaw: PIW, 1973), 2: 893–1075, 900. All translations from the Polish are my own.
2. D. Nichol Smith, ed., *Eighteenth-Century Shakespeare Criticism* (London: Oxford University Press, 1963), 125.
3. Quoted from Barbara Lasocka, "Polski Szekspir klasyczny (i romantyczny)," in *Od Shakespeare'a do Szekspira*, edited by J. Ciechowicz and Z. Majchrowski (Gdańsk: Centrum Edukacji Teatralnej, 1993), 95–105, 99.
4. See Lasocka, "Polski Szekspir klasyczny (i romantyczny)," 100.
5. Christoph Martin Wieland, *Gesammelte Schriften*, edited by E. Stadler, 10 vols. (Berlin: Weidmann, 1911).
6. Simon Williams, *Shakespeare on the German Stage, Volume 1: 1586–1914* (Cambridge: Cambridge University Press, 1990), 52.
7. Johann Wolfgang von Goethe, *Sämtliche Werke*, 40 vols. (Stuttgart and Berlin: J. G. Cotta, 1902–1907). "Zum Shakespears Tag," 36: 3–7; and "Shakespeare und kein Ende," 37: 30–50. Translation by Randolph S. Bourne in *Landmarks of Shakespeare's Criticism*, edited by Robert F. Wilson, Jr. (Amsterdam: Rodopi, 1979), 51.
8. Goethe, in *Landmarks of Shakespeare's Criticism*, 53.
9. Consider in this connection the German distinction between *Tragoedie* and *Trauerspiel*.
10. Jerzy Got, *Na wyspie Guaxary* (Crakow: Wydawnictwo Literackie, 1971), 224–45.
11. See Zbigniew Raszewski, *Krótka historia teatru polskiego* (Warsaw: PIW, 1990).
12. Andrzej Żurowski, *Szekspiriady polskie* (Warsaw: Pax, 1976), 211.
13. Compare, for example, nos. 11 and 12 of *Hamburgische Dramaturgie* on ghosts in Shakespeare and Voltaire. See Gotthold Ephraim Lessing, *Werke*, edited by Karl Eibl et al., 8 vols. (Munich: C. Hanser, 1970–1979), vol. 4.
14. Raszewski, *Krótka historia teatru polskiego*, 97–98.
15. August Wilhelm Schlegel, *Vorlesungen über dramatische Kunst und Literatur* (1811), in his *Kritische Schriften und Briefe*, edited by Edgar Lohner, 6 vols. (Stuttgart: W. Kohlhammer, 1962–1974), vol. 6.
16. Lasocka, "Polski Szekspir klasyczny (i romantyczny)," 102.
17. Ibid., 103.

Route 66: The Political Performance of Shakespeare's Sonnet 66 in Germany and Elsewhere

Manfred Pfister

Für Kurt T. v. R. in alter Freundschaft

I

ONCE UPON A TIME—OR, TO BE MORE PRECISE, IN FEBRUARY 1999—I was in Zagreb to give a couple of lectures, to hear what people thought about the new Croatia, and to discover for a conference paper I was planning whether Shakespeare's sonnet 66, "Tired with all these, for restful death I cry," had been used there as well as in Germany to ventilate political frustration and dismay over the powers that were and those that be. On my last evening there, after a week of pestering—to no avail!—my colleagues at the university with my question as to any political bells that sonnet 66 might ring with them, I went to see *Shakespeare in Love* together with Giga Graèan, a distinguished Croatian journalist. I sympathized with her hurt patriotic pride over seeing the coast of Illyria—which is, after all, the Istrian or Dalmatian, and thus the Croatian coast—whisked away to the Bermudas or the Bahamas; and, of course, my own sonnet 66—which, after all, is only marginally about Shakespeare in love—did not feature either. No matter: by then, I had already abandoned my Route 66 in Croatia.

After the film we went to the bar of the Gavella Drama Theater for a quiet talk over a few drinks. We did manage to have the drinks, but our talk was constantly interrupted by friends of Giga's—writers, actors, stage designers—who, one after another, intruded upon us with their laments about how bad things were and how frustrated they felt with current cultural politics in Croatia. It was already long after midnight when the last one left us. Giga, exhausted by now, leant back and, between one draw from her cigarette and the next, murmured to herself rather than to me: "Tired with all these...." I flared up from my late-night stupor: "Who's speaking now—you or . . . ?" "How come," she said, "you, an Anglicist and a German professor at that, and not remember your Shakespeare? Don't you know sonnet 66, 'Tired with all these, for restful death I cry'? Everybody knows it here. It has been translated at least five times in Tito's Yugoslavia and was sung on stage during a highly controversial production of *Macbeth* back in the early seventies, in 1973. Later it even became a hit, when one of our most popular singers, Ibriça Jusic, sung it in concerts and recorded it. And if you buy me a last coffee, I promise to send you the record."

When the record arrived, I could, of course, not understand the exact words of the Croatian rendering, but the singing voice and the music manage to speak across language barriers, and particularly when, as here, the musical language is that of the international protest songs of the 1960s and 1970s, drawing upon various ethnic traditions.[1] Its first line, as I have learned, is rendered in racy vernacular as "Fed up with all these . . ." and, in the repetition of this verse after each of the quatrains, the song emphasizes the structure of sonnet 66. Its hammering series of eleven anaphoric and parallel lines stress the urgency and bitterness of its indictment of a society in which integrity and creativity are frustrated. The success of this song on Yugoslav and Croatian stages, concert platforms, and records clearly shows that Shakespeare's indictment of his own society manages to speak across historical barriers, and that its catalogue of abstract oppositions between "captive good" enslaved, disempowered, humiliated, corrupted, and distorted by "captain ill" lend themselves readily to applications to other, yet equally oppressive situations. It is the very abstraction and schematic structure of this sonnet that help to open it up to ever-new historical and political contexts. Shakespeare's text, however, does not only provide the images, the argument, the structure, and the *Gestus* here; the cultural prestige of its author also protects the protest and indictment against legal sanctions. Censoring it and tongue-tying its singer would mean censoring and tongue-tying the canonical Shakespeare himself, to whom *all* authority pays lip service.

II

The popularity and admiration that sonnet 66 enjoys in Croatia and, as we shall see, elsewhere on the Continent, contrasts sharply with the disregard or, at best, lukewarm responses it has found with Anglo-American critics and scholars. In what is still the best commentary on the whole cycle, Stephen Booth's *An Essay on Shakespeare's Sonnets*, it is relegated to a footnote and the appendix.[2] The introductory notes in the scholarly editions hardly go beyond pointing up in which ways it deviates from the other sonnets of the cycle: its anaphoric structure, which completely overrules the conventional division in quatrains; the parallelism of its stichomythic lines, which does not suggest any logical progression and seems to pile up at random ever new examples of social abuses; the marginalization of the central theme of the sonnets—love—to which it only turns in the last line, actually the last hemistich:

> Tired with all these, for restful death I cry:
> As to behold desert a beggar born,
> And needy nothing trimmed in jollity,
> And purest faith unhappily forsworn,
> And gilded honour shamefully misplaced,
> And maiden virtue rudely strumpeted,
> And right perfection wrongfully disgraced,
> And strength by limping sway disablèd,
> And art made tongue-tied by authority,
> And folly, doctor-like, controlling skill,
> And simple truth miscalled simplicity,
> And captive good attending captain ill.
>   Tired with all these, from these would I be gone
>   Save that, to die, I leave my love alone.[3]

> [Bins müde auf den Tod, ich könnte schrein—
> mitanzusehn, wie Tugend betteln geht
> und blankes Nichts sich bläht in Narretein,
> und wie Beständigkeit verraten steht
> und Ehre an den falschen Mann gewandt
> und Mädchenscheu mißbraucht wird, roh geschändet
> und wirkliche Vollkommenheit verkannt
> und Kraft durch Kriecherei geschwächt verendet,
> und wie der Staat die Geister mundtot macht
> und Torheit Können prüft und dirigiert
> und Wahrheit als Einfältigkeit verlacht—
> kurz: wie das Gute dient, das Böse führt.
>   Bins müde, möchte gehen—doch sterben hieße,
>   daß *in all dem* mein Lieb allein ich ließe.[4]]

It appears to be remarkable only in what it lacks. That these absences and deviations might be a way of highlighting this particular sonnet by setting it off from the rest and thus attributing a crucial status to it, does not seem to come readily to the learned minds of scholars. Closer critical engagements with this sonnet are rare and recent. Helen Vendler, though, identifies line 9, "And art made tongue-tied by authority," as its metapoetic center, which reveals "this wearily reiterative and syntactically poverty-stricken *and . . . and* sonnet" as an instance of what it speaks about, namely art being tongue-tied by authority.[5] And, less incisively and persuasively, a more recent editor of the sonnets, Katherine Duncan-Jones, riding her numerological hobbyhorse, claims a special significance for it on the mere basis of its number 66, ever since St. John's *Revelation* associated with "universal corruption."[6]

Continental critics, however, have, ever since World War I, frequently and enthusiastically singled out this particular sonnet. Some of them are referred to in the "New Variorum" edition published during World War II, and its editor, Hyder E. Rollins, even endorses their view that it is "valid for the misery of *our* times," as the German critic Ernst Groth wrote in 1930, insisting only that this is "a statement surely truer of *our* times than of 1930."[7] The Italian philosopher Benedetto Croce called it "the famous sonnet 66" written "wholly in the spirit of Hamlet."[8] The anarchist Gustav Landauer, executed in 1919 for his conspicuous role in the short-lived Munich Soviet Republic, saw it as the expression of Shakespeare's bitterest despair, on a par with *Hamlet, King Lear, Timon of Athens*, and *Coriolanus*.[9] For the scholar Julius Bab it marks the crucial point where Shakespeare's "road curved into darkness."[10] Even for Friedrich Gundolf, the disciple of Stefan George's reactionary circle of aesthetes, it belongs with "den mächtigsten Bekenntnissen des Meisters" [the most powerful confessions of the Master] and epitomizes within its compact formulas the basic material of the whole cycle and the fundamental mood of his dramas of *Weltschmerz*: "Der äußere und der innere Fluch seines Lebens, mächtig genug für seine großen Weltschmerz—oder Weltekel-tragödien, ist hier keimhaft springend, fast epigrammatisch gepreßt . . ." [The internal and external curse of his life, powerful enough to sustain the great tragedies of *Weltschmerz* and nausea, burgeons here in an almost epigrammatic compression]. The last two lines apart, which are to Gundolf a mere arabesque and a concession to convention ("fremde Schnörkel"), sonnets 66 and 129 are "Vorspruch oder . . . Endurteil zu den ungeheuren Panoramen der sittlichen und sinnlichen Zerrüttung, die . . . dennoch erscheinen als die herrlichsten Bejahungen der menschlichen Stärke und Fülle" [the prologue to, and the final judgement on, the enormous panoramas of moral and sensual corruption represented in *King Lear* and *Antony and Cleopatra*].[11] Writing from within the "Third Reich," Joseph Gregor extolls it as "das ergreifendste und schönste" [the most deeply moving and the most beautiful of the sonnets].[12] Against this background, it does not seem all that surprising that the closest readings of sonnet 66 I have come across are by two non-Anglo-Saxon critics and that both of them approach the sonnet via its appropriations in the cultures of their respective countries, Marina Tarlinskaja's study of its Russian translation,[13] and Ulrich Erckenbrecht's richly annotated anthology of its German renderings,[14] which first launched me on my Route 66.

III

Such readings of sonnet 66, if not directly political, clearly respond to the political situation of the reader, and relate what makes the sonnet-speaker cry out against in bitter anguish to the moral chaos and the political oppression of their own times. In this sense, Karl Kraus's publication of his versions of Shakespeare's sonnets in 1933 was timely.[15] For Kraus, a Viennese Jew, great satirist, and political journalist, the shutters were coming down with Hitler's *Machtergreifung* or "Seizure of Power" and his art became tongue-tied—indeed, "silenced" as his translation says—by the new Fascist authorities. As he famously remarked: "Zu Hitler fällt mir nichts ein" [As to Hitler, there is nothing that would come to my mind]. His public readings of *Timon of Athens* in 1914 had been one of his ways of evoking the apocalyptical horrors of the oncoming World War, the "Last Days of Mankind" (*Die letzten Tage der Menschheit*, as the title of his play has it); now, at another crucial turning point of European history, he again protested in the name and voice of Shakespeare against the rising tide of inhumanity. Here, as always, his translations and adaptations were not primarily motivated by philological considerations, but by the need to respond to the political situation.[16]

In the same year, a posthumously published article by the distinguished Jewish-Austrian scholar Leon Kellner argued, in what was to be his last essay, against all reductively biographical and topical readings of the sonnets that would contain their meaning and relevance within Elizabethan bounds. Then, turning to 66, for him "the pearl among the sonnets," he insists upon its timeless validity beyond any possible topical references to particulars of Shakespeare's own political and private situation: "es ist nicht ein Wort darin, das nicht auch heute volle Geltung hätte" [there is not a single word in it which has not its full value today].[17] Written just before his death in 1928, facing the rampant growth of racism that had already cost him the chair of English at Vienna University in 1914, the political thrust is both guarded and obvious.[18]

Two years later, in 1935, Lion Feuchtwanger embarked upon the third and last novel of his *Wartesaal* trilogy, his series of *Waiting Room* novels, which were to depict the "Wiedereinbruch der Barbarei in Deutschland und ihren zeitweiligen Sieg über die Vernunft" [the return to, and irruption of, barbarism in Germany and its temporary victory over reason] in a vast panorama stretching from 1919 to 1939, from the end of the World War I to the beginning of World War II.[19] Feuchtwanger, a German-Jewish writer with strong left-wing sympathies, had fled from Nazi persecution to the South of France as early as 1933. He had set his new novel, *Exile* (or *Paris Gazette*, as it was entitled in the English translation appearing in the same year, 1940) in the contemporary Paris of German émigré composers, writers, and journalists fighting against the Nazi regime, their own frustrations, and each other. One of them is the young and highly gifted poet Harry Meisel. He has written a cycle of short stories with the title "Sonnet 66," which uses Shakespeare's sonnet not only as its title and epigraph, but as the backbone of its structure: each verse of the sonnet is turned into a bitter and cynical story set in Nazi Germany, "thus drawing its own Shakespearean rhyme and reason from what happens under Hitler":

Das Manuskript trug den Titel "Sonett 66," und als Motto war vorangesetzt jenes Sonett Shakespeares, das mit den Worten beginnt: "Müd alles des, schrei ich nach Ruh im Tod," und das in großartigen, verzweifelten Versen die Verderbnis der Zeit anklagt. Da spreizt sich hohles Nichts in Glanz und Herrlichkeit, reinster Glaube wird unheilvoll verstrickt, goldenes Ansehen schändlich an Lumpen vergeben, Kraft durch krummes Regime vertan, Leistung in Staub getreten, Persönlichkeit verbannt, der Kunst wird durch die Obrigkeit die Zunge gebunden, Verstand muß sich vom Wahnsinn verarzten lassen, überall werden Gut und Schlecht ins Gegenteil verkehrt. Harry Meisel hatte den kühnen Versuch unternommen, zu jeder Zeile des Sonetts eine Geschichte zu schreiben, spielend im Dritten Reich, und sich so auf die Hitlerschen Ereignisse seinen Shakespeareschen Vers zu machen.[20]

[The manuscript had the title "Sonnet 66" and Shakespeare's sonnet beginning with the words "Tired with all these, for restful death I cry" and denouncing in glorious and despairing verses the corruption of the time served as its epigraph on the first page. Here hollow nothing struts in glamour and glory, purest faith is fatally ensnared, gilded honour is shamefully conferred upon scoundrels, strength is wasted by a crooked regime, achievement trodden into dust, personality banished, art is tongue-tied by authority, reason forced to let itself be doctored by madness, and everywhere good and evil are reversed. Harry Meisel had made the bold attempt to write a story for each of the lines of the sonnets, set in the Third Reich and thus drawing his own Shakespearean rhyme and reason from what happens under Hitler.]

We, the readers, are never given any of these stories, but we are given Shakespeare's sonnet twice: first in the brilliant prose paraphrase I have just quoted, then, as the motto to the second book of *Exile*, in Feuchtwanger's own verse translation, modeled in parts on Stefan George's. In both cases, Shakespeare's last verse is omitted, the one verse—Gundolf's "arabesque"—that links up sonnet 66 with the love theme of the sonnet cycle. Stripped of its *volta*, "Save that, to die, I leave my love alone," the sonnet becomes an even starker indictment of political evil and an even more despairing cri du coeur. There is nothing left that would promise consolation or compensation, neither love nor religion; there is only the Hamlet-like suicidal death-drift that frames the eleven indictments as its last line repeats the first: "Des alles müd, schrei ich nach Ruh im Tod"—not, as with Shakespeare's penultimate verse, in the subjunctive ("Tired with all these, from these *would* I *be gone*"), but as a declaration of intent ("Tired with all these, I cry for rest in death"). In the end, Harry Meisel will, indeed, find a suicidal death.[21] And his friends will see in his own "Sonett 66" and in Shakespeare's sonnet 66: "The meaning of Harry's life enshrined, the revolt of Man against Nothingness breaking in upon him, the great *quand même*":

> Ist er zugrunde gegangen? Da ist noch das "Sonett 66." Das "Sonett 66" ist der Sinn von Harrys Leben, es ist das Aufbäumen eines einzelnen gegen das hereinbrechende Nichts, es ist das "quand même." Das Messer des Strizzi hat den Körper Harrys erledigt, aber dem "Sonett 66" hat es nichts anhaben können. Das "Sonett 66" wird leben, wenn kein Hahn mehr kräht nach denen, die heute so gewaltig das Maul aufreißen.[22]

> [Has he been annihilated?—There is still "Sonnet 66." The meaning of Harry's life is enshrined in that "Sonnet 66," the revolt of Man against Nothingness breaking in upon him, the great *"quand même."* The knife of the petty criminal had killed Harry's body but could do no harm to "Sonnet 66." "Sonnet 66" will live when nobody will care a straw about all those that brag so mightily today.]

Harry's great *quand même* is the great "Trotz alledem," which, in Ferdinand Freiligrath's translation of Robert Burns' "For A' That and A' That," had already inspired the radical democrats in the nineteenth century[23]: now it gives exiled German and German-Jewish intellectuals the moral strength to persist in their apparently hopeless struggle during the darkest period of our history.

It was Feuchtwanger's novel above all, which drew the attention of a wider, and particularly a politically aware, audience to Shakespeare's sonnet 66. It soon became, as Ulrich Erckenbrecht put it memorably, "die Erkennungsmelodie der Kriegsmüden, die 'Lili Marleen' der Intellektuellen" [the identification tune for all those tired and disgusted with war, the "Lili Marleen" of the intellectuals].[24] Hanns Eisler, perhaps the most prominent of the *entartete* (or "degenerate") composers escaped from Fascist Germany, set it to music in his Hollywood exile in 1939, eliminating, like Feuchtwanger, the last line with its consoling turn towards the private and the erotic.[25] He also eliminates verse 6, "And maiden virtue rudely strumpeted," presumably because it may be understood too exclusively in sexual terms. What remains is a grim and powerful decalogue of social and political abuses, mounting in its tone from fatigue and frustration to anger, and framed by the verbatim repetition of the first line at the end. Eisler's setting, dodecaphonic in technique yet approaching free atonality at places, follows Shakespeare's structure of end-stopped lines and, through brief piano interludes, breaks up the sonnet into four parts (Shakespeare's lines 1–4 / 5-7-8-9 / 10–12 / 13). At the center of the composition (bars 33 to 35 of 58), its heart of darkness, we hear the beat of the line "And art made tongue-tied by authority," with its beat emphasized by the surprising change from legato to staccato-portato chords in the piano accompaniment, by the long notes of the singing voice and by more than usually shrill dissonances.[26]

In Russia, where Feuchtwanger's novel was first published, Dmitri Shostakovich set Boris Pasternak's translation of 1940 to music,[27] and produced three versions of it as part of his *Six Romances after Raleigh, Burns, and Shakespeare* (opus 62, 62a, 62/140), two during the Stalingrad years 1942/43 (the first for bass voice and piano, the second for bass and grand orchestra) and one as late as 1971 (for bass and chamber orchestra).[28] This in itself shows how adaptable sonnet 66 is to changing political circumstances and purposes: in its overdetermined generality and abstractness it can be held up as a mirror to Stalin's or Brezhnev's Russia as well as to Hitler's Germany—or to all of them at the same time. Sonnet 66 is here the penultimate of a cycle of six songs, preceded by Sir Walter Ralegh's grimly humorous sonnet "To his Son," and three songs by Robert Burns, "Oh wert thou in the cauld blast," "Macpherson's Farewell" and "Comin thro' the rye, poor body," which continue the somber mood and the themes of imminent death and of love in times unpropitious for love-making and set the tone for it; what follows it is a scherzo march after the anonymous "King's Campaign" (a campaign from which only the king returns), which foregrounds once again the grim humor drowned in the elegiac rendering of Shakespeare's sonnet. The performance of the sonnet here rises to an impressive high-seriousness by repeating with little variation the same musical phrase for each verse, by the regular and monotonous beat of a funeral march, the plangently sonorous bass voice, the deep register of the orchestral accompaniment and the funeral bell sounding throughout it the death knell for all hopes. The series of indictments again, as in Eisler's version, reaches its climax in line 9, "And art made tongue-tied by authority," which is set off from the rest by a heightening of the voice—which reaches, in bar 42, at the Russian word for "mouth," its highest note, C flat—by the increasing resonance of the bell, and by a break in the continuity of the orchestration. The surprising turn in the concluding couplet from political frustration to love is also highlighted in this setting by a pause, the further darkening of the register and a moving change of key from the predominant, if unstable, G major to E-flat minor.

IV

The further fortunes of sonnet 66 in Germany also demonstrate its adaptability to changing situations. What had given form, a vocal habitation and a name—the prestigious and protective name of Shakespeare—to writers suffering under Fascism before and during the war, became a sounding board for dissident voices after the war. This is particularly true for the Eastern part of the divided Germany, the German Democratic Republic (GDR). Erckenbrecht's anthology offers no fewer than ten translations that respond to the situation in East Germany. Read in their chronological order, they record seismographically the growing frustration with the project of forging a socialist society without democratic consent, which resulted in ever more subtle mechanisms of repression and surveillance, and "the increasing awareness that the evils depicted in sonnet 66 did not arise from distortions within a basically just society (as originally supposed), but that they were an integral part of it."[29]

The first East German translation of the sonnet is that of the poet Stephan Hermlin, written in 1945 and revised in 1976.[30] Shakespeare's sonnet here becomes part of our German *Trümmerliteratur*, the "literature of ruins and shambles," and of the zero hour of reconstruction. Its indictment of a world upside-down looks as much back at the horrors of Fascism and the war as at the present moral chaos and the formation of new powers and divisions. Some of the words in Hermlin's translation accentuate a political reading, for instance "Wort" for Shakespeare's "art": "Das Wort von Macht gebunden welkt dahin" [The word, fettered by might, wilts away] for "And art made tongue-tied by authority." Hermlin as a poet was deeply concerned with the power—and the impotence—of words; he was to become a prominent member of the East-Berlin Deutsche Akademie der Künste in 1952 and later Secretary of its "Sektion Dichtung und Sprachpflege" [Section for poetry and the cultivation of language] and in these capacities tried to defend the freedom of speech, literature, and the word. The festival of "Junge Lyrik" [Young Poetry], which he organized in 1962, was regarded as a provocation by many academicians and members of the politburo and cost him his secretaryship.[31] Among the young and contentious poets presented by him were Volker Braun, Rainer Kirsch, and Wolf Biermann—all three of them to become translators or propagators of sonnet 66. As Volker Braun wrote in retrospect: "Das Sonett 66 war, unter unsern Verhältnissen, *Mode*" [Sonnet 66 was, in our circumstances, a *fashion*].[32] And Rainer Kirsch, compiling a mini-anthology of translations of the sonnet in his collection *Ordnung im Spiegel* [Order in the mirror], pointed out that, in Hermlin's translation, "Shakespeares bestürzende Botschaft trifft uns so, als wäre sie vor 470 Jahren für uns geschrieben," meaning that Shakespeare's startling message had proved its grim topicality in our world as if it had been written for us 470 years ago.[33] To translate, it became a samizdat way of publicizing one's anger and despair at the perversion of socialist ideals in the *real existierende Sozialismus*, the "Actually Existing Socialism." And to make the message unmistakable, though still protected by the mantle of Shakespearean authority, they used certain catchwords or catchphrases that indicated the target: *Ehrenspangen* [military bars] for "gilded honour" (Volker Braun), *Kunst und Wissenschaft* [arts and sciences] for "art" (Hans Hübner), *Apparat* (Christa Schuenke) or *amtlich* (Volker Braun, Hubert Witt) for "authority," and *Privilegien* for "jollity" (Stefan Stein). Or, they changed the register completely, twisting the first verse from melancholy to vulgar outrage, as in Ronald M. Schernikau's free rendering: "ihr kotzt mich an, ich würd jetzt gerne gehn" [You make me puke, I feel like leaving]—in the sense of leaving the GDR, the "to be or not to be" question for dissidents in those years.

Shakespeare's sonnets are the sonnets of a dramatist, a playwright. They do not only show this in their interaction of four characters, their frequent metaphors of acting, or the self-characterization of the speaker as a man of the theater; they are theatrical also in suggesting a live voice and body speaking and gesticulating. It does not, therefore, come as a surprise that there have been several attempts to actually stage them.[34] One of these attempts was made in the GDR at the Staatsschauspiel Dresden in 1985 and repeated, with considerable alterations, in 1987 at the Bayerische Staatsschauspiel München. The director, Wolfgang Engel, did not aim at a well-made play, but produced a postmodernist performance using twenty-nine of the sonnets to explore their ambiguities of gender, the instability of character and plotting, and problems of language and the poet's art. These problems also had a social and a political dimension, which Engel highlighted in his performance, his "persönlicher Offenbarungseid," as he put it, his "personal oath of manifestation," involving not only his sexual preference.[35] Under such auspices, sonnet 66, of course, was bound to occupy a focal position. It was indeed, as Engel said, "das geistige Zentrum der Regiekonzeption" [the spiritual center of his theatrical realization of the sonnets] and was emphasized by being presented in six different versions. Its first words—in Hubert Witt's translation: "Müde von alldem"—was actually planned to provide the title for the whole performance, but censorship intervened here and the programme already printed with that title had to be pulped at the last moment.[35]

In the Munich production, which was also televised by the Bayerische Rundfunk, sonnet 66 is led up to by sonnet 76, "Why is my verse so barren of new pride," which is here turned from monological self-questioning to a dialogue between patron and poet, an interrogation of the poet by the patron. From here we move via brief interpolations from Hamlet's great soliloquy, in particular his list of grievances (3.1.72–78), that prepares us for "our" sonnet, to snatches from sonnet 121, where the poet asserts his own identity against the detracting rumors circulating about him in an envenomed society. When we finally reach sonnet 66, we find its uncommonness foregrounded in the uncommon way in which it is delivered—as a rather formal recitation addressed to the audience, as a commentary upon, an indictment of, the present times and the present world, the here and now, in which lovers find it hard to love and artists hard to work. A note of politically committed poetry invades the Renaissance sonnet cycle and the postmodern performance at this point, a note resounding with the dissident connotations the sonnet has garnered in its half-century of political applications.

Of course, poems and artistic performances do not bring down Walls or Iron Curtains, but they register and reinforce dissidence and subversion. The company that staged the performance, the Staatsschauspiel Dresden, had already acquired a certain fame or notoriety for being one of the leading *perestroika* groups in the country; in autumn 1989, when the Berlin Wall did come down, it proved to be particularly active in contributing to the *Wende* or the revolution by staging it both inside and outside the theater.[37]

In these heady days and weeks, sonnet 66 once again was to play a prominent role: It is the first of December 1989, less than a month after the fall of the Berlin Wall and we are in Leipzig in the Messehalle II. The well-known poet, songwriter, and singer Wolf Biermann, invited by the dissident *Neues Forum*, gives his first concert in what is still the GDR. His expulsion from the GDR as persona non grata in 1976 had created a nationwide stir and polarized the cultural establishment in East Germany, and this background gives a symbolic resonance to his homecoming after thirteen years. What he sings is a series of new songs responding to the current events and looking back at the GDR. Among the songs with which he rises to the political occasion, there is—you will no longer be surprised now—"Shakespeare, das 66. Sonett," which he had translated and set to music early in 1989, when nobody had yet realized how imminent the implosion of the GDR was.[38] A year later, a studio recording of it was released, together with other timely songs and ballads, on his record *Gut Kirschenessen. DDR—ça ira!*[39] Here, as before in the televised concert, the contentious *Liedermacher* (or, songwriter) between East and West cries out his and the sonnet's exasperation with great emotional intensity, modulating his voice from pathos to sarcasm and reinforcing his disgust at the seemingly endless catalogue of abuses with his own guitar accompaniment, which oscillates between ironically romantic *cantilena* and the breathless drive of impassioned chords. And the word that frames the sonnet, "müd" or "müde" [tired], is given special emphasis by being repeated at the beginning and drawn out into a cri de coeur that disrupts the melodic line.

As in his early mentor, Stephan Hermlin's first postwar version, in Biermann's song Shakespeare's sonnet is made to perform in a transitional period of turmoil and disorientation and is opened up to readings that look both backwards and forwards: in the reunited Germany art may no longer be "geknebelt von der Obrigkeit" [tied and gagged by authority], but with alternative ideals vanishing quickly in the takeover bid, the remaining decalogue finds new fields of relevance. At the same time, Biermann's song proves once again that the very sonnet that speaks *of* art being tongue-tied by authority lends itself particularly well to speak *out against* authority tongue-tying art.

V

My last section is yet to be written—as I have not yet reached the end of Route 66 and am still traveling, asking people along my road whether they know anything about the further fortunes of sonnet 66. Here are a few of my most recent findings, some of them gathered in Murcia, Spain, of all places, at the conference on Shakespeare in Europe in autumn 1999. No, none of my Spanish, Portuguese, or Italian colleagues knew anything about sonnet 66 being put to critical service by dissidents in Franco's Spain, Salazar's Portugal, or Mussolini's Italy, or the Italy of the *anni di piombo* or the *mani pulite*. But there were also a number of colleagues from Eastern European countries at the conference and they proved extremely helpful in furthering my quest.

There was Isabela Staikova, an Anglicist from Sofia and wife of the well-known theater director Ludmil Staikov. She told me that her husband had told her about Vladimir Svintilla, who, in 1976, published the first complete Bulgarian translation ever of Shakespeare's sonnets: He knew all of them by heart, both in the original, in Russian translations, and in his own, and enjoyed reciting them at academic or social gatherings. Late on such convivial occasions, when wine or vodka had already mitigated fears and inhibitions, it sufficed that someone in the group shouted "66" and he did his sonnet 66 act—a performance of the English original to be followed by translations and improvised adaptations, each one of them rising more boldly and pertly to the occasion and making Shakespeare's sonnet speak out against the Shivkov regime in ever more pointed references to its social, cultural, and political abuses. The mere number 66, in this context, came to function as a samizdat shorthand for dissidence.

In neighboring Romania, relentlessly policed by Securitate, there were—to my and my Romanian friends' knowledge—no public or semi-public uses of sonnet 66, though I have been told that many lovers of Shakespeare could not help but think of Madame Ceaucescu's academic pretensions and snigger among themselves when reading of "folly, doctor-like, controlling skill."[40]

I also met Martin Hilský, who holds the chair of English at Prague's Charles University and is the most recent Czech translator of Shakespeare's sonnets. The publication of his bilingual edition in the mid-1980s was celebrated with a reading of the sonnets at the National Theater. On that occasion, he told me, the recitation of sonnets 66 and 94 ("They that have power to hurt") solicited a particularly warm response—also because its political message and application was reinforced by a theatrical effect that was as simple as it was powerful: the stagehands just lowered the iron, the safety curtain, at the actor reciting them, thus creating a visual metaphor of oppression and authority tongue-tying art.

Other recent uses of sonnet 66 in Europe I found by sheer serendipity. Studying—for reasons quite unrelated to my quest along Route 66—the poems of the distinguished Belgian poet, translator, painter, film and theater director Hugo Claus, I came across his Dutch version of "Tired with all these" in a cycle of fifteen sonnets after Shakespeare that was first published in 1988.[41] Claus only adopts three of the grievances from Shakespeare's endecalogue of abuses and replaces the rest with four powerful metaphors clearly targeted on the political stagnation and corruption of contemporary Belgium:

> Soms bidden om een kwieke dood.
> Want wat waarde heeft moet schooien.
> Terwijl onbenul wordt aangepoot
> kan waarheid het bij ons niet rooien.
>
> De raketten van een schandelijke legering
> worden gecelebreerd.
> De wetten van een ontrouwe regering
> Worden gekostumeerd.
>
> Het goede is doodmoe.
> Het kwaad is commandant.
> Adieu, moeras van mijn land,
> ik wil zinken als een steen.
> Waarom ik het niet doe?
> Ik laat haar nog niet alleen.[42]

Another surprise encounter with sonnet 66 also had a Flemish-Dutch background—a background that reaches back to the early

1990s when the Belgian theater director Luk Perceval began to think about condensing the complete cycle of Shakespeare's history plays into one performance. He was later joined in this project by the Flemish writer Tom Lanoye and the outcome of their joint venture was then presented under the title *Ten Oorlog* [Into battle] in Ghent in 1997. Attending *Schlachten!* [Slaughter], the German version of this vast and devastating twelve-hour panorama of political power-play, intrigue, perversion, and corruption at the Deutsches Schauspielhaus Hamburg one sunny day of spring 2000, I was alerted from my state of mental exhaustion induced by five or six hours of theatrical excess, when I suddenly and briefly heard the voice of sonnet 66.[43] It was at the very end of *Henry V,* here *Der fünfte Heinrich*, at the last moment before the midway break between the first set of three plays and the second and therefore at a place that gave to it a particular emphasis: "La Falstaff," Shakespeare's Falstaff figure queered into a transvestite and into Hal's surrogate mother and lover and serving as chorus and commentator to the play, laments his rejection and the Prince's betrayal of his homosexual love to patriarchal reasons of state, authoritarian law and order, and to the French Princess, in a long and moving monologue unscripted by Shakespeare, while King Henry makes love to "laughing Cathérine" on stage. Their sexual climax coincides with his emotional and rhetorical climax, and it is at that point that La Falstaff recovers a Shakespearean voice, the voice of sonnet 66, its concluding couplet, in Klaus Reichert's German translation of Tom Lanoye's Flemish translation:

> Ich bin so müd . . . Am liebsten ging ich gleich . . .
> Doch totgehn mag ich nicht . . . Denn wenn ich sterb,
> Laß ich mein Liebstes mutterseelallein . . .[44]

The last words of the sonnet are the last words of La Falstaff, and sonnet 66 has the last word before the lights go out on him and on the first part of the whole cycle. The homosexual connotations of Shakespeare's sonnets are thus made to reinforce the sexual politics of the entire performance, which adds onto Shakespeare's catalogue of grievances one that remains mute in the sonnet itself—the free flow of affections "disablèd" and humanity "disgraced" by patriarchal regulations of desire.

Finally, quite a number of friends and colleagues drew my attention to a particularly prominent performance of sonnet 66— prominent, that is, in Eastern Europe. Our sonnet featured—or even starred—in a Georgian film that has occasionally been shown at festivals and in film clubs in the West but has quickly gained a cult status amongst dissidents throughout Eastern and Central European countries—including the GDR, where a semi-official attack upon it as a distortion and defamation of history occasioned a storm of protest—and immediately came to be widely considered as a sign of the tide of changes that were soon to sweep across the Warsaw Pact states.[45] Tengiz Abuladze's film *Repentance* (*Monanieba*) was completed in the Orwellian year 1984, but was screened only once that year and then shelved. Its general release in 1986 was due to the personal intervention of both Gorbachev and his foreign minister from Georgia, Eduard Shevardnadze, and this in itself turned the film into an harbinger of glasnost.

The film is set in a provincial Georgian village, in which Varlam, the local mayor, has just died. Despite repeated attempts to bury this important man, his body continues to appear. A mysterious woman is put on trial and we learn that she, who has lost both parents and many innocent friends under Varlam's vicious, despotic rule, is responsible for the exhumations. As the truth about his monstrous inhumanity is gradually revealed in surreal imagery any repentance and forgiveness gives way to the exposure and indictment of brutal tyranny. The tyrant and *revenant*, a grotesque composite of Hitler (his moustache), Mussolini (his black shirt), and Stalin's KGB chef Lavrentij Berija (his nose-nippers or pince-nez) has, as is often the case with despots, a soft spot for music, poetry, and the fine arts, and he frequently breaks out in poetic flights, singing arias from Verdi operas or reciting from the treasures of Russian and Georgian poetry.

At one crucial moment, where he parades his artistic talents to his future victims, he first delivers Manrico's famous stretta from the third act of *Il Trovatore* and then adds, as a further token of being a man of the highest cultural accomplishments, Shakespeare's sonnet 66, pedantically giving the author's name and the sonnet number at the end.

When I first saw the film I took this recitation of sonnet 66 as a particularly cynical appropriation of dissident voices by the oppressor himself. In the meantime, however, I have been enlightened by professor Igor Shaitanov, Head of English at Moscow University and member of the jury for the Smirnoff Prize for Literature, the Russian equivalent of the Booker, that there is a further depth of meaning, another way of understanding the uses of the sonnet here: sonnet 66, together with sonnet 130, were the only two sonnets from Shakespeare's cycle canonized by the Soviet cultural authorities; they were singled out for popularization in children's readers and were on all scholastic and academic curricula. But why, you may wonder. Well, sonnet 130, "My mistress' eyes are nothing like the sun," was celebrated as a proletarian, down-to-earth realist critique of the aristocratic and decadent cult of Petrarchan love, and sonnet 66 was extolled as Shakespeare's prophetic indictment of the abuses of capitalism and the corruptions of the West. Against that background, Mayor Varlam's performance of sonnet 66 can be seen as both the cynical appropriation of dissident voices and the re-affirmation of a well-known affirmative reading of the poem by those in power. Abuladze's grim irony cuts both ways, engaging with a dissident and an affirmative reading of the sonnet at one and the same time.

At this point, where things get really difficult and confusing, I break off my quest along Route 66—at least for the time being.

Notes

An earlier version of this article was published in *Shakespeare Jahrbuch* 137 (Bochum: Kamp, 2001), 1–17.

1. Ibrica Jusic, *Ne dajte da vas zavedu*, Jugoton, Stero LSY-66049, track 9.
2. Stephen Booth, *An Essay on Shakespeare's Sonnets* (New Haven: Yale University Press, 1969), 36 and 203.
3. John Kerrigan, ed., *Shakespeare: The Sonnets and A Lover's Complaint* (Harmondsworth, UK: Penguin, 1986), 109.
4. Günter Plessow, from an unpublished translation of Shakespeare's sonnets.
5. Helen Vendler, *The Art of Shakespeare's Sonnets* (Cambridge: Harvard University Press, 1997), 310.
6. Katherine Duncan-Jones, ed., *Shakespeare's Sonnets,* The Arden Shakespeare, 3d ser. (London: Nelson and Sons, 1997), 242.
7. Hyder E. Rollins, ed., *The Sonnets*, A Variorum Edition of Shakespeare, 2 vols. (Philadelphia: Lippincott, 1944), 1:175.
8. Benedetto Croce, *Ariost. Shakespeare. Corneille*, translated into German by Julius Schlosser (Zürich: Amalthea, 1922), 180. The original dates from 1920.
9. Gustav Landauer, *Shakespeare. Dargestellt in Vorträgen*, 2 vols. (Frankfurt am Main: Rütten und Loening, 1920), 2:360.
10. Julius Bab, *Shakespeare* (Stuttgart: Union Deutsche Verlagsgesellschaft, 1925), 211.
11. Friedrich Gundolf, *Shakespeare: Sein Wesen und Werk*, 2 vols. (Berlin: Georg Bondi/Helmut Küpper, 1928), 1:650f.
12. Joseph Gregor, *Shakespeare: Der Aufbau eines Zeitalters* (Wien: Phaidon, 1935), 546.
13. Marina Tarlinskaja, "On Equivalence in Translation: Shakespeare's Sonnet 66 and Ten Translations into Russian," *International Journal of Slavic Linguistics* 30 (1984): 85–129.
14. Ulrich Erckenbrecht, ed., *Shakespeares Sechsundsechzig: Variationen über ein Sonett* (Göttingen: Muriverlag, 1996); for bibliographical references see also Annette Leithner-Braun, "Shakespeares Sonette in deutschen Übersetzungen

1787–1994," *Archiv* 232 (1995): 285–316; and Eymar Fertig, "Nachtrag zur Bibliographie 'Shakespeares Sonette in deutschen Übersetzungen 1787–1994,' erweitert durch szenische und musikalische Gestaltungen. Berichtszeit: 1784–1998," *Archiv* 236 (1999): 265–324.

15. Karl Kraus, *Shakespeares Sonette. Nachdichtung* (Wien: Fackel, 1933).
16. Rüdiger von Tiedemann, "Karl Kraus und Shakespeare: Plädoyer für eine genauere Betrachtung," *Arcadia* 111 (1979): 1–21, 8.
17. Leon Kellner, "Shakespeares Sonette," *Englische Studien* 68 (1933/34): 57–80, 75.
18. See Hannah Arnold, "Leon Kellner," in *Neue Deutsche Biographie*, vol. 11 (Berlin: Duncker & Humblot), 477–78; see also Erckenbrecht, *Shakespeares Sechsundsechzig*, 27.
19. Lion Feuchtwanger, *Exil. Roman* (Berlin: Aufbau-Verlag, 1963; first published in Moscow 1939—only the first two vols.—and in Amsterdam 1940), 845.
20. Ibid., 145.
21. Ibid., 410.
22. Ibid., 413.
23. Robert Burns, *Liebe und Freiheit: Lieder und Gedichte*, edited by Rudi Camerer (Heidelberg: Lambert Schneider, 1988), 319f.
24. Erckenbrecht, *Shakespeares Sechsundechzig*, 28.
25. Hanns Eisler, *Gesammelte Werke*, Series I: *Vokalmusik*, vol. 16: *Lieder für eine Singstimme und Klavier* (Leipzig, 1976), 66–69; a 1977 recording from the Paul-Gerhardt-Kirche Leipzig is on Hanns Eisler, *Lieder und Kantaten im Exil*, Berlin Classics, 009229BC.
26. Oliver Engelen, "Über Inhalt und Form in Text und Musik: Zwei Vertonungen von Shakespeare-Sonetten" (1999), an unpublished seminar essay that opened my ears to the subtleties of the score.
27. See Tarlinskaja, "On Equivalence in Translation," 113.
28. Dmitri Shostakovich, *Shest romansov na slova anglistikikh poetor/Sechs Romanzen nach englischen Dichtungen für Bass und Klavier, op. 62*, edited by Christoph Hellmundt (Leipzig: Deutscher Verlag für Musik, 1972), 29–34; there is a recording on *Gedichte op. 143a—Romanzen op. 62/140—Aus jüdischer Volkspoesie op. 79*, Capriccio, track 11.
29. Maik Hamburger, in a letter to the author.
30. See Erckenbrecht, *Shakespeares Sechsundsechzig*, 154; Fertig, *Nachtrag*, 290.
31. *"Die Kunst hat nie ein Mensch allein Besessen": Dreihundert Jahre Akademie der Künste*, edited by Akademie der Künste Berlin (Berlin: Henschel, 1996), 637f.
32. Erckenbrecht, *Shakespeares Sechsundsechzig*, 30.
33. Rainer Kirsch, *Ordnung im Spiegel* (Leipzig: Reclam, 1985), 100–105.
34. Cordelia Borchardt, "'As an unperfect actor on the stage'? Dramatisierungen der Sonette in England und Deutschland," in *Shakespeares Sonette in europäischen Perspektiven*, edited by Dieter Mehl and Wolfgang Weiß (Münster: LIT, 1993), 322–38.
35. Michael Raab, *Wolfgang Engel*, Regie im Theater (Frankfurt am Main: Fischer, 1991), 53.
36. See Fertig, *Nachtrag*, 296.
37. Raab, *Wolfgang Engel*, 48.
38. Hannes Stein, "Na siehste—all dies stachelt ja dein Lieben noch: Zu Wolf Biermanns Übertragung von Shakespeares 73. Sonett," *Shakespeare Jahrbuch West* (1990): 167–70, 170.

39. Wolf Biermann, *Gut Kirschenessen. DDR—ça ira!*, Wolf Biermann Liederproduktion, 1998 (originally EMI Electrola, 1990), track 11.

40. Kurt W. Treptow, ed., *A History of Romania*, (Iaşi: Center for Romanian Studies, 1996), 552.

41. Hugo Claus, *Gedichten. 1948–1993* (Amsterdam: De Bezige Bij, 1994), 961; cf. also *Gedichte. Niederländisch und Deutsch*, selected and translated by Maria Csollány and Waltraud Hüsmert (Stuttgart: Klett-Cotta, 2000), 146f.

42. Here is a rough and ready prose translation: "Sometimes to pray for a swift death. / For what is of value must beg. / While stupidity is praised / Truth cannot abide with us. // Missiles made of a shameful alloy / Are celebrated. / The laws made by a corrupt government / Are dressed up in finery. // The good is tired to death. / Evil is commander. / Adieu, swamp of my land, // I will sink like a stone. / And why don't I? / I cannot leave her alone."

Recently, Paul Franssen of Utrecht University has drawn my attention to an instance in which sonnet 66 was used for political purposes in the Netherlands. In 1999, when Bram Peper, then Minister of the Interior and previously Mayor of Rotterdam, was accused of fraudulent practices, the poet and alderman Manuel Kneepkens made use of Arie van der Krogt's translation of this sonnet, "waarin de dichter zijn woede de vrije loop laat" [in which the poet gives free rein to his anger], by reading it our during the heated debates in the city council of Rotterdam, rubbing in its obvious topical relevance. See Arie van der Krogt, "Want winst leidt tot verlies, verlies doet winnen," *Folio (Shakespeare-Genootschap van Nederland en Vlaanderen)* 7, no. 1 (2000): 5–16, 15.

43. See Maik Hamburger,"Salzburger Schlachteplatte," *Shakespeare Jahrbuch* 136 (2000): 209–12.

44. Tom Lanoye/ Luk Perceval, *Schlachten!*, Programmbuch des Deutschen Schauspielhauses in Hamburg und der Salzburger Festspiele (Frankfurt am Main: Verlag der Autoren, 1999), 130.

45. See Marcela Euler, "Pokajanie (Die Reue)," in *Metzler Film Lexikon*, edited by Michael Töteberg (Stuttgart: Metzler, 1995), 464–66.

Shakespearean Fascist: A. K. Chesterton and the Politics of Cultural Despair

G. D. White

> Shakespeare was the greatest thinker of this or any other age."
> —A. K. Chesterton

Providing an essay with a title such as this for a book on Shakespeare in Europe, I am aware that my definition of the term "fascist" plays an exceptionally significant role. In discussing the aesthetic vision of A. K. Chesterton, the former theater critic of the *Stratford Herald* and editor of the *Shakespeare Review* in the late 1920s, who became an internationally important ideologue for the far right, I use the term to describe the consistent elements of his mature [*sic*] political philosophy. These include adherence to an extreme antidemocratic nationalism with strong elements of racism and, particularly, anti-Semitism. The significance of these beliefs—and indeed, of Chesterton himself for Shakespeare scholarship—is the disquieting fact that his political convictions emerged in large part from his preoccupation with Shakespearean aesthetics. This preoccupation led Chesterton to the conclusion that the cultural decay he saw in interwar Europe (most specifically in England), demanded a spiritual rebirth built on a model of English nationhood. His vision of this rebirth crystallized around the metaphysics of Shakespearean drama.

The fascism that Chesterton espoused in his later political career, though never holding direct power in Britain, is kin to a range of European and American far-right political groupings, some of enormous historical and contemporary influence. Through investigation of the role of the aesthetic in Chesterton's political views we may shed light on the ways in which idealist conceptions of literary production can be employed to legitimate ultraconservative, nationalist, and generically fascist ideologies. In the case of Shakespeare,

Chesterton's enthusiasms mark an extreme example of the danger of idealizing literary production as a transcendent category.

From Shakespeare to Fascism: Chesterton's Journey

Chesterton's Shakespeare criticism is an example of an idealizing cultural voice that elevates the artist to heroic status and bemoans the collapse of cultural value. As such, it is very much of its moment, characteristic of the cultural despair that preoccupies commentators across the modernist movement in Europe. For some critics, artists, and practitioners, such despair led to a loose sympathy with the immersive idealism of nascent fascism. For others it rendered them the direct assistants of tyranny, though often through a complex bargain with later fascism's hatred of formal experimentation. (Joseph Goebbels was, famously, an expressionist novelist who tamed his artistic radicalism, Hans Johst an expressionist laureate whose desire for cultural renewal led him to become Hitler's most favored playwright.) As David Baker suggests in his biography of Chesterton: "The Fascist generation was typified by the 'disinherited mind' of the marginal intellectual all over Europe."[1]

In his critical celebration of Shakespeare as the aesthetic champion of spiritual truths, Chesterton provided a relatively common conservative account of the playwright. However, it was in the "aesthetic education" that Shakespeare offered that Chesterton also located the rationale for his symptomatic fascist despair. In its use of apparently respectable critical commentaries to approach political ideas, his work provides an instructive example of the co-option of an iconic cultural figure to legitimate extreme political opinion.

Before taking on the role of right-wing ideologue in Oswald Mosley's prewar British Union of Fascists, Chesterton held a career as a respected theater commentator, a critic for local and national newspapers, and as an articulator of a model of Shakespearean identity that a rebuilt Memorial Theatre should serve. Chesterton worked as editor and theater critic for the *Stratford Herald* between 1924 and 1928, and was editor of the *Shakespeare Review* during 1928. He continued to write theater criticism when he became editor of the *Torquay Times* between 1928 and his joining the BUF in 1933. He published a volume of his criticism, *Adventures in Dramatic Appreciation*, in 1931, as well as two publications related to the redevelopment of the Memorial Theatre.

From 1933, A. K. Chesterton was a member of the BUF, though he split from the organization prior to the Second World War as a consequence of Mosley's increasingly dictatorial tendencies. After the war he established the League of Empire Loyalists—a group dedicated to the defense of supposed British global supremacy. In his later years he became a founder member of the National Front, an influential, though electorally relatively unsuccessful, right-wing group in England in the 1970s. The anti-Semitism and racism that had underpinned his work in other organizations became the key to this new movement's philosophical perspective. Chesterton died in 1973, but the critical construction of Shakespeare as an artist-philosopher, drawn up in Chesterton's early friendship with a schoolteacher acquaintance whose writings on Shakespeare he encouraged—G. Wilson Knight—remained a constant part of this influential Fascist's vision.

SHAKESPEARE AS VISIONARY: CHESTERTON'S DRAMATIC CRITICISM

Chesterton's dramatic criticism is largely the conventional appraisal of performance and production, often self-deprecatingly presented as the apologetic musings of a journalist unqualified to comment on matters of high culture. However, it exhibits two clear tendencies. One is the desire to discover in contemporary drama the execration of postwar democracy for its failures to learn the lessons of the First World War. The other is to celebrate the overarching genius of Shakespeare as a philosopher and knower of human truths:

> To deduce a moral from his works is as easy, or as difficult, as it is to deduce a moral from the workings of nature. Shakespeare delved deeply into the human heart; he explored every recess of the human mind . . . he was counsel for every warring factor in man's life, but he was never more than counsel . . . he never sought to judge.[2]

It is clear from this criticism that Chesterton employed a model of drama that focused on the playwright and performer as the "unacknowledged legislator," as the articulator of a synthesis of human and political experience and desire beyond that obtainable through other discourses. Shakespeare stands here as an artist-hero with a Nietzschean supremacy of vision and an ability to stand above the glib didacticism of the politician.

During the late 1920s, Chesterton's *Shakespeare Review* was already involved in the project of national renewal.

The one thing needed is a new spirit in the land, and that spirit can only be created by superimposing upon the literacy of the nation a real education which will enable it to reject the cheap and nasty, and feed its brain on better things. Our own solution is that it should feed its brain on the best of all things—the works of William Shakespeare.[3]

The *Review* published Wilson Knight's early exploration of the aesthetic autonomy of Shakespeare's vision, "The Poet and Immortality," and it is here that Chesterton's biographer, David Baker, detects an overlap between the two writer's views of Shakespeare's genius.[4] According to Baker, Wilson Knight's criticism suggested that "all true art, properly interpreted in its own poetic terms, is capable of providing us with a truth beyond sterile intellectual rationalism; and such a message is buried in Shakespeare's *Hamlet*, which contains a tragic dialectic of beyond-good-and-evil amorality."[5] This fed neatly into Chesterton's own search for an inspirer of nationalist rebirth. Furthermore, Wilson Knight's championing of the British cultural tradition of the "poet prophet" supported the "simplistic faith in Britain as the supreme poetic nation" that attracted and infected Chesterton's own nationalism.[6] In a 1926 essay entitled "Shakespeare's Detachment and Modern Progress," Chesterton was already articulating that vision of cultural regeneration, and of eternal values contrasted with modern, soulless democracy, which he saw exemplified in Shakespeare's visionary overview.[7] Chesterton's idealization of the poet's role later provided a philosophical basis for his conviction that contemporary democracy concealed "truth," while it was only through metaphysical contemplation of this truth that a vision of renewal might be found.

Chesterton's own radicalism in the period after the First World War meant that his championing of Shakespeare was not part of a general attempt to seek solace in a classical tradition. Rather, he embraced the attacks on bourgeois morality that characterized a range of post–First World War drama, and was an engaged critic of the discursive dialectics of Shaw. As with so many other European refugees from the war, he found it difficult to square the peacetime world with the blood sacrifice he had witnessed. He wrote appreciatively of the film of Erich Maria Remarque's *All Quiet on the Western Front* for exposing the "strange eruption" known as war-fever, and he saw in the film an articulation of his own experiences of the war.[8] These had left him severely distrustful of militarism.[9]

Yet the experience of war also provided Chesterton with that generally low regard for contemporary democracy, which shaped his view of a world in need of redemption. His vision of the postwar milieu suggested that the purity of horror experienced by the soldier made the caviling of everyday life intolerable. "In the war, a man's soul was stripped naked; he could not for the life of him disguise a yellow streak. In postwar England, however, a yellow streak could be wrapped up in a coat of many gorgeous colours, and cads and cowards masqueraded as the salt of the earth."[10] The tone of despair shown here, highly reminiscent of the expressionist moment in Germany, led Chesterton into increasingly strident commentary on the weaknesses and failings of the contemporary world.

The repeated assertion of the essentialist world view, of soul and spirit, into which his model of warfare fits, is directly related to that idealist model of literature which seeks to set the poet-artist above the commonplace self-deceivers and didacts of the ordinary world. In Chesterton's case it allowed an ambitious radicalism to co-opt Shakespeare as a key legitimating figure. As such it is an example of the misrecognition of political as aesthetic values that characterizes the interwar politics of the far right in Europe and that so troubles the margins of modernism, leading many into a sympathy with the hoped-for purifying force of fascism.

In his analysis of fascism and dramatic spectacle Roger Griffin suggests that "Fascism . . . emerges when populist ultra-nationalism combines with the myth of a radical crusade against decadence and for renewal in every sphere of national life."[11] Griffin also suggests that it is anticonservative: although it may evoke mythic national ideas and models, it will aim to embody them as eternal within the new order, which it establishes.

This definition is for Griffin a careful attempt to discriminate across the wide range of right-wing movements in twentieth-century Europe, and is designed to prevent the lumping of other traditions into the fascist model of cultural despair. It makes the regenerative nationalist metaphysics of Wilson Knight's *Christ and Nietzsche* clearly distinct from the philosophizing of the European fascist regimes.[12] However, Knight's conclusion that a providential plan may have required Nazism to exist in order for the political moderation exemplified by Shakespeare's nation to flourish in its aftermath may indicate that he also suffered from a "mild case of cultural despair."[13] In Chesterton's work, nationalist myth-making and its political expression in the fascist moment were more explicitly linked.

Shakespeare and Nationalist Myths

Wilson Knight's later work retained the idealization of visionary achievement. He praised Shakespeare's authorial intention to outline in *The Tempest* "a myth of the national soul."[14] Furthermore, he suggested that the play dramatizes in Caliban's worshiping of Stephano "that utter miscarriage of all true valuation which lurks within every denial of highest sovereignty."[15]

By this point, Wilson Knight and Chesterton's avowed political sympathies had diverged, and Chesterton's aesthetic thinking had been reworked into the factionalism and pamphlets of his political party life. However, the ideal of nationhood that remains central to Wilson Knight's criticism was still mystified in similar terms to those employed by Chesterton. The suggestion that Shakespeare operated as the true visionary of his native realm is a work, in Wilson Knight's hands, of poetic reconstruction, forcing a reading of moderate, liberal, and civilizing British history into the dramatic structure of Shakespearean text (the co-option of the apparently liberal tendencies of the teacher of Shakespeare within the frameworks of varying degrees of nationalist ideology are well documented).[16]

Other of Chesterton's journalistic writings from his time in Stratford give a flavor of a similar desire to assist the placing of Shakespeare as an integral element in the mythic identity of England. In describing the work of the director of the Memorial Theatre before its 1926 fire, he provided a vivid expression of the significance of the aesthetic in the unification of a national body:

> Mr Bridges Adams brings people face to face with their own dreams. He works with spiritual essences as his materials, and in the results of his labours audiences see before them the population of their own romantic and spiritual worlds. The warring elements within them are made to take on the cloak of poetry and stand exultant . . . testifying to the grandeur of the imagination of man.[17]

This account then slides into an hagiographic celebration of the generic "great man," linking the Elizabethan imaginer with the contemporary royal family as Chesterton quotes from the address of the Duke of Windsor at the opening of the replacement building. The future abdicator is quoted declaring that "Shakespeare's genius is yet universal, and evokes the homage of the men of all nations."[18]

This claim for the universality of Shakespeare as a cultural icon is, ironically, part of the conscious construction of a specifically English cultural tradition (expressed here by a figure whose own life shows some of the contradictions inherent in such a project) that forms a thread in subsequent conservative constructions of the playwright. More recently, the current Prince of Wales produced an evocation of Shakespeare's universality as similarly rooted in the local elements of "Englishness":

> Shakespeare's language is ours, his roots are ours, his culture is ours—brought up as he was in the gentle Warwickshire countryside, educated at the grammar school in Stratford, baptised and buried in the local church.[19]

The model of a mythic nationalism, encoded in the burgeoning Shakespeare project with which Chesterton's journalism is connected, is a key element in Chesterton's later projection of a revolutionary nationalism. Here he sought to link the "great men" directly with the people, rather than with the sclerotic processes of democracy, and his seeking out of an active engagement with political life facilitated the assimilation of his aestheticized politics within the program of the British Union of Fascists. Championing the superior vision and moral judgement of the artist led Chesterton to marginalize his own humble status as critic and to celebrate the "new man" who might lead the fascist renewal—rather as Wilson Knight celebrates Prospero's control over his island as an image of developing English nationalism. Chesterton's desire for this ideal man made him a fervent early supporter of Mosley—though it later swung into equally passionate bitterness as he fell away from the movement. From here began the journey towards the extreme anti-Semitism, racism, and conspiracy theorism that has made his later paranoid ramblings such as *The New Unhappy Lords* a favorite of far-right and white supremacist organizations.[20]

Conclusion: Cultural Optimists

Griffin suggests that it is not, in fact, cultural despair that characterizes Fascism, but rather cultural optimism and the desire for transcendence.[21] Despair is the necessary precursor to the desire for a new age. In this respect, we might consider Chesterton's attachment to Shakespeare as characteristic of a prefascist condition. His journalism and criticism provided a space in which to articulate a vision of a debased contemporary world and to idealize the work of the aesthetic imagination that Shakespeare embodied. Griffin's analysis establishes a restricted definition of an ideologically fascist theater that seeks the triumph over decadence of a redemptive "new man." Chesterton's work looks to such a regeneration and claims that it should take its inspiration from the philosophical model offered by Shakespearean drama.

As Baker recounts, Wilson Knight felt that Chesterton "could have been a very great power in dramatic criticism if things had gone that way in his life."[22] In fact Chesterton turned to find transcendence in the political arena, underpinned by the inspiration of the aesthetic. In his final editorial for the *Shakespeare Review*, Chesterton moved towards the political consummation of his aesthetic ideas in the practice of politics:

> The need for spiritual leadership has never been more insistent than it is to-day, when the human race, lost in a maze of its own making, is stumbling towards a precipice which none has eyes to see.[23]

In doing so, Chesterton suggested that the poet's visionary role was not, in the end, to bring the fascist regeneration to pass, but rather to legitimate it, to articulate ideas that, correctly "interpreted," would establish a model for the soul of the fascist nation. For Chesterton himself, Shakespeare's work provided the inspiration for a monstrous English nationalism that shared many characteristics with those movements that dominated Europe in the 1930s, and that continue to lay claim to cultural legitimacy today.

Notes

The epigraph is from A. K. Chesterton, "Some Modern Criticism," quoted by David Baker, *Ideology of Obsession: A. K Chesterton and British Fascism* (London: Tauris, 1996), 109.

1. Baker, *Ideology of Obsession*, 35.
2. A. K. Chesterton, "The Ethics of *Timon of Athens*," in *Adventures in Dramatic Appreciation* (London: T. Werner Laurie, London, 1931), 74.
3. A. K. Chesterton, editorial in *Shakespeare Review* 1, no. 1 (1928): 5.
4. G. Wilson Knight, "The Poet and Immortality," *Shakespeare Review* 1, no. 6 (1928): 407–15.
5. G. Wilson Knight, quoted in Baker, *Ideology of Obsession*, 100.
6. Baker, *Ideology of Obsession*, 102.
7. A. K. Chesterton, "Shakespeare's Detachment and Modern Progress," *Shakespeare Review* 1, no. 2 (1928). Quoted in Baker, *Ideology of Obsession*, 107–8.
8. A. K. Chesterton, *Adventures in Dramatic Appreciation*, 19.
9. Chesterton's response to the film is in striking contrast to attitudes in Nazi Germany, where its antimilitarism led to it being banned.
10. Chesterton, *Adventures in Dramatic Appreciation*, 10.
11. Roger Griffin, "Staging the Nation's Rebirth: The Politics and Aesthetics of Performance in the Context of Fascist Studies," in *Fascism and Theatre: Com-*

parative Studies on the Aesthetics and Politics of Performance in Europe 1925–1945, edited by Gunther Berghaus (Providence, R.I.: Berghahn Books, 1996), 13.

12. G. Wilson Knight, *Christ and Nietzsche* (Oxford: Staples Press, 1948).

13. Baker, *Ideology of Obsession*, 98.

14. G. Wilson Knight, "The Shakespearian Superman," in his *The Crown of Life* (Oxford: Oxford University Press, 1947), 255.

15. Wilson Knight, "The Shakespearian Superman," 254.

16. See David Johnson, *Shakespeare and South Africa* (Oxford: Clarendon Press, 1996); Richard Wilson, "NATO's Pharmacy: Shakespeare by Prescription," in *Shakespeare and National Culture*, edited by John J. Joughin (Manchester: Manchester University Press, 1997); Jonathan Dollimore and Alan Sinfield, eds., *Political Shakespeare* (Manchester: Manchester University Press, 1985).

17. A. K. Chesterton, *Brave Enterprise: A History of the Shakespeare Memorial Theatre, Stratford Upon Avon* (London: J. Miles and Co., 1936), 26.

18. Chesterton, *Brave Enterprise,* 52–53.

19. H.R.H. The Prince of Wales, "Introduction," in *The Prince's Choice: A Personal Selection from Shakespeare* (London: Hodder and Stoughton, 1996), 5.

20. A. K. Chesterton, *The New Unhappy Lords* (London: Berence Press, 1965).

21. Griffin, "Staging the Nation's Rebirth," 14.

22. Baker, *Ideology of Obsession*, xiii.

23. A. K. Chesterton, "Perspective on the Cotswolds," *Shakespeare Review* 1, no. 6 (1928): 391.

Shakespeare: Man of the Millennium

Boika Sokolova

THE TITLE OF THIS PAPER WAS PROMPTED BY THE RESULTS OF THE poll conducted at the end of 1998 among 45,000 listeners of the *Today* program on BBC Radio 4. Shakespeare, by a very narrow margin, beat Sir Winston Churchill and grabbed the title of "Personality of the Millennium." *The Times* of 2 January 1999 explained the choice as acclaim "for his timeless writing, poetic vision and profound humanity."[1] This, I believe, expressed the views of many listeners. To give weight to the estimate of the newspaper, Stanley Wells and Lisa Jardine were asked to comment on the choice. I strongly doubt that either of them voted in the poll, nor did they suggest anything towards the assertion of a timeless humanity. Their scholarly opinions then, like mine, cannot explain the vote in the terms of the newspaper, but offer a venue for a discussion of Shakespeare's legacy in our time in history.

Stanley Wells gave three reasons for Shakespeare's popularity. First, the basic nature of the situations in his plays, "things that people have to struggle to put up with and things they enjoy." Second, the complex positioning of the individual, not only in society, but in relation to his "place in the universe and man's relationship with God or whatever we think of as God" (*The Times*, 3). Third he ranked the skillful construction of his plays.

On the other side of the same newspaper page, Lisa Jardine passionately held a different line: "On the eve of the millennium," she wrote,

> we might ask if Shakespeare is much more than a convenient empty box to put things into. His plays and poems have acquired an all-purpose quality which has gone way beyond that breadth of vision for which he was long revered, and which fans might once have dubbed the mark of his "genius." . . . Shakespeare has become a cipher, one of those iconic figures . . . who can be filled with any consumer message you fancy . . .

his contribution to the sum total of human well-being was restricted to lingering words rather than lasting deeds."[2]

It is in the context of these two opinions, rather than that of the poll, that I can position myself more comfortably, because they provide a framework for a sensible debate, which poll results obliterate in their categorical monosyllabic assertiveness. My perspective in this debate is that of an Eastern European whose experience of Shakespeare is colored by this fact.

My perspective on Shakespeare is to approach him as a moral and political focus for at least three generations of Eastern European directors and audiences. For those in the theater, the words of Shakespeare were a constant reminder of the lasting deeds of human spirit and a source of hope. In this context, the resilience of Shakespeare's drama against the pressures of monolithic ideology was produced through the intellectual coauthoring and partnership with the directors of the postwar generations. For millions of people Shakespeare's plays were as important as the discovery of penicillin, to use Lisa Jardine's example of lasting deeds. And more than that, they were a medium for communicating truths unspeakable and horrors unfathomable, a way of exorcizing the pent-up tensions of the system where they were kept prisoners, ultimately a tool of its subversion and demise.

To return to what Stanley Wells has given as reasons for Shakespeare's longevity is indeed to stress the basic nature of situations of human experience on which his plays are based. The Bulgarian director Vili Tsankov has a similar opinion—"It is not human character that Shakespeare is so good at, it is human action, what humans do, in basic situations."[3]

In our book *Painting Shakespeare Red,* Alexander Shurbanov and I have defined another internal reason for Shakespeare's wide appeal and adaptability, which lies at the heart of his artistic method: "Drama, by definition, is dialogical, it is the meeting point of often conflicting attitudes to a chosen object. However, most dramas, like most artistic products in general, strive to transcend the dialogical status and attain a conclusive synthesis of attitude and meaning. Shakespeare's drama is rather exceptional in that it does not seem to strive to any such final transcendence, a peculiarity defined by the tradition of liberal humanists as his proverbial elusiveness."[4]

It was indeed the openness of structures, the interplay of different points of view, the inconclusiveness of the moral stance that made

Shakespeare adaptable to the needs of a variety of discourses, and that imbibed the political in the constrained intellectual conditions of communist totalitarianism.

Another reason can be discovered in the position of the theatrical institution in European society as it emerged at the time when Shakespeare wrote his plays. Great as it is, Shakespeare's verse is not the major reason for his fame. Neither Goethe, nor Pushkin, for example, is a lesser poet. Goethe especially, is a better thinker, when it comes to the systematic expression of ideas. But it is Shakespeare, whose major poetic work is for the *theater*, that has had such a tremendous impact in Europe and beyond. The theater has secured for him a life that cuts across national frontiers, aesthetic styles, fashions, and ideologies, and has carried him through history, not as an icon to be revered and emulated but as a creative partner.

As a medium, the theater offers a specific public experience different from those offered by other media. In the communist world, where the politicized public brutally invaded the private and where public pageantry required compulsory attendance, the theater was a place for people to go by choice, a privately darkened emotional space. The unique personal presence of the actor, the director's interpretation, the muffled response of those sitting in the dark auditorium, were so different from the brightly-lit public celebrations, where multitudes marched under banners and deafening music. These "bands of brothers," gathering at performances that would sometimes last for a few weeks or run for a few seasons, depending on the immediate concerns of the censors, were the exact opposite of the multitudinous celebrations which reduced humans to ciphers. In the theater people were individuals partaking of a common experience out there, in the public space, equalized humans were like "fish-eggs," to use Mikhail Romm's phrase from his remarkable film *Simply Fascism*.

The positioning of the theater at the interface of the political establishment with the less structured world of popular social life has always been a source for its strategies of self-preservation and the root of its relative freedom. In the autumn of 1999, Chinese President Jiang Zemin made a controversial visit to Great Britain. Most of the media covering the event exposed the deep gap between the government's hypocritical assertion of human rights and its readiness to forget ethical issues, on which it had recently gone to war, under the pressures of commercial and political interest. One of the strands of the narrative around the visit was often mentioned but never discussed. It is to do with Zemin's visit to the Globe.

While Buckingham Palace with a smile unrolled its red carpets, the theater had had a different reaction, impossible to discover in the newspaper coverage. Before agreeing to the visit, artistic director Mark Rylance had sent a letter to the President expressing his own stand as well as that of his troupe on human rights. Only then did he agree to put on a "rehearsal" of *Julius Caesar*, a play belonging to a past season. The respective scene was chosen with tact and point. Not the assassination, of course, but the quarrel, between Brutus and Cassius from act 4, scene 2—the moment of tragic collapse of the singleness of purpose of the old comrades, due to their obvious human weaknesses.[5]

In the rather unpalatable political equation the Globe Theater managed to negotiate its position of saying-unsaying, a familiar stance in Eastern Europe. I am not of course suggesting a similarity of situation, but rather a broad analogy. No one would have closed the Globe had it refused the visit. However, one can imagine a large dose of unpleasantness and pressures surrounding such an act.

The way the theater gave in, comes to show something that older Eastern Europeans know all too well: that being "in" differs, depending on how you behave when you are there. Being "in" with a difference is precisely what Shakespeare provided for many of them when half of the continent was relinquished to the Soviet Union. The deal was made, then, soon after the Iron Curtain fell. Both acts were effected by the runner-up for the "personality of the Millennium" contest on Radio 4, Sir Winston Churchill. Millions were left with a terrifying legacy, including the poet's words and the politician's deeds.

Under the new circumstances, as parliaments stopped being forums for political and social debate, the theater took over some of these functions. While the official ideologues presented Shakespeare as a great precursor of communism, theater directors used his subversive imagination to show the relevance of these old texts to the here and now of their audiences.[6]

The play which became the focal point of the pressures of the time was *Hamlet*. No other drama by a European author has traveled so well, has seen so many modifications, and has been so malleable as well as distinctly itself at adoption. The play's enigmatic quality, its dynamic reality enveloped in silences and nonaction, its slipping point of view, the ceaseless strife of its characters against powers they cannot overcome, made it the ideal vehicle for probing into the Eastern European condition.

For nearly a century and a half before that, *Hamlet* had been an instrument of self-analysis across Europe, representing national concerns—be they German, Russian, Polish, or others—at moments of crisis. For the isolated postwar Eastern Europeans, the play gained a new significance—it provided a link in cultural memory, a sign of discontinuity with the past, and little by little, a diagnosis of a common present. For some years after the war, the stages were still inhabited by doubting, philosophical, weak Hamlets, a reflex of a tradition crushed against the wall of imposed normative optimism. Starting in the mid-1950s, *Hamlet* became a play about the present, and a major political drama. This process came to a head in 1964, a year of particular importance to the fortunes of the play in Eastern Europe.

Writing during the Second World War, Bertolt Brecht had been among the first to break away from the idea of *Hamlet* as a work of national self-mirroring.[7] For Brecht, *Hamlet* was a play of the depravity of the "criminal ruling classes" at a time of war, a story of the tragic discrepancy between one's reasoning and one's action.[8]

The new Eastern European politicization of the play, its lifting above the national and into the analysis of a social system, took shape slowly in the course of the two decades, following the events that prompted Brecht's reading. The first critic to describe the nature of the change was Jan Kott in *Shakespeare Our Contemporary* (appearing in Polish in 1961, in French in 1962, and in English in 1964). This work is the subtext to much of what happened with Eastern European *Hamlet*s, without necessarily being a direct influence. The new accent, which Kott discovered in Polish productions of the late 1950s, was watching and enquiring.[9] *Hamlet* was turning into a modern play about life in a police state run by murderous tyrants.[10]

The tendency to activate structural levels and elements of the linguistic texture, which appealed directly to modern audiences, became a way of bringing in *Hamlet* through the back door into political dissent. In the freer conditions of Poland, some, like Jerzy Grotowski, had started dazzling experiments, unthinkable in other places in Eastern Europe. His *Hamlet* of 1964 was a major event, whose fame spread by word of mouth and attracted directors from other countries who traveled to Poland to see the production. In this version, the play was

> not so much cut as re-written and re-cast: Hamlet was set in opposition to the rabble, an emancipated intellectual (then a fashionable term of sociological description), a hysterical Jew, versus a primitive though clever, coarse, yet vigorous anti-Semitic crowd with low pleasures and low aspirations; each party being an unattractive reflection of current social and cultural prejudices and stereotypes.[11]

This was clearly a Polish *Hamlet*—the material was handled in a novel, uncompromisingly experimental way by the director. It had nothing to do with official prescriptions for dignified optimistic remoteness. *Hamlet* pulsated with modern history.

Across the border, in the harsher circumstances of the GDR, *Hamlet* was also wrested from the dire constraints of socialist realism. In the GDR, the strength of theory was much more powerful than in any other communist country, as were the ropes of control, implementation, and observation of theoretical postulates. The oppressive situation there is comparable only to that in the Soviet Union, which however had a much stronger group of dissidents among the intellectuals. That is why in the GDR the dogma was undermined not directly but through the clever implementation of its own postulates, particularly the principle of populism and the work of Bertolt Brecht. Normative communist aesthetics had its bluff called through new, pungently modern translations, that revealed to the audiences levels of meaning and immediate relevance, often invisible in older canonic translations. Thus the directors Adolf Dresen and Maik Hamburger re-translated the play for their 1964 Greifswald production. It was quickly removed from the stage because it "was too saucily vernacular to fit the image of Hamlet as a hero of socialist humanism."[12]

Robert Weimann's *Shakespeare and the Popular Tradition in the Theatre*—first published in East Berlin as *Shakespeare und die Tradition des Volkstheaters* (1967)—provided an important exploration of the populist paradigm, which theoretically justified the need for experimentation with nonillusionist theatrical devices in circumstances bogged by mimetic reflectionism.[13] Weimann wrote in the wake of a tradition of Marxist criticism, with a history of internal differentiation of which his own book was yet another example, and in the context of Brecht's theatrical reform.

In the 1930s, Soviet Marxist critics of the sociological school were severely criticized for upholding the stance that Shakespeare could not be credited with progressive views, because he was a poet of the dying aristocracy and the emerging bourgeoisie. This theoretically stood in the way of the attempts to place him as a precursor of communism, an exercise in cultural politics that the new political order ruthlessly implemented. Critical attitudes had to adjust. What came to the fore were the active nature of Shakespeare's heroes, their struggle to change their circumstances (a proto-image of class struggle), the shared nature of the language of aristocratic and low characters, meaning the popular side of the social and linguistic structures of the plays. Soviet theory coined the all-embracing term "realistic method," invoked to bridge the gap between Shakespeare's obvious pastness and the new appropriation of his work, which, in terms of theatrical presentation, meant observation of psychological Stanislavskian conventions of acting and staging, compounded with optimistic readings of the plays.

Writing in the 1960s, Weimann highlighted the nonillusionistic nature of Renaissance theater and distinguished between the conditions in which a play was originally produced and its meaning in the present.[14] Theoretically, he spanned the gap between past and present by including in the argument the changeable factor of interpretation as an antidote to the single-message socialist realist dogma. Weimann's complex and sophisticated argument was a meeting point of Marxist critical theory and Brechtian theatrical practice, which had a liberating effect on the theater in the GDR.

Where it comes to theater practice in other Eastern European countries, however, it was not theory but the politically meaningful innovative style of Brecht that was most successfully used to justify experimental innovation, not only of the Brechtian kind. Jan Kott's powerful influence can be explained through the free nature of the Polish theater of which he became a chronicler and to the specific reception of existentialist ideas in the conditions of the communist system. Though Kott's critical model is a closed existentialist one, where mankind is confronted by a meaningless, cruel, and absurd universe, in Eastern Europe this was a fundamentally politically *oppositional* model.

Writing from an entirely different theoretical position, Kiernan Ryan has summed up Shakespearean tragedy as obliging us "to confront without illusions the appalling cost of beliefs whose absorption dooms people to destroy not only others but themselves, making a cruel farce of their conscious intentions."[15] Eastern European theater read existentialist and absurdist ideas precisely in this light, revealing the unbridgeable rift between the ideology and the destruction of the individual. This is the context that created the dialogue between Brecht and Kott as central to "the new 'internationalization'" of *Hamlet*.[16] This is something I believe to be true of Shakespeare's legacy as a whole.

*Hamlet*s originating from the Soviet Union also had a tremendous impact. Grigory Kosintzev's 1964 film externally obeyed all the rules of positive presentation of cultural heritage required by the ideologues. It reaped highest praise from the establishment for all the wrong reasons. Kosintzev's hero, played by Innokentii Smoktunovskii, was interpreted by official criticism as someone who is not a doubter, who can clearly see through time and his complex fate, an active hero placed in the unbearable conditions of an oppressive past. While the paid hacks of the system saw in the film the optimistic overcoming the reactionary forces of history, to the common cinemagoer this Hamlet was an epitome of the state of the intellectual in a world of oppression, "a man who can say no to all kinds of lie . . . though he does not know how to struggle with lie."[17] Hamlet knew that his awareness of the rotten affairs in the state of Denmark could bring about no change, but there was a dangerous charm in his heroic noncooperation and death. The Aesopian narrative was so powerful that the film became an immediate success for reasons that were light-years away from those of official criticism.

After Smoktunovsky's, the other unforgettable Hamlet which took Eastern Europe by storm, was created by Vladimir Visotsky at Yury Lubimov's Tanganka Theater in Moscow in the early 1970s. Aesopian remoteness was totally abandoned. A nervy young man in jeans, armed with a guitar, this Hamlet was not at all a passive nonconformist, ready to sacrifice himself in a gesture of superior intelligence. He was bitter, murderous, hurting, grappling with all his energy with the mediocrities invested with power who surrounded him. He was really dangerous. Unlike Kosintzev's historical as well as abstract set, Lubimov's stage showed something much closer to home—a tattered ambiance of moving curtains, hardly shielding the personal and intimate from the public, a perfect place for spying—a reality the inhabitants of "real socialism" unmistakably identified with their own communal existences. The shabbiness of life, the threatening cadences of Visotsky's intonations, the harsh melodies of his guitar spoke of an uncompromising young generation and its bristling anger.

Everywhere *Hamlet* was turning dissident. Using the power of the demotic, again in 1964, the Bulgarian director Leon Daniel played the Brechtian card. His Sofia production spoke through a new translation in harsh everyday tones.[18]

Illusionist realism was swept away. The set was a tattered makeshift tent that lent no dignity to the events. Hamlet was a neurotic, suspicious of big words. He nobly refused to collaborate but was cautious, inactive, rather than heroic. His general stance was that of Kosintzev's hero, who would appear on the screens a few months later, but was deprived of his intellectualism. Daniel's Hamlet was a reduced human being from whom the oppression of life had taken a moral toll. Daniel's hero, like Kosintzev's, was deciphered by criticism as condemning the evils of class society. His was also a highly unsettling voice of the post-Stalinist era, who confronted its audience with prickly questions: "How far can you get through noncollaboration?" and "Where do you end as a moral being if you do not react to oppression?"

Daniel's production aired the preoccupations of a generation, which had savored liberalization after the demise of Stalinism, and all the more keenly felt the grip of the system. Brecht provided an excellent justification for asking unpleasant questions. The results, more often than not, ran against the grain. Politics and new expression could be found in him; the texts of venerable Shakespeare, the sacred cow of literary progress as invented by communist literary hierarchies, were the obvious site for such interpretation. No censor could find fault with that.

The 1970s saw new developments. Romanian director Dinu Cernescu placed his Hamlet in a world of total betrayal (1974). His ghost was a hoax, Horatio himself in disguise with the aim of putting the foreigner Fortinbras on the throne; Gertrude and Ophelia were traitors; the world of the play was controlled by men in black uniforms, silent supernumeraries who were always present. The critic Snezhina Panova, typically refusing to admit that modern political implications expressed the gist of Cernescu's reading, has aptly noted that he "has rather tried to reveal the truth of the reality surrounding Hamlet, a reality understood in the existentialist sense: as a closed situation which offers no way out."[19]

The tendency to see in *Hamlet* this darkest of sides of Eastern European experience reached a high degree of realization in the production by the Bulgarian director Vili Tsankov (1982).[20] Its striking feature was that the play had been made a mixture of overtly political chronicle drama with tragic satire and the grotesque. Tsankov's directorial concept involved the disentangling of an ever more complicated political game, conducted and controlled by Claudius, and his attempts to conceal a horrid mystery. The inhabitants of Elsinore were a mass of benumbed, evil, soulless automatons moving around without a thought of their own, propelled only by animal instincts. Their gestures were those of puppets, their intonations affected, their behavior fully ritualized. Techniques of the Japanese theater were appropriately used to highlight this effect.

The atmosphere was tense—"brazen cannons" were daily cast, "implements of war" were imported from abroad. In these circumstances, Laertes, the son of Claudius's first minister, expresses a wish to leave the country. The King is suspicious. He needs the guarantee of Laertes's father. With a stern look, he urges the old man to commit himself publicly. Bailing people out of Bulgaria in this manner was not unfamiliar at that time. It was clear what lurked behind the usurper's mind: Laertes might return with foreign troops to fight against the crown (as, in a way, he does). By saying yes to his departure, Polonius pawns no less than his head. Next, the prince himself wants to leave. Certainly, no one would let him go. In the director's words, even his mother joins in: "Please, please, stay with us. We love you so!"[21]

Ophelia's dementia opened a dangerous chink in the success of this masquerade. Madness tore off her mask of restraint and all of a sudden she became uncontrollable and dangerous. As she went around raving, she drew the sword of one of the guards and pointed it at the king and queen. Everyone was stunned. In an interview Vili Tsankov stated that he had attempted to represent a situation from his own experience:

> Wives and mistresses of members of Politburo and their sons liked to mix with our lot. From them I have heard the most terrible stories about those circles. Imagine how dangerous the madness of such a woman would have been for all concerned. She knew their unseemly secrets and could now spread them far and wide.[22]

The unnatural social mechanism shown at work in the production had managed to absorb everybody, including its most formidable opponent, the clear-minded dissident prince. The finale was especially eloquent in this respect. Hamlet was forced to join one of the many ceremonies of the court, which happened to be the ceremony of his own physical destruction. The duel was staged as a carefully designed ballet and Hamlet performed the steps prescribed for him by the choreographer. Murderer and victim became interchangeable in this weird dance. The dissident as the tyrant's fool—as the tyrant's tool perhaps? A thought that, together with that of the frightening resilience of the secret guards, has most awfully plagued post-totalitarian years in Eastern Europe.[23]

The postwar East European dramatic tradition enriched Shakespearean interpretation through the uncompromising inclusion of the political. Whether by way of open experiment, Marxist Brecht, communist populism, or oppositional existentialism, his plays, *Hamlet* in particular, were used to express a traumatic common experience. Their interpretations discarded the idea of the essentially human and transcended the narrowly national as they powerfully conjured up the dire consequences of prison life on moral values and the difficult triumphs of the human spirit in the conditions of communism.

Of course, there are other Shakespeares, like the one of the listeners of Radio 4 for whom he is a national poet, and many, many others.

Eastern European Shakespeare nowadays is also no more what he used to be. He has become part of other narratives and moved on to new horizons.

What is his meaning for Europe in the context of the millennium? I will evade the futility of this question by quoting one of John Fuller's *Balkan Sonnets*:

> That swirling from Archangel to Gibraltar
> Signals the sort of weather we are under.
> We know that maps, like institutions, alter
> And sticky days give way to evening thunder.
> The globe turns round and countries shift their borders,
> And satellites observe the tanks and clouds.
> Only the rain will not respond to orders.
> Only the sky will not break up like crowds.
> The wonder is that Europe can survive:
> Like a great dinner-service, chipped and cracked,
> Reconstituted, lost, its use unlearned,
> While all the guests are flushed by half-past five,
> Mindful of precedence but not of tact.
> The talk too loud. The odd chair overturned.[24]

If not a man of the millennium, Shakespeare is certainly an element in the glue that has kept our chipped dinner-service together, and this is no mean an achievement at the end of the bloodiest millennium in human history.

Notes

1. Alexandra Frean looks at why Radio 4's *Today* listeners voted the Bard of Avon "Personality of the Millennium," *The Times* (London), 2 January 1999, 3.

2. Lisa Jardine, "Lingering Words rather than Lasting Deeds," ibid.

3. Unpublished interview given to Alexander Shurbanov and Boika Sokolova in July 1999.

4. Alexander Shurbanov and Boika Sokolova, introduction to *Painting Shakespeare Red* (Newark: University of Delaware Press, 2001).

5. This information comes from one of the guides in the Globe and seems to be the official story given to visitors. For this information I am grateful to Hilary Taylor.

6. See Kiernan Ryan, *Shakespeare*, 2d ed. (New York: Prentice-Hall, Harvester Wheatsheaf, 1998). See especially chapter 3, 70–106.

7. Manfred Pfister, "Polish and German Hamlets in Dialogue," in *Hamlet East-West*, edited by Marta Gibińska and Jerzy Limon (Gdańsk: Theatrum Gedanense Foundation, 1998), 23.

8. Reference quoted by Jan Kott, *Shakespeare Our Contemporary*, translated by Bolesław Taborski (London: Methuen, 1967), 54.

9. Kott, *Shakespeare Our Contemporary,* 48. This was Roman Zawistowski's production, designed by Tadeusz Kantor (1956).

10. For a full and interesting discussion of Polish Hamlets, see Marta Gibińska, "Shakespeare's *Hamlet* in Polish Theatres after 1945," in *Shakespeare in the New Europe,* edited by Michael Hattaway, Boika Sokolova, and Derek Roper (Sheffield, U.K.: Sheffield Academic Press, 1994), 159–74. In *Hamlet East-West,* see also Manfred Pfister, "Polish and German Hamlets in Dialogue" (16–31); and Joanna Walaszek, "Andrzej Wajda—*Hamlet* Four Times" (109–24).

11. Marta Gibińska, "Shakespeare's *Hamlet* in Polish Theatres after 1945," in *Shakespeare in the New Europe,* 167.

12. Manfred Pfister, "Hamlets Made in Germany, East and West," in *Shakespeare in the New Europe,* 83.

13. See Manfred Pfister, "Hamlets Made in Germany," 84; and Dennis Kennedy, "Shakespeare without his Language," in *Shakespeare, Theory and Performance,* edited by James C. Bulman (London: Routledge, 1996), 141–43.

14. Kennedy, "Shakespeare without his Language," 142.

15. Ryan, *Shakespeare,* 75.

16. Pfister, "Polish and German Hamlets in Dialogue," 23.

17. Quoted by Mark Sokolyansky in "Hamlet in the Russian Culture of the Period of the Thaw," in *Hamlet East-West,* 118–24.

18. Leon Daniel used the then-unpublished translation of the play by Valery Petrov.

19. Snezhina Panova, "Obiknovenniya chovek vuv fokusa na vnimanieto" [Ordinary man in the focus of attention], *Otechestven Front,* December 25, 1974.

20. At Sofia Theater in Sofia, Bulgaria.

21. Vili Tsankov, *The Silver Web* (Sofia: Raivil, 1998), 36–48.

22. Vili Tsankov, during an unpublished interview with Alexander Shurbanov and Boika Sokolova, July 1999.

23. The section about Tsankov's *Hamlet* closely follows the text that appeared in Shurbanov and Sokolova, *Painting Shakespeare Red.*

24. John Fuller, *Balkan Sonnets,* in *The Times Literary Supplement,* 1 January 1993, 11.

Part III
Translations

More Alternative Shakespeares

Dirk Delabastita

Research Traditions

As we all know too well, the endless complexities of cultural reality merely proliferate in our study of that reality. Hence the great diversity that characterizes the academic landscape, perhaps most immediately visible in the multitude of disciplines, subdisciplines, and branches sharing research and teaching activities between them. To name just a few of them within the humanities: history, rhetoric, philology, linguistics, discourse analysis, literary studies, theater studies, translation studies, and gender studies. I select these few (sub)disciplines because each of them might be germane to our present undertaking, but also because their mere juxtaposition suffices to call to mind the historicity of our academic traditions. Academic disciplines do not exist of their own nor have they always been here. Rather, as sets of responses to reality, disciplines are locked into one another by an ever-shifting network of relationships that show complex patterns of continuity and discontinuity as alliances, enmities, bonds of neighborliness, or distances between (sub)disciplines are formed, suspended, or redefined.

The divisions between disciplines and subdisciplines are of an institutional nature, determining as they do which department we work in, which journals we subscribe to, which conferences we attend, and of which academic associations we are members. In addition, and more fundamentally, they will determine the canon of relevance and correctness that we have to observe as individual scholars with respect to basic variables such as object, corpus definition, objectives, methods, analytical concepts, critical vocabulary, and standard references. Last but not least, acceptance into a discipline can benefit the individual researcher socially by the intellectual authority and symbolical power it bestows on him/her, as well as by the direct and indirect material rewards of an academic career.

This is, of course, where the individual researcher's private interests dovetail with the agenda of the discipline.

The institutional differences and the conceptual differences do not always coincide. Poststructuralist sociology and poststructuralist literary criticism communicate more smoothly with each other (across the conventional disciplinary borderlines) than a poststructuralist literary critic with a follower of myth criticism (within the same institutional setting). In fact, calls for more interdisciplinary or transdisciplinary work are heard more distinctly and more widely than ever before, suggesting that the existing correlations between institutional and conceptual divisions are getting looser and looser. So, we have to reckon not only with the diversity of material and social infrastructures that make up the landscape of academia, but also we often must cut across these institutional borderlines, with the different conceptual systems by means of which we construct, organize, and communicate our knowledge about reality—in other words, with the huge diversity of competing theories and methodologies (research paradigms, scholarly discourses, academic "fashions") that inhabit the institutional spaces. Institutions notoriously have their own kind of inertia, but the dynamic of conceptual change often succeeds in overcoming this force and in causing institutional borderlines to be redrawn. This usually happens first in the more responsive sectors of academic life (postgraduate programs, journals, book series, associations, one-off research projects) and only at a later stage (if at all) in its less flexible areas (undergraduate and graduate programs, faculty structures, and other long-established institutes). Controversy and change may also affect the very borderline between "academic" discourses and practices and "nonacademic" ones. Thus, many of us are far less confident nowadays than in the heyday of structuralism about whether we can draw a clear line between the specific expertise of the university-based translation specialist (at the "meta"-level) and that of the practicing translator who may have half a dozen of Shakespeare translations to his credit (at the "object"-level) while perhaps having few or no academic credentials.

Shakespearean Translation

The above reflections deal with what we might term (a bit pompously, perhaps) the sociology of research. What are their implications for the theme of this book? The point I would like to insist on making in this essay is that of the polyphony of the different "voices" we hear talking about Shakespearean translation. When we review the bibliography on Shakespeare translation, or when we take a closer look at lists of participants at conferences and seminars devoted to Shakespeare translation, we cannot help being struck by the variety of intellectual and professional backgrounds represented there. Insofar as I can see, the following are the most important professional and disciplinary constituencies that have generated interesting work on Shakespeare translation:

- the translators themselves
- actors and theater directors
- theater critics
- literary reviewers
- linguists
- translation scholars
- Comparative Literature scholars
- English Literature scholars
- historians of the various national literatures
- theater historians in the various national traditions

These different groups have a different relationship to the reality of Shakespeare translation, homing in on different parts or aspects of it, occupying different positions along the cline of participation/observation, having different objectives, theoretical references, and methods. This diversity of approaches may seem fertile and full of promise. All that seems necessary is for these complementary projects to team up to produce a comprehensive, balanced, unbiased, and therefore "definitive" understanding of what translating Shakespeare is really about.

This is certainly an exciting perspective and one that is valid up to a certain point. But we also have to accept that differences in scope, aim, method, concepts, and the like may be too profound for an effective dialogue to be possible at all. Every group will, often unconsciously and tacitly, proceed from a number of axiomatic principles that it is unwilling or unable to part with, and such differences have to be considered very carefully before we wax lyrical on the ecumenical prospects of interdisciplinary research. To quote a typical example, many of the experts on Shakespeare translation fail to show the faintest awareness of concepts, models, and debates in Translation Studies. While it seems only natural that everybody in the field of Shakespeare translation should take note of the achievements of Shakespearean scholarship, relatively few seem to be taking the trouble to acquaint themselves with the ABCs of Translation Studies. The result of such a lack of common ground is mutual noncomprehension and even more often noncommunication. In other words, polyphony often spells cacophony, not contrapuntal harmony.

This discord has tended to conceal the fact that one voice is conspicuously missing from the babbling chorus of discourses on Shakespearean translation: that of mainstream Anglo-American Shakespeare studies. The Anglicists who do get involved are usually scholars working at overseas, non-Anglophone universities. This fact was recently noted from the inside of the discipline by the distinguished Shakespearean scholar Inga-Stina Ewbank, writing in the equally distinguished *Shakespeare Survey*, where she described "the study of translations" as no more than "a stepchild . . . to the immensely fertile body of current Shakespeare studies . . . an interesting and harmless occupation for researchers abroad."[1] Ewbank's clear-sighted admission of collective guilt can be traced back to her personal—Scandinavian and multilingual—background; it is unfortunately matched by few other instances. Among the other exceptions that come to mind (and which I am happy to record in the present context) are the papers by some prominent English Shakespearean scholars contained in *Shakespeare in the New Europe* of 1994.[2]

It is possible to justify this blatant lack of interest by referring to the notion of a fair and efficient division of labor in the humanities. After all, since we cannot all be doing the same things at the same time, we should somehow confine ourselves to what we happen to be best at. Since "native" Shakespearean scholars are as a rule less familiar with the translating languages and the receptor cultures and may perhaps find it more difficult to get access to relevant archives and libraries, they might as well leave the whole business to overseas scholars, who can thus turn their marginal position into a strength. As I want to suggest later in this paper, there is more to the neglect than these practical considerations, however reasonable they sound in themselves.

Translation as a Form of Rewriting

While it would be foolhardy to try and sum up the state of the art of the discipline in the space of a few paragraphs, it is vitally important to note here that debates in contemporary translation theory have moved way beyond the traditional view of translation as the mere replacement of source-language words and grammar by so-called "equivalent" target-language words and grammar.[3] This is not to say that linguistic models have been abandoned altogether, but most linguistically oriented translation scholars have resorted to more comprehensive and more flexible models than that of sentence-rank analysis, namely by drawing on advances made in subdisciplines such as text linguistics, sociolinguistics, pragmatics, critical discourse analysis, and the like. On the other hand, many translation scholars have taken what is sometimes called the "cultural turn," integrating linguistic approaches into (or even downright rejecting them in favor of) theories that foreground the various cultural functions of translation and which in a number of cases embrace an explicit political agenda (like gender studies or postcolonial theory). Such theories have tended to decenter the original text in a number of ways:

- Notions of "equivalence" or "identity" of meaning between source text and target text are jettisoned, along with the idea that the source text embodies a single, stable, and transhistorical intention or meaning that can be recovered in its sameness by the translator (or by the translation scholar or the literary critic, for that matter).
- Translations are seen as representations (produced in and for a specific historical context) of the original text (which was produced in and for a different historical context) and as such they have to negotiate differences (without ever being able to erase them) between at least two linguistic, textual, and cultural systems. Insofar as this negotiation takes place at the point of reception, the scholar has to direct his/her attention to the conditions and constraints in the receptor culture that create the terms in which this reconstitution of the foreign text takes place. This involves the consideration of the translators' individual situation, as well as their wider cultural, economic, and ideological contexts, including the institutional frameworks which regulate the whole translation process (like translator training, commissions and contracts, working conditions, patronage, censorship, distribution, remuneration, and copyright arrangements).
- Not only has there been a general shift of attention away from the source text/culture to the target text/culture, in addition we seem to be witnessing a strong tendency to break down the very source/target duality. This is most programmatically the case in theories bearing a poststructuralist stamp with their built-in mistrust of pure "origins" and of binary distinctions. But empirical reality already offers enough evidence to cast

doubt on the binary source/target opposition. Consider the use of indirect translation that was standard practice in eighteenth- and nineteenth-century Shakespeare translation in Europe, but which exemplifies a principle that is really much more general: namely, that translations rarely derive from a single source. Having to position itself with respect to the multiple editorial, critical, and translational traditions to start with, every translation of Shakespeare is willy-nilly (like every Shakespearean "original," for that matter) a profoundly hybrid text, depending as it does on a multitude of past and contemporary texts and discourses to which it refers through imitation, critique, or avoidance.

- We are left with a very flexible type of theory, which rejects any hypostatized concept of translation and which dissolves the older notion of source/target "equivalence" into a complex fabric of textual relations and interdependencies. Having thus called off the search for the Holy Grail of "perfect" or "ideal" translation equivalence, modern translation theory is ready to envisage many different kinds and degrees of interlingual mediation. Not surprisingly, translation scholars are now seen taking an active interest in phenomena like subtitling and dubbing for film and television (to be sure, a major application of Shakespearean translation nowadays!), interpreting, refugee claimant hearings, bilingual poetry, translingualism, international business communication, software localization, and so on—phenomena that would formerly have been denounced as forms of "adaptation" or worse and thereby placed beyond the pale of the discipline.

Importantly, this widening of the perspective encourages the discussion of preliminary questions such as whether there will be translation in a culture in the first place, and how much, for whom, out of which culture. After all, there are other ways to deal with texts and speakers that resort to a foreign language. These include ignoring them, imposing your own language, subjecting them to ethnic cleansing, or (more constructively) learning their language, or agreeing to share a lingua franca. Studying where, when, and why Shakespeare does *not* appear in translation appears to be just as relevant as investigating the cases where he does.

Insofar as the source text gets decentered and translation is contextualized, the concept of translation loses its hard edge and we can come to understand it in terms of a general theory of discourse where it appears as a form of "reading" and "rewriting" or as a kind of "text-processing" besides many others. This idea might be exemplified by the accompanying diagram, Figure 1, which presents a grid of intertextual and metatextual operations with a few Shakespearean examples added for some of the possibilities listed.[4] The grid crossbreeds Roman Jakobson's famous distinction between *intralingual, interlingual,* and *intersemiotic* translation with the standard set of textual operations as distinguished by classical rhetoric, revived by transformational grammar and here pressed into service as carriers of intertextuality. The one comment that the model requires is that it should not be understood as trying to pigeonhole in distinct categories what is, of course, a multifarious and protean reality. Two examples will amply illustrate this point:

- The 1974 comic strip version of *Hamlet* by Gotlib and Alexis was placed in the INTERSEMIOTIC/DETRACTIO box of the model. Barely eleven pages long, it drops most of the play's action and dialogue and it rewrites the story in the new semiotic medium of the comic strip. But the text in question is at the same time a montage of the original (TRANSMUTATIO) in that it completely reshuffles the play's chronology; there is much that it adds (ADIECTIO) in order to achieve its burlesque and parodistic effect; and the dialogues are in French, involving an INTERLINGUAL transposition as well.
- Holger Klein's 1984 bilingual edition, arranged in the INTRALINGUAL/ADIETIO box for want of a more adequate single label, is another case stubbornly resisting classification. This impressive two-volume publication brings together a new edition of the original, a (German) prose translation, a list of (English) text variants, and more than 650 pages of line-by-line comments combining interpretive criticism with a discussion of both editorial and translational choices.[5]

The scheme is, therefore, not meant as a normative or rigid typology but as an adaptable set of descriptive possibilities. It is all the more important to keep this in mind, since our postmodern culture seems to be favoring Shakespearean rewritings that nibble away at the established genre distinctions—or even downright collapse them in a provocative swipe at tradition. Take the case of *Ten Oorlog* [Into battle], a Flemish version of Shakespeare's Wars of the Roses cycle by theatre director Luc Perceval and author Tom Lanoye, written for an ambitious marathon production by the Blauwe Maandag Compagnie that premiered in 1997 and has met with considerable critical acclaim.[6] This Shakespearean rewriting not only

transformation \ code	identical **Repetitio**	non-identical **Adiectio**
intralingual	mise-en-abyme ("The Murder of Gonzago") allusion anthology citation, quotation imitation plagiarism ready-made parody, pastiche, travesty	blurb epilogue, prologue paratexts preface sequel
text edition	facsimile edition reprint	amplified edition (*The Tragedy of Hamlet told by Horatio, with the full text of Shakespeare's Hamlet*, 1956) annotated edition (Holger Klein, 1984) interpolation
interlingual	literal translation word-for-word translation	annotated translation amplified translation pseudotranslation
intersemiotic	reading recitation theater performance	illustrated edition (*The Pictorial Edition of Shakspere. Hamlet*, 1839)

	non-identical	
Detractio	**Transmutatio**	**Immutatio**
abstract digest fragment summary synopsis title	anagram collage montage	paraphrase rewriting writing back offshoots
abridged edition censored edition (*The Family Shakespeare,* 1807) simplified edition (*Shakespeare Made Easy*)	concordance (Marvin Spevack, 1973) critical edition (Harold Jenkins, 1982) variorum edition (H. H. Furness, 1877) hyper-edition (*Editions and Adaptations of Shakespeare,* Chadwyck-Healey)	emendation palimpsest
abridged translation censored translation	translation in hypertext environment	free translation adaptation *belles infidèles*
comic strip version (Gotlib & Alexis, 1974) soundtrack (Argo) painting (D. G. Rossetti)	film version in hypertext environment	film adaptation (Laurence Olivier, 1948) television adaptation (BBC-TV / Time Life) stage adaptation (David Garrick, 1742) adaptation for puppet theater (bunraku version, Osaka, 1956)

Figure 1

conflates various modes of translation (including extremes of "literal" and "free" translation) but mixes them with several other intertextual strategies such as citation, phonetic transcription, montage, pastiche, synopsis, and so on. Anachronisms abound, Shakespearean high culture is systematically blended with popular culture, and various Dutch-language registers converge with French and with late-twentieth-century urban English slang to produce a curious and transgressive heteroglossia. At every level, this production shows a typical postmodern eclecticism that is bound to clash with any but the most flexible theory of translation.

Translation and Edition

The chief merit of the scheme in Figure 1 may therefore be that it situates the different types of translation among a wide of range of conventional and less conventional forms of "rewriting." With these, translation shares the paradoxical quality of being the source text's only witnesses and means of communicative survival in spite of necessarily being *different* from it in form, meaning, or effect. The model cuts the umbilical cord between original and translation and accepts that there is no way to undo the historical difference— only different ways of negotiating this difference and highlighting or masking it.

The model therefore encourages us to think about any Shakespeare translation in terms of choices and decision processes, and thus in terms of constraints and historical contexts. To press this point a little further and in more concrete terms, I would like to explore the hypothesis that much can be gained by comparing translation with another conventionally well-established form of rewriting, namely text edition. The two show striking similarities with respect to their possible functions (like representation, mediation, canonization, ideological recuperation, or innovation), to the types of textual intervention that they tend to involve (standardization, domestication or foreignization, annotation), to the claims they typically make (claims to "authenticity" and "fidelity"), to the critical vocabulary that their assessments resort to (from "distortion" to "precision"). Indeed, upon reflection, one can only be amazed that the two have almost never been studied in conjunction.[7]

A virtually virgin territory is here awaiting scholarly exploration. There is, first of all, the circumstance that translation and edition cover considerable common ground. I am referring here not just to the obvious fact that many translations are bilingual editions, but also to those "monolingual" translations where the translators do not content themselves with following one source-text edition, but produce their own source text out of the available sources, editions, and variants. Less obtrusively than the bilingual edition but just as effectively, such translations subsume the role of the editor under the translator's task.[8] In addition to such cases of actual overlap, translation and edition often show remarkable resemblances, which may rely on mere typological analogy, or on a genetic relation of textual dependence. Shakespeare translations are usually written on the basis of modern editions (and of the whole critical tradition in which these are embedded) and this situation clearly makes translators dependent on prior textual and hermeneutic choices made by the editors. This is certainly the main explanation (though probably not the only one) why the editorial and critical traditions of Shakespeare's works and their translational history have occasionally run along almost perfectly parallel lines. No work of Shakespeare's exemplifies this situation more clearly than the Sonnets, for which the pattern of reception has proceeded on almost identical principles on both sides of the Channel:

- the Sonnets were not included in the first "complete" editions/translations (they were excluded, for example, or relegated to an appendix) and have kept a slightly ambivalent status within the canon ever since
- their discovery both in England and abroad was linked with a growing interest in Shakespeare's life and person, which tended to favor nonfictional, biographical readings of the poems;
- on account of the poems' possible hints at promiscuity and homosexuality in Shakespeare's private life, such nonfictional readings generated some embarrassment which was often circumvented by subjecting the sonnets/translations to ingenious allegorical readings and/or to actual textual interventions. The latter may be confined to forcing the poems into a more edifying narrative frame by a simple change of their order. Certain editions/translations, however, had recourse to the more dramatic measure of altering the gender of some of the poetic personae (*he* becomes *she*, *friend* becomes *ma bien-aimée*) to dispel the suggestion of same-sex love.

There is no intrinsic reason why the relation of dependence between translation and text edition should have to be a one-way process, but, typically and regrettably, that's what it usually is. Every translation incorporates or constitutes an act of total interpretation; many translators are known to be superbly sensitive readers; and, whatever their individual talents, their position outside the source language and culture usually gives them a keen awareness of the "materiality of that language, the opacity of the signifier, the role of language as a system, and the obscurity and historicity of the cultural fabric of meaning," more so than with the native speaker whose reading is more likely to lull itself into an assenting recognition of misleadingly familiar patterns.[9] Looked at this way, translations present a vast exegetical potential, but editors have systematically declined to tap it. Modern Shakespeare editors and commentators bend over backwards to bring out every single subtlety of Shakespeare's text, but practically none in the English tradition seems to have taken the trouble of consulting existing translations as key witnesses of the diverse ways in which certain passages *can* be read and *have been* read.

Consider the case of Shakespeare's ambiguities, puns, and quibbles, many of which were spotted or attested just years or decades ago owing to the combination of hard historical work and interpretive ingenuity in critics or editors like John Dover Wilson, William Empson, Eric Partridge, Molly Mahood, and their followers. In point of fact, looking at the body of existing translations, we have to conclude that many of these brilliant "discoveries" had actually been made earlier by the guild of translators. This is not to say that all translators had actually understood these subtle puns or ambiguities as such, but different translators appear to have disambiguated puns *in different ways*, so that the picture emerges of readings that are complementary in their respective partialities. The mere collation of such incomplete translations or "mistranslations" thus produces a surprisingly accurate sense of the possible semantic range of Shakespeare's words.[10] If translations, through their easy availability and their interpretive explicitness, are among the most valuable documents for exploring both the interpretive history of a Shakespeare text and its semantic virtualities, why is it that editors (and critics) are not taking note of them?

SHAKESPEAREAN STUDIES AND TRANSLATION

Ever since its inception as a professional, academic discipline in the late Victorian age and the early twentieth century, the study of Shakespeare was a strongly insular affair. Shakespeare himself had of course become international property. In many European nations he played a major role in the development of national identities and of new aesthetic paradigms, being one of the key figures in the history of preromanticism and romanticism. As early as 1856, Albert Lacroix published a substantial monograph on the *Influence de Shakspeare sur le théâtre français jusqu'à nos jours* [The influence of Shakspeare on French theater to the present day], showing how the emerging research community of literary historians and comparatists on the Continent was quick to recognize the spread of Shakespeare as an important field for investigation.[11] Nor was Shakespeare's spread limited to Continental Europe. Recent studies have documented his absorbtion by American culture, as well as the ways in which copies of Shakespeare's works soon followed the flag to all corners of imperial Britain.[12] Shakespearean criticism in Britain and the U.S. meanwhile remained essentially a matter *by*, *for*, and *about* native Britons and their legitimate heirs, with little or no attention given to the history or the problems of translating Shakespeare.[13] Thus, the *New Companion to Shakespeare Studies*—a book that, as the blurb indicates, prides itself on presenting "an up-to-date and authoritative introduction to the whole field of Shakespeare studies"[14]—remains all but silent on translation. Not surprisingly, when the book came out in a German version, it was felt necessary to add a chapter on "der deutsche Shakespeare."

There have been those rare occasions when Anglophone Shakespeare critics could not help confronting the issue of translation themselves. One such occasion was the launch in 1974 of a new journal, *Shakespeare Translation* (later renamed *Shakespeare Worldwide*) under the auspices of the International Shakespeare Association. The first issue was prefaced by a few well-wishing "Messages from Scholars" (meaning established Shakespearean scholars from British, American, and Canadian universities). Significantly, the new journal thereby sought to borrow its legitimacy from the orthodox Anglophone Shakespearean community. No less significantly, it failed to obtain it in the final analysis. The well-wishers display a wide range of manners and opinions—including polite interest and genuine encouragement, along with patronizing airs and imperial sentiments of flattered superiority—but one that is definitely missing from the catalogue is the sense that the new journal might have any relevance whatever for the core activities of the discipline "itself" and that some sort of real investment might be called for on its behalf. Whatever the reality behind the journal's business arrangements, there is irony and symbolism in the fact that the journal has its editorial headquarters in faraway Japan and that it appears to be stuck on the fringe of the academic journals market. When John Lawlor, one of the well-wishers, wrote in his message, "scholars in Great Britain will follow [the journal's] fortunes with particular interest and approval," one cannot help suspecting that the "approval" must have been larger than the "interest" and that Lawlor knew neither was going to be large enough to make any difference to the routines of the "scholars in Great Britain."

Translation was the Cinderella of Shakespeare studies, which remained the more or less exclusive property of the Anglo-American academic establishment. It has been noted that the marginalization of translation is a fact of Anglo-American literary culture in general, and that it is the corollary of an essentially romantic concept of authorship that sees the text as immediately expressing the writer's unique personality and inner vision.[15] The text is a transparent self-representation of the author, expressive of his/her intention, meaning or thought. Since translation, being a derivative product, implies the risk of clouding or distorting these original realities, it must be avoided or treated with extreme caution. This notion goes hand in hand with another romantic concept of lasting influence: that of the organic nature of the work of art, expressed most dogmatically by the new critics' "heresy of paraphrase." All aspects of "form" and "meaning" are fused in the text into an indivisible unity that cannot be reproduced except in its own terms. This view is bound to have an "heresy of translation" trailing in its wake.

What makes the case of Shakespeare different—though the difference is certainly one of degree, not kind—is the undisputed and indisputable canonized status of Shakespeare as the ultimate icon of literary art, a status that bestows on him a wisdom and authority of almost metaphysical depth and therefore a universal, transcendental quality. The worldwide spread of Shakespeare must accordingly be construed as a self-generated process that was written in the stars from the beginning and that has merely followed its own inner logic. Looking into the precise circumstances of this process is not just, therefore, a futile exercise, but also a slightly disrespectful one insofar as it seems to cast a shadow of skepticism on Shakespeare's divine genius. Shakespeare is a paradigm of original creation himself:

> . . . look thorough
> This whole book, thou shalt find he doth not borrow
> One phrase from Greeks, nor Latins imitate,
> Nor once from vulgar languages translate . . .[16]

Precisely to the same extent, Bardolatry requires that Shakespeare's works be spared the injury of translation themselves. The translation of Shakespeare becomes an almost impossible reality to think.

Foreign Accents?

However, since the mid-eighties a rather dramatic series of changes have swept across the field of Shakespeare Studies, showing the effect of the introduction into English departments of modern Continental theory. One of the channels through which these new theories and philosophies have reached a broad Anglophone readership is the excellent series *New Accents* (Methuen, later Routledge), whose very title inadvertently points at their foreign, non-English origin. Two books in the series, *Alternative Shakespeares* (1985) and its sequel (or replacement) *Alternative Shakespeares Volume 2* (1996), belong to the most notable statements of this new paradigm in Shakespeare studies.[17] As these two successive volumes evince, the new Shakespearean paradigm has been characterized by variety and change, but what appears to be common to all its strands is a commitment to putting Shakespeare back in history. This move is often signalled by fitting the word "*Shakespeare*" with scare quotes or indeed by the use of the plural *Shakespeares*. A "dead, white, male" author if ever there was one, Shakespeare's canonized status is no longer taken for granted as a kind of "natural" condition, but analyzed as a man-made construction and a symptom of a specific set of stereotypes, values, positions, and interests. The idea of an "eternal," transhistorical Shakespeare is replaced by that of a series of multiple, often contradictory inscriptions and appropriations.

This new approach involves two complementary projects that have by now in broad circles dislodged the once standard critical procedure of "close reading":

- Relating Shakespeare's works more firmly to the contexts of Elizabethan and Jacobean England by seeing them as complex, possibly ambiguous discursive responses to its social (ideological and institutional) realities;
- Concentrating on the "afterlife" of Shakespeare, seen not as a story of how a proper appreciation of Shakespeare's genius is progressively and justly unfolding itself, but as a series of rewritings of Shakespeare "forged in, by, and for a specific time

and place, and in response to the pressures of a particular context."[18]

Either way, the axiom of a universal Shakespeare is superseded by the twin ideas of difference and historical contingency. This is, of course, where the notion of Shakespeare in translation might (or should) step in as an intrinsic aspect of his "afterlife." But it does not. Let us glance at three recent instances of this oversight. The first example is *Shakespeare's Caliban: A Cultural History*, an excellent study that analyzes the extraordinary range of metamorphoses that have marked the tumultuous career of Caliban, Shakespeare's alleged prototype of colonial oppression.[19] Notwithstanding the study's strong awareness of the connections between Shakespeare and cultural imperialism and its wealth of documentation, it usually overlooks non-English-language sources. This is particularly evident in its "Part III: Receptions," which discusses an impressive array of rewritings of *The Tempest* across different genres and media. The different chapters there look at stage adaptations, operatic versions, criticism, cartoons, history writing, the iconographic tradition, cinema versions, and so on, covering just about every area of our grid of metatextual relationships (Figure 1), except the translational history of the play.

Second, there is *Alternative Shakespeares: Volume 2*, Terence Hawkes's collection of essays that sports its pluralism in both title and blurb—"is there really more than one Shakespeare? . . . the different versions emerge in a wide variety of cultural contexts"— but that essentially confines this pluralism to cultural contexts where English is spoken. The problematics of translation as an instance (or an emblem) of rewriting and pluralizing Shakespeare is sidelined almost completely. When the term "translation" is used at all, it more often than not appears in an overtly figurative sense (as on page 146, where one contributor centers the discussion on Orsino's "semiotics of bowel movements, translated into polite privatized discourse, or vowel movements"). True, on the opening page, the editor of the volume aptly notes Shakespeare's "deep and complex . . . penetration of English-speaking culture *and beyond*" (italics added), but exactly what is meant by "English-speaking culture" these days, or indeed in former days? And when and how and why was it, and with what kind of effect, that Shakespeare clambered, or was pulled, across the language barrier to reach the space "beyond" English? And if it is true that English is getting bigger and bigger and that the space "beyond" it is getting smaller and smaller, would this not be an interesting perspective from which to reconsider Shakespeare's status as the jewel in the crown of the English language? Such questions force their way into the volume via a few casual phrases, but then they are left to themselves without the beginning of a systematic answer.

My last example is *Current Shakespeare*, a special issue of the *European Journal of English Studies* guest-edited by John Drakakis.[20] While Drakakis addresses the "host of cultural *differences*" invoked by a "*European* journal of *English Studies*" (267; emphasis in original), the notion of linguistic diversity was apparently not meant to be part of this concept of difference within Europe. Both in the articles and in the reviews section, questions about multilingualism and translation are hardly present—with the interesting, useful, and somewhat odd exception of Terence Hawkes's essay on the representation of Welshness in Shakespeare. This exception is interesting, because it shows how Cardiff-based Hawkes is sensitive to issues of linguistic borders, asymmetries, and forms of border crossing. Hence its usefulness as a reminder that linguistic difference has always existed and is strongly asserting itself as a domestic reality within the "English-speaking world," not just something that may inconvenience lovers of Shakespeare abroad. But Hawkes's paper also makes one wonder why the multilingual concerns it raises remain so conspicuously absent from his *Alternative Shakespeares 2*.

Far be it from me to suggest that the work referred to is lacking in quality or pertinence, or that all Shakespeareans should instantly and collectively interrupt their work to rush to the nearest M.A. or Ph.D. program in Translation Studies. But I do want to highlight the fact that translation constitutes a problematic blind spot in contemporary Shakespeare Studies. This neglect is all the more blatant given the commitment of the new paradigm in the discipline to the project of "historicizing" Shakespeare and given its commitment to the notion of "difference." Other aggravating circumstances include its postimperial stance. After all, empire has used Shakespeare as an instrument of hegemonic English, while various nationalisms and minorities, too, have resorted to Shakespeare and to Shakespeare translation as instruments of resistance, subversion, self-definition, and emancipation.[21] Finally, one might consider the growing fascination of contemporary Shakespeare studies for sexual identities. Both the traditional rhetoric of translation (most offensively in a phrase like *les belles infidèles*) and the historical reality of literary production suggest that the relation between original and translation is very much a gendered one. If this is indeed so, the suppression of translation in current Shakespeare criticism bespeaks a hidden "masculine" position of originality and authority that introduces a jarring note to the sophistication of its gender criticism. In short, the neglect of translation contains vestiges of essentialist, patriarchal, and imperial thinking about language that the new generation of Shakespearean critics ought to find difficult to accept by their own standards.

Contemporary criticism questions the "universality" of Shakespeare in terms of various realities that create group identities and interests, power structures, and ideologies, which in their turn underlie the various appropriations of Shakespeare. Among these divisive realities gender, race, and class have by critical custom been enshrined as a sacred trinity (one also finds the odd reference to realities like nation, territory, religion, ideology, sexual orientation, empire, ethnos, economy, or variants thereof). To be sure, each of these has to be taken very seriously, but why is the factor of language habitually missing in such lists as a possible principle of hegemony, exclusion, or ideology-building, and therefore as a possible generator of partial Shakespeares? Whatever factor it is that unites and divides constituencies of Shakespeare readers/rewriters, such factors are looked for, deconstructed, and challenged within an area that is staked out in advance: that of the English language and its forms and variants. Language is duly studied as a conceptual system, a subject-forming system, a body of ideological inscriptions, or whatever. But insofar as "language" is more often than not equated with "English," the latter sets itself up as a normative filter of "relevance" that is blind to its own exclusionary effect. As a medium of cultural analysis, English is generally unaware of how it forces multilingualism and other languages into minority positions while claiming such virtues as transparency, neutrality, and universality for itself. In short, the systematic neglect of Shakespearean translation within English Studies is not an entirely innocent fact politically. Being one among many other "scandals of translation" (Venuti), it raises wider issues about the hegemony of English that may be too large for this paper to take on board, but that do deserve scrutiny and debate.

But, to conclude, I would like to return to the sociological perspective that I started out with and shift the debate to a different kind of empire building: that which goes on within Academia and where the key players are the authorities, publishers, editors of journals, and their distribution agencies, and of course you and me, jostling as we all are for degrees, for tenure, promotions, international publications, and for credibility and intellectual prestige generally. To put it crudely, a strict monopoly of English, involving the exclusion of other languages and therefore translation, most readily serves the immediate interests of the majority of academics in the field of English and Cultural Studies, no matter how progressive-minded they are. The overall context of Shakespearean studies is complexly defined by different factors such as increased mobility (the combined result of cheaper travel, of electronic and digital networking, and of the richer supply of student grants and exchange schemes), changes in the labor market (with more highly qualified academics having to scramble for fewer good jobs) and the cutthroat competition in the publishing market. In this kind of context, it would make little sense for "native" Shakespeareans to venture into the less familiar terrain of multilingualism, foreign languages, cultural crossings, and the like, where they would be more likely to be beaten at their chosen game. Far safer for them to entrench themselves in their Englishness and to avoid playing the foreign card, which is not only poorly rated by the current standards of relevance in the Anglo-American home environment but which risks becoming the trump card of the increasingly mobile and ambitious foreign competitors on the labor market.

Being at the symbolical and economic center of the field, Anglo-American Shakespeareans are in a position to set the agenda for their discipline and in doing so they will understandably protect their own interests in an increasingly international and competitive environment. The case of the "non-native" scholars and "overseas" departments of English literature presents too many local variations to permit generalization. But one significant trend is nevertheless visible: most English Literature specialists *extra muros* appear to be adopting an assimilationist policy that makes them suppress their linguistic and cultural difference in an effort to gain full acceptance by the canonized centers of English Studies in Britain and the States. Insofar as they perceive their professional advancement in the field of English Studies as dependent on validation by the Anglo-American orthodoxy (in the form of degrees, publications, or critical acclaim), they will be happy to espouse the latter's current agenda and end up being its most orthodox champions. They would seem to be in the best position for exposing the scandal of translation, instead they become part of it. It is probably through publications like the present that we shall have to find a way out of this impasse.

Notes

1. Inga-Stina Ewbank, "Shakespeare Translation as Cultural Exchange," *Shakespeare Survey* 48 (1995): 1–12, 1.

2. Michael Hattaway, Boika Sokolova, and Derek Roper, eds., *Shakespeare in the New Europe* (Sheffield: Sheffield Academic Press, 1994). Further noteworthy exceptions include Dennis Kennedy, ed., *Foreign Shakespeare: Contemporary Performance* (Cambridge: Cambridge University Press, 1993); and Michael Mullin's project "Our Shakespeares: Shakespeare across Cultures" (in progress), but on the whole they are few and far between.

3. For a useful introduction, see Mona Baker, ed., *Routledge Encyclopedia of Translation Studies* (London: Routledge, 1998); among the leading journals in the field, *Target* (John Benjamins, 1988–) and *The Translator* (St Jerome, 1995–) deserve a special mention.

4. The grid is based on Hendrik van Gorp, Dirk Delabastita, and Rita Ghesquiere, *Lexicon van literaire termen*, 7th ed. (Deurne: Wolters Plantyn; Groningen: Martinus Nijhoff, 1998), 504–5. Its prototype is to be found in Hendrik van Gorp, "La traduction parmi les autres métatextes," in *Literature and Translation*, edited by James S. Holmes, José Lambert, and Raymond van den Broeck (Leuven: Acco, 1978), 101–16. The Shakespearean examples take *Hamlet* as a source; they have been culled from a variety of sources, including Gerhard Müller-Schwefe, *Corpus Hamleticum: Shakespeares HAMLET im Wandel der Medien* (Tübingen: Francke, 1987).

5. *Hamlet Englisch/Deutsch. Herausgegeben, übersetzt und kommentiert von Holger M. Klein*, 2 vols. (Stuttgart: Philipp Reclam Jun., 1984).

6. For a review of the performance and a description of the translation strategies, see the articles by Jozef de Vos and Ton Naaijkens in *Folio (Shakespeare-Genootschap van Nederland en Vlaanderen)*, 5, no. 1 (1998). This production has meanwhile been translated for the German stage.

7. The institutionally entrenched division of labor mentioned in the first section of this paper has much to do with this neglect. Textual studies now seems to have left the niche it had all to itself as a "technical" subdiscipline within Shakespeare studies as a whole and to have opened up to wider issues of historical and theoretical interest (including text genesis, literary reception, hermeneutics, textual stability, and hypertext). But this disciplinary shift has apparently not been sweeping enough to extend to the study of translation. There are, as always, the proverbial exceptions to prove the rule (the "Arbeitsgemeinschaft für germanistische Edition," for example, organized a symposium on *Edition und Übersetzung. Zur wissenschaftlichen Dokumentation des interkulturellen Texttransfers*, held in Osnabrück in March 2000). Translation scholars, in their turn, have also failed to address the close affinity of text edition to their own research field. See Edoardo Crisafulli, "The Translator as Textual Critic and the Potential of Transparent Discourse," *The Translator* 5, no. 1 (1999): 83–107.

8. Another point worth mentioning here is that translations themselves—especially canonized ones like those by Letourneur, Schlegel/Tieck, Hugo, or Burgersdijk—have often appeared in different editions, reprints, revisions, and adaptations, making it necessary to apply to them (no less than to the Shakespearean originals) the operations of bibliographical research and text criticism.

9. Martin A. Kayman, "Theorizing English in Europe," *European Journal of English Studies* 1, no. 1 (1997): 10–32, 15.

10. For some telling examples from *Hamlet*, see Dirk Delabastita, *There's a Double Tongue: An Investigation into the Translation of Shakespeare's Wordplay, with Special Reference to "Hamlet"* (Amsterdam: Rodopi, 1993), 273–74.

11. Albert Lacroix, *Histoire de l'influence de Shakspeare sur le théâtre français jusqu'à nos jours* (Brussels: Th. Lesigne, 1856).

12. See Michael Bristol, *Shakespeare's America/America's Shakespeare* (London: Routledge, 1990); and David Johnson, *Shakespeare and South Africa* (Oxford: Clarendon Press, 1996).

13. There are of course certain exceptions. To quote one, the professionally more advanced state of German philology enabled Gervinus and a few other nineteenth-century German-language scholars like Elze and Ulrici to secure an audience during the formative years of academic Shakespeare studies in Britain and America. See Hugh Grady, *The Modernist Shakespeare: Critical Texts in a Material World* (Oxford: Clarendon Press, 1991), 44.

14. Kenneth Muir and Samuel Schoenbaum, eds., *A New Companion to Shakespeare Studies* (Cambridge: Cambridge University Press, 1971).

15. Lawrence Venuti, *The Scandals of Translation: Towards an Ethics of Difference* (London: Routledge, 1998), 31 ff.

16. From Leonard Digges, "Upon Master William Shakespeare, the Deceased Author, and his Poems" (printed in Shakespeare's *Poems*, 1640). My source is *The Oxford Shakespeare*, edited by Stanley Wells and Gary Taylor (Oxford: Oxford University Press, 1986), xlvi.

17. See John Drakakis, ed., *Alternative Shakespeares* (London: Methuen, 1985); and Terence Hawkes, ed., *Alternative Shakespeares: Volume 2* (London: Routledge, 1996).

18. Hawkes, *Alternative Shakespeares: Volume 2*, 3.

19. Alden T. Vaughan and Virginia Mason Vaughan, *Shakespeare's Caliban: A Cultural History* (Cambridge: Cambridge University Press, 1991).

20. John Drakakis (guest editor), *Current Shakespeare*, special issue of *European Journal of English Studies* 1, no. 3 (1997).

21. See, for example, Annie Brisset, *Sociocritique de la traduction: Théâtre et altérité au Québec (1968–1988)* (Longueuil, Canada: le Préambule, 1990). It has also appeared in English as *A Sociocritique of Translation: Theatre and Alterity in Quebec, 1968–1988*, translated by Rosalind Gill and Roger Gannon (Toronto: University of Toronto Press, 1996).

"Telling what is told": Original, Translation and the Third Text—Shakespeare's Sonnets in Czech

Martin Hilský

IN THE 1990S FOUR CZECH TRANSLATIONS OF THE COMPLETE COLLECtion of Shakespeare's sonnets appeared. Within five years, the Prague scene saw the publication of complete sonnet cycles in Czech by Miroslav Macek (1992), Břetislav Hodek (1995), Jarmila Urbánková (1997), and myself (1997). Since the previous three complete renderings of the sonnets had appeared at considerably longer intervals, with Antonín Klášterský's translation of 1923, followed in 1955 by Jan Vladislav's and by Zdeněk Hron's in 1976. Was the sonnet fever of the 1590s (launched posthumously by Sir Philip Sidney in 1591 and lasting approximately ten years) so infectious that its virus has survived four hundred years, mysteriously to re-emerge in the Prague of 1990s? Is the feverish sonneteering of the Czech translators in the 1990s a mere coincidence? Is it, perhaps, an outcome of the cultural pluralism and the free market introduced in Czechoslovakia after 1989? Or is it symptomatic of the contemporary cultural environment in which reproducing and recycling have become the dominant cultural mode?

"Recycling" is a word commonly connected with garbage and waste, and its associations are ecological. In a sense, all translations are specific kinds of textual and cultural recycling. Shakespeare's sonnet cycle is recycled in every translation and I wish to embrace this persistent re-recycling as a positive activity. In one of the most beautiful sonnets of the cycle, Shakespeare concludes with a couplet in which cyclical motion in nature is used as a metaphor of writing verses:

> For as the sun is daily new and old,
> So is my love still telling what is told.[1]

"Telling what is told" provides a footnote to the contemporary proliferation of translations: it is a cultural analogy to the natural cycles and recycles.

It is obvious that in our time the process of re-presenting, re-producing, reinventing, reimagining, rereading, reinterpreting, re-editing, and retranslating Shakespeare has dramatically accelerated and continues on an unprecedented scale and with unprecedented intensity. And it is no less obvious that the plurality of translations has affected our perception of the status, value, identity, and meaning of literary texts, both original and translated.

Shakespeare's sonnet cycle begins in a fairly conventional way, since it is a rewriting, in fact a translation, of a well-known Renaissance treatise on procreation in beauty. That treatise was included in Thomas Wilson's *Arte of Rhetoric* (1553) under the title *Epistle to Persuade a Young Gentleman to Marriage*. It was, in fact, a translation of Erasmus's *Encomium matrimonii* [In praise of marriage] which, in its turn, was a free translation or rewording of Plato's *Symposium*: "There is a certain age at which human nature is desirous of procreation—procreation which must be in beauty and not in deformity, and this procreation is the union of man and woman, and it is a divine thing," says Plato in the translation by Benjamin Jowet.[2] Since Shakespeare was as familiar with Wilson's rhetorical manual as he was with Ovid's *Metamorphoses* in the Golding translation, it is more than likely that he knew Erasmus's *Encomium* from that source. His sonnet is, therefore, not only a translation but a translation of a translation, and his text is at least three times removed from its original source text.

Erasmus's *Encomium* was an immensely popular piece of Renaissance marriage propaganda, and it is striking that Shakespeare did not hesitate to translate the popular manual into poetry. Not only the main theme of the *Encomium* but also Erasmus's central metaphors reappear in the procreation sonnets, like images of husbandry, tillage, and grafting. "Death is ordained for all mankind, and yet . . . nature gives us a certain immortality . . . as a young graft buddeth out, when the old tree is cut down," says Erasmus.[3] In Shakespeare were read:

> And all in war with Time for love of you,
> As he takes from you, I ingraft you new.
> (sonnet 15, lines 13–14)

If a man refuses to marry and have children "what punishment is he worthy to suffer, that refuses to plough the land, which being tilled, yieldeth children," asks Erasmus.[4] And Shakespeare takes up this image in sonnet 3:

> For where is she so fair whose uneared womb
> Disdains the tillage of thy husbandry?
>
> (sonnet 3, lines 5–6)

Examples of Shakespeare's borrowings or translations from Erasmus could be multiplied. The main difference between Erasmus and Shakespeare, however, is that Shakespeare writes in verse—that is, in the sonnet form. Intriguingly, the very existence of the English sonnet was a product of translations from Petrarch. The form of the sonnet, inherited by Shakespeare, was the outcome of persistent cultural recycling that began in twelfth-century Provence, and continued in Giacomo da Lentino's transformations of the musical form of the Provençal *canzone* into the verbal structure of the Sicilian sonnet. And it was through Petrarch that the sonnet form, in translations by Wyatt and Surrey, migrated to England.[5]

The practice of translation is inscribed into both the form and content of sonnet 1; its traces run so deep that the question arises what is original in it. The answer to that question surely lies in the action of the sonnet, its linguistic performance. The sonnets not only *say* something but also *do* something, and what they do or perform may be quite different from what they say.

Even a cursory reading of sonnet 1 reveals that something happens in its second quatrain:

> But thou, contracted to thine own bright eyes,
> Feed'st thy light's flame with self-substantial fuel,
> Making a famine where abundance lies,
> Thyself thy foe, to thy sweet self too cruel.
>
> (sonnet 1, lines 5–8)

This event is signaled by the word "But" and it may be described in many different ways. In contrast to the smooth, unambiguous, and uneventful statement of the first quatrain, the sonnet suddenly accelerates its tempo, and the deeply ambiguous "contracted to thine own bright eyes" is followed by a quick succession of oxymoronic phrases ("Making a famine where abundance lies," "Thyself thy foe, to thy sweet self too cruel"). These lines are also translations of Ovid's story of Narcissus and Echo, but there is a moment of surprise that makes them strikingly original. The concentration of meaning achieved through the oxymoronic patterning of images is heightened by the sudden thickening of the language, most conspicuously presented in line 5. "Feed'st thy light's flame with self-substantial fuel" is a mouthful, to say the least. The line contrasts with the fluency and quiet, almost placid pace of the first quatrain (disturbed only by the rippling sound of "heir" and "bear" in line 4). The language of this line is contracted to itself as much as the friend's bright eyes and Shakespeare's language here actually performs the self-abuse of which it speaks: it almost literally *eats itself* and performs the action suggested by the self-directed, suicidal cannibalism of "gluttony."

The main theme of the so called "procreation sonnets" (1–17) may be seen as Shakespeare's translation of death: the friend should marry, have children, and through breeding ensure his immortality. Children are seen as the best insurance policy against death:

> This fair child of mine
> Shall sum my count, and make my old excuse.
> (sonnet 2, lines 10–11)

To have children is also interpreted as an act of usury:

> That use is not forbidden usury
> Which happies those that pay the willing loan.
> (sonnet 6, lines 5–6)

It is, in fact, an act of usury at the best possible interest rate:

> Ten times thyself were happier than thou art,
> If ten of thine ten times refigured thee.
> (sonnet 6, lines 9–10)

If I am not mistaken, the interest rate of having children offered in the sonnet is the incredible 1000 percent, being much more than the Banco di Genoa, Banco di Rialto, or Florentine bankers (260 percent) could charge.

The metaphoric energy of these sonnets links the sexual act and breeding with various money transactions or translations, mainly usury, and it is not surprising that the word "use" could be used both for usury and the sexual act. Shylock echoes those procreation sonnets in his famous speech on Jacob's and Laban's sheep in which he quotes Genesis 30: 25–43.[6] Jacob peeled certain wands, stuck them up before the fulsome ewes who conceived, and in due time dropped particolored lambs. The word-play of "ewes," "Jews," "use," and "usury" in this passage is unusually complex and even an experienced translator who is used to such verbal usages will have a translation problem par excellence here.

The second mode of survival suggested in the Sonnets is the act of writing. The metaphoric link between making children and writing poems becomes apparent long before sonnet 15, where the theme is stated explicitly and then restated in many other sonnets. Sonnet 11 speaks of Nature, whose intention is to store the beauty of the friend, but the friend, as the dramatic speaker puts it in the concluding couplet, in his turn must enable Nature to do so by having children:

> She carved thee for her seal, and meant thereby,
> Thou shouldst print more, not let that copy die.
> (sonnet 11, lines 13–14)

The act of printing obliquely mirrors sexual act and the metaphor is supported by the image of the seal, which does not denote the wax but signet or the stamp imprinted in the wax.

Can one, as a translator, resist the temptation of seeing the reproduction of the self, suggested in the sonnets, as an act of translation? Children or progeny, as presented in the procreation sonnets, are "copies" or "translations" of their fathers (mothers are in this early modern generative transaction somewhat shoved aside). In this concept, a translation is related to the original as an offspring is to his parent, and various sonnet translations may be viewed as the progeny of Shakespeare's sonnets. The purpose of these translations is to keep Shakespeare's sonnets alive in the cultural and linguistic communities other than English. The genetic metaphor for translation may have its dangers, but it also has the advantage of preserving diversity within similarity. Children usually take after their parents but they also develop into autonomous and independent persons having their own minds. They even talk back to their parents. Translations, like children, talk back to the parental authority of the original texts.

The view that translations are copies of their originals is still very widespread among the lay readers unaffected by recent translation theories. But that idea is based upon the post-Renaissance notions of "originality" and "copy." We use the word "copy" mainly in its pejorative sense, implying derivativeness, debasement, being secondhand. For the Elizabethans, copies could not be so easily separated from their originals since the word "copy," among other things, signified "printer's copy," being a pattern from which a copy was made. Such a copy was, more often than not (and in

Shakespeare's plays and poems always), the only "source text" available, and copies were made from it. In other words, copies were as much *productive* as well as *reproductive* devices, and the role of the original and copy was mixed in them. Moreover, in Shakespeare's time the word "*copia*" suggested abundance, wealth, and copiousness, concepts that captured the very opposite of the derivative paucity of the word "copy" as we usually understand it now.

It is no longer feasible to suppose that there is a possibility of one good (or ideal, or normative) translation of the sonnets. The very number of translations raises a simple but important issue of correspondence or equivalence. What is Shakespeare's in the sonnet translations? The only honest answer to this question is "not one single word." Since the sonnets consist of words, and since poetry is first of all the craft of the words, this commonplace can be more intriguing than it seems to be at first sight.

If we accept the traditional model of translation based on equivalence, or the greatest possible equivalence, then the value judgement implied is: the more the translation approaches to the original text, the better it is. If we accept this view, then, an ideal translation would be complete identity. This is impossible, for obvious reasons. Some *difference* between the original and the translation is not only inevitable but desirable. That difference is always present but it becomes most manifest in the dual editions in which the translation and the original directly look or gaze at one another.

In the dual language edition of the sonnets, it is not an original text and a copy of it that face one another but *two poems*, moreover two *different* poems. These two poems interact in a dialogue that is not only about Shakespeare but also about two languages and two cultures. The mirror is a great Shakespearean metaphor permeating the plays and the sonnets. The mirror-like edition, by the arrangement of the two texts, represents or materializes that metaphor. The purpose of such editions is to suggest as many *possibilities* of their reading as possible. The original text, the translation (together with notes and introductory study, if they are provided) are Shakespearean mirrors in which the meaning of the sonnets is not reflected but refracted. These multiple refractions constitute the third text.

The third text is produced by the interaction of the two texts facing one another. It does not have a material shape since it is not printed on the page. It is written neither by Shakespeare, nor by the translator, but by the reader himself. The reader "writes" the third text in his or her mind whenever he or she reads the two texts simultaneously and compares them.

The third text, however, is not a *tertium comparationis*, meaning an ideal and invariant text that both the source text and the target text have in common. The third text, as I am using the term, is not based upon similarity or identity but on a *difference* and *diversity*. It can be defined as a semantic tension existing between the text of the original and the text of the translation. The mirror-like arrangement of the two texts thus breaks the illusion that the translation is a replica of Shakespeare and emphasizes the *otherness* of the translation. One might say that the third text enriches the reading of the sonnet by another dimension that does not consist in the mere catalogue of semantic losses in the translation but reflects back upon the meaning of the original. It foregrounds those aspects of the meaning that would remain hidden in a "one-dimensional" (that is, either exclusively English or exclusively Czech) reading of the sonnet.

At this point it is important to note that each translation produces its own third text, and that there are as many third texts as there are readers of the sonnets. But it is equally obvious that in spite of these individual differences the shared language and culture of, say, Czech readers will generate a different order of meanings and responses than those generated by Spanish, French, Italian, German, Dutch, or Scandinavian readers. Let me, therefore, briefly discuss certain linguistic norms ("langue") and cultural presumptions shared by all Czech translators (and readers). I shall not be able to describe all the systemic differences between English and Czech, but only those that are relevant to the translation and reading of the sonnets and to the third text of the dual language editions.

The first obstacle any Czech translator of Shakespeare's sonnets has to face is the different semantic density of the two languages. Most words in English have one to two syllables, whereas most Czech words have two or three syllables. A sonnet line may, therefore, have four semantic units (or cores) in English but only three in Czech. The concluding couplets of many of Shakespeare's sonnets often consist of monosyllabic words only (as in sonnets 18, 26, 43, 103, 115, 134, 146, 147, and 149). Any attempt to imitate single syllable cadences of English in Czech is doomed to failure. There is a natural tendency in Czech to extend the number of syllables in order to get all the meanings into one line but the cultural norm of the Czech sonnet translations, established in the nineteenth century, requires the sonnet line to have ten (or eleven) syllables at most.

Six out of seven existing Czech translations of sonnet cycle rigorously respect the ten or eleven-syllable line, and only one translator (Jan Vladislav) decided to use the twelve- or thirteen-syllable line.

The resulting effect is interesting. Vladislav enlarged the room of the sonnet by two syllables and transformed the couplet into the Czech variant of the French regular alexandrine. Because of the enlarged space, he can move more freely in a confined sonnet space. Yet he loses the pressure so characteristic of Shakespeare's sonnets. The mellifluousness of his alexandrine proves to be a hindrance rather than an asset and, on the contrary, the very difficulty of compressing the Shakespearean meanings into ten Czech syllables generates the sense of compactness. As it often happens in translations, an obstacle, a *difficulty* may be a positive force and produce pressure and meanings that would have been hard to achieve under different conditions. The trick of good translations often seems to be to turn the obvious disadvantages of their target language into assets.

One of the most difficult problems of translation is to render the music of Shakespeare's sonnets. The difficulty does not lie so much in the rhyme patterns, since in Czech the rhyming possibilities are greater than in English (due to inflections and varied verbal forms). Shakespeare's grammatical rhymes like "usest—refusest" and "receivest—deceivest," all of them occurring within the second quatrain of sonnet 40, would be perceived as unimaginative in Czech, and Czech translators would consider it their duty to invent better rhymes.

The stress or accent, which is shifting in English and often falls upon the second syllable of a word, is fixed in Czech and falls invariably on the first syllable. This means that the natural meter in Czech poetry is trochaic. There is some beautiful Czech poetry written in iambic verse (Karel Hynek Mácha's romantic poem *Máj* [May]), but it is rare and its effect is vastly different from the iambic verse in English. In spite of the prevailing "trochaic" tendency of the Czech poetry, in all Czech translations of Shakespeare's sonnets (except the first translations written in the nineteenth century) the iambic meter became normative, and there are no translations using trochee. The practice of the sonnet translation thus works against the Czech linguistic and literary norm. Czech translators of Shakespeare's sonnets (and plays) are faced with an impossible task: they must find ways in which the naturally falling meter of Czech can be transformed into the rising meter of Shakespeare's sonnets.

One of the most interesting and intriguing problems of the sonnet translation into Czech is gender. Czech language is much more gendered than English. Czech nouns, adjectives, and many verbal forms (especially in the past tense) are gendered, in the sense that there are different forms for masculinity and femininity. This linguistic quality is crucial for the cultural meaning of the sonnets since some of the key words in the sonnets are affected by it. The English word "lover," for example, is used both for women and men whereas in Czech there are two forms of this word distinguished by their gender: "milenec" (he-lover), and "milenka" (she-lover). The English word "friend" is also gendered in Czech, offering "přítel" (he-friend) and "přítelkyně" (she-friend).

It is a well-known fact, established by generations of scholars, that Sonnets 1–126 are addressed to a young man. But only in a relatively small number of the sonnets is their male addressee explicitly represented by means of grammar. In other words, most of the sonnets in the first group are *silent* about the gender of the addressee, and this ambiguity is fundamental for the meaning of the sonnets. The gender speaks more explicitly in Czech and it is more difficult to be silent about it than it is in English. The androgynous quality of many Shakespeare sonnets can be rendered into Czech only if extreme effort is exerted to conceal the gender. But Czech translators must hide not only the gender but also the effort expended on hiding it.

In Czech translation, more sonnets of the first group are grammatically gendered than in English, and the prevailing tradition is to address them to a man. There were some attempts in the nineteenth century to address them to a woman, reflecting some well-known attempts of the English editors to change the sex of the addressee and neutralize the awkward suggestion that the English national poet, husband and father of three children, could be suspected of homoerotic passion.[7]

Czech translators of Shakespeare's sonnets respect fully the form of the English sonnet, although this sonnet form never took roots in Czech poetry. Czech sonneteering was mostly in the Petrarchan fashion, and the Italian sonnet has been far more productive in Czech literature than the English sonnet. Yet all the translations of Shakespeare's sonnets, from the 1860s to the present day, have respected the form of the English sonnet.

It is significant that the first Czech translations of the sonnets were written in the time of the Czech national revival, and their purpose was to demonstrate that the Czech language was capable of the highest forms of expression. Shakespeare as a cultural icon of Europe was used as a test of cultural and poetic competence, as a kind of entrance ticket to Europe, and the sonnets and plays carried connotations of sacredness. Czech translations of the sonnets represented one of the ways in which the Czech community of the nineteenth century, politically powerless, could acquire some cultural power and survive. In the power of the word (meaning Shakespeare's word in translation) the voice of the powerless could be heard. Shakespeare's word in Czech translations was, in an important sense, a substitute or compensation for the political power that was absent.

I want to end with a statement on the task of a Shakespeare translator as I understand it:

1) To translate Shakespeare is to be faithful to Shakespeare but not less faithful to one's own language and culture. Arguably, the translator is even more faithful to his own language and culture. This duplicity, this divided allegiance of the translator, cannot be described by a simple antinomy of *traduttore/ traditore,* but it rather suggests a possibility of an intercultural and interlingual dialogue.

2) Shakespeare's sonnets not only say something but also *do* or perform something, and what they do may be quite different from what they say. In other words Shakespeare's sonnets are first of all language in action, and one of the most important tasks of the translator is to represent in his own medium the nature of that action (including its rhythm, its pace, and tempo).

3) Shakespeare's sonnets are not crossword puzzles that must be solved, but *poems* whose meaning is in continual *flux*. To translate Shakespeare's sonnets is to be faithful not to the words but to their *semantic energy*, their semantic currents, undercurrents, and countercurrents, their changing pressure of meaning.

4) The sonnets are so much alive today not because they contain "great ideas" or "eternal and unchanging truths," but reveal paradoxes, tensions, and contradictions of our being in the world.

5) The sonnets are a gift, one of the most generous gifts Shakespeare has bequeathed us. The primal task of Shakespeare's translators is to present that gift to the large and ever increasing international community of readers whose English is not their mother tongue but an acquired language, or who read the sonnets in languages other than English and perceive them in a cultural environment radically different from that of Shakespeare himself or the English Renaissance. The task is enormously difficult since it requires that the linguistic competence, the skills of a literary scholar and cultural historian, as well as the artistic creativity of a poet be combined in one person.

Notes

1. William Shakespeare, *The Sonnets*, edited by G. Blakemore Evans, The New Cambridge Shakespeare (Cambridge: Cambridge University Press, 1996), sonnet 76, lines 13–14.
2. Plato, *Symposium*, translated by Benjamin Jowet. The translation by Jowet is different from the Czech translation by Frantisek Novotný.
3. See Katherine M. Wilson, *Shakespeare's Sugared Sonnets* (London: Allen & Unwin, 1974), 148.
4. Wilson, *Shakespeare's Sugared Sonnets*, 149.
5. Michael R. G. Spiller gives a fascinating account of the genesis and transformations of the sonnet form in his *The Development of the Sonnet* (London: Routledge, 1992).
6. *The Merchant of Venice*, edited by John Russell Brown, The Arden Shakespeare (1961; reprint, London: Methuen, 1984), 1.3.66–85.
7. There is only one contemporary translator (incidentally one of the leading right-wing politicians of the country) who did not hesitate to change the sex of the sonnets. The concluding couplet of Sonnet 63, for example, reads:

> His beauty shall in these black lines be seen,
> And they shall live, and he in them still green.
>
> (sonnet 63, lines 13–14)

In Miroslav Macek's translation, "his" is changed into "her" and "he" into "she."

Royal and Bourgeois Translators: Two Late-Nineteenth-Century Portuguese Readings of *The Merchant of Venice*

Filomena Mesquita

ON 27 NOVEMBER 1877, *THE TIMES* PUBLISHED A REVIEW OF KING D. Luís's translation of *Hamlet* entitled "A Royal Translator. *Hamlet, drama con cinco actos.* Lisboa. 1877." In this review, the monarch is praised for having "conferred a great boon on his country by giving to the Portuguese Nation their first translation of Shakespeare."[1]

As in many other European countries, the second half of the nineteenth century in Portugal saw the appearance of a number of translations of Shakespeare's plays into the vernacular, where the tendency had previously been to imitate or adapt them. In her review of the translations published between 1856 and 1879, Carolina Michaëlis de Vasconcelos, a philologist also well known to Spanish Shakespearean scholars, stated that southwestern Europe was finally waking up to the genius of Shakespeare. Evidence was to be found in at least two of the translations under analysis, indeed close translations of the Bard's texts—"wirklichen Übersetzungen" or "real translations" with literary aspirations.[2] Among other things, Michaëlis praised the king's efforts in rendering an honest and clear, albeit prose representation of the ideas in the text, particularly since it was his first attempt at translation and because he had, according to her, worked directly from the original.[3]

The second of the texts referred to by Michaëlis was the 1879 translation of *Hamlet* by Bulhão Pato. Michaëlis displayed an obvious sympathy for the royal translator and adopted a somewhat deprecating tone when considering the efforts of Bulhão Pato. She praised the merits of Pato's style, the coordination between form and content, and stressed the translator's success in capturing both the color and individual style of each character as well as keeping to the original use of verse and prose. However, she was rather keen on putting the merits of the translation down to the author's vast experience as a man of letters, and a mature poet in his own right. Besides, Pato is portrayed as a cunning translator who relies heavily on other well-known European versions of the original rather than the *true* Shakespearean text.[4] According to Michaëlis, Pato followed the French/Hugo school of translation too closely, sacrificing the romance language structure while betraying his own literary positions, whilst D. Luís tried to dress up the Bard's thoughts in Portuguese (or French) clothing.[5]

The manifest glee about the coming benefits for the Portuguese people from the translations of Shakespeare's plays, albeit clichés of the time, seem particularly interesting if put into context with the cartoon by Rafael Bordalo Pinheiro, a prominent contemporary journalist and commentator, better known for his political and social caricatures.[6] In the late 1870s and early 1880s, Bulhão Pato occasionally used Shakespearean characters and scenes to illustrate the relationship between the crown and the government, to get at the king or his ministers, often emphasizing the ineffectiveness of the liberal regime and the dubious nature of power allegiances under the constitutional monarchy. This picture was published in Pinheiro's satirical journal—the year Bulhão Pato published his translation of *The Merchant of Venice*—and it was entitled "Shakespeare and the Constitution. The latest version," referring directly to the frequent and regular amendments to the text of the constitution but also to the fact that the king's translations were known to be rather poor (as we shall see, the king had by then also published a translation of *The Merchant of Venice*). The dialogue reads:

—What state you're in, Master Shakspeare!
—It's all your friend's doing, my dear lady!

The female figure is a clear representative of Pinheiro's style of caricaturing the underprivileged: a short, robust, dark-skinned, and poor old woman of the people, much abused by the regime and by politicians. The ethnic contrast is more than evident: D. Luís (1838–89; ruled 1861–89) was of German descent and is commonly portrayed in Pinheiro's work as a short, fat, fair-skinned, blond man, this time with his back to the viewer, brandishing a pen as a warrior might a sword, and hiding a scrunched up manuscript of *Hamlet* behind his back. His pen shining brightly like a torch, he is shown in an attempt to enlighten the nation, and at the same time to see into the composition of the government, represented as a troupe of politicians in witches' guise. Poor Will stands in between these two stocky characters, sympathizing with the old hag who manages to evince a lot more physical and textual stamina than himself.[7]

As in *The Merchant of Venice*, letters and people, bonds, pounds of flesh, words, vows, and human bodies intermingle in complex levels of metaphor and metonymy. Here the Bard appears frail but gentlemanly in his tall body; in spite of the tattered clothes, set out in sharp contrast with the ethnicity of the other figures. His laurel-crowned head dominates the body and invites us to look at the other headgear: Fontes Pereira de Melo, the head of the cabinet, is the power figure wearing the crown, whilst the king displays his navy cap.[8] Shakespeare's bald, globe-shaped head and the white collar are reminiscent of the Chandos portrait by John Taylor, which "reigned as the popular favorite" in Victorian England.[9]

The two versions of *The Merchant of Venice* I propose to discuss in this paper are by the same two authors who translated *Hamlet* and also came out, interestingly enough, within two years of each other: the king's in 1879 and Bulhão Pato's in 1881.[10] Up to a point, I have read the latter as something close to a direct response to the former, involving both ideological and literary challenges to the royal version. Bulhão Pato (1829–1912), a writer and journalist, began his career as a representative of the ultraromantic school, producing highly lyrical poems of folkloric inspiration, telling sad tales of passion and country love. In the 1870s, he followed the new social and realist vein, which grew as a reaction against the romantic excesses of the time; he also wrote some satirical poems of social criticism, charged with a rather unrefined popular pseudo-realism.[11] As we have already seen, he also published some translations, and it is certainly not without interest in this context that he dedicated his version of *The Merchant of Venice* to the Portuguese statesman, deputy, and parliamentarian António de Oliveira Marreca (1805–1889), a man of the Portuguese "Regeneration," the liberal political regime that took over around 1850, after five decades of internal fighting and general instability.

Oliveira Marreca, himself also a journalist and writer, was first and foremost an economist, a defender of protectionist policies in favor of the rudimentary national industries, and against the unlimited adoption of the doctrines of free trade.[12] Significantly, he was not only a prominent representative of liberal radicalism but, between 1880 and 1883, he also played an important role as one of the founding members of the Republican Party.[13] Indeed, republicanism gained momentum at this stage in Portugal's history, imbued by a nationalist spirit that grew around rather grandiose

Shakespeare and the Constitutional Chart. The latest version. 1881 (Courtesy of Museau Rafael Bordalo Pinheiro. Divisão de Museus e Palácios—Câmara Municipal de Lisboa).

commemorations of the tercentenary of the birth of the Portuguese national poet, Luís de Camões, in 1880, and also following the debate over the signing of the Treaty of Lourenço Marques (1879), which was to give Great Britain not only the right to build a railway connecting the Transvaal in South Africa to the coast through the Portuguese colony of Moçambique, but also free transit throughout the area as well as navigation, commercial, and fiscal privileges.[14]

Interestingly, then, between the years 1879 and 1881, a republican faction shaped itself in opposition to Portugal's growing economic dependence in relation to Great Britain. This dependence had been dominating national life throughout the century. Naturally, it had an economic and a colonial dimension, but its impact is further illustrated by the fact that this dependence was also related to the strengthening of the royal House of Bragança and of the most conservative social groups in the country, being the "Ancien Régime" aristocracy, the landed agricultural elite, and the church.[15]

We find fascinating the way in which Camões was rediscovered as cultural capital by the republicans at around the same time. He became the epitome of a Portuguese golden age, to contrast with the then-current experience of economic collapse and political disillusionment in the face of the evidence of all the unfulfilled promises of progress that the liberal revolution had proclaimed. As this nationalistic cultural process took place, Britain's own national poet was also being rewritten into the dependent culture. It is thus significant that Pato's translation should be so explicitly dedicated to a republican.

Again in response to King D. Luís's prosaic rendition of the text, devoid of any critical apparatus or introduction, Pato furnished a considerable number of scholarly notes on both lexical and editorial aspects of the text, an appendix with Ser Giovanni's *Il Pecorone*, as well as valuable references to alternative European translations, which would seem to add support to Michaëlis's objections to his method of work. At about the same time, we know how prominent the scientific study of Shakespeare had become in Britain and on the Continent, for example, with its progressive commercialization of new and intellectually respectable editions of the texts.[16] Pato's use of other translations, such as François-Victor Hugo's, August Wilhelm Schlegel's, François Guizot's and the Marqués de Dos Hermanas, whose work he much admired, is in keeping with the scientific spirit of the times and the professionalization of literature.

The king's first translations, by contrast, were published in small, anonymous editions; his name did not appear on the title page because the books were designed as personal gifts from the king.[17] In accordance with a somewhat outmoded aristocratic practice, the royal work was originally not meant to circulate as a commodity in the modern market.[18] It is ironic, therefore, that Pato's text is extant only in its first edition, while D. Luís's far less interesting translation is one of the very few versions of *O mercador de Veneza* available in the Portuguese market at present, in a bilingual, pocket size, paperback format. It is also likely to be the first contact that Portuguese students have with Shakespeare's text before they turn to the English original.

Needless to say, the days of comparing the relative merits of translations are long gone. I am not interested in establishing whether any of these versions (or any combination of the two) reaches the status of the literary achievement of the Schlegel-Tieck Shakespeare, or whether further attempts at translating *The Merchant of Venice* into Portuguese have got anywhere near an optimum state of perfection, according to an evolutionary view of language or translation techniques.[19] As has been pointed out by the editors of *European Shakespeares*, there is a need for "a higher degree of contextualization of the translations, which means the interaction between translations on the one hand, and literary and nonliterary phenomena in the target system, or neighboring systems, on the other."[20] Translations are in themselves acts of reading and rewriting that take place in a particular cultural moment in time, and the very act of re-reading a translation, from the distance of over a century, sets off a truly complex system of cultural exchanges.[21]

In the suggestive words of Inga-Stina Ewbank: "Translation is never a purely philological activity but a collusive re-creation in which cultural differences cling to grammar and syntax and history mediates the effect even of single words."[22] I shall be concentrating precisely on "single words," on particular options and preferred readings that are significant both in terms of the specific political, economic, social, and cultural context of the late nineteenth century, and also of my own critical concerns when dealing with the play. I would also like to look into the ways in which cultural contextualization is effected: how do we put together these orders of information? How do we begin to explain the links in the cultural exchange between three eras: early modern England, late nineteenth-century Portugal, and again Portugal (or is it Europe?), at the verge of the new millennium?

To address these issues, I will begin with the translation of the expression "royal merchant," from the Duke's plea (in act 4, scene 1) to Shylock: "Enow to press a royal merchant down."[23] Whilst the king translates the adjective "royal" by "o mais opulento"—(80: "o mais opulento negociante," meaning "the wealthiest dealer")—thus picking up the metaphorical undertones of "royal" in its specific association with "merchant," Pato opts for a literal version—"um *real* mercador"—and an extended note is added in which he justifies his choice by quoting Warburton at length, via Dos Hermanas.[24] Pato's preoccupation with explaining the legitimate use of *royal/real* in a mercantile context, referring to Venetian historical detail and scholarly authorities, suggests an explicit challenge to the king's reluctance in applying the term *royal* to a mere merchant, or dealer, as he chooses to translate "merchant" in the specific context.[25] There is an explicit divergence between the two texts in this instance that, interestingly, points towards the very construction of the moneyed figures, both in their relation to early modern society and in their equivalents in contemporary Portugal.

Whereas the former example concerns the representation of class, the next introduces the issue of gender. Pato uses the very same adjective D. Luís applies to Antonio, *opulento*, to translate Bassanio's description of Portia, in 1.1.161—"In Belmont is a lady richly left." His version reads: "Vive em Belmonte uma *opulenta* herdeira" (20), or, literally, "A wealthy heiress lives in Belmont," transposing to the text the identification of the character in the "Dramatis Personae" ("*Porcia*, rica herdeira," or "*Portia*, a wealthy heiress"). The king, on the other hand, opts for a fairy tale beginning to Bassanio's speech which seems more coherent with the original:

> No castelo de Belmonte pousa uma jovem herdeira, bela, que não há expressões condignas para elogiar a sua beleza; ninguém a iguala em qualidades brilhantes e prendas. (21)

> [In the castle at Belmont dwells a young heiress, so beautiful that there are no words adequate to praise her beauty; no one equals her in bright qualities and gifts.]

Shakespeare's inversion and use of the passive voice explicitly constructs Bassanio's vision of the woman as a passive fairy-tale figure, which the rest of the speech confirms, a strategy further supported by his self-fashioning as a heroic Jason. The rhythm and wording of the king's version are semantically suggestive of that atmosphere and of this model of woman in Shakespeare.[26] D. Luís's reading of Portia does not concern itself particularly with the aristocratic nature of her wealth and status, but it does insist on a certain level of ladylike character decorum. This is particularly evident when he translates Portia's final comment in act 3, scene 2—"Since you are dear bought, I will love you dear" (312)—as "quantas ânsias me tem custado! mas aumentam o meu amor" (70), meaning "how much anguish it has cost me! but it has increased my love." Pato preserves the pun but also draws attention to it by taking two lines for it instead of one:

> Se caro vos comprei, encarecido
> Por vós será também o meu affecto
>
> (117–18)

On one level this translates as:

> Since I have bought you dear, dearer
> My love for you shall also be.

Alternatively, since there is another level of ambiguity in the Portuguese ordering of the words, it may also read: "endeared / By you shall also my love be." The result in the first line is that, while punning with the economic dimension of the situation, Portia could simply be declaring her growing love for Bassanio. However, as the second rendering reveals, Portia could just as well be charging Bassanio with turning that love into an increasing expense. The latter's heroine is a wealthy, privileged woman with a strong character, one who plays with language, gender difference, and sexual stereotyping.

When the cross-dressing is announced and Portia speaks of:

> ... such a habit
> That they shall think we are accomplished
> With that we lack,
>
> (3.4.60–62)

Pato opts for a close translation:

> em trajo tal que hão de suppor
> Que nós temos aquillo que nos falta,
>
> (125)

which means:

> in such a habit that they shall think
> We have what we lack.

Tellingly, D. Luís's rendering reads: "mas debaixo de um tal disfarce, que lhes será impossível reconhecer-nos" (74). Translated back into English, this yields: "under such a disguise, that it will be impossible for them to recognise us."[27]

The interest and implications of these details (and there are many more), it seems to me, must lie in the complex network of issues involved in the act of translation: what are the translator's main or manifest concerns? How does the immediate historical and cultural context *interfere* with the act of translation? Who is the potential reader of each version? What difference would it have made had any of these translations been made for the stage?

In 1784, 84.4 percent of the Portuguese population was illiterate, as were 89.3 percent of all Portuguese women: although the percentage was lower in the major cities (64 percent), the numbers suggest the existence of a rather limited reading public.[28] However, in the cities, especially in Lisbon, theatergoing had become a very important social activity; although tickets were too expensive for the common people, the theater became a favorite meeting place for the bourgeoisie, as well as a stage for political and ideological change.[29] Whereas in the early part of the century, Portuguese theaters were dominated by French taste, by melodrama, ultraromantic historical plays, and comic opera, the "Regeneration" explored the ideological potential of the stage by inspiring a form of social drama with realist and didactic aspirations, aimed at a bourgeois, urban public.[30] The stories were set in urban settings rather than castles, palaces, or dungeons, and they involved characters drawn from contemporary society, such as aristocrats (usually ruined), members of the new moneyed classes and bourgeoisie, representatives of the new nobility, but also of the honest and hard-working laboring classes that sustained the first stages of Portuguese capitalism.[31] So, although the two *Merchant*s under consideration in this essay were not translated for the stage, the emergent bourgeois setting of the play, the class power relations that trigger the plot, down to the importance of marriage, of credit, and of the usurer, as we shall see later, are highly significant to the general context of the new culture at the receiving end of the translation process.

In effect, culture and intellectual as well as political activity were in the hands of the more privileged members of the bourgeoisie and of the liberal professions. The industrial, productive bourgeoisie that contributed to the radical economic transformations under way dealt with the lucrative exploration of the colonies (Brazil and, later in the century, Africa), with international trade (which was deeply dependent upon Great Britain) and, notoriously, with money itself, with the growth of the banking system and the increasingly popular operations of financial speculation.[32] The credit system underwent a great boom in the third quarter of the century, and the social aspirations of certain ranks of the bourgeoisie grew accordingly. The liberal state made access to titles of nobility rather easy for certain political sectors close to the regime, and D. Luís is said to have granted as many titles between 1866 and 1880 as his mother and brother had done together.[33] Soon the figure of the new nobleman, known as "o barão," or the baron with his social aspirations and ostentatious display of wealth and ambition, became an object of satire.[34]

In the drama, as in some of the satirical literature of the period, which Pato also cultivated, one finds the constant reappearance of social themes and types: financial ruin, debts, and material difficulties, irrepressible social ambition and the corrupting power of money, love stories across the social spectrum, and often a providential inheritance. The characters included the ruined aristocrat, the rich heiress, the humble but hard-working hero whose honesty, true love for the right woman, and perseverance, guaranteed that he would succeed in winning her and prosper at the same time, thus embodying a process of social mobility that allowed the petit bourgeois to identify with the aspirations and rewards of the upper echelons of society.[35]

Also a significant number of plays included a usurer as the hero's antagonist, a representative of the new wealth or of the new rapacious nobility. These plays show a manifest social and moral concern with the ways in which wealth was acquired and money was perceived to affect people's lives, and at the same time a necessity of drawing clear moral distinctions between industrial and productive capitalism, on the one hand, and usurious capital and financial dealings, on the other.[36]

Given this particular cultural context, the choice of *The Merchant of Venice* as the object of study and translation in Portugal seems to be perfectly justified. There are, after all, remarkable similarities between the type of plays I have just described and the plot of Shakespeare's play. However, the parallels are not transparent or unproblematic. In nineteenth-century England, romantic taste and its "fascination with passionate individuality and exotic difference" turned *The Merchant of Venice* into the second most popular play, after *Hamlet*, and the Victorians strengthened this tendency by turning Shylock into the play's most picturesque and prominent character.[37] It was precisely in 1879 that Henry Irving's production at the Lyceum Theater not only established this type of reading but also the play as one of the author's tragedies.[38]

On the Portuguese stage, the villain usurer was an important stock character, but he was not a Jew. Officially, there were no Jews in Portugal, since it was not until as late as 1821 that the tribunal of the Inquisition was abolished.[39] The first half of the nineteenth century was a period of profound liberal anticlericalism. As part of this process, Eugène Sue's *The Wandering Jew* (1844) became widely known in the 1880s, after Luís Maria Bordalo's 1842 play entitled called *O Judeu* [The Jew], and the publication in 1866 of Camilo Castelo Branco's *O Judeu: Romance Histórico* [The Jew: A Historical Novel], the story of the life and death of António José da Silva, a Portuguese dramatist born to one of the heirs of a traditional noble family after his marriage to a new-Christian woman. The novel is the story of two generations' efforts to flee the Inquisition, and is deeply critical of the corrupt alliances between Catholic institutions and the ruling classes in the late seventeenth and early eighteenth centuries.[40] Between 1893 and 1901, Pato himself used the image, or rather the stereotype, of the Jew in some of his verse satires, as well as a humoristic, cautionary tale entitled "Um Judeu que escapou a Shakespeare" [The Jew who escaped Shakespeare], about a shipwreck off the Azores coast in which there was a Jew who couldn't stop screaming and lamenting the fact that, in order to save the vessel and themselves, the crew had to throw overboard their cargo of bags of wheat—"the grandiose avarice of that Shylock" manifested itself over the loss of the bags in which the grain was stored, the only part of the goods that had not been insured.[41]

The portrayal of Jews in contemporary literature was ambiguous, stereotypes on the one hand, and heroic, long-suffering figures on the other. Equally ambiguous seem to me the two nineteenth-century imaginings of Shylock into Portuguese, central to this essay. Both Shylocks are, to a certain extent, close renditions of Shakespeare's character, and thus open to complex layers of ambiguity and ironic readings, whether the translators chose to replace the various insults he is subjected to by a variety of softer synonyms, not to fall into a repetitive style (the king), or went for a closer and crude version of those insults (Pato). The latter, however, offered an interesting variation (too lengthy to quote here) on the "Signior Antonio, many a time and oft / In the Rialto you have rated me" speech (1.2.101–24). Given that in Portuguese this is also in verse and with frequent, although not absolutely regular, use of rhyme, the figure of the usurer attains a marked level of dignity in this first stage confrontation with the Christian merchant. It effectively shapes our perception of the character and of the play's debate over the morality of economic models they personify. In neither text, however, is there any attempt to redeem Shylock at the end, nor much of an interest in exploring the tragic vein of the play's fourth act.

This is, of course, a complex project that would not be complete without looking also at the ways in which the princes of Morocco and Arragon are translated.[42] Not having space here to look at this now, I will, instead, draw attention to one last particularly fascinating detail whose effect reveals not only the complexities and challenges of Shakespearean texts and the need to contextualize the translations of those texts, but also the problematic nature of these efforts at contextualization.

On the last page of the book of his translation of *The Merchant of Venice*, Bulhão Pato adds a list of errors in which he introduces not only a few minor corrections, but also the following:

> Act 4—"Qual é o mercador, qual o judeu?"/ Which is the merchant, which the Jew? should read as—*Qual é o mercador, qual é Antonio?/ Which is the merchant, which is Antonio?*

There is no justification for this change. At the end of his list of errors, Pato adds: "Mais alguns erros que escaparam, facilmente os emendará o leitor," meaning: "Any further mistakes that have escaped me, will easily be corrected by the reader." It almost implies that the first version is to be included in that list of errors.

Is Pato's a licit, acceptable translation of the famous question "Which is the merchant here? and which the Jew?" (4.1.170). What are we to make of the new version, given that we have become so keen on interpreting Portia's question as a sort of proof that there should be no obvious reasons why a *royal* merchant should look that different from a Jew? On the one hand, the new formulation reinforces that liberal reading, and Portia's obliteration of the figure of the Jew does indeed imply that the two characters are indistinguishable, and all she wants to do is to satisfy her immediate curiosity as to the identity of the man who is not only extraordinarily generous but has also just come between herself and her hard-found husband. But couldn't it be read otherwise, as a way of emphasising the ethnic and moral difference at the basis of their antagonism? That is to say, were they in nineteenth-century Portugal perceived as sufficiently different to warrant a form of "tampering" with the Bard's text, cleansing it of an apparently ineffective question given the immediate dramatic context of the Duke's reply: "Antonio and old Shylock, both stand forth."[43]

But the point rests precisely on erasing Shylock from this particular moment in the text when the two forms of capital have to re/present themselves before the law and declare their respective identities. My main concern in this paper has been precisely that: a first step towards studying the relationship between two texts and a variety of contexts through the ambiguities and instability of the representation of money and the mercantile system.

NOTES

I would like to thank my colleagues, Professor Maria Manuela Delille and Professor Irene Vaquinhas, for their invaluable assistance in the preparation of this text.

1. Quoted in Alice Pestana, "The King of Portugal's Translation of *Hamlet*" (1877), in *Alice Pestana 1860–1929: In Memoriam* (Madrid: Julio Cosano, 1930), 248–63.
2. Carolina Michaëlis de Vasconcelos, "Shakespeare in Portugal," *Jahrbuch der Deutschen Shakespeare-Gesellschaft* 15 (1880), 266–97, 266 and 285.
3. Ibid., 288.
4. Ibid., 290–93.
5. Ibid., 291 and 294.
6. The cartoon is taken from *Fontes Pereira de Melo nas Caricaturas de Bordalo Pinheiro*, Museu Rafael Bordalo Pinheiro (Lisboa: O Museu, 1988), 196.
7. The semicircle of figures at the top are mounted on brooms like witches and stand for the government of the time, headed by the mustachioed and crowned figure in the middle, António Maria Fontes Pereira de Melo, the most prominent politician.
8. The headgear the king wears is quite obviously not the crown but a navy cap. Having been brought up to be an official of the navy, which he loved, D. Luís ascended to the throne by accident, after the untimely death of his elder brother in 1861. He was also an amateur cello player, a painter, and a translator, about whom the following was written: "The Queen and Fontes are his true teachers, the only true friends H. M. the King D. Luís ever had. Maria Pia taught her husband to be a king. Fontes Pereira de Melo taught his master to be a politician." Fialho de Almeida, *Os Gatos*, quoted in Francisco Carvalho Louro and Graça Mendes Pinto, "Introdução," in *D. Luís I: Duque do Porto e Rei de Portugal*, edited by Isabel da Silveira Godinho (Lisbon: Palácio Nacional da Ajuda, Printer Portuguesa, 1990), 15–24, 23–24.
9. Richard Halpern, *Shakespeare among the Moderns* (Ithaca, N.Y.: Cornell University Press, 1997), 163.
10. D. Luís de Bragança, *O mercador de Veneza* (Mem Martins: Publicações Europa-América, 1988); Bulhão Pato, *O mercador de Veneza* (Lisbon: Typographia da Academia Real das Sciencias, 1881). All page references to these translations will be given in the text.
11. See António José Saraiva and Oscar Lopes, *História da Literatura Portuguesa*, 6th ed. (Oporto: Porto Editora Lda, n.d.), 764–65.
12. Luís Reis Torgal and João Lourenço Roque, eds., *História de Portugal*. Vol.

5: *O Liberalismo, 1807–1890* (Lisbon: Printer Portuguesa, 1993), 143; Vítor Sérgio Quaresma, *"A Regeneração": Economia e Sociedade* (Lisbon: Publicações D. Quixote, 1998), 70–75; António Almodovar and José Luís Cardoso, *A History of Portuguese Economic Thought* (London: Routledge, 1998), 81–82.

13. See Torgal and Roque, *História de Portugal*, 239.

14. See S. Sideri, *Trade and Power: Informal Colonialism in Anglo-Portuguese Relations* (Rotterdam, Netherlands: Rotterdam University Press, 1970), esp. chapter 7 on "Foreign Capital and Development: Another Feature of Dependence," and chapter 8 on "Colonization and Specialization" (145–200); Torgal and Roque, *História de Portugal*, 308; *História Comparada: Portugal, Europa e o Mundo* (n.p.: Sociedade Industrial Gráfica, 1997), 169.

15. Miriam Halpern Pereira, *Política e Economia: Portugal nos Séculos XIX e XX* (Lisbon: Livros Horizonte, 1979), esp. chapter 6 on "O Comércio com Portugal e o desenvolvimento económico da Grã-Bretanha," and chapter 7 on "Comércio e poder político," 129–41.

16. See Gary Taylor, *Reinventing Shakespeare: A Cultural History from the Restoration to the Present* (New York: Weidenfeld & Nicholson, 1989), chapter 4 on "Victorian Values," 162–230.

17. In a letter to Queen Victoria dated January 4, 1878, which accompanies the gift of his first translation, D. Luís writes: *"Je vous prierai cher tante, de vouloir accepter un petit travail à moi. J'ai entrepris la traduction en portugais, des oeuvres d'un des plus grands genies, c'est à dire Shakespeare. Je viens de terminer "Hamlet" et je vous* [sic] *de le recevoir. J'espère bientôt pouvoir vous remettre "Merchant of Venice," "July and Romeu" et "Richard III." J'occupe le temps qui me reste de mes affaires à faire connaitre en Portugal la litterature Shakespirienne qui etait tout a fait inconnue."* Quoted in Louro and Pinto, "Introdução," 23.

18. According to the Paris-based periodical *A Illustração*, the profit from the sale of the second edition of *Hamlet* was entirely given to the association of nurseries for children, one of the queen's charities, and three hundred copies of *The Merchant of Venice* were sold in favor of Lisbon's abandoned children's asylums. See *A Illustração* 6, no. 22 (20 November 1889), 351. The king seems to have been aware of the amateur nature of his endeavors: of an evening, he would read aloud extracts from his translations to figures of the court and the government whom he really wanted to bore; see Louro and Pinto, "Introdução," 23.

19. See Peter Wenzel, "German Shakespeare Translation: The State of the Art," in *Images of Shakespeare: Proceedings of the Third Congress of the International Shakespeare Association, 1986*, edited by Werner Habicht, D. J. Palmer, and Roger Pringle (Newark: University of Delaware Press, 1988), 314–23.

20. See Dirk Delabastita and Lieven D'hulst, introduction to *European Shakespeares: Translating Shakespeare in the Romantic Age*, edited by Dirk Delabastita and Lieven D'hulst (Amsterdam: John Benjamins, 1993), 9–21, 18.

21. See Inga-Stina Ewbank, "Shakespeare Translation as Cultural Exchange," *Shakespeare Survey* 48 (1995): 1–12, 7 and 9.

22. Ibid., 6.

23. See *The Merchant of Venice*, edited by John Russell Brown (1955; reprint, London: Methuen, 1977), 4.1.29. Further references to this edition will be given in the text.

24. Pato, *O mercador de Veneza*, 224. Pato had already translated "royal" literally (113), in 3.2.238, whereas the king opted for "honrado negociante," or honorable merchant (68).

25. Both authors often alternate between the words "mercador" and "negociante" for "merchant."

26. D. Luís's marriage was also in itself a form of quest, which he had to carry out after ascending the throne. He wrote to Queen Victoria, asking for the hand of her daughter Alice in marriage, but his request was denied on religious grounds. He then considered other European princesses, finally choosing Princess Maria Pia of Savoy, daughter of the recently crowned king of Italy, whose progressive liberal connections made the marriage very attractive to Portugal's own liberal government. See Louro and Pinto, "Introdução," 23.

27. In 1886, Camilo Castelo Branco, a prominent novelist, wrote a review of the King's translation of *Othello*, praising his accuracy and care in rendering the brutality and rudeness of the emotions and the language of the play. He recommended that, at readings of this play, young ladies should be advised to leave the room and to come back only when Iago leaves the scene. He added jokingly: "The young ladies have probably already heard him sing under Brabantio's window; but did not understand him." See Camilo Castelo Branco, *Esbôço de Critica. Othello: O Mouro de Veneza* (Oporto: Livraria Civilização, 1886), 30.

28. See, respectively, Maria de Lourdes Lima dos Santos, *Para uma Sociologia da Cultura Burguesa em Portugal* (Lisbon: Editorial Presença, 1983), 15; and *História de Portugal*, edited by Torgal and Roque, 451.

29. See Lourdes L. dos Santos, *Para uma Sociologia*, 40 and 64.

30. Ibid., 65–66; there were six theaters in Lisbon in 1870 (40).

31. Ibid., 90. For the association between the Regeneration regime with the Portuguese capitalist system, see the contemporary economist, politician, and thinker Oliveira Martin[s], *Portugal Contemporâneo* (1881), quoted in Torgal and Roque, *História de Portugal*, 320.

32. See Sideri, *Trade and Power*, 145–56; Pereira, *Política e Economia*, 71 and 143; Manuel Villaverde Cabral, *O Desenvolvimento do Capitalismo em Portugal no Século XIX* (Lisbon: A Regra do Jogo, 1977), 16; Torgal and Roque, *História de Portugal*, 291–309; António José Telo, *Economia e Império no Portugal Contemporâneo* (Lisbon: Edições Cosmos, 1994), 37–42; Quaresma, *"A Regeneração,"* 77–83; *História de Portugal*, 387ff.

33. Torgal and Roque, *História de Portugal*, 449.

34. Pereira, *Política e economia*, 6; Santos, *Para uma Sociologia*, 17.

35. M. de Lourdes L. Santos analyzes the plots of nine plays written and performed in Lisbon between 1854 and 1867, in her chapter "O 'Drama Social,'" *Para uma Sociologia*, 56–92.

36. Lordes L. dos Santos, *Para uma Sociologia*, 75.

37. James C. Bulman, *The Merchant of Venice*, Shakespeare in Performance (Manchester: Manchester University Press, 1991), 26–27.

38. Ibid., chapter 2 on "Henry Irving and the Great Tradition," 28–52; and John Gross, *Shylock: Four Hundred Years in the Life of a Legend*, part 3: "Interpretations (1600–1930)" (London: Chatto & Windus, 1992), 89–186, 89–145.

39. Torgal and Roque, *História de Portugal*, 225.

40. See Camilo Castelo Branco, *O Judeu: Romance Histórico* (1866; reprint, Lisbon: Livraria Editora, 1919).

41. Respectively "Os Judeus Novos," in *Hoje: Satyras, Canções e Idyllios* (Lisbon: Typographia da Academia Real das Sciencias, 1888), 81–87; *A Dança Judenga: Satyra* (Lisbon: Typographia Academia, 1901); and "Um Judeu que escapou a Shakespeare," in *Memorias. Quadrinhos de Outtras Epochas*, vol. 3 (Lisbon: Typographia da Academia Real das Sciencias, 1907), 221–25.

42. In relation to this particular point, there is another interesting difference in the translation of the exchange between Lorenzo and Launcelot on the topic of the

Moor's pregnancy by the latter (3.5.34–39), in which the king's choice is to conflate the disturbing aspects of this woman's otherness with the play's explicit anxiety regarding miscegenation by leaving the "Moor" out of the text, whilst Pato chooses to eradicate the word "Negro." Thus we have: "Lor. I shall answer . . . better than you can the getting up of the Negro's belly: the Moor is with child by you Launcelot!" D. Luís renders it at follows: "Muito mais fácil será para mim . . . do que a ti, Lanceloto, justificares-te das consequências de uns teus negros amores que eu conheço perfeitamente" (76). In modern English this would read: "It will be much easier for me . . . than for you, Launcelot, to explain the consequences of your Negro/black loves, of which I am perfectly informed." Pato translated "Mais facilmente me justificara eu de tal acusação . . . do que tu da gravidez da moira. A moira, Lanceloto, está assim por tua causa" (130). This is best retranslated into English as: "It would be easier for me to justify myself against such an accusation . . . than for you to explain the Moor's pregnancy. It's because of you, Launcelot, that she is in the state she is."

On this question see Kim F. Hall, "Guess Who's Coming to Dinner? Colonisation and Miscegenation in *The Merchant of Venice*," *Renaissance Drama* 23 (1992): 87–111.

43. *The Merchant of Venice*, 4.1.171. There is a second correction to this very passage that follows immediately upon the former: Pato decides that the Duke does not need to call Shylock "old" and we do not need to feel sympathy for him, in "Antonio and old Shylock, both stand forth" (171), and gives us this final version: "Antonio, e vós, Shylock, aproximae-vos (Antonio, and you, Shylock, come closer). The earlier translation had been literal.

Part IV
Productions

Shakespeare and the Cold War

Dennis Kennedy

THE HISTORY OF THE INTERPRETATION AND PERFORMANCE OF SHAKEspeare in the postwar period is complex, of course, and I am concerned here with only one portion, if a rather neglected one: the relationship of the English national dramatist to the international situation in Europe in the years from 1945 to about 1965. My chief point is that Shakespeare was used in Western and Central Europe as a site for the recovery and reconstruction of values that were perceived to be under threat, or already lost—though often both the supposition and the proposed manner of recovery were a long way from logical. In fact, in the four centuries of Shakespeare performance in Europe since the English Comedians ventured into Braunschweig, the postwar period of the twentieth century may turn out to be one of the most curious.

Festivals in Ruins

The crucial year is 1947, when plans for material recovery in Europe were well underway and intellectual awareness of the vast amount of work remaining began to sink in. Before turning to the political situation, it is worth recalling that on the cultural front the most significant development was "The Week of Dramatic Art in Avignon," the first attempt at the Avignon Festival, inaugurated in September 1947 only weeks after the first Edinburgh International Festival opened. Avignon was founded by the great French actor and director Jean Vilar, who oversaw it until his death in 1971. Vilar thought of theater, in his own phrase, as a "public service in exactly the same way as gas, water or electricity." For him drama transcended class barriers and political differences by celebrating timeless themes, and Avignon gave him the opportunity to test his thesis on a large scale in a country still shocked by the years of occupation and the psychic and material devastation that accompanied the Liberation. If Sartre and Camus were devising an existentialist response to the human condition in the face of the war, Vilar proposed to use the festival setting to retrieve a classical equilibrium. He thought the project important enough to put up 300,000 francs of his own money, more than a quarter of its total capital in the first year, the rest coming from the city and the state.[1] Avignon was a utopian scheme, but one that took seriously the warning that civilization as Vilar understood it might have been destroyed, and that French bourgeois culture might still be destroyed in the aftermath of war. He spoke about his founding motivations in an interview in 1964:

> In 1947, the year of the first Avignon Festival, we said that the theater lacked oxygen. We had suffered the pain of war, of occupation. We still had rationing. Transportation by rail, by bus, by car was still very difficult.... Whereas the theater under the occupation had been a meeting place for Parisians, filled with a fervent public, ready to welcome the young and all their efforts (as authors, performers, directors, painters, etc.), suddenly after the Liberation it had to find a new reason for being, and not only artistically. The theater, a much-loved social center for the French, became once more just a place like any other. The theaters rapidly became the object of exploitation pure and simple.... The Liberation had liberated the people; it did not liberate professional institutions [*les métiers*].[2]

From Vilar's perspective the Avignon Festival was a scheme for the maintenance of memory, a re-creation of an European past.

For that re-creation Vilar chose as his first production in September 1947 the same play that Rudolf Bing used at Edinburgh in August: *Richard II*. The venue at Avignon helped in selecting the text: outdoors in the Court of Honour of the Palace of the Popes, with three thousand seats in front of the monumental fourteenth-century walls. This would be a classless place, Vilar thought, without the trappings and the divisions of the nineteenth-century playhouse, despite the evocation of the medieval papacy. Performance there depended on large-scale vocal delivery and gesture, rich period costumes, and a sense of ritual that resembled High Mass.[3]

The opulence and ceremony on stage must have heartened an audience aware of themselves as survivors in a ruined world. And aware of themselves, in Vilar's view, as inheritors of high art: "theater is only of value, like poetry and painting," he said, "when it does not give way to costumes, to the tastes, to the ordinary social needs of the masses."[4] The Papal Palace heightened the meaning of a play about a royal history from the same era, collapsing the past upon the past in an uncertain present. *Richard II* played in Paris, on tour, and reappeared at Avignon for the next six years. It even went to Edinburgh in 1953.

Vilar was not an aesthetic interventionist. He thought a director should never interpose himself between text and audience, though his acting in the title role was very powerful and many critics thought it the greatest part of his career. But his emphasis was on the humanity of the main character. Harold Hobson noted that the king was "of no more account than any other human being; the emphasis is laid not upon him, but upon the whole human race. . . . [I]t comes out of M. Vilar's hands almost a new play and one of great imaginative power."[5] As Jean Jacquot comments in his history of Shakespeare in France, choosing a Shakespeare history play in 1947 was Vilar's response to the need of the time for some kind of faith in the future.[6] His belief in the reconstructive potential of the arts is further apparent in his early desire to include lectures, discussions, poetry readings, cinema, music, and dance in the festival. The festival idea spread widely under Vilar's influence, so that by 1960 there were some fifty arts festivals in France, while his lead in staging plays with historical settings in ancient surroundings was followed in the 1950s all over the south of France.[7] It happened in Italy as well: Giorgio Strehler opened the Piccolo Teatro in 1948 with *Richard II*. Luchino Visconti directed *As You Like It* that same year in Rome, designed in surrealist style by Salvador Dalí, and in the summer of 1949 *Troilus and Cressida* in the Boboli Gardens in Florence, designed by Franco Zeffirelli with "unparalleled magnificence of costumes and circus-like pageantry."[8] Cultural reconstruction seemed to lend itself to the idea of the festival, a self-congratulatory celebration of the amount of recovery already accomplished; the ancient ruins spoke of a romantic continuity with the past.

What was it about Shakespeare that encouraged these theatrical institutions to use him so flagrantly as a banner? Arts in the classic mould appealed to many people after the war because they represented an imagined continuity with a calmer, more ordered world. Shakespeare, and particularly a play like *Richard II*, with its dependence on artifice and ceremony amid cold-blooded politics, engaged precisely what seemed to have been threatened or lost, a sense that some human endeavors moved outside of time, some elements of life might be free of the harsh taint of history, some values could transcend pain and death. The liberal democracies felt they had narrowly escaped the destruction of the humanist values that they had claimed as central to their wartime cause. The defeat of the Axis had been couched in moral terms—nothing exceptional about that, of course—but building a peace and rebuilding Europe needed commitment to something more than mere survival. Reviewing the assaults on humanity that resulted from unprecedented global aggression, national leaders could easily conclude that Europe must return to solid, well-tested, Christian values, values traditionally claimed to reside in high art, or to be supported by it. The right-of-center governments that led France, Italy, West Germany, and some of the smaller states for much of the postwar period positioned themselves as custodians of those values. Even when their parties were racked with scandals of corruption or espionage, they managed to suggest that they were inheritors and preservers of the past.

The worries over reconstruction were enough in themselves to foreground high principles and high art, but the perceived threat to Europe by the Soviet Union added immensely to the purpose. In the first years after German surrender, when the fronts were "congealing" (to use the contemporary term), a mounting desperation overtook the victorious Western powers. As Eric Hobsbawm writes, the Cold War was based on the Western belief that "the future of world capitalism and liberal society was far from assured." This thought may seem "absurd in retrospect but [was] natural enough in the aftermath of the Second World War." Many observers expected a worldwide economic crisis after 1945, and Washington, which of course set the foreign policy agenda for the West for the next half-century, feared large-scale trouble because "the belligerent countries, with the exception of the United States, were a field of ruins inhabited by what seemed to Americans hungry, desperate, and probably radicalized peoples, only too ready to listen to the appeal of social revolution and economic policies incompatible with the international system of free enterprise, free trade and investment by which the USA and the world were to be saved."[9]

The year 1947 was crucial for theater institutions and crucial in international politics. In March, President Harry Truman outlined the Truman Doctrine, which effectively constructed the frame for the Cold War: "At the present moment in world history nearly every nation must choose between alternative ways of life," he said. In a clear reference to Soviet moves in Europe, he announced that henceforth U.S. policy would "support free peoples who are resisting attempted subjection by armed minorities or outside pressure."[10] In June, General George Marshall, Army Chief of Staff during the war and now Truman's Secretary of State, offered a plan to deal with the "great crisis." In a ten-minute address at the Harvard commencement—he was receiving an honorary degree along with Robert Oppenheimer, General Omar Bradley, and T. S. Eliot—Marshall held that the world and "the way of life we have known is literally in the balance" and proposed that only the U.S. could provide the necessary financial credit and material assistance that would ensure the continuation of a free Europe. "There is widespread instability," he noted; "there are concerted efforts to change the whole face of Europe as we know it, contrary to the interests of free mankind and free civilization."[11] The U.S., which he held to be "an integral part" of the European culture, had a moral obligation to step into the breach. The Marshall Plan, with its massive aid for war recovery, was to be the carrot. Less than two months later the stick came along, when the National Security Act of 26 July 1947 created the CIA.

When Stalin installed satellite governments in Eastern Europe and tried to close off Berlin, when Mao ordained a revolutionary people's government in China and supported a parallel revolution in Korea, official U.S. opinion, already sensitized to the horrifying results of aggression in Europe, had concluded by 1950 that godless communism was in quest of world domination. Some of the obsessions and paranoia of the Cold War that followed were directly attributable to an American presidential dread not so much of Stalin's belligerence as of a loosening of the alliance which kept anarchy and revolt off the streets of London, Paris, and Rome. It is doubtful that politicians in Western Europe were quite so panicked about the Soviet threat, especially in light of the rapid demobilization of the Red Army, reduced from almost twelve million in 1945 to three million by late 1948.[12] But certainly Europeans shared the fear that social upheavals could disrupt the international capitalist system. Indeed the frightening harvest of 1946 and the horrendous winter of 1946–47, the worst on record, conspired to increase those fears and to drive Western Europe more firmly into NATO, the American camp, and the rhetoric of the Cold War.

That rhetoric grew harsher in the U.S. of the 1950s, of course, driven by the House Unamerican Activities Committee and the persecutions conducted by Joseph McCarthy in the Senate. Nixonian red-baiting became a vital element of national politics for a decade of paranoia, set off with the first atom bomb test by the USSR in 1949, compounded by the hydrogen bomb in 1953 and the launching of Sputnik in 1957. Though it is clear that nuclear war was the last thing either superpower wanted, even a sophisticated thinker like John Kennedy knew that with his religious disadvantage he could win the presidency only if he out-Nixoned Nixon. His electioneering speeches in 1960 seem now to be vastly out of touch with the actual state of the Cold War, as when he claimed that "the enemy is the communist system itself—implacable, insatiable, unceasing in its drive for world domination. . . . This is not a struggle for supremacy of arms alone. It is also a struggle for supremacy between two conflicting ideologies: freedom under God versus ruthless, godless tyranny."[13] As one who grew up in that nerve-racking environment, I can attest that when I was studying Shakespeare at a university in San Francisco in 1960 there was a clear and palpable sense in the classroom that we were engaged in an enterprise of battle against the world: escape from Civil Defense drills, bomb shelters, canned goods and bottled water in the basement, and Mutual Assured Destruction.

After the work of Michael Bristol and Hugh Grady, it is now widely accepted that American Shakespeare Studies in the period were dominated by an ideology of retreat from the present. To Hardin Craig, for instance, Shakespeare was a refuge; he promoted the view that the dramatist was aloof from or even diffident to any cause, and that the job of the present generation was to perpetuate his timelessness. In 1948 Craig claimed that Shakespeare's genius, like Chaucer's and Goethe's, was thoroughly objective:

> His works are written from the point of view of general humanity, which means that they have in them the minimum of affectation, formalism, dogmatism, egotism, and prejudice. They are about life, about people and about recurrent human situations.[14]

In the introduction to his complete edition of the works, which I used in class those forty years ago, Craig wrote that Shakespeare "gives us in his plays life patterns that are continuous in the history of the human race."[15] Hope for a better future, and even for the defeat of world communism, was grounded in the permanent values in Shakespeare; a sixteenth-century playwright would show the way out of postwar materialism and malaise, the loss of spirituality and the alarms of the Cold War. To take an example with a different effect, Cleanth Brooks and Robert Heilman produced criticism with an "aura of necessary trafficking with a corrupt world" that helped make sense of the era of McCarthyism by insisting that it was possible to back away from taking sides in reading Shakespeare's politics: a kind of abstract expressionism of criticism, a "subjectless" idealism of withdrawal.[16] American Shakespeare discourse often was in congruence with American Cold War discourse, and both found their way forcefully into Europe. To some commentators, Shakespeare was to be a cultural Marshall Plan.

Dividing the Kingdom

I back up now to peer into the darkest heart of Europe: Berlin in 1945. One of the most remarkable circumstances of the time was how fast the theaters reopened in May. The Renaissance theater had escaped destruction and was producing two weeks after surrender; six more theaters were operating before the year was out. The next year, with the city still filled with rubble, hundreds of performances of various types were available.[17] In a study of the cultural and intellectual life in Berlin immediately after the war, Wolfgang Schivelbusch notes that in its first season the bombed-out Deutsches Theater in the Soviet sector mounted ten productions under Gustav von Wangenheim, including three classics: Lessing's *Nathan the Wise*, Molière's *School for Wives*, and *Hamlet*.[18] Wangenheim, a communist who had been in Russian exile, was a political choice for the job. His *Hamlet* opened on 11 December 1945, but the director and cast had been selected more for their socialist credentials than for talent or appropriateness, and the result was a "mingle-mangle" of styles and ideologies. But the rapidity with which *Hamlet* was staged in postwar Germany shows just how consequential Shakespeare was going to be in the cultural reconstruction of the German nation—or rather, of the two German nations, for he became equally important East and West. Though it is usually assumed that the reasons were different, in both the Federal Republic of Germany and the German Democratic Republic Shakespeare was seen as a method of connecting with prewar culture.

That was most apparent in the West, of course, where much of politics and culture hoped to retrieve life before the Nazi period. As Wilhelm Hortmann puts it, people sought the same thing in the crowded theaters as in the crowded churches: "reassurance, guidance, spiritual orientation, some form of hope, not flat confrontation with the unthinkable and ineffable." Starting in 1949, Adenauer's fourteen-year term of office as chancellor set a tone of quest for a restored humanity. The theater sought not revolution as after World War I but wished instead "to regain lost humanist traditions," and the regeneration would be a safe and conservative one. As early as 1948, Bertolt Brecht on his return to Germany saw this desire as an attempt to carry on as usual, repressing all the huge falsity of the time. In one of the most telling analyses of the postwar situation, he said that "everybody is afraid of the demolition without which reconstruction is impossible."[19] Audiences flocked to Shakespeare. From 1945 to 1955, the annual average was about one thousand nights of performance for Shakespeare compared to less than 150 for Brecht. In the two decades after 1955 Shakespeare was undoubtedly in first place among playwrights in the number of productions and the number of total performances. Schiller was considerably behind, and only after 1971 did Brecht begin to gain on his Elizabethan model.[20]

One of the best directors of the period, Gustav Rudolf Sellner at Darmstadt, provides a cogent example of how this retirement from accountability played out. Like Vilar, Sellner believed in submission to the text; only by serving the dramatist was it possible to convey the universality of the work. His withdrawal from the present took the form of ritualized staging. In his *Midsummer Night's Dream* of 1952, the interest was almost exclusively on ritual and archaic tragedy. He departed entirely from illusion, and from Mendelssohn's music, by treating the work as a representation of elemental forces. A new abstract score by Carl Orff provided the center of the interpretation and controlled much of the tone. The set was simple, with abstract mobiles hung from the flies like giant leaves, lit by colored light, red for the palace, green for the woods. The characters were without much individuality: they were present to take part in a ceremony of timeless proportions. "In Sellner's theatre," a critic wrote later, "Man was always seen under existential, never under sociological aspects."[21] A new formalism was taking shape to support even further the notion that displaying Shakespeare was enough in itself—it was not necessary or even desirable to expound upon the specific import the plays might have in the present. Their universality was assured because there had been no attempt to convey meaning.

It is not surprising that West Germany evaded both the totalizing mentality and specific social implication in its use of Shakespeare in the 1950s. As an emergent liberal democracy it had much to prove and much to make up for; Adenauer Restoration was above all fixed on rebuilding Germany while convincing the victors that it was not the same old Germany. Ideas were dangerous, and for a while West German thought and art could pretend to avoid them. How was it different in the East? In the GDR, ideology was constantly foregrounded; artists without proper and approved analysis were deemed reactionary and could be condemned. Yet we find that a similar concern for established values dominated Shakespearean issues in the first decades after the war. Since Shakespeare was officially important in the Soviet Union, his position in the new German workers' state was doubly assured. Leninist orthodoxy maintained that Shakespeare wrote at the cusp of historical change from feudalism to capitalism, and that his characters often show a dawning awareness of the threats to humanity the new order will bring: a humanist reading based on materialist analysis. Theater was valued in the GDR—somewhat paradoxically for an antibourgeois state—because it referred to a grander and more generous scale of human endeavor. It was a place for teaching, but also a home for what was elevated in the spirit.

Thus a number of productions at the Deutsches Theater and elsewhere remained relatively free of overt political statements and often, like the Wangenheim *Hamlet* in 1945, took refuge in a generalized Renaissance-ism. As Maik Hamburger puts it, "Restoration of humanist values on a rationalist, atheist basis was, in fact, the main concern of subsequent Shakespeare productions in East Germany through the 1950s."[22] There was one important socialist achievement in performance of the time: "directors made a closer scrutiny of social relations in Shakespeare's plays and achieved a much clearer delineation of plebeian figures which had often enough been summarily treated as trivial comic relief." Brecht and the Berliner Ensemble would further refine the theatrical techniques for class analysis, and spread them across Europe. But as the Brechtian style was not incorporated into Shakespeare production in the GDR until the next decade, theaters were not fully equipped, methodologically speaking, to present Marxist interpretations of the work. It was only after the Ensemble's production of *Coriolanus* in 1964, and the publication of Robert Weimann's book *Shakespeare und die Tradition des Volkstheaters* [*Shakespeare and the Tradition of Popular Theater*] in 1967, that the techniques useful to a materialist explication of Shakespeare in performance became widely known.[23]

Shakespeare as Cold Warrior

Ironically the Brechtian mode was first developed for Shakespeare in France and Italy, notably in the productions of Roger Planchon and Giorgio Strehler. Both had seen the Berliner Ensemble and met Brecht before his death in 1956, and both immediately saw the potential for Shakespeare of his general method. In 1957 Planchon staged an adaptation of *Henry IV* in Lyon that used Brechtian devices effectively to comment on the power struggles in the text, and particularly to reveal the social and economic distinctions between the proletariat, foot soldiers, nobles, and the church. Mimed scenes were interpolated that showed the "sufferings of the common man or the harshness of the ruling classes."[24] The play was entirely deromanticized: Hotspur was stabbed in the back while Prince Hal was fighting him in the front. Strangely coincident, just a few days later Strehler opened *Coriolanus* in Milan, in a modernized translation; the production "stressed essentials through a rigorous monochrome" that gave the audience time to think—each fragmented scene was identified by a placard that commented on its significance.[25] In the title role Tino Carraro was a "paranoic dictator" who managed to suggest nonetheless that the play was political tragedy with thoroughly modern applications.[26]

My point is not to elucidate the Brechtian methods, which are well known. I wish instead to stress the importance of a socialist approach to Shakespeare that developed in the West at the end of the 1950s. The populist dramaturgy begun by Vilar in 1947 had a decade later become an overtly Marxist one and was used more and more as a dissident exclamation in the capitalist countries of Europe. Nowhere was this more surprising than in England, where Peter Hall, overwhelmed by the power and clarity of the Berliner Ensemble's productions in London in 1956, founded the Royal Shakespeare Company (RSC) four years later using Brecht's organizational model and performance methods as his cornerstones. It seems particularly strange that a company sponsored by the queen—the Royal Shakespeare Company, as the joke went at the time, has everything in its name but God—should mark itself as so politically engaged, and there is huge doubt that it ever was. Nonetheless important productions in the first years clearly placed social issues in the foreground, even if they often remained ambiguous about what conclusions should be drawn about them. And the RSC was not alone in preferring Shakespeare. An era of unprecedented prosperity saw a significant increase in the number of Shakespeare productions everywhere in Britain and Europe, enabled by huge increases in public spending.

Of course Shakespeare had been presented before the war in a variety of Marxist clothes. What was different about Marxist Shakespeare in the 1950s in Europe was the presence of the Cold War, which lent any criticism of the West made from within a heightened voice, and contextualized it with the knowledge that an alternative to the capitalist system was living next door: as Coriolanus says, there is a world elsewhere. Why did liberal governments in the West fund companies that presented work critical of the capitalist order?

In a sense they were trapped into it, or embarrassed into it, by the fact that it was being done in that "elsewhere." East and West, arts councils were locked in a cultural arms race. If John Le Carré is right, the Cold War was a "looking-glass war," in which the enemies stared at each other across the front and saw only their own reflections. The greatest irony of the period is that a figure of high art status like Shakespeare was enlisted into the socialist cause by West European Marxists, while after 1968 directors in the Eastern Bloc would be using him to critique and undermine the socialist system in place there. "Dissident Shakespeare" had different meanings depending on where you were, but on both sides of the Iron Curtain it was likely to be well funded.

In the Eastern Bloc there was never any doubt that supporting high art ventures was the state's responsibility, a duty that conveniently combined continuity with the past with propaganda about the virtues of a socialist government. Though France and Germany had long traditions of public subsidy, it was only after the war that countries like Italy, England, and the U.S. began to toy with the notion that financial support for the theatre might be a national task. There is little doubt that the sums spent on the arts by the governments of Western Europe were at least in part designed as counterpropaganda for the East, and designed to support bourgeois notions of freedom. Ironically, Western nations relied on a quasi-socialist redistribution of wealth to arts organizations, in order to bolster the virtues of a free-market economy.

It is well known by now how deeply implicated the secret services were in cultural financing. In her exhaustive study *Who Paid the Piper?*, Frances Stonor Saunders detailed the extraordinary extent of the CIA's involvement in European cultural affairs, funding—always indirectly, sometimes at three removes of money laundering—intellectual journals (most famously *Encounter*), book publication, conferences, travel, writers, orchestras, recordings, films, tours of ballet, theater, and jazz groups, radio broadcasts, and of course the entire network of the Voice of America. Most of the American payouts in Europe were channeled through or connected to the Congress for Cultural Freedom, a strange and often opaque organization, first located in Berlin, then headquartered in Paris in the 1950s. A cross between a State Department cultural affairs agency and an active propaganda device, with a reasonably intact front, the Congress had almost limitless money to promote artists, critics, and events sympathetic to American policy, or somehow indicative of the virtues of the Western way of life. I am not claiming that the CIA paid for Shakespeare performance; I have not seen any evidence of that, though it would certainly be in keeping with the type of high status and modernist art that the cultural mandarins in the "company" favored. But I do suggest that the large support for Shakespeare in Europe during the Cold War was part of a web of government spending, overt and covert, that had as its object the promotion of the superiority of liberal democracy and the capitalist system.

In 1962 Kenneth Tynan presented a parody of the Congress for Cultural Freedom on *That Was the Week that Was* on the BBC:

> "And now, a hot flash from the Cold War in Culture," began the sketch. "This diagram is the Soviet cultural bloc. Every dot on the map represents a strategic cultural emplacement—theatre bases, centres of film production, companies of dancers churning out intercontinental balletic missiles . . . a massive cultural build-up is going on. But what about us in the West? Do we have an effective strike-back capacity in the event of an all-out cultural war?" Yes . . . the good old Congress for Cultural Freedom, which, "supported by American money, has set up a number of advanced bases in Europe and elsewhere to act as spearheads of cultural retaliation. These bases are disguised as magazines and bear codenames—Encounter, which is short for 'Encounterforce Strategy.'" A "Congress spokesman" [then] . . . boasted of a cluster of magazines, which were a "kind of cultural NATO," the aim of which was "Cultural containment . . . a ring around the pinkoes . . . we [have] a historic mission. World readership. . . ."[27]

The turning point in the Cold War history of Shakespeare came in 1961 with the publication of Jan Kott's *Shakespeare Our Contemporary* in Polish, followed the next year by a French edition and in 1964 by a translation into English.[28] If the Cold War had been lurking in the shadows of Shakespeare studies and performance since 1945, with Kott's work it entered without disguise and with a new language. His book made the divide in approaches apparent. Brecht's followers saw Shakespeare as a force for social change in the present; Kott saw him as our contemporary precisely because the world does not change. Not for Kott the Marxist belief that progress is possible through the actions of human beings; Shakespeare showed us, he claimed, that we could not escape the cyclical nightmare, the beast within our sexuality, or the "grand mechanism" of history. Abandoning his Marxist background after the Soviet invasion of Hungary, Kott became in his critical work a supporter of the dominant Western belief in individualism. As John Elsom astutely points out, by retaining the old trust in the universality of Shakespeare but moving it directly into the realm of the "contemporary," Kott hinted that directors in the East could use the mask of Shakespeare to "comment on current affairs without fear of censorship" from Stalinist regimes.[29]

Kott's influence on Shakespeare production in the 1960s and 1970s was enormous, and one still can see productions, especially of the comedies, that claim to derive from his thought. The most famous, of course, was Brook's *King Lear* for the RSC in 1962, which was overwhelmingly driven to convey a world without affect, a world of universal annihilation. Kott's most widely read chapter, "King Lear or Endgame," called upon Beckett's play to explain the clownish atrocity of Lear and Gloucester. *Endgame*, first produced in Paris in 1957, is the quintessential Cold War drama, showing a remnant of life in the "shelter," an entropic universe, a metaphorical and theatrical space made up of absences. The disintegrating body and the closure of narrative are its most significant features, where the blind Hamm who cannot stand and the sighted Clov who cannot sit are doubled images of Cold War impotence that is not quite able to end: "there are no more sugar plums," in Clov's famous litany, no more bicycle wheels, pain killers, biscuits, coffins, or people. "Outside of here it's death," says Hamm. *Endgame* became for Kott a model for understanding the absurd within Shakespeare's tragedy—and Brook seemed to swallow the idea whole. Brook himself wrote that "Lear is for me the prime example of the Theatre of the Absurd, from which everything good in modern drama has been drawn." Certainly Brook gave the ultimate compliment of a cold warrior when he added that "Kott is undoubtedly the only writer on Elizabethan matters who assumes that every one of his readers will at some point or other have been awoken by the police in the middle of the night."[30]

Though the production was at pains to use a number of Brechtian devices, from its anti-illusionist creation of the storm scene to bringing up the houselights during Gloucester's blinding in an attempt to implicate the audience, they were apolitical in implication. Brook's *Lear* was focused on the individual, not the social group. It assumed Kott's existentialist premise: the anti-Marxist premise that the world is a cold and unchanging place, that human progress is not possible since men and women are beasts at heart. Nowhere did this theme resonate more loudly than in Eastern Europe, where people living under Stalinist regimes felt powerless to alter their lives and lived in fear of repression and retaliation. Admitting that his *Lear* did not connect with spectators on its tour to the U.S., where audiences felt remote from its themes of absence and loss, Brook noted that "the best performances lay between Budapest and

Moscow."[31] The production must be acknowledged as one of the first—perhaps the very first—major performance of Shakespeare that appeared in the socialist countries that used Kott's coded method to critique, implicitly and only half-intentionally, the politics of the Iron Curtain. Brook's *Lear*, born of the Cold War, produced in the year of the Cuban Missile Crisis, visually indicating holocaust and devastation, more than anything else evoked the policy of Mutual Assured Destruction.

I must re-emphasize that my study of reconstructive Shakespeare does not tell the whole story of his performance in the period. Nevertheless it is clear that the international situation gravely affected some important moments in that history, and this becomes even clearer when we look at the 1970s. As the worst frights and dreads of the Cold War faded, as the Viet Nam war ended and China opened to the West, new concerns like inflation and an energy crisis occupied the global picture, and Shakespeare production moved away from confidence in the dramatist's immediacy and rectitude. From Stratford to Berlin directors lost the edge of the old political conviction, which had been born of opposition between two superpowers competing for hearts and minds; as Shakespeare performances multiplied, the challenge became one of style rather than statement; both Brecht and Kott receded as influential forces. By the early 1980s an advanced director like Ariane Mnouchkine could claim that "Shakespeare is not our contemporary and must not be treated as such . . . he is distant from us, as distant as our profoundest depths." Both she and Brook switched to intercultural methods to mark Shakespeare's distance: a return to the call of universality without contemporary overtones, Shakespeare formalized, exoticized, globalized, festivalized, marathonized.[32]

Institutional theaters and international festivals grew in size and economic importance as they moved away from the reconstructive goals that Vilar established immediately after the war, and Shakespeare productions and festivals now thrive almost worldwide. I can give a simple example of the global reach: in 1964 there were four Shakespeare productions or adaptations in Tokyo; in 1994 there were thirty-three, more than in London.[33] Despite all this activity, compared to the postwar period much Shakespeare performance is adrift, either unexamined in its purpose or relying on heritage appeal, in keeping with postmodern or consumerist notions of cultural production. The Shakespeare born of commitment receded as the Cold War receded, just like the institutions of espionage. A huge increase in cultural tourism has kept the big classic theaters going, even if they must often chase spectators and corporate sponsors through appeals to a nostalgic past that no one quite believes in. The most financially successful classic theater company in Britain is the new Globe in Bankside, a theater that draws audiences not through the quality of its productions, much less for their social or intellectual content, but because they are packaged as a pleasing adventure experience.

In Eastern Europe the change did not occur so quickly. The censorious powers of the socialist states, coupled with the Kottian tradition of using classic texts as coded messages about the present to foil repressive regimes, kept Cold War Shakespeare alive through much of the 1980s. But since the fall of the wall, and the attendant decline in state subsidies in the countries behind the rusted Iron Curtain, theaters have rapidly caught up with the condition of post–Cold War Shakespeare in their aesthetics and their funding. I do not want to sound nostalgic about life under communism, but it is undeniable that many fewer interesting productions of Shakespeare occur twelve years after *die Wende* than occurred under the harsh hands of official Marxism. Instead of a banner for elevated values, Shakespeare is most often another product for marketing and display. It is helpful to recall that Habermas has said that the events of 1989 and 1990 in Eastern Europe were "a catching-up revolution."

What else could we expect? No matter what high ideals might be ascribed to Shakespeare, no matter what claims for his poetic power, dramatic supremacy, philosophic virtue or moral instruction, it is highly unlikely that we will ever see again the same level of public subsidy or the same degree of commitment to his production that went hand-in-hand with the Cold War in Europe. In the face of vast competition within the entertainment industry, it is actually surprising that there is so much Shakespeare about these days. The most convincing explanation for the prevalence of Shakespeare in a market economy, and especially in Hollywood-funded films, is that his work is public domain property with high name-recognition. In Shakespeare performance the Cold War is definitely over, and the capitalists have won.

Notes

1. Jean Vilar, *Le Théâtre, Service Public et Autres Textes*, edited by Armande Delcampe (Paris: Gallimard, 1975), 471.
2. Vilar, *Le Théâtre*, 468 (my translation).
3. Dennis Kennedy, "The Language of the Spectator," *Shakespeare Survey* 50 (1997): 29–40. This and other aspects of the general topic are discussed from a different perspective in Dennis Kennedy, *Looking at Shakespeare: A Visual His-*

tory of Twentieth-Century Performance, second edition (Cambridge: Cambridge University Press, 2001).

4. Vilar, *Le Théâtre*, 472.

5. See Samuel L. Leiter, ed., *Shakespeare Around the Globe: A Guide to Notable Postwar Revivals* (New York: Greenwood, 1986), 573.

6. Jean Jacquot, *Shakespeare en France: Mise en scène d'hier et d'aujourd'hui* (Paris: Le Temps, 1964).

7. David Jeffery, "France: Towards *création collective*," in *European Theatre 1960–1990: Cross-cultural Perspectives*, edited by Ralph Yarrow (London: Routledge, 1992), 11–44, 18–19.

8. Mario Praz, report in *Shakespeare Survey* 3 (1950): 118.

9. Eric Hobsbawm, *Age of Extremes: The Short Twentieth Century, 1914–1991* (London: Michael Joseph, 1994), 230–31.

10. Frances Stonor Saunders, *Who Paid the Piper?: The CIA and the Cultural Cold War* (London: Granta, 1999), 25.

11. Ibid., 24.

12. Hobsbawm, *Age of Extremes*, 232.

13. Martin Walker, *The Cold War and the Making of the Modern World* (London: Fourth Estate, 1993), 132.

14. Quoted in Michael D. Bristol, *Shakespeare's America/America's Shakespeare* (London: Routledge, 1990), 158.

15. *The Complete Works of William Shakespeare*, edited by Hardin Craig (Chicago: Scott, Foresman, 1951), 13.

16. Hugh Grady, *The Modernist Shakespeare: Critical Texts in a Material World* (Oxford: Clarendon Press, 1991), 129.

17. Wilhelm Hortmann, *Shakespeare on the German Stage: The Twentieth Century* (Cambridge: Cambridge University Press, 1998), 175–76.

18. Wolfgang Schivelbusch, *In a Cold Crater: Cultural and Intellectual Life in Berlin, 1945–1949*, translated by Kelly Barry (Berkeley and Los Angeles: University of California Press, 1998), 63–64.

19. Hortmann, *Shakespeare on the German Stage*, 179–80.

20. Ibid. 181.

21. Quoted in Hortmann, *Shakespeare on the German Stage*, 203.

22. Maik Hamburger, "Shakespeare on the Stages of the German Democratic Republic," special section in Hortmann, *Shakespeare on the German Stage*, 372.

23. This seminal study was translated into English several decades later, and appeared as Robert Weimann, *Shakespeare and the Popular Tradition in the Theater: Studies in the Social Dimension of Dramatic Form and Function*, edited by Robert Schwartz (Baltimore: Johns Hopkins University Press, 1987).

24. Jean Jacquot, report in *Shakespeare Survey* 13 (1960): 127–28.

25. Mario Praz, report in *Shakespeare Survey* 12 (1959): 114.

26. Ossia Trilling, review in *World Theatre* 13, no. 1–2 (1964): 97.

27. Saunders, *Who Paid the Piper?*, 340–41.

28. Jan Kott, *Shakespeare Our Contemporary*, translated by Bolesław Taborski (New York: Anchor Books, 1964).

29. John Elsom, *Cold War Theatre* (London: Routledge, 1992), 78. See also Dennis Kennedy, ed., *Foreign Shakespeare: Contemporary Performance* (Cambridge: Cambridge University Press, 1993).

30. Peter Brook, *The Shifting Point, 1947–1987* (New York: Harper and Row, 1987), 89 and 44.

31. Peter Brook, *The Empty Space* (New York: Atheneum, 1968), 21–23.

32. See Dennis Kennedy, "Shakespeare and the Global Spectator," *Shakespeare Jahrbuch* 131 (1995): 50–64.
33. Ryuta Minami, "A Chronological Table of Shakespeare Productions in Japan, 1866–1994," in *Shakespeare and the Japanese Stage*, edited by Takashi Sasayama, J. R. Mulryne, and Margaret Shewring (Cambridge: Cambridge University Press, 1998), 255–331.

Spanish Productions of *Hamlet* in the Twentieth Century

Rafael Portillo and Mercedes Salvador

THE STAGE HISTORY OF SHAKESPEARE'S PLAYS IN SPAIN BEGAN IN October 1772, when playwright Ramón de la Cruz staged his own translation, *Hamleto, rey de Dinamarca* [Hamlet, king of Denmark] in Madrid. *Hamleto*, however, did not follow the English text but instead a somewhat free translation in Spanish of a 1769 free version in French by Jean-François Ducis who, in turn, imitated an earlier rendering by P. A. de La Place, published in 1745.[1] Such emblematic scenes as Polonius's death, the play-within-the-play, and Ophelia's madness were missing, as they had previously been regarded contrary to French taste and hence cut. On the other hand, the protagonist was promoted to the position of king, since, according to the principles of legitimacy, the French adaptors had similarly decided that a monarch should always be succeeded by his own son. We must bear in mind that, at that time, French culture dominated Spanish learned and scholarly circles, while English still remained an "exotic" and practically unknown language. The Madrid production of *Hamleto* was a fiasco, among other reasons because the main characters were played by actors and actresses specialized in comic roles (Vicente Merino, Catalina Tordesillas, Polonia Rochel), and because José Espejo, who played Claudius, was too old for the part.[2] Presumably, the staging of a Shakespearean tragedy took the Madrid audience by surprise, as they were not yet familiar with subjects and modes that would be more acceptable in a proper romantic context.

A few years later, in 1798, Leandro Fernández de Moratín's translation of *Hamlet* from the original English text was published in Madrid. This new version would be reprinted, imitated, and even plagiarized on numerous occasions throughout the nineteenth and twentieth centuries. Despite its success as a printed work, however, it was never staged, as theater producers rejected it on the grounds that Shakespeare's text was unsuited to Spanish theater practice, which at that time required adherence to the three classical unities, compliance with certain rules of decorum, and a clear-cut moral message. According to these criteria, the English *Hamlet* was regarded as being full of "irregularities" and "far-fetched" elements. In the prologue to his translation, Moratín himself strongly criticized certain aspects of the original text, such as its "coarse" dialogues "capable only of provoking laughter in a wine-sodden, rude populace."[3] A conventional tragedy in the French style, such as Ducis's, seemed therefore more appropriate. In any case, the influence of Moratín's version can still be traced in such character names as "Ricardo," "Guillermo," and "La Sombra"—corresponding to Rosencrantz, Guildenstern, and The Ghost, respectively—which appear in the cast-lists of well-known contemporary productions."[4] Furthermore, such place-names as "Elsingor" for Elsinore and "Witemberga" for Wittenberg have been retained in some twentieth-century printed versions.[5]

After that first 1772 failure, *Hamlet* would not be seen again until 1825, when Carnerero's own translation of the Ducis text was staged in Madrid. Although Carnerero inserted passages from Moratín's translation, and even if the performers were now better suited to their roles, this new production once more received a cold response.[6] Similarly, a Spanish version of *Macbeth*—translated from the original text by José García de Villalta—was produced in Madrid in 1838, but without success. After this new fiasco, Shakespeare's tragedies would not be staged in Madrid for some time. The situation was no better in Barcelona, with no productions of *Hamlet* until 1866, when Ernesto Rossi's Italian company performed it there.[7]

The most popular Shakespeare play in the early nineteenth century was *Othello*, which had been first performed quite successfully in Madrid in 1802. It was a free translation—by Teodoro de la Calle—of Ducis's 1792 French version.[8] It was performed in many towns. As a matter of fact, Othello became so familiar a character, that it was soon identified with the person who played the role, namely, Isidoro Máiquez, a Cartagena-born actor who had been taught in Paris by the famous tragedian Talma. In later years, there appeared several burlesque versions of the famous tragedy, which would give rise even to certain *zarzuelas* (Spanish operettas).[9] The long-lasting popularity of *Othello*—even if it presented considerable discrepancies with the original English text—may have been due, not only to Máiquez's impressive performance in the title role, but to the fact that jealousy, cuckoldry, and the battle of the sexes have always excited Spanish theatergoers. It is not surprising, then, that the second most popular Shakespeare play in the late nineteenth and early twentieth centuries was *The Taming of the Shrew,* shown under such "exciting" titles as *La doma de la bravía* [The taming of the shrew], *La bisbetica domata* (an Italianized version of the same title), *La fierecilla domada* [The taming of the little wild beast], and even *Las bravías* [The shrews], a *zarzuela* with music by Ruperto Chapí, first staged in 1896.[10]

As for the remaining plays of the Shakespeare canon, only a few were produced in the main theaters of Spain in the period 1830–60. The most popular one at that time, apart from those mentioned above, was *Richard III*, which was presented in free translations of French versions, under such odd titles as *Los hijos de Eduardo* [Edward's sons] or *Ricardo III, Segunda Parte de los hijos de Eduardo* [Richard III, The second part of Edward's sons]. The story of King Richard III may have seemed attractive to Spanish romantic circles, as he was presented as a cruel tyrant who, according to the new revolutionary trends, deserved deposition and death; as the plot allows for several significant female roles, it lent itself particularly well to the aims of contemporary Spanish companies, some of which were in fact led by women. The acceptance of *Richard III* as a drama must have brought about the 1828 Madrid success of Ventura de la Vega's *Shakespeare enamorado* [Shakespeare in love]—in turn, a translation of Alexandre Duval's French comedy *Shakespeare amoureux* [Shakespeare in love], first performed in Paris in 1804.[11] Both Duval and Ventura de la Vega present young William Shakespeare in love with an actress who is rehearsing *Richard III* in London; the Spanish version of Duval's play was revived successfully throughout the nineteenth century. The other "history plays" were never staged, possibly because producers thought that their subject was alien to Spanish culture; only in recent years has a translation of *Richard II* (by A. Luis Pujante) been performed successfully in Madrid and elsewhere.

Shakespeare's tragedies would not be produced again until the late nineteenth century, when several Italian theater companies performing in Italian (Adelaida Ristori's, Ernesto Rossi's, Giovanni Emmanuel's, Ermete Novelli's, and a few others) visited Madrid and Barcelona. One of these, Ermete Zacconi's, put on *Amleto* [Hamlet] at the Tívoli Theater, Barcelona, as late as February 1923.[12] These productions exerted a considerable influence on Spanish theatergoers and added to an increasing taste for Italian operas based on Shakespeare plots (like Verdi's or Rossini's). The result was that new dramas were incorporated into the hitherto slim

Shakespeare repertoire consisting of *Othello, Romeo and Juliet*, and *Richard III*. Thus *The Taming of the Shrew, Antony and Cleopatra, King Lear*, and *The Merchant of Venice* also came to be staged and revived. It was in this context that *Hamlet* was produced again, and now quite successfully, even if it was spoken in Italian. This made it possible for a new Spanish version—Carlos Coello's three-act *El Príncipe Hamlet* [Prince Hamlet]—to be staged in Madrid (at the Español Theater) in 1872; it had been written at the request of actor Antonio Vico (who played the title role) and was often revived in Madrid and Barcelona in the last two decades of the century.

An outstanding case is a Catalan *Hamlet* for male amateurs, "translated and arranged for the Catholic stage" [Traduhit i arreglat á l'escena católica] by Ángel Guerra (a pseudonym of Father Gaietá Soler), which was published in 1898.[13] The text, strongly indebted to both Ducis and Moratín, was clearly designed for the religious indoctrination of young men. That is why female characters were omitted and, at the same time, Claudius's life was spared. The Ghost appeals in fact to Hamlet's mercy, and the Prince, instead of killing his uncle, forgives his crime and lets him get away free. Claudius, in his turn, repents and exclaims: "May Heaven bless your noble heart!" [¡Mes benehesca / lo cel ton noble cor!].[14]

Hamlet has often been produced in the twentieth century, even if it is by no means Shakespeare's most popular drama in Spain: *The Taming of the Shrew* was clearly a favorite with the Madrid and Barcelona audiences in the period prior to the Civil War (1936–39) and *A Midsummer Night's Dream* has held sway for the last few decades. By way of example, three different productions of this comedy (in Spanish) could be seen in Madrid in 1993; but there have also been performances in English, Galician, Catalan, and Basque, special children's productions, and even puppet-shows based on the play. This essay, however, will focus on *Hamlet*, always regarded by a fair number of actors, directors, and scholars as a particularly challenging drama.

According to Par, *Hamlet, Princep de Dinamarca* [Hamlet, Prince of Denmark], especially translated by Antoni Bulbena i Tosell for the Catalan stage, was published in Barcelona in 1910.[15] A prose adaptation entitled *El Intérprete de Hamlet* [The Hamlet actor], being a tragicomedy based on the Hamlet story, was first performed at the Principal Theater, Zaragoza, in 1915, and was then revived at Madrid's Princesa Theater in 1915.

In the early 1920s, Ricardo Calvo and his company staged López-Ballesteros and González Llana's free-prose translation of

Hamlet in Madrid; it received a warm reception, and was often revived.[16] When it was shown at the Español Theater, Madrid, in January 1923, it got enthusiastic reviews in the press.[17] The text—a six-act version heavily indebted to Moratín's—had been specially devised for the stage, and relied on the scenographic resources of contemporary Spanish theaters. To begin with, it required fairly elaborate painted scenery, some of which was used several times in the same performance: for instance, the backdrop for the opening scene also served for the Ghost's apparition and, later on, for some other outdoor scenes. Mignoni, a famous theater artist, was praised for these settings.[18] Ricardo Calvo's and Carmen Seco's performances in the roles of Hamlet and Ophelia respectively, were also acclaimed.[19] A contemporary photograph shows Calvo dressed up for the title role and, curiously enough, he resembles Don Juan Tenorio rather than Prince Hamlet; it must be borne in mind that it was then customary—and even compulsory—for all Spanish leading actors to possess a Don Juan Tenorio outfit, as Zorrilla's famous play used to be revived every year in early November.[20] *Hamlet* became such a landmark in Ricardo Calvo's career that he chose this play and this same role for his "benefit night" in 1923 and again in 1930.[21] It indicates that the play already enjoyed a considerable reputation in the early decades of the century.

The script followed the original English text but avoided certain difficult situations and long scenes and speeches, thus shortening Shakespeare's play and adjusting it to the two hours of an average performance. By contrast, the printed version includes passages that had been traditionally omitted in nineteenth-century Spanish renderings, probably due to their technical complexity. The dialogue between Hamlet and the Ghost is here preserved, and directions indicate entrances and exits in full detail:

> Hamlet y la Sombra entran por la derecha del espectador, habiendo salido de la escena por el lado opuesto. La Sombra entra primero y Hamlet la sigue.

> [Hamlet and the Shadow enter right, after having exited left. The Shadow enters first, and Hamlet follows him.]

The graveyard scene is presented in a realistic manner, since real earth, and even bones, are required:

> mientras canta [el sepulturero] metido dentro de la fosa, arroja paletadas de tierra sobre el escenario; por último, arroja también una paletada de huesos.

[the gravedigger sings inside the grave as he casts a trowelful of earth on the stage; he eventually casts a trowelful of bones as well.]

The play-within-the-play does not include the dumb show, as it was probably considered redundant. The final duel, which results in Hamlet's death and subsequent funeral procession, brings this version to its conclusion. This must have been a novelty, as most nineteenth-century renderings had simply avoided the hero's death.

Another remarkable production, based on the prose version in four acts by Fernando de la Milla, was staged by Juan Santacana at the Pavón Theater, Madrid, in 1928. De la Milla's was, again, a quite free rendering heavily indebted to nineteenth-century sources, most of which relied on Ducis and other French adaptators. It was not a real translation of the English play and, in addition, several significant scenes were either cut or shortened, while some soliloquies disappeared or were turned into prose dialogue. "O that this too too solid flesh would melt" was part of a conversation with Ophelia in which most of the poetic images were missing. It seems that both De la Milla and Santacana had aimed at presenting a conventional, romantic, and even melodramatic hero whose violent actions and outbursts could be morally justified; for that reason, they made him apologize to Horatio for the deaths of Polonius and Ophelia in this rather clumsy manner:

> HAMLET: Yo maté a Polonio. Pero ¿fuí yo, o fueron sus enredos, oficiosidades y bellaquerías? . . . Ofelia se ahogó porque perdió el juicio. Perdió el juicio . . . porque yo maté a su padre. Yo maté a su padre porque no soy dueño de mí desde que también mataron al mío . . .[22]

> [HAMLET: I killed Polonius. But was it I, or was it his tricks, flatteries and evil-doings that killed him? . . . Ophelia drowned herself because she lost her wits. She lost her wits . . . because I killed her father. I killed her father because I am not in control of myself since someone killed mine . . .]

Certain characteristic episodes were discarded as well, namely, the Fortinbras-Norway plot, the hero's trip to England, the dumb show (3.2), the King's prayers, and even the deaths of Hamlet and Laertes. Claudius was here killed by Laertes just as Horatio shouted "¡Viva Hamlet, Rey de Dinamarca," or "Long live Hamlet, King of Denmark!"[23] However, the Ghost or Sombra—which was played by the same actor who played the gravedigger—became quite important in this version, although most earlier productions had avoided having the Ghost on stage at all.

Santacana's was a modern-dress production, apparently the first one to be seen in Madrid, even if, as some press reviews pointed out, he was simply following the example of earlier London, Berlin, and New York productions.[24] The first *Hamlet* in modern costume to be seen in Britain had in fact been staged by the Birmingham Repertory Company at the Kingsway Theatre (London) in 1925.[25] A contemporary photograph of the Madrid theater shows the graveyard scene: Horatio wears a modern Spanish cloak, Prince Hamlet appears as a high-rank military officer, and the gravediggers are characterized as contemporary peasants.[26] The painted backdrops were also considered rather innovative, as they had been designed in a very stylized manner. The only drawback was the faulty diction of Santacana and several other actors, which the audience sometimes found difficult to understand.[27]

The Civil War marked the end of an era in Spanish drama. In spite of increasing difficulties, however, theaters never stopped completely, not even in Madrid when it was under siege, for as César Oliva points out, Salvador Soler and Milagros Leal staged *Hamlet* at the Eslava Theater just as soldiers were fighting only a few miles away. That was probably the only Spanish version of the play to be performed in the period 1936–39.[28] Then, in the aftermath of the war, although Shakespeare—being English—had become suspicious in the eyes of orthodox fascists, *Hamlet* would be performed again.[29] The first significant production was played by Alejandro Ulloa's repertory company; it was first staged in Barcelona and was revived quite successfully in 1945, touring around Spain. Ulloa played the title role, Luis Orduña was Claudius, and the part of Ophelia was played by Ana María Campoy. Adolfo Marsillach, who would later become a famous actor and director, made his theater debut in the role of Laertes.[30]

Hamlet was also played by director Cayetano Luca de Tena, who used poet José María Pemán's text, entirely rendered in verse. It was first staged at the Español Theater (Madrid) in 1949. This same version would later be produced by the Lope de Vega Theater Company—directed by José Tamayo—and would go on a tour in South America. Now, for the first time since 1772, the dramatic plot was offered in its entirety, as Pemán preserved all the episodes in their original sequence. Many elements which had traditionally been cut in previous renderings—the Fortinbras story, the meeting with the players, the nunnery scene, the dumb show, the trip to England, the dialogue with Osric, the duel, and Hamlet's death—were all included here, some for the first time.

Pemán, however, did not translate or follow Shakespeare's text, as he was only interested in the story, which gave him a good excuse to write his own script. His hero was quite different from Shakespeare's; his was actually a romantic, Christian, even Roman Catholic, young prince, forever hesitating, forever repenting of his previous conduct and who, far from being carried away by passion and revenge, appeared as an innocent victim in a corrupt and wicked world. The romantic aspect of the character was particularly emphasized in the "To be, or not to be" soliloquy—actually a series of ten quatrains—spoken by Guillermo Marín. The actor posed as the famous Rodin statue "The Thinker" while the stage remained dark except for a spot, lighting him from below. Hamlet kept reminding the audience that he was incapable of making up his mind; at one particular moment, he stated, seated musing on a rock:

> muero entre dudas y vacilaciones,
> desandando caminos, como en la playa el mar.
> . . . Basta ya, duda eterna . . . ¡Basta ya!"[31]

> [I die in the midst of doubts and hesitations
> retracing my steps, like the sea on a beach . . .
> Enough, eternal doubt . . . that's enough!]

There were several allusions to Hamlet's "profound Christian beliefs." In a dialogue with Horatio he asserted: "And I have already my own pathway, traced out by God" [Y yo tengo un camino que es Dios quien me lo marca, 1788], and added: "Since you are in a state of grace. . . . Being acquainted with him is sinful enough" [Pues te hallas en estado de gracia. . . . Conocerle ya es pecado, 1788]. The king himself appeared as a devout and pious Catholic penitent who prayed on a kneeler thus:

> No pretendo engañarte, Señor . . . Ésta es mi mano
> manchada en sangre. Mira . . . Si tú quieres, Señor . . .
>
> (1754)

> [I do not mean to deceive you, Oh Lord . . . This is my hand
> stained with blood. Look . . . If you want, Oh Lord . . .]

Pemán tried to smooth out rude or obscene expressions, and he virtually censored Ophelia's songs, which in his version lost all sexual implications. Ironically, the only negative criticism of Pemán's script in the press was that he had followed Shakespeare's text too closely, thus creating a rather lengthy and "learned" version. Critics, though, were unanimous in praising the quality of his verse.

Neither Pemán nor Luca de Tena seems to have been aware of the geographical features of Denmark, as they prepared a rather odd setting for the entrance of Fortinbras and his army, namely "A mountainous landscape close to Elsinore" [Paisaje de sierra en las proximidades de Elsinor, 1766]. They might have been influenced by the famous Olivier film—released one year earlier (1948)—which showed cliffs and a castle on a hill. Also, they seem to have insisted on the cold climate of Scandinavian countries, as Francisco alluded to snow: "Thanks for this relief. It is snowing" [Se agradece el relevo. Está nevando, 1701].

A striking and rather controversial production was Armando Moreno's, based on a script by Nicolás González Ruiz, which was first performed at the Griego Theater (Montjuich, Barcelona) in 1960; it then went on a tour of Spain, and was revived at Barcelona one year later. The title role was played by Moreno's twenty-four-year-old wife Nuria Espert. She was not the first "female" Hamlet to appear on a Spanish stage, as Sarah Bernhardt had played that part in Madrid in 1899. Some years later, at least two Spanish actresses had followed her example, namely Gloria Torres and Margarita Xirgu. Torres, as the leading actress in Salvador Martínez's Company, had played that role some time before the Civil War; Margarita Xirgu's *Hamlet* had been staged in Argentina in 1938.[32] The idea of having a woman in that role must have appealed to Spanish artists in the early twentieth century, since Zuloaga painted a young lady dressed up as Prince Hamlet while posing in front of the Segovia "Alcázar," an ancient Spanish castle.[33]

However, Moreno's production, which had initially attracted a great deal of attention, met with harsh and rather negative criticism, as many people found Nuria Espert's work unsatisfactory. One reason for wanting to play that challenging role was her admiration of Sarah Bernhardt. And since Armando Moreno had viewed Prince Hamlet as a romantic teenager devoid of passion and sexual appetite, Nuria Espert did not have to pretend to be a man; her part did not demand a definite sexual role.[34] This is precisely what infuriated some critics, who argued (in a somewhat male-chauvinistic way) that Shakespeare's original character required a manly and confident performer instead of Nuria Espert.[35]

González Ruiz translated directly from the English, but had to shorten the text to adjust it to a normal running time. His version was highly praised. It was a spectacular and rather grand production, with three-dimensional scenery by Sigfrido Burmann that incorporated the old moat and walls of Montjuich, thus producing the impression of a massive castle, not unlike the setting of Olivier's film, by now a standard reference. A sketch published in *La Vanguardia Española* showed Nuria Espert's hairstyle with the characteristic short fringe of Laurence Olivier in the role of Prince Hamlet.[36] Critics also traced back certain details of the closet scene to Olivier's film.[37]

A remarkable and heavily subsidized production, directed by José Tamayo, was staged at the Español Theater, Madrid, in December 1961. It was based on a prose translation by playwright Antonio Buero Vallejo following the English text, which would eventually become a successful printed work. Hamlet was played by Adolfo Marsillach, who had become a leading actor by this time. Lighting had a very important function here, as it allowed for quick and smooth scene changes, and also suggested different settings. The music, arranged by Cristóbal Halffter, was one of the highlights of the performance. This production opened with a very successful preview in the early evening, followed on the same day by a disastrous first performance proper; according to Marsillach, nearly everything went wrong, including his own voice, which he nearly lost.[38] The Ghost or *la Sombra* was then visible, with a special actor for the part. This would be one of the first versions to make the character of the Ghost important, and it was also the last to have him appear in full view on stage; as most later versions have replaced him with sound and lighting effects. Hamlet's dialogue with his father's ghost took place on a high platform, probably in imitation of the Olivier film. There is a curious anecdote about this particular scene: on New Year's Eve, as the Ghost was saying "Adieu, adieu, Hamlet. Remember me," he added in a humorous tone "and a happy New Year to you," which made the audience roll in the aisles with laughter.[39]

There was now, for the first time, a serious attempt to break away from the old, traditional, romantic stereotype of an innocent, doubting Hamlet, since Buero tried to show him and Ophelia as ordinary, weak, imperfect, human beings. Stage directions in the text help stress, for example, that Ophelia is not sincere when speaking to her father:

Lo ha dicho bajando los ojos y sin convicción: tal vez miente.

[She has said that while looking down, unconvinced. She may be lying.]

Next, she "avoids his glance" [rehuye su mirada, 48]. Further stage directions in the "nunnery scene" hint that Hamlet and Ophelia may have had sexual intercourse in the past; so when he alludes to her honesty and beauty, Buero adds: "He, mockingly, looks up and down at her beautiful body, that he may have possessed" [Burlón, mira de arriba abajo el bello cuerpo que tal vez fue suyo, 71]. And she "looks down, perhaps regretting past indulgencies, and laments" [baja los ojos, quizá arrepentida de pasadas generosidades, y se lamenta, 71–72].

One of the most outstanding aspects of that production was the fact that Buero Vallejo, being an experienced playwright, preserved the majority of allusions and episodes relating to theater and drama. He included, for instance, Hamlet's dialogue with the players about the war of the theaters, the Pyrrhus speeches, the dumb show, and the entire play-within-the-play, here rendered in verse.

After that production, *Hamlet* has often been present on the Spanish stage. Alejandro Ulloa and his company performed Agustín de Rojas's version at the Barcelona Theater (Barcelona, 1963), and it was then revived on several occasions. Ulloa, who had already played the part of Prince Hamlet in the early 1950s, undertook that role once again, with Carolina Colom as Ophelia; both of them were acclaimed in press reviews.[40] A very different type of arrangement was the outdoor production based on Terenci Moix's Catalan version, which was first staged in the open—in two different venues in Barcelona in 1979—and then taken to the Comedia Theater, an indoor playhouse in Madrid in 1980. Another Catalan production by the "Talleret de Salt" Company, based on a translation by Maurici Farré, was staged at the Regina Theater, Barcelona, in 1989.

Álvaro Custodio—a Spanish Republican exile from 1939 to 1974—produced *Hamlet* in Mexico in the 1960s.[41] He had become the director of a company known as the "Teatro Español de México" [Spanish Theater of Mexico], which in 1968 performed Custodio's own verse translation at the Chapultepec Castle; the old building was turned into Elsinore for this purpose. One year later, the same company revived it at the Hidalgo Theater, México D.F.; a two-level platform was built for that occasion.[42]

The complexities and subtleties of Shakespeare's text have not prevented amateur groups from producing the play, which is regarded by some drama schools as a compulsory step in the training of future actors and actresses. The Seville High School of Drama produced *Hamlet* in the late 1980s, and then again in 1999, this time directed by Emilio Rivas. Similarly, the Madrid High School of Drama staged Ignacio García's text in 1988.

Foreign companies also contributed to the increasing popularity of the play in the late 1980s and throughout the 1990s in the course of various theater festivals held in several Spanish cities, especially Madrid and Barcelona. Playwright Tom Stoppard produced his own adaptation of *Hamlet* for actors and puppets, enacted by the "Teatar I.T.D." (Yugoslavia) at the Olympia Playhouse, Madrid, in 1984, under the direction of Zlatko Bourek. Five years later, in 1989, the "Théâtre de Nanterre-Amandiers" Company staged a French version directed by Patrice Chéreau at the "Mercat de les Flors" in Barcelona. Two other companies—"Der Kreis Theater" from Austria (1990) and another one from Argentina (1992)—visited Barcelona and staged their own productions of *Hamlet*.[43]

The most luxurious, expensive, and ambitious production to date has undoubtedly been a heavily subsidized project undertaken by the "Centro Dramático Nacional" [Spanish National Dramatic Center]. It was promoted by José Carlos Plaza, who had just been appointed director of that institution. Plaza had commissioned Vicente Molina Foix to translate Shakespeare's drama, adapting it to his own artistic requirements, and the resulting text—a free-verse rendering—was published as a bilingual edition and then sold at the foyer of the theaters, just as the play was being performed. It was first staged at the María Guerrero Theater, Madrid, in 1989, and then taken on a long tour around Spain, although the cast was slightly different. Press reviews were mostly positive and enthusiastic, as Molina Foix had made critics believe that his version and Plaza's production were a real landmark in theater history. He erroneously argued that *Hamlet* had not been staged in Spain for thirty years.[44] His version of *Hamlet* had followed Shakespeare's English text very closely, even if he made some obvious mistakes when translating significant passages. Though forced to shorten speeches and dialogues to adjust his script to the prescribed running time, the performance still lasted nearly four hours. Certain secondary characters—Cornelius, Voltimand, and the English ambassadors—were missing, and several items were changed; one of the Elsinore players, for example, was a woman.

A considerable amount of public money was lavished on this period-costume production, presented to the media as a first-rate "cultural" event, since it was the masterpiece of the greatest theater genius. So, very popular and expensive actors and actresses—such as José Luis Gómez (Hamlet), Alberto Closas (Claudius), and Ana Belén (Ophelia) were engaged for the main parts. Settings, costume, lighting, and sound effects all showed that it had been designed as a grand, costly, spectacular show. However the result was rather disappointing, as most of the visual effects were purposeless. For instance, the Ghost did not appear on stage, even if the costume designer had prepared a full armour for him.[45] His voice could just be heard offstage, as water fell in a cascade from the ceiling and red lights flashed. According to the published text, the Ghost's voice should be that of the actor playing Hamlet, but the audience missed that detail as they were busy looking at the special effects. In general terms, it was a very lengthy, tedious, rhetorical, and static performance, which did not contribute to making Shakespeare's drama popular but discouraged prospective theatergoers.

The latest Spanish production, and the last of the twentieth century, was the "Teatre Lliure" version, first staged in a Catalan translation by Joan Sallent at the Grec Theater (Barcelona, July 1999). It was directed by Lluís Homar, who also played the title role. A few months later it was taken on tour throughout Spain (1999–2000); this time they used a Spanish verse translation by A. Luis Pujante, which reproduced the spirit and rhythm of Shakespeare's original text.[46] The stage-business evolved around a huge rostrum with steps, and characters spoke as they climbed up and down, which seemed somewhat awkward at times. Only eleven players managed to take on all roles, and that entailed doubling; the Ghost, which was perfectly visible, was played by the actor who also enacted one of the players and a priest at Ophelia's burial. Lluís Homar played a convincing Hamlet, but he appeared to be much older than either Gertrude or Claudius. One of the most striking aspects of this production was that Rosencrantz and Guildenstern behaved in a clown-like manner. On the whole, it was a fairly innovative stage rendering of the play.

Hamlet first became important in the Spanish theater repertoire in the late nineteenth century, once the romantic mood was finally accepted. Since then, it has gradually increased in popularity, which would explain why first-rate actors and actresses—Calvo, Xirgu, Marsillach, Espert, Gómez, Ana Belén, and so on—performed it throughout the twentieth century. However there is, as yet, no distinct national tradition in its stage presentation, as companies have mostly relied on what has been done abroad. In fact, they imitated French and Italian adaptations first, then British, German, or even American productions, and eventually, film versions of the play, especially Olivier's. To a certain extent, the Spanish theater image of Prince Hamlet is still that of a romantic, old-fashioned, nineteenth-century hero.

Up to the first half of the twentieth century, Madrid set the example for all other productions, including those staged in Barcelona. However, in later years and particularly after Franco's death, Barcelona companies produced their own versions and adaptations regardless of what was done elsewhere. One of the reasons for this was the attempt to promote Catalan, and Shakespeare, being a foreign author, lent himself to an endless series of translations.

Hamlet is not yet Shakespeare's most popular play in Spain, perhaps because both plot and characters are still relatively alien to Spanish taste and culture. This would explain the continuous rewriting of the original text. In most productions, directors commissioned well-known writers to provide the company with a suitable acting script, usually in prose. However, those versions were seldom real translations from the English, and did not follow Shakespeare's drama closely. The entire plot of *Hamlet* was shown for the first time in 1949. It was in the course of Luca de Tena's production based on Pemán's text, even if that verse rendering was quite free. But it was only in the last quarter of the century that real translations from the English were actually used for the stage (Molina Foix's, Pujante's and so on).

One of the main objections that Spanish theater companies may have had to the play was that its female roles were not important enough, at least, when compared with that of Prince Hamlet. For this reason, leading actresses such as Torres, Xirgu, and Espert dared to play the title role, even if some of them met with hostile criticism. Since the role of women in theater circles is substantial now, it is not unlikely that an all-female cast *Hamlet* will be seen in one of the Spanish professional playhouses in the near future.

Notes

1. Alfonso Par, *Representaciones Shakespearianas en España*, 2 vols. (Madrid: Victoriano Suárez, 1936), 1:21–26; and Paul Benchettrit, "Hamlet at the Comédie Française: 1769–1896," *Shakespeare Survey* 9 (1956): 59–68.

2. Par, *Representaciones,* 1:25–26.

3. Ynarco Celenio [Leandro Fernández de Moratín], *Hamlet* (Madrid, 1798), Prologue (no page number): "capaces sólo de excitar la risa de un populacho vinoso y soez."

4. For instance, such productions as Ricardo Calvo's (based on López-Ballesteros and González Llana's version, 1923), Santacana's (based on De la Milla's free translation of *Hamlet* [Madrid: Prensa Moderna, 1928]), Luca de Tena's (based on Pemán's free version, 1949) and José Tamayo's (based on Buero Vallejo's text, 1961) all included "Ricardo," "Guillermo," and "La Sombra" in their cast.

5. Both Ángel Guerra's Catalan version (1898) and López-Ballesteros and González Llana's text (1923) refer to "Elsingor." Guerra's and Buero Vallejo's versions render "Witemberga" and "Vitemberga" respectively. See *Hamlet, drama en tres actes y en vers*, translated by Ángel Guerra [= Gaietá Soler] (Barce-

lona, 1898); and *Hamlet, príncipe de Dinamarca*, translated by Antonio Buero Vallejo (Cádiz: Escelicer, 1962).
  6. Par, *Representaciones*, 1:70–74.
  7. Par, *Representaciones*, 2:75.
  8. Par, *Representaciones*, 1:26–37.
  9. A very popular burlesque was *El Caliche* [literally "The whitewashed man"]—first performed in Madrid in 1828—which was very often revived. Other famous nineteenth-century parodies were *Otelo, el moro de Valencia* [Othello, the Moor of Valencia], *Otelo, el moro de Magnesia* [Othello, the Moor of Magnesium], and *Otelo, el moro de Sarriá* [Othello, the Moor of Sarriá (meaning, from a poor quarter in Barcelona)]; see also Francisca Íñiguez Barrena, *La parodia teatral en España (1868–1914)* (Sevilla: Universidad de Sevilla, 1999), 59. A *zarzuela*, *El Otelo del barrio* [Backstreet Othello], was performed in Madrid in 1921; the music was composed by Jacinto Guerrero. See Dru Dougherty and María Francisca Vilches, *La escena madrileña entre 1918 y 1926* (Madrid: Fundamentos, 1990), 380.
  10. See Íñiguez Barrena, *La paradia teatral,* 126; Dru Dougherty and María Francisca Vilches, *La escena madrileña entre 1926 y 1931* (Madrid: Fundamentos, 1997), 406.
  11. See Ventura de la Vega, *Shakespeare enamorado, comedia en un acto, escrita en francés por A. Duval y traducida al castellano* (Madrid, 1831); and Alexandre Duval, *Shakespeare amoureux. Oeuvres complètes*, vol. 5 (Paris: Barba, 1822).
  12. Josep M. de Sagarra, *Crítiques de teatre: "La Publicitat," 1922–1927*, edited by Xavier Fábregas (Barcelona: Institut del Teatre, 1987), 418–22.
  13. Ángel Guerra [Gaietá Soler], *Hamlet, drama en tres actes y en vers* (Barcelona, 1898).
  14. Ibid., 46.
  15. Alfonso Par, *Contribución a la bibliografía española de Shakespeare* (Barcelona: Publicaciones del Instituto del Teatro Nacional, 1930), 102.
  16. Luis López-Ballesteros and Félix González Llana, *Hamlet* (Madrid: Prensa Popular, 1921).
  17. *ABC*, 18 January 1923, 22.
  18. *ABC*, 20 January 1923, 27.
  19. *ABC*, 18 January 1923, 22.
  20. See *Blanco y Negro*, 28 January 1923, n.p.
  21. On these two performances see respectively *Blanco y Negro*, 28 January 1923; and *El Sol*, 3 January 1930, 3.
  22. De la Milla, *Hamlet*, 67.
  23. De la Milla, *Hamlet*, 76.
  24. *ABC*, 2 July 1928, 38.
  25. See Anthony B. Dawson, *Hamlet*, Shakespeare in Performance (Manchester: Manchester University Press, 1995), 83–84.
  26. *Blanco y Negro*, 8 July 1928, n.p.
  27. See *ABC*, 2 July 1928, 38; and *Blanco y Negro*, 8 July 1928, n.p.
  28. César Oliva, *El teatro desde 1936* (Madrid: Alhambra, 1989), 24.
  29. See Julio Martínez Velasco, "Representaciones del teatro de Shakespeare en Sevilla desde 1930," in José Manuel González Fernández de Sevilla, *Shakespeare en España* (Zaragoza: Pórtico, 1993), 341–77, 348.
  30. For a detailed account of this production, see Adolfo Marsillach, *Tan lejos, tan cerca: Mi vida* (1998; reprint, Barcelona: Tusquets, 1999), 83–91.
  31. *Hamlet*, translated by José María Pemán, in his *Obras Completas*, vol. 4 (Madrid: Escelicer, 1949), 1768.

32. Antonina Rodrigo, *Margarita Xirgu* (Madrid: Aguilar, 1988), 347–48.
33. See photo in *El País*, 9 May 1999, 46.
34. See *La Vanguardia Española*, 28 July 1960, 21; and *Primer Acto*, July–August 1960, 60.
35. *La Vanguardia Española*, 30 July 1960, 25.
36. *La Vanguardia Española*, 28 July 1960, 21.
37. *Primer Acto,* July–August (1960), 60.
38. See Adolfo Marsillach, *Tan lejos, tan cerca: Mi vida*, 222–23.
39. Marsillach, *Tan lejos, tan cerca*, 225.
40. *La Vanguardia Española*, 8 November 1963.
41. *Hamlet: traducción castellana, edición y estudio*, translated by Álvaro Custodio (Tarragona: Tarraco, 1977).
42. See Álvaro Custodio, *Hamlet* (1977).
43. See José Manuel González Fernández de Sevilla, *Shakespeare en España* (Zaragoza: Pórtico, 1993), 531–32.
44. González Fernández de Sevilla, *Shakespeare en España*, 224.
45. See *Hamlet*, translated by Vicente Molina Foix (Madrid: Publicaciones del Centro Dramático Nacional, 1989), Introduction (n.p.).
46. *Hamlet*, edited and translated by Ángel-Luis Pujante (Madrid: Espasa Calpe, 1994).

Apocalyptic Beginnings at the End of the Millennium
Stefan Bachmann's *Troilus and Cressida*

Sylvia Zysset

> *Thersites*: Lechery, lechery; still wars and lechery; nothing else holds fashion.
>
> *Aeneas*: Hark, what good sport is out of town today!
> *Troilus*: Better at home, if "would I might" were "may."
> —*Troilus and Cressida*

WHAT HELPS THE PERFORMANCE OF A SHAKESPEARE PLAY BECOME A popular and critical success at the end of the millennium? How can postmodern playfulness be employed to entertain, empower, and challenge audiences into reconsidering their lives in the world of today? A 1998 production of *Troilus and Cressida* performed in Salzburg, Austria and in Basel, Switzerland suggests some possible answers to these questions. Could this end-of-millennium production have traveled successfully to other European countries, or are its concerns and the success of its techniques limited to a particular cultural environment of Western Europe?

One-and-a-half years before the end of the millennium and amidst growing, media-hyped hysteria surrounding the big date, thirty-two-year-old Swiss director Stefan Bachmann came to Basel to become the youngest-ever artistic drama director at a Swiss municipal theater. He and his team introduced themselves to the local audience with Shakespeare's *Troilus and Cressida*, the play that inspired them to select for their entire first season the theme of "Apocalypse." To mark any beginning with a motto like this suggests a paradox, which the production itself also embodied in the conflicting messages it conveyed: a hopeless vision of a doomed patriarchal society in which every ideal is exposed as a delusion or ideological construction, presented with a captivating joy of acting and of the theater as a whole. The production was coproduced by, and first performed at, the Salzburger Festspiele. Here the opening-night audience as well as many of the big-name German and Austrian critics pooh-poohed the production as a simplistic, comic reduction of what Shakespeare had intended.[1] In Basel, though, Bachmann and his team's performance of the play enjoyed a highly favorable reception. *Troilus and Cressida* soon became a sold-out success, particularly with young audiences: people lined up for returns, and extra seating had to be installed in an attempt to meet demand. This is remarkable because, like many theaters in the German-speaking world, the Basel Theater has in recent years been suffering from dwindling audience figures and a decreasing interest in the theater in general. The production's bitterly disillusioning yet also highly entertaining portrayal of the Greek and Trojan "heroes" as ridiculous and dangerous members of today's patriarchal Western society obviously hit the right note. Its success seemed to stem both from the kind of interpretation it delivered and, perhaps more importantly, from its staging and performance. Visual references to postmodern culture were combined with a stage set that facilitated an almost Elizabethan openness as well as simultaneity of place and time. The metatheatrical awareness of the actor's skills and their apparent delight in exploring and playing their parts greatly increased the audience's involvement and its sense of enjoyment.

Bachmann, whose interests span from the Bible and medieval literature to Hollywood cinema and pulp fiction, made a name for himself in Berlin's free theater scene as cofounder of the independent theater group Affekt [emotion, heat of the moment]. His stagings are frequently described as undogmatic, playful, intelligent, witty, and human. In one interview, he mentioned that the Affekt-team humorously dubbed their style "neo-conservative," since they wanted to oppose the deconstructionist *Zertrümmerungstheater* [theater of destruction] of directors like Frank Castorf, by putting stories back together again in a contemporary language.[2] Bachmann acknowledges the audience's desire for stories and makes use of the aesthetics of film, TV, comics, and video games to find a language suitable for representing the fractured nature of postmodern life. He is also a fan of Renaissance art and his productions convey a great fascination for the theater and its manifold and magical possibilities. Most importantly, he respects the importance of the actor as creator, allowing his actors to take center stage and develop a strong individual presence as performers. This kind of staging opposes the single viewpoint of modernist director's theater by creating a polyphony of contradictory but equally valid voices. The emphasis on single scenes as engaging and entertaining moments in their own right, rather than predominantly on the single overarching development of the plot, is furthermore reminiscent of the performance style of Elizabethan theater. Bachmann and his dramaturg Matthias Günther felt that *Troilus and Cressida* was particularly suited to exploring the balance between fractured moments and a story line.[3]

A theater company's ability to draw a regular audience depends largely on its success in forging a bond of complicity with the local population. Bachmann is aware that actors are key factors in this process. He insists that he is part of a large, creative team—many of the actors, directors/dramaturgs, and designers from the Affekt-team accompanied him to Basel—and not the sole person responsible for artistic success, stressing the value of the ensemble idea and the mutual trust it allows an artistic team to develop.[4] This, too, seems a typical feature of postmodern artistic work and marks a break from modernist director's theater.

Questioned about his feelings towards Switzerland, Bachmann describes the country as a very unreal island in the rest of Europe: clean, conservative, protected, and obsessed with security.[5] To him, "Berlin is dirtier and more real."[6] He criticizes Switzerland's unwillingness to take a decisive stand in major issues, to participate in the creation of a unified Europe, or to face up to its own growing internal problems (unemployment, racism, disorientation) and its past: "The Swiss are world champions in sweeping things under the carpet."[7] However, he believes that the façade is now slowly cracking and that this will finally cause stronger emotional outbreaks in the country. As a theater practitioner, he wants to trace such cracks and reflect on current moods in Swiss society with irony, seriousness, and humor. When questioned about the two famous moralists and critics of Swiss hypocrisy, Friedrich Dürrenmatt and Max Frisch, Bachmann mentions with some regret that it is difficult for people of his own generation to present moral views of society, since today all values appear insecure and questionable; all views are relative or easily dismissed as ridiculous.[8] By allowing the actors to take center stage and by emphasising their physical presence and playfulness, Bachmann's theater does, however, manage to transport a very human quality.

Salzburg

Forging an allegiance with the audience was obviously more difficult in Salzburg than in Basel; there were acoustical problems, and the free-standing stage did not fit well into the space of a converted cinema. Many opening-night visitors regarded Bachmann and his actors' grotesque debunking of the heroes as an instance of simplification and a mark of disrespect for Shakespeare's play rather than a truthful rendition of its attitude. In their opinion the Bard was not taken seriously enough. It was felt that there should have been a greater sense of mourning for lost ideals.[9] Given the fact that the whole story was presented from Thersites' perspective, it was difficult to tell whether some critics' objections were really directed against the director or the play itself. Yet a number of critics did applaud Bachmann's ability to mediate between a problematic play and topical concerns. Some added that the three-hour performance was entertaining and enjoyable. This, however, seems to be a dangerous compliment in the German cultural world, where distinctions between "entertaining" and "serious," between "popular" and "high-brow" culture are still more sharply drawn and pertinent than in the Anglo-American world. In light of this seemingly unavoidable distinction it becomes clear that Bachmann's style—and indeed this "problem play" itself—would necessarily plunge critics into a conflict. One Austrian critic said: "If it weren't the worst thing that you could possibly say about a theater production in the high-culture business [Hochkulturbetrieb], the verdict would have to be: excellent entertainment!"[10] Benedict Nightingale in *The Times* seemed blissfully unaware of this typically "German" problem. In a review headed "Salzburg's Wild and Crazy Guise—Austria's festival has madcap productions to surpass Edinburgh's," he concluded:

> The production ... catches the callow sexuality, the raw machismo and the dark humour that have combined to make Shakespeare's cynical portrait of love and war speak so strongly to our era ... the evening is almost too generous with telling, original detail. I have never seen the play more boldly or brilliantly staged.[11]

The Swiss critics who traveled to Salzburg for a sneak preview were also more willing to engage with the production's stance: "Dismantling the Heroes—Stefan Bachmann's Promise," "Loud Mouths Like Us," and "Carefully Observed Affection" were titles of their reviews. The director, one Swiss critic concluded, makes it clear

> that philosophy resigned long ago in the face of all-corrupting dissipation and love of violence. ... [W]hat are the Trojans and Greeks to

[him]? Idiots: he doesn't mourn for them, he laughs at them. That he doesn't place himself above them gives the whole undertaking the air of a confession or manifesto: look here, this is where we stand at the end of the millennium.[12]

BASEL: MUSIC, LANGUAGE, TEXT, AND CULTURE

In the following I will try to shed light on some aspects of this *Troilus and Cressida* production as it was presented in Basel. The categories are based loosely on the benchmarks Patrice Pavis chooses for discussing intercultural Shakespeare performances.[13]

The production opened with strange, eerie music resounding from the stage. Members of the audience described it as primeval, uncanny, and unsettling. It was produced by two young Swiss musicians playing instruments and producing vocal sounds related to those used in traditional Swiss folk music (alphorn, harmonium, yodelling) and yet very different from these, having been mixed with music traditions from many different cultures (like the digeridoo or Tibetan overtone singing). Like a Greek chorus, they were present throughout the production, commenting on the unfolding action in their strange, wailing, giggling, menacing, and plaintive tones. For a Swiss audience this type of music may have been particularly intriguing. The sounds were in a way familiar, normally associated with a very traditional, conservative type of Swiss culture particularly unpopular with younger people. Yet here the elements of a specifically national culture appeared to have dissolved into an unexpected, international context and to touch on a deeper level of shared human—or perhaps animal—emotions, prior to language.[14] This made sense in a play that locates sex and war as the driving forces of human nature and exposes culture as a carefully constructed cover-up. The musicians' performance made a strong impression on critics and audiences, and they were frequently applauded spontaneously during the performance. This musical and vocal (but nonverbal) commentary also increased the many-faceted nature of the play, adding new levels of tone and feeling to the language spoken. Both director and dramaturgs were impressed by the rich and varied language styles of the original. They commissioned a new translation, reworked it substantially during rehearsals, but were not entirely satisfied with the result. One problem, said Günther, is the fact that people today are not used to listening closely and perceiving the details and nuances of spoken language that the Elizabethans were familiar with.[15] The language-like musical commentary did much to reintroduce this rich aural dimension.

The German prose translation was modern, shifting between formal and colloquial registers. Developed with the actors to achieve the greatest possible "speakability," it was clear that they enjoyed playing about with the translation spontaneously: Agamemnon threw in expressions typical of the German Chancellor Helmut Kohl, whereas Odysseus first ignored and then turned to Achilles with feigned surprise: "Ach!—illes!" (3.3.95; "Ach" meaning something like "Oh! so sorry! I didn't notice you"). In some cases snippets of the original were preserved, but used in a way typical of young people, who lace their Swiss-German with English words and expressions that are "cool" and "in": Troilus rushed onto the walls of Troy in an attempt to stop the fighting, calling "Peace!" (1.1.85) and reinterpreting the word in an appropriately modern way by holding up two fingers of each hand to form the peace sign. "Fair play," and "fool's play" were similarly preserved in the final act, creating yet another of the production's numerous links between sports and war.

Stage, Costume, and Culture

The free-standing wooden stage was set up in the foyer of the Basel Theater, between the main stage and the entrance doors, which lead out onto a heavily traveled piazza. A certain similarity to the Elizabethan theater as a public, communicative (and more intimate) space was aimed at, in an attempt to bring the theater closer to the town and its inhabitants.[16] The stage was made of light wood and shaped in a rough, open semicircle, with walls jutting out unevenly into the large foyer. This encouraged the fictional space to fuse with that of the audience seated opposite, on what is normally a wide flight of stairs. The set remained the same throughout the play, one of the aims being to accentuate the simultaneity of parts of the action and enable filmlike transitions from one scene to the next. All sites of the stage were multifunctional and indeterminate, evoking certain specific associations at different moments. Presumably these were very individual for different members of the audience. In a certain light the blue sky of the back wall evoked Swiss painter Ferdinand Hodler's symbolically charged alpine landscapes. The light pine wood and slight backward tilt of the walls of Troy reminded one of the Swiss Alps, though only momentarily, when a musician stood on them in the opening scene, and played an unusual kind of alphorn (the "Alperidu"). Were the walls of Troy meant to refer to the Swiss "Alpenfestung" [alpine stronghold]? Were the two musicians, watching the action from a safe distance up on the wall, an ironic commentary on the Swiss role in international politics? Returning from battle, the Trojans lined up under a row of showers on the right stage wall. The shower gel they used turned out to be stage blood: at first sight this image evoked the horrible reality of battle and wounded bodies, but it soon turned into the spectacle of men spreading enemy blood over their torsos with sadistic relish or narcissistically applying the proof of their military valor like make-up. These associations highlight an important quality that distinguished all elements of the production: its ability to provide certain recognisable signs and images that triggered multiple and contradicting associations, allowing the audience mentally to play around them.

Wilhelm Hortmann believes that the success of a postmodern Shakespeare production depends on its ability to engage the spectators' productive imagination and emphasises the importance of the visual as a means for tapping into the collective subconscious of the audience.[17] He mentions the difficulty of devising an appropriate set design for *Troilus and Cressida*: "Historical costumes are liable to make an audience . . . rebel against the staginess of the 'cursed theatre Greeks,' modern uniforms may evoke the wrong associations, while the choice of a completely different frame of scenographic reference . . . can rob the play of important dimensions."[18] Peter Sieffert's 1983 Mannheim production of the play transferred the action to the world of rival gangster clans in Atlantic City, New Jersey, bombarding the audience with so many specific references that it acted as a straightjacket to the imagination. Dieter Dorn's 1986 Munich production was more successful because it avoided the "trap of a too-definite visual setting." The costumes did not indicate any definite place or period, being compiled of a mixture of—to European eyes—exotic cultural references: African, Mexican, Native American, Kabuki Theater. This evoked an indeterminate cultural atmosphere, archaic and eternally valid. Trevor Nunn's 1999 production at the National Theatre seems to have employed similar methods; it avoided clear references to the present, but emphasized ideas of colonialism and fear of the "foreign" or "other." The white Greeks were furnished with timeless Greek attributes, the dark-skinned Trojans were situated within an Oriental frame of reference.[19]

Bachmann's production was equally successful in creating a "contradictory, yet suggestive, indeterminacy" and opening up a vision of the human condition in general, but he employed cultural references that were more recognizable (temporally and geographically speaking) for a Western European audience.[20] The costumes were representative of postmodern Western culture, strongly influenced by America. At the same time they exaggerated and highlighted the ridiculousness of modern macho "war-dress." The jeans-clad Trojans were rigged out to varying degrees with a brand of ultra-modern sportsgear and video game armor: motocross boots, ice hockey, and American football shoulder- and kneepads, even plastic breastplates complete with logos. War-equals-sports associations were strengthened by signaling Trojan alarums with an ice hockey interval horn. The Greek leaders also sported ludicrous shoulder-pads and breastplates, though these were less obviously modern. Their whole look was shoddy and passé: drab brown clothes—half suits, half uniforms—combined with unfashionable elements from the sixties and seventies. "Die Schreibtischtäter-Liga" commented a number of critics—the league of desk-bound culprits. Others were reminded by their garb of the "chic of the erstwhile GDR-provinces." Interestingly, the *Times* critic, while describing the Trojans as "Power Rangers returning from a game of rollerball," was reminded by the Greeks of "cheaply dressed Albanian refugees." The connection between the Greek leaders and German politicians was particularly stressed in the Greek war council scene (1.3). Agamemnon's resemblance to German chancellor Helmut Kohl—both visually and aurally—was much noted, as was Odysseus' gradual transformation from the commitment of a Joschka Fischer to the demagogic tones of Joseph Goebbels.[21] The more specific political references were German and, of course, the Swiss always enjoy laughing about their prominent neighbors much more than about themselves. This production (unlike others, later in the season) did not criticize specifically Swiss characteristics and failings, but rather exposed more universal problems in human societies. It was not aimed particularly at a Swiss audience, but more generally at a German-speaking one.[22] However, recent conservative voting results strongly suggest that the theme of a reactionary patriarchal society very much needs addressing in this Switzerland. Could *both* these facts have contributed to its success?

Acting Style

The production was found both enjoyable and thought-provoking because the characters were more than just simple, garish cartoons—although they were often that too. The acting style aimed neither at total psychological identification, nor encouraged the audience to distance itself completely in a Brechtian manner. Bachmann didn't deconstruct Shakespeare's characters until there was nothing left under their discarded masks. Rather, he employed the actors as mediators full of humor, irony, and honesty to bring the characters into close contact with contemporary theatergoers. Their joy at playing helped forge a complicity between actors and audiences across the "fourth wall," encouraging people on either side of the "curtain" to laugh and despair at behavior only too familiar to themselves. The performance style was also energetic and physical: younger Trojans repeatedly rushed up the wall of Troy, disappearing over its top in flying leaps, momentarily evoking a skateboarder's half-pipe. This energy, combined with the honesty the actors displayed concerning their bodies, seemed to captivate especially younger members of the audience. Troilus and Cressida appeared naked in their first scene; the actors playing Paris, Patroklos, or the enormously fat Achilles ruthlessly, humorously, and endearingly exaggerated and used their own physical shortcomings to mock the characters they were portraying.

In the book *Mephisto ist müde—welche Zukunft hat das Theater?* [Mephisto is tired—what is the future of the theater?], practitioners and scholars discuss the current crisis of German-speaking theater.[23] They conclude that if the theater wants to survive the growing competition from other media, it must reconsider what makes it unique as opposed to film, TV, or virtual reality.[24] Many believe that this unique feature is the immediacy and physical presence of actors onstage, their interaction with the audience in creating an experience that has no safety net, and will never be quite the same next time round. Erica Fischer-Lichte writes that in the present high-tech era, "[t]he theatre appears to be one of the last residues where human beings still communicate directly with each other in public, one of the few places in which . . . the magic of bodily presence can still be felt today."[25] The theater then must try to find its own suitable aesthetic practices concerning "perception, body, and language."[26] Theatergoers have an advantage over film or TV audiences since they can be "freed from the constraint of deciphering prescribed "readings" or "messages." If metatheatrical elements highlight the experimental nature of the stage presentation, theatergoers can become aware of themselves as perceiving subjects,

> relating (their) own "discoveries" to those of the artists. Then theater going is a creative act and the performance a product of the theatregoer's active participation.[27]

This seems to Fischer-Lichte an appropriate form for the theater to engage with our time, the only way in which it can still have an "emancipatory function." This cannot be effected by authors (or directors) who patronize actors and audiences in an attempt to convert them to their interpretation of reality, no matter how critical and progressive their messages might be. Emancipation cannot be achieved by "restricting the theatre-goers' possibilities of perception and interpretation, only by constantly expanding and dynamizing them."[28]

Central Themes of the Production

The main method of linking the play with present Western culture was the emphasis on correlations between war, sports, and play. Medieval chivalric ideals were compared to the equally fictional and questionable ideals embodied by the true heroes of modern popular culture: sports champions, free-style wrestlers, video-game fighters, or Hollywood heroes. This was not just a superficial way of updating the play visually. Rather, it was used to raise general questions about the nature of patriarchal societies and the fatal interrelations between power, sexuality, aggression, and pleasure that they perpetuate and idealize. "Last round of the heroes" was Bachmann and Günther's working title and their means of linking the war/sports-complex to the idea of Apocalypse. Since the myth determines (and the audience knows) that Achilles must and will kill Hector, a large part of this play consists of people hanging around, waiting for the fatal encounter to occur. The currently omnipresent idea of Apocalypse could be seen as an equally dangerous myth, seducing people into accepting it and its inevitability. The production offered no alternatives, it even emphasized the sense of circularity and inevitability within which humanity is caught by reversing the age structure one might expect in the play. The Trojan side, often described as the old-fashioned chivalric idealists, was reduced to its younger members Paris, Hector, Troilus, and Aeneas. The first two self-consciously and somewhat desperately trying to preserve their mythical image (by means of flashy clothes and amphetamines), the younger two idealistic, hyperactive, and neurotic; all unquestioningly perpetuating age-old patriarchal ideals and power structures. The Greeks were portrayed as the outdated generation of 1968, now grown fat and complacent; the generation of the fathers whose once new ideas have degenerated into stale or self-serving political poses.

The two women (Helena and Cressida) played along with the game; it was obvious that the system was too large and well-established for them to change it. Helena seemed caught in a Hollywood dream of beauty and romance; an aging diva who couldn't believe her charms had faded (the director mentioned Liz Taylor as role-model.)[29] Both she and Paris were forced continually to stage their own myth (complete with toe-sucking incident), to try to convince the Trojans that theirs was the greatest love affair ever and worth the human sacrifices of war. Fortunately, even these characters were more than cartoons: near the end of the play Helena appeared through a door in the starry sky of the stage's back wall—as if from a dream, or like an old woman absentmindedly stepping into the wrong room—to stare down in disbelief at the dying Patroklos in the battle raging below. Her expression suggested that she would be drowning the thought of what she had helped (and been used) to bring about in alcohol or antidepressants a minute later.

Although Cressida was perceived by director and actress to be a different character in each of her scenes—they did not want to give her a unifying psychological characterization—the different snapshots of her personality could still be read as a logical development.[30] Her cool, sulky, cheeky pose at the beginning soon appeared to be an attempt to hide vulnerability caused by deeper feelings. Her sadness when told she had to leave Troy seemed more desperate and deeply felt than Troilus's obsessive talk of fidelity. The production emphasized that in some ways Troilus abandons Cressida immediately after their first night together, even before his brothers arrive. When he drew back the sheets, he was lying in bed beside the naked Cressida, himself in full armor, then tried to sneak out of the room undiscovered. Abandoned by all the Trojan men, even her uncle, one could not blame Cressida for losing any ideals of love she might still have had and giving in to Diomedes, who, if nothing else, was at least a more seductive lover than Troilus.

The production was interested in the difficulty or impossibility of expressing feelings of love today. Both Troilus and Cressida were beautiful, but also rather aseptic, like characters from an American teen TV series or a safe-sex advertisement. Instead of any "natural" and impulsive declarations and acts of love—as one might expect from Romeo and Juliet, said Günther, who called this: "Romeo and Juliet in real life"[31]—they seemed terribly self-conscious and insecure, distrustful of each other's feelings and the concept of love itself, as well as weighed down by the knowledge of what such scenes are supposed to be like in the movies. The pressure of trying to live up to that image was aggravated by having Pandarus as audience under the sheets with them.

Cressida turned into a focus of sympathy, but she also remained an ambiguous character, not just a victim, although she never had the slightest chance of changing anything. When Pandarus dragged her onto a ramp to watch the passing Trojan heroes, she commented on their ridiculous procession with the exaggerated and listlessly performed impression of an American cheerleader. While her clothes and Sharon Stone looks made her the ideal female to be chosen for this type of sideline supporting act, her stance showed exactly what she thought of it. And yet, even though she asserted herself as an ironic commentator, she could not help occupying and acting out the part of passive spectator that the patriarchal structures of the game—here cleverly highlighted by the visual sports comparison—relegated her to. Like Helena she was a toy, an idealized status symbol and excuse for male aggression. All she could do was make the best of it.

The production implied that there is no reason for hope if these societal structures remain intact, nor any likelihood of them changing. At the end of the play Achilles offered Hector a cigarette. While they were chummily smoking together, Achilles slit Hector's throat from behind, then licked the bloody knife. Only two pictures and a quotation in the program booklet possibly suggested an alternative. On the first page two photos were provocatively juxtaposed: at the top, in the famous Alfred Eisenstadt photo, an American sailor on V-J Day in 1945 kisses a woman in a celebratory gesture, aggressively bending her backwards in a vice-like grip so that she is in danger of losing her balance, while people in the street smile their approval. Underneath, another "kissing" man is shown from a similar perspective, bending over a wounded comrade (presumably in Viet Nam), performing mouth-to-mouth resuscitation. An aggressive, overpowering versus a life-giving male "kiss," both in the context of war, depicted with no comment. On the next page a quotation by George Tabori: "There are a hundred different ways of saying 'No more war!' or 'I love you,' but in the end only one of them might perhaps turn out to be convincing."

Questioning and exploring gender roles in serious and humorous ways seems to be an important concern in Bachmann and his team's productions.[32] Although the possibility of change appeared nonexistent within this *Troilus and Cressida*, both the positioning of it at the beginning of at least three years' work in Basel and the playful relish with which male behaviorisms were exposed offered some positive counterbalance.[33]

The Basel Theater's drama division, headed by Bachmann's artistic team, was awarded the prestigious title "Best (German-speaking) theater of the year, 1998/99" by German, Austrian, and Swiss drama critics.[34] The subsequent Basel theater season was entitled "Der Bürger" (the bourgeois) with a distinctly male bias in the definite article, a motto that seems to be even more clearly, or should one say more stereotypically and provocatively directed at Switzerland and the Basel audience. It need come as little of a surprise that Bachmann moved on to Shakespeare's Greek comedy, the most frequently performed Shakespearean comedy in the German-speaking world, the "bourgeois hit" *A Midsummer Night's Dream.*

NOTES

The epigraph is from *Troilus and Cressida*, edited by W. Brönnimann-Egger, Englisch-deutsche Studienausgabe der Dramen Shakespeares (Tübingen: Francke Verlag, 1986), 5.2.189–90 and 1.2.109–10, respectively.

 1. A number of factors contributed to this predominantly negative reception at the swanky Austrian festival. I will be able to mention only a few below.
 2. See the interview in *Der Spiegel* 17 (1999): 231.
 3. Early discussion between Bachmann and Günther concerning ideas for staging the play. The typescript of this talk was kindly made available to me by M. Günther.
 4. The ensemble system is still quite common in Germany and the German-speaking part of Switzerland, as opposed to France and the French-speaking part of Switzerland, which favor the en-suite system. It is interesting to note that the permanent company seems to be regaining popularity in Britain, with Trevor Nunn partly reverting to this system at the National Theatre (opening the company's first season with *Troilus and Cressida*), and Peter Hall's attempt to establish a repertory company.
 5. Interview "Behütet, sauber und sehr irreal," *Tages-Anzeiger*, 21 July 1998. Unless stated otherwise, all translations from the German in this paper are my own.
 6. "Von Null auf Hundert in sieben Jahren," *Cosmopolitan* 2 (1999): 54.
 7. Interview "Behütet, sauber und sehr irreal," *Tages-Anzeiger*, 21 July 1998.
 8. "Behütet, sauber und sehr irreal," *Tages-Anzeiger*, 21 July 1998.
 9. See, for example, Peter Iden, "Die blödsinnig gewordenen Helden," *Frankfurter Rundschau*, 20 August 1998.
 10. Wolfgang Reiter, "Machos und Muskelprotze," *Profil*, 24 August 1998.
 11. Benedict Nightingale, *The Times* (London), 26 August 1998. Patrice Pavis speaks of the "Zadekian conflict of moralising and opening up," which Peter Zadek explains as the result of his own confrontation with English and German (theater) culture. England, in Pavis's words, is "a country where theatre has remained an entertainment, a craft rather than an art, and where performance does not carry any philosophical or political message" (see Patrice Pavis, "Wilson, Brook, Zadek: An Intercultural Encounter?" in *Foreign Shakespeare: Contemporary Performance*, edited by Dennis Kennedy [Cambridge: Cambridge University Press, 1993], 282). His provocative statement is seconded by Dennis Kennedy's

claim that "English Shakespeare is no longer a political and rarely an intellectual challenge" (*Foreign Shakespeare*, 301). In Zadek's work, the English approach conflicts with what the director himself calls the "German tendency to think in moralising terms" (*Foreign Shakespeare*, 282; quoted from Peter Zadek, *Das wilde Ufer: Ein Theaterbuch* [Köln, Kiepenheuer und Witsch, 1990], 186).

12. Barbara Villiger Heilig, "Maulhelden wie wir," *Neue Zürcher Zeitung*, 20 August 1998.
13. Patrice Pavis, "Wilson, Brook, Zadek: An Intercultural Encounter?," 271. Pavis chooses the following benchmarks:

1. The global discourse of the production;
2. The use of actors;
3. The relationship of the performance to the text and its translation;
4. The theatrical representation of culture: the manner in which the production shows culture (or cultures) on stage;
5. The type of interculturalism and its relationship to Shakespearean tradition.

14. "Excellent, continually surprising, amazing: the music playfully integrated into the production by Balthasar Streiff, the alphornist and Christian Zehnder, the acrobat of throat and sounds. They created atmosphere, mood, myth; sounds that are understood" (*Münchner Merkur*, 20 August 1998).
15. Taped interview that I conducted with Günther at the Basel Theater, 18 June 1999.
16. Discussion with Bachmann, Günther, and actors at the English Department, Basel University, 2 November 1998.
17. Wilhelm Hortmann, "Word into Image: Notes in the Scenography of Recent German Productions," in Kennedy, *Foreign Shakespeare*, 233.
18. Kennedy, *Foreign Shakespeare*, 240.
19. Patricia Benecke, "In Love with Shakespeare," *Neue Zürcher Zeitung*, 24 March 1999.
20. Hortmann, in Kennedy, *Foreign Shakespeare*, 240.
21. Joshka Fischer was a colorful and controversial member of the Green Party in Germany, who became Minister of Foreign Affairs in the coalition government of Gerhard Schröder.
22. Discussion, English Department, Basel University, 2 November 1998.
23. *Mephisto ist müde—welche Zukunft hat das Theater?*, edited by Lothar Schöne (Darmstadt: Wissenschaftliche Buchgesellschaft, 1996).
24. A number of authors in the book believe that German theater has been able to revolve for too long in a "l'art pour l'art" world of its own, due to the very high subsidies it enjoyed for a long time, giving its prime attention to directors and critics and ignoring the interests of authors, actors, and especially audiences. German theater is the most highly subsidized in the world—Swiss theater somewhat less so—but recent cuts have alerted theater practitioners to the fact that half-empty auditoriums at elitist performances are not (only) a sign of a high intellectual standard.
25. Erika Fischer-Lichte, "Von der Magie leiblicher Gegenwart," in Schöne, *Mephisto ist müde*, 157.
26. Ibid., 158.
27. Ibid., 165.
28. Ibid.
29. Typescript, preliminary discussions about the staging, Spring 1998.

30. Discussion at the English Department, Basel University, 2 January 1998.

31. Taped interview, Basel Theater, 18 June 1999.

32. Bachmann and his team's first Basel season, Christine Richard, the critic from the *Basler Zeitung*, wrote:

Was in den meisten Inszenierungen erfrischend durchbrach, war auch ein neues Geschlechterbild: schwächere Männer, stärkere Frauen . . . die martialischen Helden danken in den Inszenierungen ab, sie wollen sich zumeist lieber ihrem Privatleben zuwenden—und werden wider Willen hineingerissen in Krieg und politische Konflikte. Gesellschaftskritik—ästhetisch aufbereitet nicht als harter Affront, sondern mit spielwitziger Beweglichkeit, auch mit Selbstironie oder kalter Verzweiflungsswut . . . *BAZ*.

[What manifested itself refreshingly in most productions was also a new gender image; weaker men, stronger women . . . the martial heroes retire in the performances; mostly they would rather devote themselves to their private lives—and are drawn unwillingly into war and political conflicts. Social criticism—aesthetically constructed not as a harsh affront, but with witty and playful agility, as well as with self-irony and the cold anger of exasperation . . . *BAZ* (19–20 June 1999).]

33. Bachmann said that he wanted to get the Apocalypse theme over and done with before the millennium, in order to have a free head for other things. See interview "Die Lust an der Apokalypse" [The pleasure of the apocalyptic], *Neue Luzerner Zeitung*, 11 September 1998. The season ended in June 1999 with a festival and an apocalyptic all-night performance that lasted until sunrise.

Shakespeare's History Plays in Belgium: Taken Apart and Reconstructed as "Grand Narrative"

Jozef de Vos

THE THEATER OF THE 1960S AND 1970S, IN FLANDERS AS WELL AS IN the rest of Europe, was marked by a demand for contemporary relevance. As a result it became common practice for directors to fashion Shakespeare's plays according to a particular interpretation or even to impose the "relevant" reading of the play upon the production. Audiences thus were presented with a Marxist *Coriolanus*, an absurdist *Lear*, and a "flower power" *Twelfth Night*.

The eighties witnessed an even more radical approach, in which plays were subjected to a process of deconstruction. The best Flemish example of this tendency was *King Lear*, directed by Jan Decorte for the theater company Het Trojaanse Paard (1983). This production, which lasted for six hours, made use of a nearly complete text in an almost literal translation. By deliberately playing against the text and using the literal and therefore sometimes grotesque translation, the company undercut the play's emotional and pathetic content. Setting and costumes marked the icy atmosphere of the production. On stage, feelings of fear and pity were absolutely avoided. The fundamentally ironic tone appeared most clearly in those scenes traditionally charged with emotion. A transparent theatricality—as in the storm scene, where the cosmic dimensions were deliberately negated by the scanty means of producing it—as well as an almost cartoonlike treatment of the characters, also contributed to the overall desecrating, antiheroic tenor of the production.

In the wake of Jan Decorte, many mainly small-scale productions followed that seemed to cultivate the ironic mode of presenting the text and an acting style that aimed at deconstructing character. All the more surprising was the production of *Ten Oorlog* [Into battle], which in 1997–98 baffled audiences in Flanders and The Netherlands alike, and that was recently also translated into German as *Schlachten!* [Massacre].[1] *Ten Oorlog*, produced by Blauwe Maandag Compagnie (Ghent) and later by Het Toneelhuis (Antwerp), was a grand-scale, perhaps even megalomaniac project, the driving forces of which were the director, Luk Perceval, and the translator/adaptor, Tom Lanoye.[2] They took the bold initiative of staging Shakespeare's two tetralogies of history plays in a single production lasting a full day. In the event, they restructured the eight plays into a trilogy so that spectators could see the whole work on three consecutive nights, or, alternatively, into a single so-called "marathon" performance. Because of the production's organic unity and the effect of actors being reincarnated in later roles of the cycle, it was only in the "marathon" performance that *Ten Oorlog* could fully be experienced and appreciated. In interviews, Perceval explained that the project developed out of the idea of staging *Richard III*. In order to grasp fully the action and the significance of characters such as Queen Margaret, he became convinced that he had to stage the entire cycle. It is obvious that, working through the history plays, Perceval and Lanoye became increasingly fascinated by the material, not only for the light it shed on *Richard III*, but far more for the possibilities it offered to construct a mythical story of their own. The mythical dimension is already suggested by the structure and the religiously tinged titles of the three parts of *Ten Oorlog*. The division and the titles introduced by the adaptors are as follows:

- Part I: *In de naam van de vader en de zoon* [In the name of the Father and the Son]. Consists of: *Richaar Deuzième* [*Richard II*], *Hendrik Vier* [*Henry IV*], *Hendrik de Vijfden* [*Henry V*]. In the published version, *Henry V* is the opening play of the second part of the trilogy.
- Part II: *Zie de dienstmaagd des Heren* [Behold the handmaid of the Lord]. Consists of: *Margaretha di Napoli* [*1* and *2 Henry VI*, *3 Henry VI*, Act 1].
- Part III: *En verlos ons van het kwade* [And deliver us from evil]. Consists of *Edwaar the King* [*3 Henry VI*, Acts 2–5].

Clearly the authors were looking for and discovered a great deal of coherence in the two tetralogies, which inspired them to distill their own grand narrative. This is all the more remarkable at a time when the traditional reading of the plays as mirroring the operation of Divine Providence in English history and celebrating the establishment of the Tudor regime seems to have had its day. Parallel with the "Tudor myth" interpretation, the view that the plays must be understood as part of a larger unit has increasingly come under pressure. For one thing, we know that Shakespeare did not compose the sequence in the order of the various reigns. Moreover, the eight plays that make up the cycles show such a diversity of themes and dramatic structures that, as Michael Hattaway suggests for the *Henry VI* plays, they should be regarded as "a set of complex essays" on the politics of the fifteenth century.[3]

It is at least a remarkable and somewhat paradoxical phenomenon, then, that this radical adaptation seems to take apart the twofold cycle in order to construct a new even more comprehensive "grand narrative," as if the authors wanted to counter the fragmentation of postmodern culture. In general, the number of characters is reduced in such a way that the whole of the adaptation can be performed by a dozen actors. It is also striking that in a version that clearly intends to highlight the political layer of the plays and which carries the title *Ten Oorlog—Schlachten!* in the German translation—all military matters are either left out or reduced to slapstick scenes. The low-life episodes were also cut systematically. It probably needed two continental artists to approach the history plays in such a radically ahistorical manner. For indeed, history in a restrictive sense, anecdotal matters, and nearly all minor characters have disappeared from this new version. The reader or spectator no longer has the compelling sense of witnessing a series of events from English history. The authors deliberately remained at a distance from the concrete historical material so as to be able to transcend it and record nothing less ambitious than the evolution of western society. The 1997–98 program leaflet of *Ten Oorlog* declared that instead of a century of English history, the production aimed at creating "an impression of seven hundred years of humanity."

Shakespeare's diversified material was fashioned by Lanoye and Perceval into a more compact and coherent trilogy. Here two lines of development seem to form the axis. First, they have projected onto the text a pseudo-historical development from the Middle Ages to the present. At the same time, they have incorporated a range of original, more personal themes. Let us first trace the historical line.

A striking feature of the stage version by Perceval and Lanoye is that, although they have produced a highly idiosyncratic and radical interpretation, they stick fairly closely to Shakespeare's text in the cycle's first play. For *Richard II,* that strongly ritualistic and poetical play, Lanoye uses a slightly archaic Dutch, interspersed with

French phrases. In the production the actors, most of them stripped to the waist and wearing skirts, adopted a slow and almost ceremonial acting style. In that way a vague, mythical past associated with the courtly atmosphere of the Middle Ages was evoked. Richard, who opened the show, solemnly holding up the crown with the words "Au nom de Dieu . . . Du Roi . . . De la Patrie," is a Nero-like, effeminate figure whose queen is still a child. In the course of the play he will be humiliated and eventually be poisoned. *Ten Oorlog* clearly follows the traditional reading of Shakespeare's cycle in seeing the murder of Richard II as a curse on the royal house and the country, an original sin. The ritual but already rather decadent world surrounding Richard explodes even before the first part of the trilogy is over.

For indeed, whereas *Richaar Deuzième* is a rather faithful version of Shakespeare's play, *Hendrik Vier* and *Hendrik de Vijfden* only contain fragments of the original plays. Gone are all the low-life scenes, as well as the Glendower episode. The conflict between King Henry IV and the rebels is merely one with the Percy family. Falstaff has been metamorphosed into La Falstaff, a burlesque mixture of the La Mama type, transvestite, and diva. The grotesque elements already noticeable in the Flemish rendering of *Richard II* increasingly dominate in the adaptation of the two subsequent plays. Especially *Henry V,* which was reduced to a hilarious puppet show.

In the second part of the trilogy, characteristically entitled *Margaretha di Napoli*, most of the characters wore dark costumes with white ruffs. Their attire as well as the terrestrial globe in the setting's background vaguely suggested the Renaissance. Lanoye's diction in this part shifted into a fairly modern one. Whereas women were as good as absent in the patriarchal society that was established in Part I of the adaptation, they were given central roles in Part II. *Margaretha di Napoli* was the most radically adapted part of *Ten Oorlog*. The first part of *Henry VI* was severely cut fully to shed light upon Margaret. Not only the eponymous queen, but also Joan la Pucelle, and to a certain extent also Eleanor, can be seen as subverters of history.[4] As these women take their place in the political arena, a battle of the sexes erupts. Clearly this was Lanoye's central theme here.

The third part took the spectators right into a contemporary society, marked by violence and cynicism. The York brothers were mobsters who could have walked right out of a Quentin Tarantino movie. The archaic language of the opening play here gave way to a mixture of contemporary Dutch and American hip-hop. Some scenographic elements in this part of the trilogy as well as the acting style of Edward, for instance, who at times presented himself as a showman, suggested a connection between the degenerate nature of this society and the pervasive presence of modern media.

The pseudo-historical line that we have traced created, as it were, a fixed central axis connecting up with which the development of a number of personal themes. It also provided the framework within which the dominating theme of the political power game was explored. This was evidently a major Shakespearean theme on which the adaptors also tried to focus throughout the cycle. In *Richard II*, which *Ten Oorlog* followed fairly closely, the center of attention was the power struggle between Richard and Bolingbroke. Lanoye and Perceval clearly traced the process of humiliation to which Richard is subjected. He was gradually deprived of his "body politic," and in the production he was literally shown naked.

Particularly in *Margaretha di Napoli*, the emphasis was very much on the intrigues and the ruthless power game, to which justice becomes subservient. It was typical that the Bishop of Winchester's almost programmatic lines relating to the elimination of the Duke of Gloucester should have been divided between and therefore shared by Somerset, Buckingham, York, and Suffolk:

> That he should die is worthy policy;
> But yet we want a colour to his death:
> 'Tis meet he be condemned by course of law.[5]

For all of them policy is merely self-interest. Margaret herself in this version gradually emerged as the emblematic woman who used love and sex as a weapon in the power struggle.

In *Edwaar the King*, based on *3 Henry VI* (from act 2 onwards), the authors demonstrated the connection between power and the media. Edwaar was a performer for whose charm and talent the contemporary audience easily fall. It is slightly ironic that precisely this acting quality that is such a distinct characteristic of Shakespeare's *Richard III* was to be curtailed in *Risjaar Modderfokker den Derde* [Richard Motherfucker III]. Far more than in Shakespeare, Lanoye's Risjaar illustrated the total degeneration of power, ultimately leading to self-destruction.

The cycle in its entirety demonstrates what Jan Kott has called the "Grand Mechanism." History is presented as a ruthless power struggle in which every ruler is eventually replaced by a new one. But when the latter assumes the crown, he drags behind him a chain of crimes and, therefore, has already created the basis for a new pretender who brings the wheel full circle.[6]

In an interview, Tom Lanoye himself explained that the concept of the Great Wheel of Time and Power can be more effectively demonstrated in a sequel of plays and kings. If, moreover, one can present that sequel in one day and with the same cast, the meaning will emerge even more poignantly. In that way, the audience will experience the whole development together with the actors. Each of them first plays a major role, then a minor one, and finally submerges in the story, or the other way round. This gives rise to a full, ritual narrative in which each king also represents a particular form of exercising power. The sequel thus also becomes an essay on the use of power.[7]

The concept that allows actors to re-emerge in different roles creates a sense of repetition and degeneration. The authors skillfully make use of this in order to add some extra effects. It is significant, for example, that the actor playing Richaar Deuzième takes up the role of La Falstaff. The "feminine" aspect of Richard that is rejected by Bolingbroke is thus continued in the subversive sexuality of Lá Falstaff. The murderer of Richard (Roste) later becomes Hein (Hal) and Hendrik de Vijfden (Henry the Fifth), who in a sense is the real usurper of the crown. Another striking example is the "resurrection" as it were of the three actors whose bodies lie murdered on a huge table at the end of *Margaretha di Napoli* (Winchester, York, and Suffolk) and who reappear as avengers in the shape of Risjaar (Richard of Gloucester), Edwaar, and Sjors (George of Clarence).

Clearly, *Ten Oorlog* leaves behind the actual line of history in order to create a larger, more comprehensive, all but mythical development. Whereas most of the low-life scenes, many military episodes, and other subplots are simply cut, other "historical" elements are given a more mythical quality. A case in point is Joan la Pucelle, who in Shakespeare is a character showing different facets of a fascinating personality: popular leader, politician, Venerian figure.[8] In the adaptation, she appears merely in a vision of young Henry the Sixth, who takes up the role of the Dauphin and is challenged to fight against her. Since the role is played by the same actress who is Leonora (Eleanor), she appears as an incarnation of Hendrik's vision of ideal womanhood.

I have already mentioned the curious metamorphosis of Sir John Falstaff into La Falstaff. In recent years, critics have pointed out that Falstaff's favorite place, the Boar's Head, is not only a theatrical but also a feminized place. Falstaff is characterized very much in feminine terms and thus he threatens to effeminate the king's heir, Prince Hal.[9] At the same time he also represents the carnival attitude, a central image of which, according to Mikhail Bakhtin, is the body. He "constitutes a constant focus of opposition to the official and serious tone of authority and power."[10] Lanoye and Perceval apparently were only interested in these aspects of Falstaff and thus created the weird mixture of Mother-Lover-Transvestite who tries to prevent Hein from rejecting the feminine and subversive values he/she stands for. Far from being the many-sided character that Shakespeare created, La Falstaff thus becomes an archetypical figure.

There is another way in which the adaptation goes beyond actual history, contributing to its allegorizing tendency. For their Flemish and Dutch audiences, Lanoye has said in interviews, the names of Richmond and Kent mean very little apart from being well-known cigarette brands. The concrete historical context is not experienced as such in the continental reception of these plays, and this facilitated Lanoye's symbolical or allegorical approach. More important than the actual kingdom, for example, is the position of England as an island. In the course of the trilogy this position is strengthened in that it tries to consolidate its patriarchal structures and to protect itself against external influences, first and foremost that of woman. All important women come from France, which acquires the status of a mythological place of danger and mystery. This is where Hendrik de Vijfden goes to war and conquers his bride. It is no coincidence that this past is played by the same actress who performs the role of Margaretha di Napoli later. Italy, Lanoye argues, can be seen as the superlative of France, but also as the birthplace of the Renaissance with its fundamental changes, affecting and producing the central position of individual man. All rebellions are situated in Ireland, which thus also acquires a symbolical meaning.[11]

Parallel to the general "historical" line, or rather in close connection with it, the authors have developed a set of individual-psychological themes. In the first part, *In de naam van de Vader en de Zoon*, the struggle between father and son is a central issue. Already in *Richaar Deuzième*, the conflict between York and his son Aumale is emphasized and sharpened, if only because the role of the Duchess has been cut. But it is particularly in the conflict between Henry the Fourth and prince Hal that the conflict is further thematized. Shakespeare himself put the theme in greater perspective by creating a second father figure in Falstaff and a second son figure in Hotspur. The adaptation capitalizes on the play's central irony that precisely the unworthy son Hal will be the killer of Percy, the "ideal son," who, in Lanoye's version, inflicts a mortal wound upon the king. In the penultimate scene which ends with the king's death, the spectators witness an extended physical struggle between Hendrik and his son, in which the two rivals cling tightly to each other. This is a fine theatrical image of the ambiguity in the father-son relationship. Lanoye runs together *2 Henry IV,* act 3, scene 1 ("How many thousand of my poorest subjects/Are at this hour asleep") with the episode in act 4, scene 5, where Hal, assuming that the king is dead, takes the crown. The text, especially of Hal's reply to the king's reproach of "hunger[ing] for his "empty chair . . . before thy hour be ripe," is adapted in such a way that Hal, rather than showing himself an obedient and dutiful son, appears to despise his father. Ironically, this is precisely the attitude that is appreciated by the king, who is eventually choked by the prince.

Henk is now able to follow in his father's footsteps. Before he can do so, however, he has to shake off the influence of La Falstaff, who is to him a Mother as well as a Lover. Clearly Henk must renounce the feminine values in order to become a conqueror of France and of the French princess Catherine. As a military champion, he subdues Catherine, who is represented as a frump. Whereas in Shakespeare's version there is still an emotional aspect to the relationship between Henry and Catherine, the love affair in the adaptation is reduced to a brutal taking possession of what he has conquered.

The whole of *Hendrik de Vijfden* is in fact presented to the audience by La Falstaff, who also delivers the prologue. Before he does so, however, he takes off his female attributes such as his fake breasts and exchanges his long red gown for shirt and trousers. This shift into the role of the Chorus suggests the recuperation of the subversive and feminine forces represented by La Falstaff.

It is interesting to note the similarity with the reading of the Henriad offered by Valerie Traub, who finds a parallel construction of male subjectivity and sexuality in the plays and in psychoanalytic theory:

> The drama enacted by Prince Hal and narrativized by Freud provides a telling instance of the mechanisms by which patriarchal relations reproduce themselves. The female body, first constructed as a "grotesque" maternal body (Falstaff) which must be reproduced is displaced by the closed "classical" body (Katherine) which must be subjugated for Prince Hal to assume phallocratic control as King Henry V.[12]

Hal's rejection of Falstaff seems to assuage anxieties about their homoerotic bond as well as about the equation of woman and maternity.[13] It is indeed striking that Falstaff, and particularly his body, is often referred to in female terms. Equally striking are the military context and terms in which Henry the Fifth woos the French princess.

Valerie Traub sees the process of the rejection of the maternal and of identification with the paternal not merely as the individual psychosexuality of one character, but also as a paradigm for the cultural construction of early modern masculine subjectivity.[14] This broadening of an individual development into a cultural one is exactly what *Ten Oorlog* tries to achieve through the development of the two central thematic lines which reinforce each other.

It is also interesting to note that Lanoye has given the relationship between Henk on the one hand, and the sexually ambiguous La Falstaff (and, later, Catherine) or the other more poignancy by having the Chorus rely in more than one passage on some of the sonnets that deal with the triangle of the poet, the Dark Lady, and the young man.

The second part of the trilogy, *Margaretha di Napoli* (*1* and *2 Henry VI*) opens on a woman dressed like an angel who is playing the cello. This attractive and memorable image introduces and accompanies a few scenes with a dreamlike atmosphere, centering around Joan. The action in France seems to be reduced to what happens inside the head of Hendrik (Henry the Sixth). It is young Hendrik himself who in these scenes plays the role of the Dauphin and fights with the Maid of Orleans. This is quite puzzling to the spectator, but on realizing that the actress playing the part of Joan is also the one who takes the role of Hendrik's aunt Leonora, and that the actress who impersonates the angel will reappear as Hendrik's bride, Margaret, one gathers that the authors' objective here is to dramatize the clash between dream and reality in Hendrik's experience. The two women are his vision of ideal womanhood, a vision that is in stark contrast with the scheming and violence they are to indulge in. As a matter of fact, they will try to beat the men at their own game. Margaretha gradually emerges as the emblematic woman who uses love and sex as weapons.

After the murder of York and his son Schoon Rolandke (Rutland), the three remaining York brothers unite against Margaretha. This is the point where Lanoye's third part, *En verlos ons van het kwade* [And deliver us from evil], begins. The spectators, who so far have watched the ritualistic and mannerist world of *Richard II*, the burlesque cartoonlike presentation of *Henry IV* and *Henry V,* as well as the mixture of dream and history in *Henry VI*, are in for yet another surprise. Edwaar's opening lines—"Bruurs! Who de fok has made a rolling stone/of Daddy York, onze geliefde pa?"—set the tone for a representation of a contemporary society that has not a spark of humanity left. Edwaar is a showman and womanizer to whom all women are merely sex objects. Finally, Risjaar Modderfokker den Derde is the ultimate perversion. Cast out even by his own mother, he only hungers for power. His suicide at the very end of the cycle signifies the self-destruction of this degenerate world.

Lanoye and Perceval were not interested in the historical content of the plays, but thought they could recycle the material for their own purposes. It is therefore obvious that, rather than producing a new translation, they have chosen for a radical reinterpretation. The most conspicuous aspect of this version is its language, which mirrors the overall quasi-mythical development that the authors wanted to project into the text. Throughout the trilogy, Lanoye takes advantage of the dramatic quality and flexibility of the iambic pentameter. From the archaic language, enriched with a certain theatricality and decadence by French expressions, via the fairly modern diction of *Margaretha di Napoli*, he moves to a mind-boggling gangster rap. The number of English words increases and infects the language. At first, the originality of this procedure produces the desired shock effect, creating the appropriate cynical atmosphere, but this soon wears thin. Unlike the sparingly used French words, which add a specific flavor to the text, the profusion of English eventually turns counterproductive.

It is difficult to overstate the enormous amount of intertextuality that characterizes this late-twentieth-century version. Both Richaar Deuzième's devotion to poetry and his rather personal tastes are illustrated by having him quote the Flemish poet Paul Snoek ("Tabula rasa," in 2.1) and the Greek poet Kavafis ("Waiting for the Barbarians," in 5.2). The decadent atmosphere surrounding Richaar is suggested by Aumale's obscene version of a well-known Flemish poem by Alice Nahon ("Avondliedeken III," in 2.1). In the same vein is La Falstaff's parody of Guido Gezelle's *'t Schrijverke* [Writings] in *Hendrik Vier*, 1.1). The scene in *3 Henry VI* where Edward says he will make his brothers Richard and George duke of Gloucester and duke of Clarence respectively, is considerably expanded in *Ten Oorlog* (*Edwaar the King*, 1.1, end). Lanoye makes the scene interreflect with the name-giving scene in Tarantino's *Reservoir Dogs*, where it is the leader of a criminal gang who gives new names to its members. In addition to all the literary references, there are allusions to contemporary Flemish or Belgian culture or politics. The use of languages—Dutch with its Flemish variants,

French, English, American slang—is almost as diverse as the cultures referred to.

As I have indicated, history in the sense of the actual fifteenth century that Shakespeare evokes and the interpretation in the light of the Tudor myth almost disappear from sight in the adaptation. Instead, *Ten Oorlog* presents itself as a typical postmodern reinterpretation of the Shakespearean material. It may moreover be adduced here that throughout the trilogy there is a persistent tendency to undercut or trivialize. Richaar Deuzième, for example, is so much of a whimsical sissy that he undermines the tragic potential in that play. Nearly all scenes and characters in France are rendered in a burlesque way. Paradoxically, though, the authors have been able to reorganize and refashion the scattered pieces of this huge mosaic in such a way that a grand narrative becomes discernible which allows us to look at Shakespeare's cycles in a fresh light.

Notes

1. This German title is ambiguous. On the one hand, *Schlachten* is simply and neutrally the plural of "Schlacht" [battle]. With the exclamation mark in the German title, it acquires a more sinister meaning, "to massacre," "to butcher." The exclamation mark makes it virtually a war cry, approximating Mark Antony's "Havoc!" in *Julius Caesar*.

2. *Ten Oorlog* by Tom Lanoye and Luk Perceval, based on Shakespeare's two tetralogies of history plays. Played by Blauwe Maandag Compagnie, Ghent, Belgium. Text: Tom Lanoye; Director: Luk Perceval; Adaptation: Tom Lanoye and Luk Perceval; Dramaturgy: Luc Joosten and Hans van Dam; Scenography: Katrin Brack. First performance: Ghent, Vooruit, 22 November 1997. Published text: Tom Lanoye and Luk Perceval, *Ten Oorlog. Naar "The Wars of the Roses" van Shakespeare*, 3 vols. (Amsterdam: Prometheus, 1997). German translation: Tom Lanoye and Luk Perceval, *Schlachten! Nach den Rosenkriegen von William Shakespeare*. Aus dem Flämischen von Rainer Kersten und Klaus Reichert (Frankfurt am Main: Verlag der Autoren, 1999).

3. *The Third Part of King Henry VI*, edited by Michael Hattaway, The New Cambridge Shakespeare (Cambridge: Cambridge University Press, 1993), 4.

4. See also Phyllis Rackin, "Anti-Historians: Women's Roles in Shakespeare's Histories," in *Performing Feminisms*, edited by Sue Ellen Case (Baltimore: Johns Hopkins University Press, 1990), 207–22.

5. *The Second Part of King Henry VI*, edited by Michael Hattaway, The New Cambridge Shakespeare (Cambridge: Cambridge University Press, 1991), 3.1.235–37.

6. Jan Kott, *Shakespeare Our Contemporary*, translated by B. Taborski (New York: Anchor Books, 1966), 7.

7. Jozef de Vos, ed., *"Ten Oorlog" doorgelicht*, Special theme issue of *Documenta (Tijdschrift voor Theater)* 16, no. 2 (1998).

8. Compare *The First Part of King Henry VI*, edited by Michael Hattaway, The

New Cambridge Shakespeare (Cambridge: Cambridge University Press, 1990), 21–28.
   9. Jean E. Howard and Phyllis Rackin, *Engendering a Nation: A Feminist Account of Shakespeare's English Histories* (London: Routledge, 1997), 165.
   10. Graham Holderness, "*Henry IV*: Carnival and History," in *Shakespeare's History Plays: Richard II to Henry V,* edited by Graham Holderness (Basingstoke: Macmillan, 1992), 151–64, 154.
   11. Vos, *"Ten Oorlog" doorgelicht,* 116–17.
   12. Valerie Traub, *Desire and Anxiety: Circulations of Sexuality in Shakespearean Drama* (London: Routledge, 1992), 18.
   13. Ibid., 59.
   14. Ibid., 55.

Shakespeare on the French Stage: A Historical Survey

Isabelle Schwartz-Gastine

HENRY IV, THE KING OF FRANCE (1589–1610) AND OF NAVARRE (1572–1610), is said to have seen a play featuring the character of Falstaff, presented by some English traveling actors who performed at the court of France in 1605. The appreciative comments expressed at the time were limited to the court and its immediate environment, and it remains to be proven that the play was really Shakespeare's and not just a makeshift plot around a most successful hero, one sure to bring success and laughter. Apart from this, no further evidence of the Shakespearean corpus could be traced to this period, a time when France was struggling with the religious wars malignantly spreading over the country. In those dangerous circumstances, any reference to a work from a Protestant country could be considered as an act of treason. And for most people, personal safety came well before literary or theatrical concerns. The French theater, definitely a court occupation operating according to completely different principles than the English theater, would have restricted this kind of entertainment. There were no varied acting spaces, the action being limited to a single stage, level with and facing the audience; the back curtains, which were split in the middle, allowed for a rarely used frontal entrance, the usual openings being the two side wings.

It is also necessary to raise the issue of theoretical influences. The French drama drew its sources directly from the Ancient Greek thinkers, and it reached a climax with the strict respect of the slightly distorted "rules of the three unities" as derived from Aristotle's *Poetics*. The multiplicity of locations and the extended time schemes typical of the Shakespearean drama could in no way please French taste, which praised verisimilitude in both the action and in the text. The strict (if not stale) respect for these rules were at the core of the classical French drama; Shakespeare could be used for the matter of his plays, but the French discarded the manner of them. Playwrights might even turn directly to Shakespeare's sources (such as Ovid or Plutarch) and write "parallel" plays (mostly tragedies) according to the French pattern, so these plays could be included in the national repertoire.

Additionally, a male cast interpreting all the characters, women included, was thought almost indecent at a time when Jean Racine wrote his tragedies with only female characters, such as *Esther*, intended for an all-woman cast. And, lastly, one should not forget that recourse to violence, whether verbal or physical, was thoroughly banned from the French stage. It was either implied as an offstage act or entirely contained in constrained phrasing.

It was during the Age of Enlightenment that influences from beyond the boundaries of France could finally be felt. Because of his stubborn, repeated free thinking, Voltaire (François-Marie Arouet, 1694–1778) was exiled to England between 1726 and 1729. There, as an act of further defiance towards the authorities, but in itself an unheard-of proof of intellectual open-mindedness that later had dramatic and lasting repercussions on the literary, he endeavored to learn English, and could follow the nation's drama in the native tongue. The plays he put on at Drury Lane Theatre, however, were in direct contrast with the current trends of French literature and as such represented a daring act of rebellion against the France that had rejected him. On his return to France, he wrote some distant imitations, in regular heroic alexandrines but including the much-debated and discarded mixing of genres. These plays met with considerable success on the French stage, thus proving that the French audience was ready for a change. These plays (which were in turn translated into other European languages) were *Zaïre* (1732), which was inspired by *Othello* but set at the time of the Crusades; *La Morte de César* [Caesar's death, 1735], in which there were no female parts; and *Sémiramis*, in which he included the apparition of a ghost. The last two titles were written at the castle of Cirey in Lorraine, where he had taken refuge, and performed in the makeshift attic theater by the distinguished guests themselves. Voltaire even translated some fragments of *Hamlet* twice. He first turned it into a classic piece in heroic alexandrines; a second version was closer to the original, respecting the great variety of registers even in the vulgar or popular vein. Voltaire's early passion for Shakespeare stemming from the English revival should not be overlooked when considering his later, equally virulent condemnation, perhaps not so much of the plays but of the use of Shakespeare in French culture. And so when Voltaire witnessed the growing interest for

Shakespeare—which he himself had contributed to—he heavily criticized the then-successful translations of Pierre Le Tourneur (1737–1788) and the adaptations of Jean-François Ducis (1733–1816) in a pamphlet published under the pseudonym of Jérôme Carré, *Du Théâtre Anglais* (1761).

The eighteenth century saw complete editions of Shakespearean theater in translation. The first one was a compilation by Pierre-Antoine de La Place (1707–83), who had *Le Théâtre Anglois* published in 1746 (volumes one to five being devoted to Shakespeare), which included "Discours sur le théâtre anglais," an elaborate theoretical justification of his approach. This essay, justifying his choices in preparation for potential criticism, indicated the innovation of his approach, and demonstrated that, well before any theoretical issues had been expressed, the concepts of translation and adaptation were already much debated.[1] La Place explained why he had deliberately chosen not to translate the texts literally, but preferred to adapt the plays to suit classical French usage and taste without betraying the spirit of the original. He cut the plays into scenes whenever a character entered or left the stage, used the alexandrine for lofty speeches pertaining to the sublime or the beautiful, wrote some base passages in prose, and simply dismissed other portions or roughly summarized them. Of course, he excluded the overtly vulgar or comic, which represented an inadmissible transgression into a tragedy.

Many more translations followed, either in single volumes or in full, multivolume collections. In the twenty-volume edition of his translation, published between 1776 and 1782, Pierre Le Tourneur showed a different approach than La Place. He was very faithful to the original and followed Shakespeare's text as closely as possible. However successful his translations were as readings, they never found their way onto the stage. French audiences had to wait until Jean-François Ducis had written his tragedies, which he adapted from La Place and composed in heroic alexandrines after the classic rules. The plot and cast were much altered, certain passages were developed into long asides given by confidants, and Ducis had these plays published under his own name—Shakespeare, the original source of his inspiration, was completely omitted from the books or theater bills. So the first theatrical contact with Shakespeare in France was under the name of the adaptor without any reference to Shakespeare. However, these plays met with considerable and lasting success at the Comédie Française.[2] This success was also, in part, due to the famous tragedian François-Joseph Talma, who played the main parts until his death in 1826: *Hamlet* first performed in 1769, *Romeo and Juliet* and *King Lear* in 1783, *Macbeth* in 1784, *King John* (entitled *Jean sans terre ou la mort d'Arthur* [John Lackland, or the death of Arthur]) in 1791 and *Othello* in 1792.[3] The stagings emphasized the importance of the tragic hero, whom the adaptor had already set at the very center of the dramas. The focus was on the exploration of the dilemma that the exceptional character had to face, his hesitations and inner struggle, and his final destiny. François-Joseph Talma identified so closely with Shakespearean theater that he was even given the part of Shakespeare himself in a one-act prose comedy by Alexandre Duval, *Shakespeare amoureux* [Shakespeare in love], performed at the Comédie Française in 1804.[4] Talma is said to have tried to imitate English actors to the point of borrowing their intonation (for parts not solely Shakespearean), showing that the time had come to turn to Shakespeare in the original, and to English actors as a reference.

This new taste for Shakespeare continued to grow until it achieved considerable popularity in the nineteenth century. One must not forget that this was also the period of a great Shakespearean revival on the English stage and the beginning of regular tours abroad by the most celebrated English actors of the time. The very first visit, however, was far from successful, as anti-English feeling and the perennial feud between the two countries were at their worst in France after the naval defeats of the Napoleonic wars in 1815. Indeed, the booing was such at the Théâtre de la Porte Saint-Martin in 1822 that the performance of *Othello* had to be interrupted and the auditorium briskly evacuated.[5] But this violent rejection, grounded in fanatic nationalism and not in the arts, was criticized by more open-minded writers like Stendhal (Henri Beyle, 1783–1842), who produced a kind of romantic manifesto that was to have a very wide circulation, *Racine et Shakespeare* (1823). And when the same actors came back in 1826, their success was triumphantly acknowledged. Charles Kemble became the epitome of Hamlet, and Harriet Smithson had been such a beautiful Ophelia that the composer Hector Berlioz (1803–69) fell in love with her, embarking on a stormy and devastating marital relationship. He transposed Shakespearean themes into his music, notably in *King Lear* (1834), the much-acclaimed *Romeo and Juliet* (1839), and finally the less successful *Béatrice et Bénédict*, a light opera based on *Much Ado about Nothing*, created at Baden-Baden in 1862.

From that time onwards, the Shakespearean myth was part of the romantic inspiration in all the arts. More famous operas deserve to be mentioned: another *Romeo and Juliet* (1867) by Charles Gounod (1818–93), which received immediate success, as well as an earlier

Macbeth (1829), a lyrical tragedy in three acts by Claude-Joseph Rouget de Lisle (1760–1836), the composer of the French national anthem. The painter Eugène Delacroix (1798–1863), then at the start of his career, traveled to London in 1825 to sketch his lithographs from the original theatrical performances. *Desdémone et Emilia* (1825) was the first painting in a very productive series inspired by Shakespeare; *Les Adieux de Roméo et Juliette* [The farewells of Romeo and Juliet, 1845] was composed towards the end of this creative period. But Delacroix's greatest source of inspiration over the years was certainly the representation of Hamlet.[6] Indeed, Hamlet became the romantic hero par excellence in his black mourning outfit, full of spleen, his attention drawn inwards, absorbed by his inner meditation and procrastination.[7] The tragedy was so powerfully ingrained in French culture that it was made into an opera by Ambroise Thomas (1811–96) as late as 1868, although far removed from the original play. However, from the start of the romantic attraction for the Bard, the main adaptations took their primary source from English plays (which had themselves to be rid of former layers of rewritten and added elements) to become independent masterpieces. This was the case of the tragedy by Alfred de Vigny (1797–1863) based on *Othello*, entitled (briefly) *Le More de Venise* (1829). As expected in the case of a French author, the number of characters was reduced and the plot cleared of general speeches in order to concentrate solely on the individual fate of the hero. On the stage, the sumptuous settings by the famous artist Ciceri represented perfectly authentic views of Venice, Cyprus, and well-known palace interiors that the widely traveled members of the audience could pleasurably recognize.[8] The argument aims more at a historical reconstitution than a rendering of the Shakespearean drama. The stage fashion now favored heavy sets that could only be handled with sophisticated machinery, and necessitated long pauses in the theatrical action so that they could be changed, each one more spectacular than the previous. The plays then had to be split into tableaux, and the actors, in small numbers, developed a static way of acting, based on powerful vocal effects and hand gestures.

A new type of subject matter flourished, loosely linked with Shakespearean dramas. These plays were not an expansion of a theme nor were they based on Shakespeare, the mysterious playwright, but rather on the famous actors who favored the rediscovery of Shakespeare in their own country. One such example is *Kean ou Désordre et Génie* [Kean, or disorder and genius], written by the prolific popular writer Alexandre Dumas *père* (1802–70) in 1836, which was favorably received by audiences and is still performed occasionally today. The same author also had a hand in a *Hamlet* (1847) that was very far removed from the original, although it preserved the title.[9] The ghost only appeared at the end of the play as a representative of divine justice, condemning Hamlet to expiate his sin of having committed the murders of innocent characters in the course of his long and dutiful revenge on Claudius, the only guilty victim. This version triggered the cult devoted to "hamlétisme," the phrase coined by the symbolist poet Stéphane Mallarmé in a very influential article (*La Revue indépendante*, 1 November 1886) written after the performance of the play given at the Comédie Française, with the great tragedian Mounet-Sully (1841–1916) in the title role.[10] This is a very important trend: showing a thorough appropriation of Shakespeare as an artifact of French culture, tinged with French connotations and even representing France abroad in the arts as well as in politics.

Concurrent to this personal exploration of the themes, some translations aimed at a new evaluation of the text, freed from successive additions and conceived as a complete work. In 1821, at the beginning of his fruitful career, the historian and conservative politician François Guizot (1787–1874) rewrote Le Tourneur's versions, reincorporating the wider social and political perspectives of the plays, and his eight-volume edition was still in print forty years later. But the main literary event of the time was the work of François-Victor Hugo (1828–73).[11] A journalist by trade and the second son of Victor Hugo, he completed a translation of the Shakespearean corpus in fifteen volumes between 1859 and 1865 while the whole family was exiled to Guernsey. At an age when regular heroic verse was the current trend on stage, Hugo nevertheless opted for a prose translation closely based on the then-available Folio. So his attempt is a great novelty as it represents a unified version in which the faithfulness to the original predominates over the observance of the literary fashion. His first volume included two versions of *Hamlet*, based on the 1603 and 1604 Quartos, and (in a most visionary way) he added some apocryphal writing in 1866, such as *Edward III*. In keeping with the current trend for formidable heroes, he discarded the Folio grouping to adopt a personal classification based on character types: "tyrants," including *Macbeth, King John, Richard III*, "jealous men" with *Othello*, "tragic lovers" such as *Romeo and Juliet* and *Antony and Cleopatra*, "friends," "family" with *Coriolanus* and *King Lear*, "society," with *Measure for Measure, Timon of Athens, Julius Caesar*, "country," and "the farces." These translations, in which some say the genial father had a secret hand, are still a literary reference nowadays, but have been seldom performed on stage as they are extremely difficult to act, and can be termed a "Spectacle dans un fauteuil" [an armchair spectacle] after Alfred de Musset's title. The volumes were introduced by an essay by Victor Hugo himself, simply entitled *William Shakespeare*, which was published in 1864 to commemorate the tercentenary of Shakespeare's birth. The essay received great attention and can still be read most rewardingly today. It focuses on the mystery surrounding the character of Shakespeare, the man of experience, his fate, and the development of his career as a playwright, whom Hugo defined as one of the geniuses of humanity, along with himself.[12]

So by the middle of the nineteenth century, there was certainly a large French readership and devoted audiences for Shakespeare. As has been noted, the most frequently staged play was *Hamlet*. For instance, at the very moment when Mounet-Sully was playing the role at the Comédie Française in 1886, the great diva Sarah Bernhardt (born Rosine Bernard, 1844–1923) performed Ophelia at the Théâtre de la Porte Saint-Martin (a theater she had bought)—the reception of which was rather mitigated. In 1899, Bernhardt featured as a most daring Hamlet in Marcel Schwob's scholarly prose translation, taking advantage of her androgynous figure, which was then out of fashion and nastily criticized.[13] But all her defects she could turn to perfection, to paraphrase Cleopatra—a part she played equally with tremendous success in 1890, in an adaptation entitled *Cléopâtre* that centered on the heroine. Bernhardt had commissioned this version, as was her custom, from the prolific variety playwright Victorien Sardou (1831–1908). She had a sense of detail in the sumptuous setting (an atmosphere of the oriental harem and languid sensuality were conveyed with palm trees, sofas, cushions, and ornate materials) and in her dress (she was wearing a tailor-made copy of Cleopatra's headgear and jewels). She managed to produce a sensuous shock among her admirers as she had a real but nonpoisonous serpent moving down her breast in the part of the asp.[14] She had been a fierce Lady Macbeth in 1884; her bare feet on the stage elicited many a comment. One should bear in mind that this particular staging did not meet with the expected success on stage—she even had to sell her mansion and jewels to pay off her debts. However, her part was well publicized and passed on to posterity thanks to the extremely evocative studio portraits by the Nadars, father and son, which focus on her as an individual artist, and not on the whole staging which was said to be spectacular.[15] She played the same part on the London and Scottish stages. Indeed, she embarked on long tours around the world, as far as Russia,

America, and even Australia, not only as Racine's Phèdre, but also as Cleopatra and Hamlet (which she also performed in Denmark). As the first international star she proved a pioneer in exporting the very first French interpretations of Shakespeare to English-speaking countries. It was still a time when a most awkward confusion subsisted between the part and the performer. And in the case of Sarah Bernhardt especially, the roles were commented on in so far as they corresponded to the artist rather than the character. However, this trend kindled a wider knowledge of the Shakespearean theater.

Towards the close of the century, Shakespearean creations were extremely numerous and followed totally antagonistic principles. It was also at this time that the function of "director" emerged, putting an end to the domination of the main actors.

The symbolist movement turned to magical drama making a fantasy of *A Midsummer Night's Dream* and an eerie experience of *Macbeth*, both performed in the ruins of a Gothic cathedral in Saint-Wandrille (Normandy) in new versions by the French-speaking Belgian playwright and poet, Maurice Maeterlinck (1862–1949), whose early play after Shakespeare, *La Princesse Maleine* (1890), was most promising.[16]

Aurélien Lugné-Poe (1869–1940) found an answer to his dislike of heavy settings and the cult of the hero in the strong Shakespearean revival under the leadership of William Poel and Arthur Dillon, who had founded the Elizabethan Stage Society. In London, Lugné-Poe appreciated the use of a reconstituted Elizabethan stage and playhouse, which enabled the exploration of new (or renewed) forms of acting and interaction with the audience. After he had written his article entitled "Shakespeare sans décor" (*La Nouvelle revue*, 1897), he experimented on a one-night staging of *Measure for Measure* (1898) in a summer circus house on the Champs Elysées in Paris, with actors emerging from the auditorium and playing on an almost bare wooden stage. But his faithfulness to the Elizabethan spirit was thwarted in the somewhat deficient translation of the play that he was forced to use for financial reasons: his writer was also his backer. He returned to Shakespeare in 1913 with *Hamlet*, in a much more traditional Italian theater in the translation of Georges Duval, whose eight volumes claimed to be "entièrement conforme au texte anglais" [entirely faithful to the English text] and were "couronné par l'Académie Française" [awarded the highest honor by the Académie Française]. His wife Suzanne Després played the title role in a completely different spirit from Sarah Bernhardt before her. She was an athletic hero, well-trained in the art of fencing. She was strong, full of life and energy, bustling with action and decision, in an age of shortened hair and female emancipation. Lugné-Poe played a sly Polonius with the pretense of niceness.[17]

The naturalist director André Antoine (1858–1948) closely illustrated the famous social writer Emile Zola's manifesto "Le naturalisme au théâtre" in most memorable renderings. He offered a meticulous reconstruction of historical settings on the wide stage of his own theater. Thanks to the use of large casts he achieved sumptuous effects in the crowd scenes. *King Lear* (1905), in Pierre Loti's unabridged translation, was performed under an old Norman arch. *Julius Caesar* (1907) was a very complex evocation of Rome. And *Coriolanus* (1910) had a fixed set at the back representing antique Roman buildings covered with vines that could be partly hidden behind movable curtains featuring the interior of a house or a perspective. This clever (and rather inexpensive) device, which gave an exact reproduction of true-to-life scenery and gestures and allowed for uninterrupted performance, would be an example for all future theater, not just Shakespeare.[18]

Some theatrical groups were created that specialized solely in Shakespearean productions. Camille de Sainte-Croix had an extremely ambitious program for his Compagnie Française du Théâtre Shakespeare, founded in 1909. He would precede the plays (generally his own translations) with a series of lectures on Shakespeare and Elizabethan drama. His young actors would only give one or two performances before selected audiences, either in real theaters or in private apartments, playing against mere painted curtains so as to assure the continuity of the play and concentration on the text.

A few years later, in 1917, Firmin Gémier (1869–1933) created the short-lived Société Shakespeare, aiming at celebrating the tercentenary of Shakespeare's death (which had not been commemorated because of "Wilhelm II's expansionism") and at promoting the union between England, France, and America that had been "forged on the battlefields."[19] His intentions, which reflected the prevalent anti-German ideology, were also a personal manifesto on modern theatrical aesthetics. He advocated a large, spectacular auditorium that he compared to a circus, a very open stage with painted curtains, and would necessarily integrate some music. *The Merchant of Venice* (1917), in a free adaptation by Népoty in which he played a cunning Shylock, met with total success. *Antony and Cleopatra* (1918) was a grand show, including a cast of eighty actors and supernumeraries spread about on a wide staircase in extremely light costumes, all intended to represent the final Egyptian orgy before the battle of Actium. The impression of sensuousness conveyed by the scene was experienced as shocking at a time when so many soldiers were struggling to survive in the trenches, but it was also a strong lesson in hope and a call for victory. After the war, Gémier turned to comedies in much-abridged versions: *The Taming of the Shrew* and *A Midsummer Night's Dream*.

At the beginning of the war, Jacques Copeau (1879–1949) had still felt the need to turn to England. *Twelfth Night* (1914), performed at the Théâtre du Vieux Colombier with Louis Jouvet as Aguecheek, was meant as a homage to Harley Granville-Barker. The stage was made up of mobile areas and different levels after the Elizabethan fashion. The stylized decor, influenced by modern art and verging on the abstract, was a landmark in modern theater. He furthered this staging sobriety in *The Winter's Tale* (1920), in which he imagined even more abstract architecture with a backstage gallery.

Charles Dullin (1885–1949) chose few Shakespeare plays, but his interpretation of Richard III in 1933 was one of his most memorable parts. Mastering Far Eastern dancing techniques, he would edge his way through the complex circular setting without a sound and take over the stage as a nasty, grinning, deformed villain. His acting was all apparent softness but extreme deviousness. This of course had to be interpreted as a warning for the times to come.[20]

A few months later, a performance developed into a manifesto of dramatically opposing views. In February 1934 *Coriolanus* was performed at the Comédie Française in a biased version by the Swiss-French writer René-Louis Piachaud, which favored the patricians with delicate language and Latin undertones but emphasized the gross fickleness of the crowds and the sly, manipulating speeches of the tribunes. Large numbers of supernumeraries were featured in massive crowds of plebeians and patricians, all with their right hands extended in the Roman salute, greeting the newly elected Coriolanus on the gigantic steps of the back set. When angered by the tribunes, the citizens shifted in impressive, threatening movements that filled the stage. After a week of tumultuous evening performances, the over-excited audiences took to the streets and joined extreme-right demonstrations displaying the same Roman salute as a tribute to the newly elected chancellor of Germany and his French sympathizers. As riots developed, the performances had to be cancelled, the Comédie Française was closed, and its administrator was dismissed.[21]

It was a Shakespeare play that Jean-Louis Barrault (1910–94) chose to stage at the end of the Second World War: *Antony and Cleopatra,* for which he commissioned André Gide to produce a new translation. Since then, the interest in Shakespeare has never failed on the French stage. In fact, some plays were among the most superb, large scale stagings of the open-air Avignon Festival created by Jean Vilar (1912–71). The latter premiered a most memorable *Richard II* at the opening season in 1947. He also played a hieratic, enigmatic *Macbeth* in 1953, one obviously influenced by *The Theatre of Cruelty*, written in 1932 by Antonin Artaud, who had himself planned to stage the play to illustrate his arguments. There followed a Brechtian *Richard III* staged by Roger Planchon in 1966, a flamboyant *Richard III* by Georges Lavaudant in 1984, a staging of *Coriolanus* that was favorable to the plebeians by Gabriel Garran in 1977, and, more recently, the French premiere of *Henry V* by Jean-Louis Benoit in 2000, a play that La Place had dismissed as anti-French propaganda in a mere five-page summary in his 1746 edition.[22]

In the subsidized cultural centers built in the suburbs of the main cities after the Second World War, directors have shown Shakespeare plays along with some renewed explorations of the French classics. This choice has proved successful in captivating their large audiences, who, for some, had a rather limited cultural background. Jean Dasté (1904–94) in Saint-Etienne promoted an enthusiastic type of theater based on actors performing in a light transformable space intended to tour to remote villages. He won a young company award with his *Measure for Measure* in 1958. Ito Josué's beautiful black-and-white photographs of delighted, anonymous spectators are the best testimonies to the popular success of his *Midsummer Night's Dream*.[23]

Some other directors under the Brechtian influence aimed at bringing about a political awakening thanks to Shakespeare's repertoire. Apart from his 1977 *Coriolanus*, a play that he had already staged in a simplified version in 1964, Gabriel Garran also performed *Henry VIII* as a warning against "providential men" at Aubervilliers, in the suburbs of Paris. In another working-class suburb (Gennevilliers), Bernard Sobel chose *Hamlet*, *King John*, and *Coriolanus* in strong dialectical terms and austere sets. Roger Planchon, otherwise a Molière specialist, started his career with *Twelfth Night* and *The Merry Wives of Windsor* in 1951. In Villeurbanne near Lyons he staged *Antony and Cleopatra* and *Pericles* jointly in 1978, placing them in the context of the many military dictatorships that were spreading around the world.[24]

In the more recent past, some directors have occasionally turned to Shakespeare as a stimulating lesson in perfect theater, stagings that in fact may have proved to be outstanding successes in their personal careers. Antoine Vitez (1930–90) staged a six-hour *Ham-*

let (1982), with a completely white set designed by Yannis Kokkos. The stylized, complex lines met in the far distance of the back stage, reflecting the maze of Hamlet's infinite mind. The tall, hieratic figures of the actors moved with exaggeratedly slow gestures to emphasize the artificiality of the theatrical experience and concentrate on words as pure sounds.

Patrice Chéreau played the title role of his *Richard II* (1970) as an unconcerned clown only seeking personal pleasure (said to be autobiographical on Chéreau's part), in an elaborate set dominated by complex machines. With *Hamlet*, in a fine translation by the poet Yves Bonnefoy, Gérard Desarthes achieved great success as Hamlet, first at the 1988 Avignon Festival and later at Nanterre, near Paris. Richard Peduzzi's gigantic wooden set represented the front of a castle covering the stage, which cracked open dangerously at some crucial moments of the action; the ghost was a soldier-at-arms on a real horse that galloped onto the set, with its hooves resounding ominously on the wooden floor.[25] Chéreau recently adapted some passages of *Richard III* as an exercise for his theater students.

Georges Lavaudant's spectacular 1984 *Richard III* portrayed an attractive/repulsive tyrant (played by Ariel García-Valdés) with white make-up, huge, sensuous, bright-red lips, and a shiny, tight-fitting black outfit. The hero wore a metal casing on his crippled leg, which stamped irregularly on the wooden floor, thus announcing his ineluctable coming even before he appeared on stage. This derisive study in black seduction was such a complete contrast to Charles Dullin's 1933 interpretation.

Some directors concentrate on a particular theme through different plays of the corpus or a revisiting of their former production. This is the case with Matthias Langhoff, of East German origin, who is obsessed with the fearful memories of his traumatic past, time and time again portraying the inevitable rise of a tyrant and the sheer impossibility of existing under a totalitarian regime. He produced two versions of *King Lear*, one in Dutch (1979) and another in French (1986), a powerful but misunderstood *Macbeth* (1990), and a collage of texts entitled *Gloucester Time: Materiau Shakespeare* (1995).[26]

In 1977 Daniel Mesguich staged a striking psychoanalytical *Hamlet*, with three actors interpreting the part of the eponymous hero as a basic clinical case of split personality. Ophelia was similarly doubled into a blonde and a brunette. The space was entirely covered with mirrors that endlessly reflected the multiplied images of the characters to a sickening obsession. The free adaptation by Michel Vittoz was peppered with collage texts by the film director

Jean-Luc Godard and the playwright Hélène Cixous. Mesguich felt the necessity to go back to *Hamlet* in 1986, a version in which he played the title role as a theater director keeping outside the stage frame and manipulating the other characters at will. Mesguich's career has seen a succession of "intellectual," buoyant, and controversial explorations of the Shakespearean repertoire: *Romeo and Juliet, Titus Andronicus, The Tempest* in 1998. The latter featured an extremely sophisticated set representing a section of a capsized caravel, with the addition of Richard III's seduction of Lady Anne played as transvestite parts.

From her student days in England when she was assistant director for a *Coriolanus*, Ariane Mnouchkine has always had access to the text in the original. In 1967 her version of *A Midsummer Night's Dream*, performed in the circular space of a now-demolished circus, was much in keeping with the impending liberation of gesture and movement, her fellow student actors wallowing in furs exuding a strange animality. But she is mostly praised for her famous cycle, which ran most successfully between 1981 and 1985 including successive worldwide tours, composed of *1 Henry IV, Richard II*, and *Twelfth Night*.[27] Her own archaic French versions were played at the makeshift theater of La Cartoucherie, on a wide, bare frontal stage raked at a slight angle towards the audience and covered with beige matting. There were hardly any props or sets, only huge pieces of multicolored silks of great beauty. She started what has become a now well-established taste for Oriental transposition: the hierarchical masculine warlike code of honour of the medieval England of the two histories was set into superb kabouki living tableaux, while the feminine fluidity of transvestites was changed into harmonious katakali for the comedy.[28]

Stéphane Braunschweig had no objective reason to turn to Shakespeare: having trained with Vitez, of Brechtian sensitivity, he would explore the German contemporary repertoire (even translating the plays himself), and operas in France, Italy, and Germany. However, he chose three rather problematic plays for which he designed an extreme scenography: a slanted, white, parallel-piped set at various angles, which made it difficult for the actors to keep their balance for *The Winter's Tale* (1994)[29]; a very heavy mobile circular wooden structure for *Measure for Measure* (1997), with an English cast from Nottingham (both plays being invited to the Edinburgh Official Festival); and mobile wooden paneling for *The Merchant of Venice* (1999).[30] His was an intellectual approach that discarded realist diction and intonation and favored a sad or uncertain ending: the characters could not reach final happiness after what they had been through.

Interestingly, some English or American directors who have direct access to the original text, but who are based in France, produce most of their work in French. This is the case with Peter Brook, who in fact claimed a French influence as far back as 1965 when the Stratford season was named "the Theatre of Cruelty" after Antonin Artaud's study. This shows a very complex phenomenon of enriching interdependencies between English and French theories, as Artaud had studied many aspects of the Elizabethan theater. Now based in Paris for over two decades, Brook has experimented with his conception of an empty space for the sole purpose of a small cast and a text in the old-fashioned theater of Les Bouffes du Nord, which he keeps in a half-derelict state. In Jean-Claude Carrière's efficient prose translations, he staged *Timon of Athens* (1974), *Measure for Measure* (1978), and *The Tempest* (1990) with few basic props and essential elements of costumes as the plays have to be embodied by the actors themselves.[31] He had already staged some of the plays previously, such as *Hamlet* and *Measure for Measure*, but each time it is clearly a longing to rediscover the essence of the theatrical act. His recent *Hamlet* (2000), in English with his own subtitles, centered on the hero (played by Adrian Lester) and his inner tragedy.

An American in Paris since the 1970s, Stuart Seide has vastly explored the Elizabethan and Jacobean repertoires, not only Shakespeare. He is used to writing his own French versions of the plays as part of his dramaturgical research. *A Midsummer Night's Dream* (1984) was on a bare stage, with a magic circle; the three parts of *Henry VI* (1994) were shortened into two evenings of disturbing verbal and scenic violence, which nevertheless included disparaging anecdotes; in *Romeo and Juliet* (1999), an immense sculptural setting seemed to engulf the senses.

The name of Shakespeare currently represents a thriving "industry" in France. More Shakespeare plays are being performed than any from the French classic repertoire. Strangely enough, however, the Shakespearean corpus has not generated many major French films, not even after the recent success of English and American versions, both traditional and updated. *Les amants de Vérone* [The lovers of Verona], a color film by André Cayatte (1909–89) made in 1949 on a scenario by the poet Jacques Prévert and himself, is, however, still a highly praised masterpiece.[32]

Shakespearean creativity does not much focus on opera or the visual arts as in the nineteenth century, with Berlioz's operas or

Delacroix's paintings, yet some references might crop up in unexpected contexts such as cartoons for children, for instance, the marsh fairies of *Le Sortilège des Gâtines* [The curse of the wastelands] by W. and Y. Delporte. Contrary to the phenomenon occurring in the English-speaking world, there have been on the whole rather few modern "imitations" in the theater. Among them are the famous rewritings of *Macbeth,* ranging from *Ubu Roi* (1896), a student hoax by Alfred Jarry (1873–1907)—one of Lugné-Poe's notoriously boisterous stagings,[33] as well as one of Peter Brook's early Paris productions in 1977—to *Macbett* (1972) by the Romanian-born French playwright Eugène Ionesco (1912–94), who used a different spelling as a derisive means to combat an impending deadly tyranny. Modern plays inspired by Shakespeare do exist either as a form of rewriting (Gabor Rassov's *La vie criminelle de Richard III* [The criminal life of Richard III[34]], a modern transposition (Bernard Chartreux's *Cacodémon-Roi* [Devil-king][35]), or a sequel (Marie Ordinis's *Les Monstres de Vérone ou Le Moine et la nourrice* [The monsters of Verona, or the friar and the nurse[36]], but remain confidential and marginal.

However, Shakespeare is definitely a safe bet for the theater box-office, whether the text used be the full play or a shortened version of it focusing on one character or a particular aspect. Any title can attract vast audiences that, in fact, may sometimes form a curious mixture of rather scholarly members and much younger ones who might otherwise have a limited theatrical experience, but who could well know the new English and American films derived from the plays. And indeed, any hints at famous, popular modern filmic versions might be the new *détour obligé* that can bring back younger audiences to dark theater auditoriums through a technique of metatextual cross-references.

It regularly happens that the same plays attract the attention of several directors within a rather short period of time, as if a play could be emblematic of an age and could bring some kind of solution to a current problem or concern. Of course we are now far from the nineteenth-century trend of "hamlétisme," but it has been interesting to see the emergence of several interpretations within the same season of *Titus Andronicus, Richard III, Measure for Measure,* or *Antony and Cleopatra. Hamlet* is of course beyond these considerations as standard fare, as is *A Midsummer Night's Dream,* which are chosen by highly trained companies and nonprofessional actors alike. Shakespeare plays often attract prominent or junior directors and may well prove promising experiences for the latter, who might choose a very well-known play in a daring exploration, or a rarely performed one as a challenge (such as the *Troilus and Cressida* directed by Eric da Silva,[37] or *Cymbeline* directed by Philippe Calvario).[38]

Many companies come to France with Shakespeare plays performed in English, or in a surprising variety of other languages, and have a supportive audience.[39] The reverse exchange is equally true with the export of Shakespeare in French following a trend that was started in a visionary way by our diva Sarah.

It would occur to no one at present to turn to the English stage as a model and a source of inspiration, or to consider English companies and directors as the sole heirs to the Shakespearean heritage as has been the case on various occasions in the past from Voltaire as a young man, Aurélien Lugné-Poe in the late nineteenth century, Jacques Copeau to Delacroix. French theater directors are not attracted towards Shakespeare particularly for his Englishness but for the message offered and the theatricality of his plays. They find their own solutions, drawing their inspiration from very varied influences and not necessarily from the cultural or literary. This may be living proof that in France Shakespearean theater has in fact been integrated in the surrounding world and turned into a familiar corpus that can be explored by directors, according to their whims, tastes, and interests.

Some directors may prefer to stage a new version and so proceed to translate or adapt the text to their own vision, like Ariane Mnouchkine, Daniel Mesguich, or Stuart Seide. Some commission a particular text: for example, Peter Brook's long-term collaboration with Jean-Claude Carrière (and not only for Shakespeare) or Georges Lavaudant and Stéphane Braunschweig with Jean-Michel Déprats. Some others may use the numerous translations already in print, as Patrice Chéreau did for his *Hamlet* by the famous poet Yves Bonnefoy's version, or as Roger Planchon had done with Henri Thomas's translation of *Antony and Cleopatra*.

So if the Shakespearean corpus is blooming on the French stage, it is also thriving on the page. And it will do so even more in the future with the publication of the complete, bilingual edition with new translations, the plays edited by Jean-Michel Déprats, the most prominent present-day translator, and the poems by the fine scholar Henri Suhamy, showing that Shakespeare has definitely found roots in French culture.[40]

Notes

1. Christian Biet, "*Le Théâtre Anglois* d'Antoine de La Place (1746–1749), ou la difficile émergence du théâtre de Shakespeare en France," in *Shakespeare et la*

France, edited by Patricia Dorval (Paris: Société Française Shakespeare, 2000), 29–50.

2. The plays were temporarily transferred to the Odeon Theater for political reasons at the time of the French Revolution and the reorganization of the theaters under Napoleon I.

3. Pierre Dux and Sylvie Chevalley, *La Comédie Française* (Paris: Denoël, 1980).

4. Comédie Française Files, Bibliothèque de l'Arsenal, Paris. On the international popularity of Duval's play with Shakespeare as a fictional character, see also the contribution by Keith Gregor to this volume.

5. Press cuttings, Bibliothèque de l'Arsenal, Paris.

6. Fortunato Israel, "L'iconographie shakespearienne en France" (PhD diss., Université de la Sorbonne, Paris, 1968).

7. Catherine Treilhou-Balaude, "Shakespeare romantique: La réception de Shakespeare en France de Guizot à Scribe (1821–1851)" (Ph.D. diss., Université de Paris III, Sorbonne-Nouvelle, 1994).

8. Anne Ubersfeld, "Le drame romantique," in *Le Théâtre en France*, edited by Jacqueline de Jomaron, vol. 2 (Paris: Armand Colin, Paris, 1989).

9. Edouard Noël and Edmond Stoullig, *Les Annales du Théâtre et de la Musique* 12 (Paris: Charpentier & Cie, 1887).

10. This part was a lifelong success of Mounet-Sully as he played the part of Hamlet 206 times between 1886 and 1916 (see Noël and Stoullig, *Les Annales*).

11. Madeleine Horn-Monval, *Les Traductions françaises de Shakespeare* (Paris: CNRS, 1963).

12. Victor Hugo, *William Shakespeare*, Nouvelle Bibliothèque romantique, introduction by Bernard Levilliot (Paris: Flammarion, 1973).

13. Press cuttings, Bibliothèque de l'Arsenal, Paris.

14. Isabelle Schwartz-Gastine, "La portée d'*Antoine et Cléopâtre* au théâtre," in *Lectures de Shakespeare: "Antony and Cleopatra,"* edited by Jean-Christophe Mayer (Rennes: Presses Universitaires de Rennes, 2000).

15. Pierre Spivakoff, *Sarah Bernhardt vue par les Nadar* (Paris: Herscher, 1982).

16. Jean Jacquot, *Shakespeare en France, mises en scènes d'hier et d'aujourd'hui* (Paris: Le Temps, 1964).

17. Isabelle Schwartz-Gastine, "Lugné-Poe et son approche de Shakespeare: de Pompée à Polonius," in Dorval, *Shakespeare et la France*, 213–29.

18. Jean Jacquot, *Shakespeare en France*.

19. Firmin Gémier, "Quelques mots sur la Société Shakespeare" (1917). Bibliothèque de l'Arsenal, Paris.

20. Monique Surel-Turpin, "Charles Dullin" (Ph.D. diss., Université de Paris III, 1979).

21. Isabelle Schwartz-Gastine, "Le *Coriolan* de Shakespeare mis en scène par Gabriel Garran, 1977" (Ph.D. diss., Université de Paris VII, 1982).

22. *Avignon 50 Festivals*, sous la direction de Claire David (Arles: Actes-Sud, 1996).

23. *Jean Dasté, qui êtes-vous?* (Lyon: La Manufacture, 1987).

24. Emile Copfermann, *Théâtre de Roger Planchon* (Paris: UGE, 1977).

25. Marie-Madeleine Mervant-Roux, *L'Assise du spectateur, pour une étude du spectateur* (Paris: CNRS, 1998).

26. Odette Aslan, *Matthias Langhoff* (Paris: CNRS, 1994).

27. Anne Neuschafer and Frédéric Serror, *Le Théâtre du Soleil, Shakespeare* (Cologne: Prometheus, 1984).

28. Ariane Mnouchkine, "Le théâtre est oriental," in *Confluences: Le dialogue des cultures dans les spectacles contemporains* (St Cyr l'École, 1993).
29. "Le réel retrouvé," entretien sur *Le Conte d'hiver* avec Anne-Françoise Benamou, *Théâtre Public* 115 (January–February 1994).
30. Isabelle Schwartz-Gastine, "*Mesure pour mesure* selon Stéphane Braunschweig," *Cahiers Elisabéthains* 58 (2000): 49–58.
31. Richard Marienstras, "La représentation et l'interprétation du texte," in *Les Voies de la création théâtrale*, edited by Denis Bablet and Jean Jacquot, vol. 5 (Paris: CNRS, 1977); Georges Banu, *Peter Brook de "Timon d'Athènes" à "La Tempête"* (Paris: Flammarion, 1991).
32. Louis Chauvet, *Le Figaro*, 9 March 1949.
33. Aurélien Lugné-Poe, *La Parade*, vol. 2, *Acrobaties, Souvenirs et Impressions de théâtre 1894–1902* (Paris: NRF, 1931).
34. Gabor Rassov, *La vie criminelle de Richard III* (Paris: Le Chapeau Rouge, 1994).
35. Bernard Chartreux, *Cacodémon-Roi* (Paris: Dérives-Solin, 1984).
36. Marie Ordinis, *Les Monstres de Vérone ou Le Moine et la Nourrice* (Paris: L'Echiquier, 1995). Avignon, Festival off (1995).
37. L'Emballage Théâtre, Théâtre de Genevilliers (Paris suburb), 1988–89, modernized translation by Eric da Silva.
38. Théâtre des Amandiers, Nanterre (Paris suburb), 2001.
39. Especially at L'Odéon-Théâtre de l'Europe since the mandate of Lluis Pasqual inaugurating a systematic policy of subtitles. The first company to benefit from it in 1990 was the Royal National Theatre with a double Shakespeare bill in fact: *King Lear*, directed by Deborah Warner with Brian Cox, and *Richard III*, directed by Richard Eyre with Ian McKellen.
40. Series published by La Pléiade, Gallimard, Paris.

Bibliography: Shakespeare in European Culture

Ton Hoenselaars

THIS IS A SELECTIVE BIBLIOGRAPHY OF ACADEMIC PUBLICATIONS bearing on the issue of Shakespeare and his works in a European cultural context. It lists the specific national histories of Shakespeare reception in European countries. It also includes publications in the fields of translation, production, and criticism that theorize Shakespeare and the notion of an assumed European identity. Publications on national appropriation in more general terms as well as comparative discussions of Shakespeare in translation, production, and criticism have also been included. For a census of individual productions and specific theatre reviews, the reader is referred to the relevant sections in the journals and other publications of the Shakespeare institutions and societies (*Cahiers Elisabéthains, Folio, Shakespeare Bulletin, Shakespeare Jahrbuch, Shakespeare Survey, Shakespeare Quarterly, Shakespeare Studies, Shakespeare Translation*, and *Shakespeare Worldwide*).

Aaltonen, Sirkku. "*La Perruque* in a Rented Apartment: Rewriting Shakespeare in Finland." *Ilha do desterro: A Journal of English Language, Literatures in English, and Cultural Studies* (Brazil), 36 (1999): 141–59.

Afonso, M. J. da Rocha. "Simão de Melo Brandão and the First Portuguese Version of *Othello*." In *European Shakespeares: Translating Shakespeare in the Romantic Age*, edited by Dirk Delabastita and Lieven D'hulst, 129–46. Amsterdam: John Benjamins, 1993.

Alekseev, M. P. *Sekspir i russkaja kul'tura / Shakespeare and Russian Culture*. Moscow: Akademija nauk SSSR, 1965.

Alexander, Edward. "Shakespeare's Plays in Armenia." *Shakespeare Quarterly* 9 (1958): 387–94.

Allison, Jonathan. "W. B. Yeats and Shakespearean Character." In *Shakespeare and Ireland: History, Politics, Culture*, edited by Mark Thornton Burnett and Ramona Wray, 114–35. Houndmills, U.K.: Macmillan, 1997.

Andreyeva, Vera. *Shakespeare in Estonia*. Moscow: n.p., 1979.

Arnold, Thomas James I. *Shakespeare, in de Nederlandsche letterkunde en op het*

Nederlandsch tooneel. Bibliografisch overzicht. The Hague: Martinus Nijhoff, 1879.

Bachrach, A. G. H., J. Swart, and F. W. S. van Tienen. *Rondom Shakespeare.* Zeist: Uitgeversmaatschappij W. de Haan, 1964.

"Bardolatry Abroad." *Times Literary Supplement,* 13 April 1946, 175.

Barker, Francis. "Nationalism, Nomadism and Belonging in Europe: *Coriolanus.*" In *Shakespeare and National Culture,* edited by John J. Joughin, 233–65. Manchester: Manchester University Press, 1997.

Barker, Simon. "Re-loading the Canon: Shakespeare and the Study Guides." In *Shakespeare and National Culture,* edited by John J. Joughin, 42–57. Manchester: Manchester University Press, 1997.

Barrault, Jean-Louis. "Shakespeare et nous." *Revue d'histoire littéraire de la France* 2 (1950): 131–36.

Bartmann, H., *Grabbes Verhältnis zu Shakespeare.* Münster, 1898.

Bate, Jonathan. "The Politics of Romantic Shakespeare Criticism: Germany, England, France." *European Romantic Review* 1, no. 1 (1990): 1–26.

———. *The Romantics on Shakespeare.* Harmondsworth, U.K.: Penguin, 1992.

———. *Shakespeare and the English Romantic Imagination.* Oxford: Clarendon Press, 1986.

———. *Shakespearean Constitutions: Politics, Theatre, Criticism, 1730–1830.* Oxford: Clarendon Press, 1989.

———, and Russell Jackson, eds. *Shakespeare: An Illustrated Stage History.* Oxford: Oxford University Press, 1996.

Bauer, Roger, ed. *Das Shakespeare-Bild in Europa zwischen Aufklärung und Romantik.* Bern: Peter Lang, 1988.

Begemann, Nienke. "De Engelse komedianten in de Nederlanden." *De Gids* 127, no. 5 (1965): 398–412.

Benedix, Roderich. *Die Shakespeareomanie.* Stuttgart, 1873.

Beza, Marcu. *Shakespeare in Roumania.* London: J. M. Dent, 1931.

Bircher, Martin, and Heinrich Straumann. *Shakespeare und die deutsche Schweiz bis zum Beginn des 19. Jahrhunderts: Eine Bibliographie raisonnée.* Bern and Munich: Francke Verlag, 1971.

Blinn, Hansjürgen, ed. *Shakespeare-Rezeption: Die Diskussion um Shakespeare in Deutschland.* 2 vols. Berlin: Schmidt, 1982–1988.

———. *Der deutsche Shakespeare: Eine annotierte Bibliographie zur Shakespeare-Rezeption des deutschsprachigen Kulturraums (Literatur, Theater, Film, Funk, Fernsehen, Musik und bildende Kunst/The German Shakespeare: An Annotated Bibliography of the Shakespeare Reception in German-Speaking Countries (Literature, Theatre, Mass Media, Music, Fine Arts).* Berlin: Erich Schmidt, 1993.

Blum, Eugène. "Shakespeare in the USSR." *Shakespeare Association Bulletin* 20 (1945): 99–102.

Blumenfeld, Odette-Irene. "Shakespeare in Post-Revolutionary Romania: The Great Directors Are Back Home." In *Shakespeare in the New Europe,* edited by Michael Hattaway, Boika Sokolova, and Derek Roper, 231–46. Sheffield: Sheffield Academic Press, 1994.

Böhtlingk, Arthur. *Bismarck und Shakespeare.* Stuttgart: Cotta, 1908.

Bolin, Wilhelm. "Zur Shakespeare-Literatur Schwedens." *Shakespeare Jahrbuch* 15 (1880): 73–128.

Bonnard, George A. "Suggestions Towards an Edition of Shakespeare for French, German and Other Continental Readers." *Shakespeare Survey* 5 (1952): 10–15.

Bragaglia, Leonardo. *Shakespeare in Italia. Personaggi ed interpreti. Vita scenica del teatro di Guglielmo Shakespeare in Italia, 1792–1973.* Rome: Trevi editore, 1973.

Brandl, Alois. *Shakespeare and Germany.* British Academy Lecture. New York: Oxford University Press, 1913.

Brennecke, Ernest, ed. *Shakespeare in Germany, 1590–1700.* With translations of five early plays by Ernest Brennecke in collaboration with Henry Brennecke. Chicago: University of Chicago Press, 1964.

Brosche, Günter. *Shakespeare in der Österreichischen Nationalbibliothek: Ein Postskriptum zum Shakespearejahr.* Vienna: St. Gabriel, 1965.

Brown, Ivor. "Shakespeare og Danmark." *Berlingske tidende* (Copenhagen), 21 May 1957.

Brown, John Russell. "Foreign Shakespeare and English-speaking Audiences." In *Foreign Shakespeare: Contemporary Performance*, edited by Dennis Kennedy, 21–35. Cambridge: Cambridge University Press, 1993.

Brown, Richard. "'Shakespeare Explained': James Joyce's Shakespeare from Victorian Burlesque to Postmodern Bard." In *Shakespeare and Ireland: History, Politics, Culture*, edited by Mark Thornton Burnett and Ramona Wray, 91–113. Houndmills, U.K.: Macmillan, 1997.

Bryner, Cyril. "Shakespeare among the Slavs." *Journal of English Literary History* 8 (1941): 107–18.

Bull, Francis. "The Influence of Shakespeare on Wergeland, Ibsen and Bjørnson." *The Norseman* 15 (1957): 88–95.

Burian, Jarka. "*Hamlet* in Postwar Czech Theatre." In *Foreign Shakespeare: Contemporary Performance*, edited by Dennis Kennedy, 195–210. Cambridge: Cambridge University Press, 1993.

Burian, Orhan. "Shakespeare in Turkey." *Shakespeare Quarterly* 8 (1958), 28–29.

Burnett, Mark Thornton, and Ramona Wray, eds. *Shakespeare and Ireland: History, Politics, Culture.* Houndmills, U.K.: Macmillan, 1997.

Burt, Richard. "Baroque Down: The Trauma of Censorship in Psychoanalysis and Queer Film Re-visions of Shakespeare and Marlowe." In *Shakespeare in the New Europe*, edited by Michael Hattaway, Boika Sokolova, and Derek Roper, 328–50. Sheffield: Sheffield Academic Press, 1994.

Calgari, Guido. "Fortuna di Shakespeare in Italia e in Francia." *Hesperia* (Zurich), 3 October 1953, 191–99.

Carlson, Marvin. "Daniel Mesguich and Intertextual Shakespeare." In *Foreign Shakespeare: Contemporary Performance*, edited by Dennis Kennedy, 213–31. Cambridge: Cambridge University Press, 1993.

Chasles, Ph. *Études sur W. Shakespeare, Marie Stuart, et l'Arétin.* Paris, 1851.

Checkley, C. S. "Rumanian Interpretations of *Hamlet*." Ph.D. diss., University of Birmingham, Birmingham, U.K., 1956.

Ciglar-Žanić, Janja. "Recruiting the Bard: Onstage and Offstage Glimpses of Recent Shakespeare Productions in Croatia." In *Shakespeare in the New Europe,* edited by Michael Hattaway, Boika Sokolova, and Derek Roper, 261–75. Sheffield: Sheffield Academic Press, 1994.

Cohn, Albert. *Shakespeare in Germany in the Sixteenth and Seventeenth Centuries: An Account of English Actors in Germany and the Netherlands and of the Plays Performed by them during the Same Period.* 1865. Reprint, New York: Haskell House Publishers, 1971.

Collison-Morley, Lacy. *Shakespeare in Italy.* 1916. Reprint, New York: Benjamin Blom, 1967.

Condamin, J. "Un royal traducteur de Shakespeare, Louis, roi de Portugal." In his *Études et Souvenirs.* Paris, 1883.

Creizenach, W. *Die Schauspiele der englischen Komödianten.* Stuttgart, 1889.

Crinò, Anna Maria. *Le traduzioni di Shakespeare in Italia nel settecento.* Rome: Edizione di Storia e Letteratura, 1950.

Cronin, Michael. "Rug-headed Kerns Speaking Tongues: Shakespeare, Translation and the Irish Language." In *Shakespeare and Ireland: History, Politics, Culture,* edited by Mark Thornton Burnett and Ramona Wray, 193–212. Houndmills, U.K.: Macmillan, 1997.

Cummings, Peter. *Shakespeare in Italy: Out of the Lost Years.* Geneva, N.Y.: Library Associates, Warren Hunting Smith Library, Hobart and William Smith Colleges, 1988.

Daniell, David. *"Coriolanus" in Europe.* London: Athlone Press, 1980.

Dávidházi, Péter. "Cult and Criticism: Ritual in the European Reception of Shakespeare." In *Literature and Its Cults: An Anthropological Approach / Littérature et ses cultes: Approche anthropologique,* edited by Péter Dávidházi and Judit Karafíath, 29–45. Budapest: Argumentum, 1994.

———. "Cult and Criticism: Ritual in the European Reception of Shakespeare." *Neohelicon* 17, no. 1 (1990): 59–78.

———. "The Domestication of Shakespeare in Hungary: The Nineteenth Century." In *Shakespeare and Hungary. Special Theme Section: The Law and Shakespeare,* edited by Holger Klein, Péter Dávidházi, and B. J. Sokol. Shakespeare Yearbook 7. 37–45. Lewiston, N.Y.: Edwin Mellen Press, 1996.

———. "Providing Texts for a Literary Cult: Early Translations of Shakespeare in Hungary." In *European Shakespeares: Translating Shakespeare in the Romantic Age,* edited by Dirk Delabastita and Lieven D'hulst, 147–62. Amsterdam: John Benjamins, 1993.

———. *The Romantic Cult of Shakespeare: Literary Reception in an Anthropological Perspective.* London: Macmillan, 1998.

———, and Judit Karafíath, eds. *Literature and Its Cults: An Anthropological Approach/Littérature et ses cultes: Approche anthropologique.* Budapest: Argumentum, 1994.

De Faria, Jorge. "O primeiro tradutor português de Shakespeare." *Mundo Gráfico* 1, no. 5 (1940): 15.

Delabastita, Dirk. "*Hamlet* in the Netherlands in the Late Eighteenth and Early Nineteenth Centuries: The Complexities of the History of Shakespeare's Reception." In *European Shakespeares: Translating Shakespeare in the Romantic Age,* edited by Dirk Delabastita and Lieven D'hulst, 219–36. Amsterdam: John Benjamins, 1993.

———, and Lieven D'hulst, eds. *European Shakespeares: Translating Shakespeare in the Romantic Age*. Amsterdam: John Benjamins, 1993.

Dobson, Michael. *The Making of the National Poet: Shakespeare, Adaptation, and Authorship, 1660–1769*. Oxford: Clarendon Press, 1992.

Downs, Brian W. "Anglo-Norwegian Relations, 1867–1900." *Modern Language Review* 42 (1952): 449–94.

Drahomanov, M. "*The Taming of the Shrew* in the Folklore of the Ukraine." *Annals of the Ukrainian Academy of Arts and Sciences in the US* 2 (1952): 214–18.

Dubeux, Albert. *Les Traductions françaises de Shakespeare*. Paris: Les Belles Lettres, 1928.

Düntzer, H. *Shakespeare und der junge Goethe*. Stuttgart, 1891.

Duţu, Alexandru. *Shakespeare in Rumania: A Bibliographical Essay*. With an Introd. by Mihnea Gheorghiu. Bucharest: Meridiane Publishing House, 1964.

Egri, Péter. "Whose Immortality is It Anyway? The Hungarian Translations of Shakespeare's Sonnet 18." In *Shakespeare and Hungary. Special Theme Section: The Law and Shakespeare*, edited by Holger Klein, Péter Dávidházi, and B. J. Sokol. Shakespeare Yearbook 7. 207–34. Lewiston, N.Y.: Edwin Mellen Press, 1996.

Einarsson, Stefán. *Shakespeare á Islandi*. Winnipeg: Viking Press, 1939.

———. "Shakespeare in Iceland: An Historical Survey." *Journal of English Literary History* 7 (1940): 272–85.

Elze, Karl. *Die englische Sprache und Literatur in Deutschland*. Dresden, 1864.

Engel, C. E. "Shakespeare in Switzerland in the Eighteenth Century." *Comparative Literature Studies* 17–18 (1945): 2–8.

Engel, J. "Shakespeare in Frankreich." *Shakespeare Jahrbuch* 34 (1898): 66–118.

England, Martha Winburn. "Garrick's Stratford Jubilee: Reactions in France and Germany." *Shakespeare Survey* 9 (1956): 90–100.

———. *Garrick's Jubilee*. Columbus: Ohio State University Press, 1964.

Engle, Ron. "Audience, Style, and Language in the Shakespeare of Peter Zadek." In *Foreign Shakespeare: Contemporary Performance*, edited by Dennis Kennedy, 93–105. Cambridge: Cambridge University Press, 1993.

English, Richard. "Shakespeare and the Definition of the Irish Nation." In *Shakespeare and Ireland: History, Politics, Culture*, edited by Mark Thornton Burnett and Ramona Wray, 136–51. Houndmills, U.K.: Macmillan, 1997.

Esquerra, Ramón. *Shakespeare a Catalunya*. Barcelona: Generalitat de Catalunya, 1937.

Estorninho, Carlos. "Shakespeare na Literatura Portuguesa." *Ocidente* 67, no. 113 (1964): 114–23.

Etkind, Efim. "Shakespeare in der russischen Dichtung des Goldnen Zeitalters (1808–1840)." In *Das Shakespeare-Bild in Europa zwischen Aufklärung und Romantik*, edited by Roger Bauer, 241–61. Bern: Peter Lang, 1988.

Fabiny, Tibor. "*King Lear*'s Significance in the New Hungarian Political Context, 1989–1995." In *Shakespeare and Hungary. Special Theme Section: The Law and Shakespeare*, edited by Holger Klein, Péter Dávidházi, and B. J. Sokol. Shakespeare Yearbook 7. 191–206. Lewiston, N.Y.: Edwin Mellen Press, 1996.

Forsyth, Neil. "Shakespeare the European." In *Translating/traduire/tradurre*

Shakespeare, edited by Irene Weber Henking, 5–21. Lausanne: Centre de Traduction Littéraire de Lausanne, 2001.

Frank, Tibor. "'Give Me Shakespeare': Lajos Kossuth's English as an Instrument of International Politics." In *Shakespeare and Hungary. Special Theme Section: The Law and Shakespeare*, edited by Holger Klein, Péter Dávidházi, and B. J. Sokol. Shakespeare Yearbook 7. 47–73. Lewiston, N.Y.: Edwin Mellen Press, 1996.

Franz, Wilhelm. *Shakespeare als Kulturkraft in Deutschland und England*. Tübingen: Kloeres, 1916.

Fresco, Gaby Petrone. "An Unpublished Pre-Romantic *Hamlet* in Eighteenth-Century Italy." In *European Shakespeares: Translating Shakespeare in the Romantic Age*, edited by Dirk Delabastita and Lieven D'hulst, 111–28. Amsterdam: John Benjamins, 1993.

Friederichs, E. "Shakespeare in Rußland." *Englische Studien* 1 (1916): 106–36.

Fujita, Minoru, and Leonard Pronko, eds. *Shakespeare East and West*. New York: St. Martin's Press, 1996.

Funke, Otto. *Die Schweiz und die englische Literatur: Ein Vortrag*. Bern: A. Francke, 1937.

Garber, Marjorie. *Shakespeare's Ghost Writers: Literature as Uncanny Causality*. New York: Routledge, 1987.

Gay, Peter. "Freud and the Man from Stratford." In *Reading Freud: Explorations and Entertainments*, 5–53. New Haven: Yale University Press, 1990.

Géher, István. "Hamlet the Hungarian: A Living Moment." In *Shakespeare and Hungary. Special Theme Section: The Law and Shakespeare*, edited by Holger Klein, Péter Dávidházi, and B. J. Sokol. Shakespeare Yearbook 7. 75–87. Lewiston, N.Y.: Edwin Mellen Press, 1996.

Genée, Rudolf. *Geschichte der Shakespeare'schen Dramen in Deutschland*. Leipzig: Wilhelm Engelmann, 1870.

———. *A. W. Schlegel und Shakespeare: Ein Beitrag zur Würdigung der Schlegel'schen Übersetzungen*. Berlin: Georg Reimer, 1904.

George, Emery. "*Twelfth Night* by Two Translators: A Homogeneous Text." In *Shakespeare and Hungary. Special Theme Section: The Law and Shakespeare*, edited by Holger Klein, Péter Dávidházi, and B. J. Sokol. Shakespeare Yearbook 7. 143–67. Lewiston, N.Y.: Edwin Mellen Press, 1996.

Gervinus, G. G. *Händel und Shakespeare*. Leipzig, 1868.

Gheorghiu, Mihnea. *Shakespeare in Rumania*. Bucharest: Intreprinderea Poligrafica "Informatia," 1964.

Gibian, George. "Shakespeare in Soviet-Russia." *Russian Review* 11 (1952): 24–34.

Gibińska, Marta. "Polish Hamlets: Shakespeare's *Hamlet* in Polish Theatres after 1945." In *Shakespeare in the New Europe*, edited by Michael Hattaway, Boika Sokolova, and Derek Roper, 159–73. Sheffield: Sheffield Academic Press, 1994.

———. *Polish Poets Read Shakespeare: Refashioning of the Tradition*. Kraków: Towarzystwo Naukowe "Societas Vistulana," 1999.

——— and Jerzy Limon, eds. *Hamlet East-West*. Gdansk: Theatrum Gedanense Foundation, 1998.

Gilman, Margaret. *Othello in French*. Bibliothèque de la Revue de Littérature Comparée 21. Paris: E. Champion, 1925.

Golub, Spencer. "Between the Curtain and the Grave: The Taganka in the *Hamlet* Gulag." In *Foreign Shakespeare: Contemporary Performance*, edited by Dennis Kennedy, 158–77. Cambridge: Cambridge University Press, 1993.

Gömöri, George. "Shakespeare in Milán Füst's Writings." In *Shakespeare and Hungary. Special Theme Section: The Law and Shakespeare*, edited by Holger Klein, Péter Dávidházi, and B. J. Sokol. Shakespeare Yearbook 7. 131–42. Lewiston, N.Y.: Edwin Mellen Press, 1996.

González Fernández de Sevilla, José Manuel, ed. *Shakespeare en España. Crítica, traducciones y representaciones*. Alicante/Zaragoza: Universidad de Alicante/ Pórtico, 1993.

Goy-Blanquet, Dominique. "Warner, Stein, and Mesguich Have a Cut at *Titus Andronicus*." In *Foreign Shakespeare: Contemporary Performance*, edited by Dennis Kennedy, 36–55. Cambridge: Cambridge University Press, 1993.

Gregor, Graham Keith. "Spanish Shakespeare-manía: *Twelfth Night* in Madrid, 1996–97." *Shakespeare Quarterly* 49, no. 4 (1998): 421–31.

Greguss, A. *Shakespeare in Ungarn*. Budapest, 1879.

Grein, Jacob T. "Shakespeare in Hungary." *The Illustrated London News*, 13 December 1924, 1165.

Greiner, Norbert. "The Comic Matrix of Early German Shakespeare Translation." In *European Shakespeares: Translating Shakespeare in the Romantic Age*, edited by Dirk Delabastita and Lieven D'hulst, 203–17. Amsterdam: John Benjamins, 1993.

Grillo, Ernesto. *Shakespeare and Italy*. Glasgow: R. Maclehose, 1949. Reprint, New York: Haskell House, 1973.

Gundolf, Friedrich. *Shakespeare und der deutsche Geist*. Berlin: Georg Bondi, 1914. Revised edition of F. Gundelfinger, *Shakespeare und der deutsche Geist vor dem Auftreten Lessings*. Heidelberg, 1911.

Guntner, Lawrence. "Brecht and Beyond: Shakespeare on the East German Stage." In *Foreign Shakespeare: Contemporary Performance*, edited by Dennis Kennedy, 109–39. Cambridge: Cambridge University Press, 1993.

―――, and Andrew M. McClean, eds. *Redefining Shakespeare: Literary Theory and Theater Practice in the German Democratic Republic*. Newark: University of Delaware Press, 1998.

Gury, Jacques. "Shakespearomanie et subversion?" In *Modèles et moyens de la réflexion politique au XVIIIe siècle*. 3 vols. Lille: Publications de l'Université de Lille III, 1977–1979. Vol. 3, *Débats et combats idéologiques: sociétés de pensée, loges, clubs*, 227–41.

―――. "Heurs et malheurs de *Roméo et Juliette* en France à l'époque romantique." In *European Shakespeares: Translating Shakespeare in the Romantic Age*, edited by Dirk Delabastita and Lieven D'hulst, 187–202. Amsterdam: John Benjamins, 1993.

Gyulai, Ágost. *Shakespeare in Hungary*. London: Gale & Polden, 1908.

Habicht, Werner. "The Romanticism of the Schlegel-Tieck Shakespeare and the History of Nineteenth-Century German Shakespeare Translation." In *European Shakespeares: Translating Shakespeare in the Romantic Age*, edited by Dirk Delabastita and Lieven D'hulst, 45–53. Amsterdam: John Benjamins, 1993.

―――. *Shakespeare and the German Imagination*. International Shakespeare Association Occasional Paper No. 5. Hertford, U.K.: Stephen Austin and Sons, 1994.

——. "Topoi of the Shakespeare Cult in Germany." In *Literature and Its Cults: An Anthropological Approach/Littérature et ses cultes: Approche anthropologique*, edited by Péter Dávidházi and Judit Karafíath, 47–65. Budapest: Argumentum, 1994.

Haines, Charles Moline. *Shakespeare in France. Criticism: Voltaire to Victor Hugo*. London: Oxford University Press, 1925. Reprint, New York: AMS Press, 1975.

Hamburger, Maik. "'Are You a Party in This Business?': Consolidation and Subversion in East German Shakespeare Productions." *Shakespeare Survey* 48 (1995): 171–84.

Haraszti, Zoltán. *Shakespeare in Hungary: His Plays on the Stage and His Influence in Literature and Life*. Boston: Trustees of the Public Library, 1929.

Harbage, Alfred. "Shakespeare as Culture Hero." In *Conceptions of Shakespeare*, 101–19. Cambridge: Harvard University Press, 1966.

Harnack, O. *Über Goethes Verhältnis zu Shakespeare. Essais und Studien*. Brunswick, Germany, 1899.

Harries, Frederick J. *Shakespeare and the Welsh*. 1919. Reprint, New York: Haskell House Publishers, 1972.

Hattaway, Michael. "Shakespeare's Histories: The Politics of Recent British Productions." In *Shakespeare in the New Europe*, edited by Michael Hattaway, Boika Sokolova, and Derek Roper, 351–69. Sheffield: Sheffield Academic Press, 1994.

Hauffen, A. *Shakespeare in Deutschland*. Prague, 1893.

Hauptmann, Gerhart. "Deutschland und Shakespeare." *Shakespeare Jahrbuch* 51 (1915): vii-xii.

Hawkes, Terence. "Shakespeare's Spooks, or Someone to Watch Over Me." In *Shakespeare in the New Europe*, edited by Michael Hattaway, Boika Sokolova, and Derek Roper, 194–206. Sheffield: Sheffield Academic Press, 1994.

Hawkings, Harriet. "Shakespeare's Radical Romanticism: The Popular Tradition and the Challenge of Tribalism." In *Shakespeare in the New Europe*, edited by Michael Hattaway, Boika Sokolova, and Derek Roper, 278–93. Sheffield: Sheffield Academic Press, 1994.

Healy, Tom. "Past and Present Shakespeare's: Shakespearian Appropriations in Europe." In *Shakespeare and National Culture*, edited by John J. Joughin, 202–32. Manchester: Manchester University Press, 1997.

Healy, Thomas. "Remembering with Advantages: Nation and Ideology in *Henry V*." In *Shakespeare in the New Europe*, edited by Michael Hattaway, Boika Sokolova, and Derek Roper, 174–93. Sheffield: Sheffield Academic Press, 1994.

Heftrich, Eckhardt. "Shakespeare in Weimar." In *Das Shakespeare-Bild in Europa zwischen Aufklärung und Romantik*, edited by Roger Bauer, 182–200. Bern: Peter Lang, 1988.

Hempfner, Klaus W. "Shakespeare, Voltaire, Baretti und die Kontextabhängigkeit." In *Das Shakespeare-Bild in Europa zwischen Aufklärung und Romantik*, edited by Roger Bauer, 77–101. Bern: Peter Lang, 1988.

Henriques, Alf. *Shakespeare og Danmark indtil 1840*. Copenhagen: Munksgaard, 1941.

———. "Shakespeare and Denmark, 1900–1949." *Shakespeare Survey* 3 (1950): 107–15.

Herford, C. H. "A Sketch of the History of Shakespeare's Influence on the Continent." *Bulletin of the John Rylands Library* 9 (1925): 20–62.

Herz, E. *Englische Schauspieler und englisches Schauspiel zur Zeit Shakespeares in Deutschland.* Hamburg: Voss, 1903.

Heun, Hans Georg. *Shakespeare in deutschen Übersetzungen.* Berlin: Akademie-Verlag, 1957.

Hevesi, Sándor. *Az igazi Shakespeare és egyéb kérdések* [The Real Shakespeare and Other Questions]. Budapest: Táltos, 1919.

Hilský, Martin. "Shakespeare in Czech: An Essay in Cultural Semantics." In *Shakespeare in the New Europe*, edited by Michael Hattaway, Boika Sokolova, and Derek Roper, 150–58. Sheffield: Sheffield Academic Press, 1994.

Hoch, Horace Lind. *Shakespeare's Influence upon Grabbe.* Philadelphia: n.p., 1910.

Hodgdon, Barbara. *The Shakespeare Trade: Performances and Appropriations.* Philadelphia: University of Pennsylvania Press, 1998.

Hoenselaars, Ton. "Recycling Shakespeare in the Low Countries." *The Low Countries* 6 (1999): 203–11.

———, and Jan Frans van Dijkhuizen. "Abraham Sybant Tames *The Taming of the Shrew* for the Amsterdam Stage (1654)." *Ilha do desterro: A Journal of English Language, Literatures in English, and Cultural Studies* (Brazil) 36 (1999): 53–70.

Hogan, Patrick Colm. "Shakespeare, Eastern Theatre, and Literary Universals: Drama in the Context of Cognitive Science." In *Shakespeare East and West*, edited by Minoru Fujita and Leonard Pronko, 164–80. New York: St. Martin's Press, 1996.

Holderness, Graham. "Franco Zeffirelli (1966)." In *The Taming of the Shrew*, 49–72. Manchester: Manchester University Press, 1989.

———, ed. *The Shakespeare Myth.* Manchester: Manchester University Press, 1988.

———, and Andrew Murphey. "Shakespeare's England: Britain's Shakespeare." In *Shakespeare and National Culture*, edited by John J. Joughin, 19–41. Manchester: Manchester University Press, 1997.

Holland, Norman H. *Psychoanalysis and Shakespeare.* New York: McGraw-Hill, 1966.

Holland, Peter. *English Shakespeares: Shakespeare on the English Stage in the 1990s.* Cambridge: Cambridge University Press, 1997.

Hortmann, Wilhelm. "Word Into Image: Notes on the Scenography of Recent German Productions." In *Foreign Shakespeare: Contemporary Performance*, edited by Dennis Kennedy, 232–53. Cambridge: Cambridge University Press, 1993.

———. *Shakespeare on the German Stage: The Twentieth Century.* Cambridge: Cambridge University Press, 1998.

Huesmann, Heinrich. *Shakespeare-Inszenierungen unter Goethe in Weimar.* Vienna: Hermann Böhlaus Nachf., 1968.

Hughes, Arthur Edward. *Shakespeare and his Welsh Characters.* 1919. Reprint, Folcroft, Pa.: Folcroft Library Editions, 1973.

Inbar, Eva Maria. *Shakespeare in Deutschland: Der Fall Lenz.* Studien zur deutschen Literatur, 67. Tübingen: Max Niemeyer Verlag, 1982.
Jackson, John E. "What's in a Sonnet? Translating Shakespeare." In *Translating/ traduire/tradurre Shakespeare*, edited by Irene Weber Henking, 57–73. Lausanne: Centre de Traduction Littéraire de Lausanne, 2001.
Jacobowski, L. *Klinger und Shakespeare: Ein Beitrag zur Shakespearomanie der Sturm- und Drangperiode.* Freiburg, 1891.
Jacquot, Jean. *Shakespeare en France: Mise en scène d'hier et d'aujourd'hui.* Paris: Le Temps, 1964.
Jensen, Niels Lyhne. "Shakespeare in Denmark." *Durham University Journal* 56 (1963/4): 91–98.
Johnson, David. *Shakespeare and South Africa.* Oxford: Clarendon Press; New York: Oxford University Press, 1996.
Joughin, John J., ed. *Shakespeare and National Culture.* Manchester: Manchester University Press, 1997.
———. "Shakespeare, National Culture and the Lure of Transnationalism." In *Shakespeare and National Culture*, edited by John J. Joughin, 269–94. Manchester: Manchester University Press, 1997.
Juliá Martínez, Eduardo. *Shakespeare en España. Traducciones, imitaciones e influencia de las obras de Shakespeare en la literatura española.* Madrid: Tip. de la "Rev. de Arch., Bibl. y Museos," 1918.
Jusserand, Jean Jules. *Shakespeare en France sous l'Ancien Régime. English Shakespeare in France under the Ancien Régime.* London: T. Fisher Unwin, 1899. Reprint, New York: American Scholar Publications, 1966.
Keller, W. "Shakespeares Eindringen in Frankreich und die deutsche Shakespeare-Begeisterung." *Europäischer Wissenschaftsdienst* 2 (1942): 2–3.
Kennedy, Dennis. *Looking at Shakespeare: A Visual History of Twentieth-Century Performance.* Cambridge: Cambridge University Press, 1993. Second edition, 2001.
———, ed. *Foreign Shakespeare: Contemporary Performance.* Cambridge: Cambridge University Press, 1993.
———. "Introduction: Shakespeare without His Language." In *Foreign Shakespeare: Contemporary Performance*, edited by Dennis Kennedy, 1–18. Cambridge: Cambridge University Press, 1993.
Kiernander, Adrian. *Ariane Mnouchkine and the Théâtre du Soleil.* Cambridge: Cambridge University Press, 1993.
Kiséry, András. "Hamletizing the Spirit of the Nation: Political Uses of Kazinczy's 1790 Translation." In *Shakespeare and Hungary. Special Theme Section: The Law and Shakespeare*, edited by Holger Klein, Péter Dávidházi, and B. J. Sokol. Shakespeare Yearbook 7. 11–35. Lewiston, N.Y.: Edwin Mellen Press, 1996.
Klajn, Hugó. "Shakespeare in Yugoslavia." *Shakespeare Quarterly* 5 (1954): 41–45.
Kleber, Pia. "Theatrical Continuities in Giorgio Strehler's *The Tempest.*" In *Foreign Shakespeare: Contemporary Performance*, edited by Dennis Kennedy, 140–57. Cambridge: Cambridge University Press, 1993.
Klein, Holger, and Christopher Smith. *Hamlet at Home and Abroad.* Special issue of *New Comparison* 2 (1986).

———, Péter Dávidházi, and B. J. Sokol, eds. *Shakespeare and Hungary. Special Theme Section: The Law and Shakespeare*. Lewiston, N.Y.: Edwin Mellen Press, 1996.

———, and Jean-Marie Maguin, eds. *Shakespeare and France*. Lewiston, N.Y.: Edwin Mellen Press, 1994.

———, and Michele Marrapodi, eds. *Shakespeare and Italy*. Lewiston, N.Y.: Edwin Mellen Press, 1999.

Knight, George Wilson. *Shakespeare and Tolstoy*. London: Oxford University Press, 1934.

Knox, I. *The Aesthetic Theories of Kant, Hegel, and Schopenhauer*. New York: Columbia University Press, 1936.

Koberstein, August. *Shakespeare allmähliches Bekanntwerden in Deutschland und Urteile über ihn bis zum Jahr 1773. Vermischte Aufsätze*. Leipzig, 1858.

———. "Shakespeare in Deutschland." *Shakespeare Jahrbuch* 1 (1865): 1–17.

König, Wilhelm, Jr. "Voltaire und Shakespeare." *Shakespeare Jahrbuch* 10 (1875): 259–310.

Kott, Jan. *Shakespeare Our Contemporary*. Translated by Bolesław Taborski. Garden City, N.Y.: Doubleday, 1964.

Lacroix, Albert. *Histoire de l'influence de Shakespeare sur le théâtre français jusqu'à nos jours*. Brussels, 1856.

Lambert, José. "Shakespeare en France au tournant du XVIIIe siècle: Un dossier européen." In *European Shakespeares: Translating Shakespeare in the Romantic Age*, edited by Dirk Delabastita and Lieven D'hulst, 25–44. Amsterdam: John Benjamins, 1993.

Larroumet, G. *Shakespeare et le théâtre français: Études d'histoire et de critique dramatiques*. Paris, 1892.

Ledebur, Ruth Freifrau von. *Shakespeare in Deutschland seit 1945*. Frankfurt am Main: Akademische Verlagsgesellschaft, 1974.

Leek, Robert Henri. "Shakespeare in the Netherlands: A Study of Dutch Translations and Dutch Performances of William Shakespeare's Plays." 2 vols. Ph.D. diss., University of Auckland, New Zealand, 1972.

———. *Shakespeare in Nederland : Kroniek van vier eeuwen Shakespeare in Nederlandse vertalingen en op het Nederlands toneel*. Zutphen: Walburg Pers, 1988.

———. "'Bless Thee, Bottom, Bless Thee! Thou Art Translated!': The Bard and His Dutch Interpreters." In *Something Understood: Studies in Anglo-Dutch Literary Translation*, edited by Bart Westerweel and Theo D'haen, 139–70. Amsterdam: Rodopi, 1990.

Leeuwe, H. H. J. de. "Shakespeare op het Nederlandse toneel." *De Gids* 127 (1964): 324–39.

Leiter, Samuel L. *Shakespeare around the Globe: A Guide to Notable Postwar Revivals*. Westport, Conn.: Greenwood Press, 1986.

Levaillant, M. "Quand Shakespeare à Jersey parle à Victor Hugo." *Revue de Littérature Comparée* 26 (1952): 296–312.

Levin, Yuri D. "Shakespeare and Russian Literature: Nineteenth-Century Attitudes." *Oxford Slavonic Papers* n.s. 22 (1989): 115–32.

———. "Russian Shakespeare Translations in the Romantic Era." In *European*

Shakespeares: Translating Shakespeare in the Romantic Age, edited by Dirk Delabastita and Lieven D'hulst, 75–90. Amsterdam: John Benjamins, 1993.

LeWinter, Oswald, ed. *Shakespeare in Europe*. 1963. Reprint, Harmondsworth, U.K.: Penguin Books, 1970.

Lieblein, Leanore. "Translation and mise en scène: The Example of Contemporary French Shakespeare." In *Foreign Shakespeare: Contemporary Performance*, edited by Dennis Kennedy, 76–92. Cambridge: Cambridge University Press, 1993.

Limon, Jerzy. *Gentlemen of a Company: English Players in Central and Eastern Europe, 1590–1660*. Cambridge: Cambridge University Press, 1985.

———, and Jay L. Halio, eds. *Shakespeare and His Contemporaries: Eastern and Central European Studies*. Newark: University of Delaware Press, 1993.

Lirondelle, André. *Shakespeare en Russie (1748–1840). Étude de littérature comparée*. Paris: Librairie Hachette, 1912.

Loehlin, James N. "'Wish Not a Man From England': *Henry V* Outside the United Kingdom." In his *Henry V*, Shakespeare in Performance Series, 146–69. Manchester: Manchester University Press, 1996.

Lotheissen, F. "Shakespeare in Frankreich." In *Literatur und Gesellschaft in Frankreich zur Zeit der Revolution*. Weimar, 1872.

Lounsbury, Thomas Raynesford. *Shakespeare and Voltaire*. 1902. Reprint, New York: Benjamin Blom, 1968.

Luther, A. "Shakespeare in Rußland." *Shakespeare Jahrbuch* 84–86 (1950): 214–28.

Maanen, W. van. "*Hamlet* in Frankrijk." *De Gids* 127, no. 5 (1965): 384–97.

Magon, Leopold. "Deutschland, Shakespeare und der Norden." *Shakespeare Jahrbuch* 82/83 (1948): 136–53.

Maguin, Jean-Marie. "Shakespeare Studies in France since 1960." In *Shakespeare and France*, edited by Holger Klein and Jean-Marie Maguin, 359–73. Lewiston, N.Y.: Edwin Mellen Press, 1994.

Maley, Willy. "'This Sceptred Isle': Shakespeare and the British Problem." In *Shakespeare and National Culture*, edited by John J. Joughin, 83–108. Manchester: Manchester University Press, 1997.

Maller, Sándor, and Kálmán Ruttkay, eds. *Magyar Shakespeare tükör* [Hungarian Shakespeare Mirror]. Budapest: Gondolat, 1984.

Mamaryk, Irena R. "Woman Scorned: *Antony and Cleopatra* at Moscow's Vakhtangov Theatre." In *Foreign Shakespeare: Contemporary Performance*, edited by Dennis Kennedy, 178–94. Cambridge: Cambridge University Press, 1993.

Marder, Louis. *His Exits and Entrances: The Story of Shakespeare's Reputation*. London: John Murray, 1963.

Mark, Thomas Raymond. "Shakespeare in Hungary: A History of the Translation, Presentation, and Reception of Shakespeare's Dramas in Hungary, 1785–1878." Ph.D. diss., Columbia University, New York, 1955.

Márkus, Zoltán. "'Loyalty to Shakespeare': The Cultural Context of the 1952 *Hamlet*-Production of the Hungarian National Theater." In *Shakespeare and Hungary. Special Theme Section: The Law and Shakespeare*, edited by Holger Klein, Péter Dávidházi, and B. J. Sokol. Shakespeare Yearbook 7. 169–89. Lewiston, N.Y.: Edwin Mellen Press, 1996.

Marrapodi, Michele, A. J. Hoenselaars, Marcello Cappuzzo, and Lino F. Santucci, eds. *Shakespeare's Italy: Functions of Italian Locations in Renaissance Drama*.

Manchester: Manchester University Press, 1993. Rev. ed.: Manchester: Manchester University Press, 1997.

———, and A. J. Hoenselaars, eds. *The Italian World of English Renaissance Drama: Cultural Exchange and Intertextuality*. Newark: Delaware University Press, 1998.

McClure, Derrick. "When *Macbeth* Becomes Scots." In *Ilha do desterro: A Journal of English Language, Literatures in English, and Cultural Studies* (Brazil) 36 (1999): 29–51.

McManaway, James G., ed. *Shakespeare and England*. Review of National Literatures vol. 3, no. 2. Jamaica, N.Y.: St. John's University, 1972.

Meissner, J. *Die englischen Komödianten zur Zeit Shakespeares in Österreich*. Vienna, 1884.

Moltzer, H. E. *Shakespeare's invloed op het nederlandsch tooneel der zeventiende eeuw*. Groningen, 1874.

Monaco, Marion. *Shakespeare on the French Stage in the Eighteenth Century*. Études de littérature étrangère et comparée 70. Paris: Didier, 1974.

Moninger, Markus. *Shakespeare inszeniert: Das westdeutsche Regietheater und die Theatertradition 'des dritten deutschen Klassikers'*. Tübingen: Max Niemeyer, 1996.

Morozov, Michael M. *Shakespeare on the Soviet Stage*. Translated by David Magarshack. London: Soviet News Publications, 1947.

Moutaftchief, I. "Shakespeare and Bulgaria." *Times Literary Supplement*, 18 November 1949, 751.

Nels, S. "Shakespeare and European Culture." *The Theater* (USSR) 4 (1941): 3–15.

Nicoll, Josephine. *Shakespeare in Poland*. London: Oxford University Press, 1923.

Nulli, Siro Attilio. *Shakespeare in Italia*. Milan: Editore della Real Casa, 1918.

Nüssel, Heide. "Rekonstruktion der Shakespeare-Bühne auf dem deutschen Theater." Ph.D. diss., University of Cologne, Cologne, Germany, 1967.

Oechelhäuser, Wilhelm. "Die Würdigung Shakespeares in England und Deutschland." *Shakespeare Jahrbuch* 20 (1885): 54–68.

Oehlmann, Wilhelm. "Shakespeares Wert für unsere nationale Literatur." *Shakespeare Jahrbuch* 5 (1870): 148–53.

Orlovskaya, N. K. "Shakespeare in Georgia." In *Vilyam Shekspir, 1564–1964*. Moscow: Nauka, 1964.

Országh, Lászlo. "Quoting Shakespeare in Hungary." *New Hungarian Quarterly* 5, no. 13 (1964): 90–94.

O'Shea, José Roberto, ed. *Accents Now Known: Shakespeare's Drama in Translation*. Special issue of *Ilha do desterro: A Journal of English Language, Literatures in English and Cultural Studies* (Brazil) 36 (1999).

Ostrovsky, Arkady. "*Twelfth Night* of 1917 and the Moscow Art Theatre." *Ilha do desterro: A Journal of English Language, Literatures in English, and Cultural Studies* (Brazil) 36 (1999): 161–84.

Pancheva, Evgenia. "Nothings, Merchants, Tempests: Trimming Shakespeare for the 1992 Bulgarian Stage." In *Shakespeare in the New Europe*, edited by Michael Hattaway, Boika Sokolova, and Derek Roper, 247–60. Sheffield: Sheffield Academic Press, 1994.

Par, Alfonso. *Representaciones shakespearianas en España.* 2 vols. Madrid and Barcelona: Victoriano Suárez/Biblioteca Balmes, 1936–1940.

———. *Shakespeare en la literatura española.* 2 vols. Madrid and Barcelona: Biblioteca Balmes, 1935.

Parker, R. B. "Dramaturgy in Shakespeare and Brecht." *University of Toronto Quarterly* 32 (1963): 229–46.

Pascal, Roy. *Shakespeare in Germany, 1740–1815.* 1937. Reprint, Folcroft, Pa.: Folcroft Library Editions, 1973.

Pavis, Patrice. "Wilson, Brook, Zadek: An Intercultural Encounter?" In *Foreign Shakespeare: Contemporary Performance*, edited by Dennis Kennedy, 270–89. Cambridge: Cambridge University Press, 1993.

Pellissier, G. "Le Drame shakespearien en France." In *Essais de littérature contemporaine*, 69–109. Paris, 1893.

Pennink, Renetta. *Nederland en Shakespeare: Achttiende eeuw en vroege Romantiek.* The Hague: Martinus Nijhoff, 1936.

Petersohn, Roland. *Heiner Müllers Shakespeare-Rezeption. Texte und Kontexte.* Frankfurt am Main: Peter Lang, 1993.

Pfister, Manfred. "Hamlet und der deutsche Geist: Die Geschichte einer politischen Interpretation." *Deutsche Shakespeare Gesellschaft West, Jahrbuch 1992* (Bochum: Kamp, 1992), 13–38.

———. "Hamlets Made in Germany, East and West." In *Shakespeare in the New Europe*, edited by Michael Hattaway, Boika Sokolova, and Derek Roper, 76–91. Sheffield: Sheffield Academic Press, 1994.

Pokorný, Jaroslav. *Shakespeare in Czechoslovakia.* Prague: Orbis, 1955.

Popović, Vladeta. *Shakespeare in Serbia.* London: Oxford University Press, 1928.

———. "Shakespeare among the South Slavs, especially in Post-War Yugoslavia." *Zbornik Filozofskog Fakulteta* (Belgrade) 2 (1952): 281–91.

Portillo, Rafael, and Manuel J. Gómez-Lara. "Shakespeare in the New Spain: Or, What you Will." In *Shakespeare in the New Europe*, edited by Michael Hattaway, Boika Sokolova, and Derek Roper, 208–28. Sheffield: Sheffield Academic Press, 1994.

Potter, Nicholas. "'Like to a Tenement or a Pelting Farm'—*Richard II* and the Idea of the Nation." In *Shakespeare in the New Europe*, edited by Michael Hattaway, Boika Sokolova, and Derek Roper, 130–47. Sheffield: Sheffield Academic Press, 1994.

Price, Lawrence M. "Shakespeare as Pictured by Voltaire, Goethe, and Oeser." *Germanic Review* 25 (1950): 83–84.

Radulescu, I. Horia. "Les Intermédiares français de Shakespeare en Roumanie." *Revue de Littérature Comparée* 18 (1938): 252–71.

Raleigh, Walter Alexander. *Shakespeare and England.* London: Oxford University Press, 1918.

Ranke, Wolfgang. "Shakespeare Translations for Eighteenth-Century Stage Productions in Germany: Different Versions of *Macbeth*." In *European Shakespeares: Translating Shakespeare in the Romantic Age*, edited by Dirk Delabastita and Lieven D'hulst, 163–82. Amsterdam: John Benjamins, 1993.

Raszewski, Zbigniew. "Against some Part of Poland." *Drama* (Spring 1936): 24–28.

Rauch, H. *Lenz und Shakespeare: Ein Beitrag zur Shakespearomanie der Sturm- und Drangperiode.* Freiburg, 1892.
Reymond, William. *Corneille, Shakespeare et Goethe: Étude sur l'influence anglo-germanique en France au XIXe siècle.* Paris: Klincksieck, 1864.
Rhodes, Neil. "Bridegrooms to the Goddess: Hughes, Heaney and the Elizabethans." In *Shakespeare and Ireland: History, Politics, Culture*, edited by Mark Thornton Burnett and Ramona Wray, 152–72. Houndmills, U.K.: Macmillan, 1997.
Riedel, W. "Über Shakespeares Würdigung in England, Frankreich und Deutschland." *Archiv für das Studium der neueren Sprachen* 48 (1882).
Robertson, J. G. "The Knowledge of Shakespeare on the Continent at the Beginning of the Eighteenth Century." *Modern Language Review* 1 (1905/6): 312–21.
———. "Shakespeare on the Continent." In *Cambridge History of English Literature* 5 (1910): 283–308.
Rose, Francis. "Les Poètes elisabéthains et nous." In *Le Théâtre Elizabéthain*, 311–13. Paris: Les Cahiers du Sud, 1940.
Rothe, Hans. "Shakespeare in französischem und deutschen Gewande bei Polen, Russen und Tschechen." In *Das Shakespeare-Bild in Europa zwischen Aufklärung und Romantik*, edited by Roger Bauer, 262–82. Bern: Peter Lang, 1988.
Rowe, Eleanor. *Hamlet: A Window on Russia.* New York: New York University Press, 1976.
Rudenti, Lucio, ed. *Shakespeare degli Italiani: I testi scespiiriani inspirati da fatti e figure della nostra storia e delle nostra leggenda.* Turin: Società Editrice Torinese, 1950.
Ruppert y Ujaravi, Ricardo. *Shakespeare en España. Traducciones, imitaciones e influencia de las obras de Shakespeare en la literatura española.* Madrid: Tip. de la "Rev. de Arch., Bibl. y Museos," 1920.
Saint-Denis, Michel. "Shakespeare en France et en Angleterre." *Revue théâtrale* 26 (1954): 13–18.
Salingar, L. G. "The Soviet Public and Shakespeare." *Anglo-Soviet Journal* 3 (1942): 228–34.
Samarin, Roman Mikhailovich, and Alexander Nikolyukin, eds. *Shakespeare in the Soviet Union: A Collection of Articles.* Translated into English by Avril Pyman. Moscow: Progress Publishers, 1966.
Sasayama, Takahasi, J. R. Mulryne, and Margaret Shewring, eds. *Shakespeare and the Japanese Stage.* Cambridge: Cambridge University Press, 1998.
Schabert, Ina. "Shakespeares Geschichtsvision in romantischen Brechungen: Die Rezeption der Historien in England, 1800–1825." In *Das Shakespeare-Bild in Europa zwischen Aufklärung und Romantik*, edited by Roger Bauer, 60–76. Bern: Peter Lang, 1988.
Schlebrügge, Johannes von. "Adam Müllers Shakespeare: Ein Verbündeter im romantischen Kampf gegen Napoleon." In *Das Shakespeare-Bild in Europa zwischen Aufklärung und Romantik*, edited by Roger Bauer, 226–40. Bern: Peter Lang, 1988.
Schmidt, Alexander. *Voltaires Verdienste um die Einführung Shakespeares in Frankreich.* Königsberg, 1864.
Schneider, Lina. "Shakespeare in den Niederlanden." *Shakespeare Jahrbuch* 26 (1891): 26–42.

Schoneveld, Cees W. "The First Dutch Translation of (a Selection of) Shakespeare's Works (1778–1782)." *Dutch Crossing* 28 (1986): 38–52.

———. "Transmitting the Bard to the Dutch: Dr L. A. J. Burgersdijk's Principles of Translation and His Role in the Reception of Shakespeare in the Netherlands to 1900." In *Something Understood: Studies in Anglo-Dutch Literary Translation*, edited by Bart Westerweel and Theo D'haen, 249–69. Amsterdam: Rodopi, 1990.

Schrickx, Willem. *Foreign Envoys and Travelling Players in the Age of Shakespeare and Jonson*. Wetteren, Belgium: Universa, 1986.

Schröder, Rudolf Alexander. "Shakespeare als Dichter des Abendlandes." *Theater-Almanach* 2 (1947): 220–33.

Schulze, Brigitte. "Shakespeare's Way into the West Slavic Literatures and Cultures." In *European Shakespeares: Translating Shakespeare in the Romantic Age*, edited by Dirk Delabastita and Lieven D'hulst, 55–74. Amsterdam: John Benjamins, 1993.

———. "The Time Is out of Joint: The Reception of Shakespeare's *Hamlet* in Polish Plays." *New Comparison* 8 (1989): 99–113.

Schütt, Maria. "Hat Calderón Shakespeare gekannt? Die Quellen von Calderóns *La Cisma de Inglaterra*." *Shakespeare Jahrbuch* 61 (1925): 94–107.

Scolnicov, Hanna, and Peter Holland, eds. *The Play out of Context: Transferring Plays from Culture to Culture*. Cambridge: Cambridge University Press, 1989.

Seaton, Ethel. *Literary Relations of England and Scandinavia in the Seventeenth Century*. Oxford: Clarendon Press, 1935.

Sebestyén, Ch. "Cult of Shakespeare in Hungary." *The Hungarian Quarterly* (Budapest) 3 (1937): 154–63.

"Shakespeare in Armenia." *American Review on the Soviet Union* 6 (1945): 59–60.

Shakespeare in Deutschland 1864–1964. Bochum, Germany: Deutsche Shakespeare-Gesellschaft West, 1964.

Shakespeare in France. Special issue of *Yale French Studies* 33 (1964).

Sheen, Erica. "The Pannonians and the Dalmatians: Reading for a European History in *Cymbeline*." In *Shakespeare in the New Europe*, edited by Michael Hattaway, Boika Sokolova, and Derek Roper, 310–20. Sheffield: Sheffield Academic Press, 1994.

Shewring, Margaret. "The Politics and Aesthetics of Theatrical Languages: *Richard II* on the European Stage." In her *King Richard II*, Shakespeare in Performance, 154–79. Manchester: Manchester University Press, 1996.

Shurbanov, Alexander, and Boika Sokolova. "From the Unlove of *Romeo and Juliet* to *Hamlet* without the Prince: A Shakespearean Mirror Held up to the Fortunes of New Bulgaria." In *Shakespeare in the New Europe*, edited by Michael Hattaway, Boika Sokolova, and Derek Roper, 24–53. Sheffield: Sheffield Academic Press, 1994.

———. *Painting Shakespeare Red: An East-European Appropriation*. Newark: University of Delaware Press, 2001.

Siemon, James. "'Perplex'd beyond Self-Explication': *Cymbeline* and Early Modern / Postmodern Europe." In *Shakespeare in the New Europe*, edited by Michael Hattaway, Boika Sokolova, and Derek Roper, 294–309. Sheffield: Sheffield Academic Press, 1994.

Simmons, Ernest J. "Catherine the Great and Shakespeare." *Publications of the Modern Language Association* 47 (1932): 790–806.

———. "The Early History of Shakespeare in Russia." In *English Literature and Culture in Russia (1553–1840)*, 204–36. Cambridge: Harvard University Press, 1935.

Sito, Jerzy. "Shakespeare, Poland's National Poet." *Delos* 3 (1970): 147–58.

Slivnik, Francka. *Shakespeare v gledaliscih srednje Evrope med obema vojnama 1918–1938* [Shakespeare in the theatres of Central Europe between the two wars, 1918–1938]. Ljubljana, Slovenia: Slovenski gledaliski in filmski muzej, 1994.

Smidt, Kristian. "The Discovery of Shakespeare in Scandinavia." In *European Shakespeares: Translating Shakespeare in the Romantic Age*, edited by Dirk Delabastita and Lieven D'hulst, 91–103. Amsterdam: John Benjamins, 1993.

Solt, Andor. *Shakespeare in Hungarian Criticism during the Enlightenment and Romanticism.* Acta Litteraria: Academiae Scientiarum Hungaricae 7, no. 1–2. Budapest: Akadémai Kiadó, 1965.

Sorelius, Gunnar. "The Rise of Shakespeare 'Idolatry' in Sweden." In *Literature and Its Cults: An Anthropological Approach/Littérature et ses cultes: Approche anthropologique*, edited by Péter Dávidházi and Judit Karafíath, 67–80. Budapest: Argumentum, 1994.

———, and Michael Srigley, eds. *Cultural Exchange between European Nations during the Renaissance.* Acta Universitatis Upsaliensis. Studia Anglistica Upsaliensia 86. Uppsala, Sweden: n.p., 1994.

Sorge, Thomas. "Buridan's Ass between Two Performances of *A Midsummer Night's Dream*, or Bottom *telos* in the GDR and After." In *Shakespeare in the New Europe*, edited by Michael Hattaway, Boika Sokolova, and Derek Roper, 54–74. Sheffield: Sheffield Academic Press, 1994.

———. "Tradition and Modernization: Some Thoughts on Shakespeare Criticism in the New Europe." In *Shakespeare in the New Europe*, edited by Michael Hattaway, Boika Sokolova, and Derek Roper, 321–35. Sheffield: Sheffield Academic Press, 1994.

Sorgen, W. G. F. A. *De Tooneelspeelkunst te Utrecht.* The Hague, 1885.

Spassky, Y. "Shakespeare without End." *Theatre* (USSR) 4 (1939): 13–32.

Sprung, Guy. *Hot Ice: Shakespeare in Moscow—A Director's Diary.* Winnipeg: Blizzard Publishing, 1991.

Stadler, Ernst. *Wielands Shakespeare.* Straßburg: Karl J. Trübner, 1910.

Stahl, Ernst L. *Shakespeare und das deutsche Theater.* Stuttgart: Kohlhammer, 1947.

———. "Shakespeare heute in Europa." *Die Quelle* 2, no. 4 (1948): 11–18.

Stapfer, Paul. *Molière et Shakespeare.* Paris, 1887.

Steck, Paul. *Schiller und Shakespeare.* Frankfurt am Main: Peter Lang, 1977.

Stříbrný, Zdeněk. *Shakespeare and Eastern Europe.* Oxford: Oxford University Press, 2000.

Swart, Jacobus. "Shakespeare in vertaling." In *Rondom Shakespeare*, by A. G. H. Bachrach, J. Swart, and F. W. S. van Tienen, 75–103. Zeist, The Netherlands: Uitgeversmaatschappij W. de Haan, 1964.

———. "Shakespeare in Dutch Translation." *Delta* 7, no. 2 (1964): 31–40.

Symington, Rodney T. K. *Brecht und Shakespeare*. Bonn: Bouvier, 1970.

Szaffkó, Péter. "In Search of the 'Real' Shakespeare: Sándor Hevesi's Role in the Development of Hungarian Theatre Arts." In *Shakespeare and Hungary. Special Theme Section: The Law and Shakespeare*, edited by Holger Klein, Péter Dávidházi, and B. J. Sokol. Shakespeare Yearbook 7. 111–29. Lewiston, N.Y.: Edwin Mellen Press, 1996.

Szenczi, Miklós. *Shakespeare in Recent Soviet Criticism*. Debrecen, Hungary: n.p., 1965.

Szilassy, Zoltán. "Some New Trends and Practices in Hungarian Shakespeare Studies." In *Shakespeare and Hungary. Special Theme Section: The Law and Shakespeare*, edited by Holger Klein, Péter Dávidházi, and B. J. Sokol. Shakespeare Yearbook 7. 235–48. Lewiston, N.Y.: Edwin Mellen Press, 1996.

Taylor, Gary. *Reinventing Shakespeare: A Cultural History from the Restoration to the Present*. London: Hogarth Press, 1990.

Thienen, F. W. S. "Shakespeare op het toneel." In *Rondom Shakespeare*, by A. G. H. Bachrach, J. Swart, and F. W. S. van Tienen, 104–76. Zeist, The Netherlands: Uitgeversmaatschappij W. de Haan, 1964.

Thimm, F. *Shakespeariana from 1564 to 1864*. 2nd ed. London, 1872.

Thomas, Henry. *Shakespeare and Spain*. The Taylorian Lecture. Oxford: Clarendon Press, 1922. Reprint, Folcroft, Pa.: Folcroft Library Editions, 1974.

———. "Shakespeare in Spain." *Proceedings of the British Academy* 35 (1949): 3–24.

Thornton Burnett, Mark, and Ramona Wray, eds. *Shakespeare and Ireland: History, Politics, Culture*. Houndmills, U.K.: Macmillan, 1997.

Tieghem, Paul van. *Le Préromantisme: Études d'histoire littéraire européenne (La Découverte de Shakespeare sur le Continent)*. Paris: Sfelt, 1947.

Tittmann, J. *Die Schauspiele der englischen Komödianten in Deutschland*. Leipzig, 1880.

Turnbull, H. G. Dalway. *Shakespeare and Ibsen*. Oxford: Blackwell, 1926. Reprint, New York: Haskell House, 1971.

Ulrici, Hermann. "Goethe und Schiller in ihrem Verhältnis zu Shakespeare." In *Abhandlungen zur Kunstgeschichte als angewandter Ästhetik*. Leipzig, 1876.

———. *Über Shakespeares dramatische Kunst und sein Verhältnis zu Calderon und Goethe*. Halle, 1839.

Unflad, L. *Die Shakespeare-Literatur in Deutschland*. Munich, 1880.

Verdaguer, Isabel. "Shakespeare Translations in Spain." *Ilha do desterro: A Journal of English Language, Literatures in English, and Cultural Studies* (Brazil) 36 (1999): 87–110.

Vetter, Theodor. "Shakespeare und die deutsche Schweiz." *Shakespeare Jahrbuch* 48 (1912): 21–36.

Vielhaber, Christiane. "Shakespeare auf dem Theater Westdeutschlands, 1945–1975." Ph.D. diss., University of Cologne, Cologne, Germany, 1977.

Villemain, A. F. *Essai biographique et littéraire sur Shakespeare*. Paris, 1838.

Vočadlo, Otakar. "Shakespeare and Bohemia." *Shakespeare Survey* 9 (1956): 101–10.

Voigt, Felix A., and Walter A. Reichert. *Hauptmann and Shakespeare: Ein Beitrag zur Geschichte des Fortlebens Shakespeares in Deutschland*. Breslau, Germany:

Maruschke & Berendt, 1938. Rev. ed. Goslar, Germany: Deutsche Volksbücherei, 1947.
Vos, Jozef de. "Shakespeare in Flanders: A Study of the Theatrical, Critical and Literary Reception of Shakespeare's Work." Ph.D. diss., University of Ghent, Ghent, Belgium, 1976.
———. "Shakespeare en het culturele leven in Zuid-Nederland." *Handelingen van de Koninklijke Zuidnederlandse Maatschappij voor Taal- en Letterkunde en Geschiedenis* 32 (1978): 61–96; and 33 (1979): 131–89.
Vuraldi, Mert. *Shakespeare in der Türkei*. Frankfurt am Main: Peter Lang, 1979.
Wagner, Wilhelm. "Shakespeare in Griechenland." *Shakespeare Jahrbuch* 12 (1877): 33–56.
Weber Henking, Irene, ed. *Translating/traduire/tradurre Shakespeare*. Lausanne, Switzerland: Centre de Traduction Littéraire de Lausanne, 2001.
Weimann, Robert. "A Divided Heritage: Conflicting Appropriations of Shakespeare in (East) Germany." In *Shakespeare and National Culture*, edited by John J. Joughin, 173–205. Manchester: Manchester University Press, 1997.
Wells, Robin Headlam. "'The Question of these Wars': *Hamlet* in the New Europe." In *Shakespeare in the New Europe*, edited by Michael Hattaway, Boika Sokolova, and Derek Roper, 92–109. Sheffield: Sheffield Academic Press, 1994.
"William Shakespeare und G. B. Shaw in Polen." *Kulturprobleme des Neuen Polen* (Berlin) 4 (1952): 3–6.
Williams, Simon. *Shakespeare on the German Stage. Vol. 1: 1586–1914*. Cambridge: Cambridge University Press, 1989.
Wilson, Charles. *Holland and Britain*. London: William Collins' Sons & Co., 1946.
Wilson, Richard. "NATO's Pharmacy: Shakespeare by Prescription." In *Shakespeare and National Culture*, edited by John J. Joughin, 58–80. Manchester: Manchester University Press, 1997.
Worp, J. A. *Engelsche Tooneelspelers op het vasteland in de 16de en 17de eeuw*. Nederlandsch Museum, 1886.
Würtenberg, Gustav, ed. *Shakespeare in Deutschland*. Bielefeld, Germany: Verlag von Velhagen & Klasing, 1942.
Wurzbach, Wolfgang von. "Shakespeares *Heinrich VIII* und Calderóns *La Cisma de Inglaterra*." *Shakespeare Jahrbuch* 32 (1896): 190–211.
Yalman, Tunç. *Shakespeare in Atatürk's Turkey*. New York: Office of the Ambassador for Cultural Affairs, Republic of Turkey, 1981.
Yoland, A. "The Cult of Shakespeare in Hungary." *The Hungarian Quarterly* (Budapest) 5 (1938): 285–96.
Zacharias, Gerhard P. "Macbeth in uns." *Das neue Forum* (Darmstadt) 5 (1955/56): 113–14.
Zanco, Aurelio. *Shakespeare in Russia*. Bologna: N. Zanichelli, 1938.
———. *Shakespeare in Russia e altri saggi*. Turin: Editore Gheroni, 1945.
Zaryan, Rouben V. *Shakespeare and the Armenians*. Translated by Haig Voskerchian. Yerevan: Academy of Sciences Press, 1969.

Notes on Contributors

DIRK DELABASTITA is Professor of English literature and literary theory at the University of Namur (Belgium). He is the author of *There's a Double Tongue* (1993) and editor of *Wordplay and Translation* (1996) and *Traductio: Essays on Punning and Translation* (1997). Delabastita is co-editor of *European Shakespeares* (with Lieven D'hulst, 1993), *Vertalen historisch bezien* (with Theo Hermans, 1995), and *Under Construction: Links for the Site of Literary Theory* (with Dirk de Geest, Ortwin de Graef, and others, 2000).

BALZ ENGLER is Professor of English at Basel University (Switzerland). He has published a critical edition of *Othello* (1976), and written books on Shakespeare translation (*Rudolf Alexander Schröders Übersetzungen von Shakespeares Dramen*, 1974), the relationship between poetic texts and their modes of communicating (*Reading and Listening: The Modes of Communicating Poetry and their Influence on the Texts*, 1982), and literature as performance (*Poetry and Community*, 1990). He is the editor of three collections of essays: *Das Festspiel* (with Georg Kreis, 1988), *Writing & Culture* (1992), and *European English Studies* (with Renate Haas, 2000).

MARTA GIBIŃSKA is Professor of English Literature at the Jagiellonian University in Cracow (Poland), and President of the Polish Shakespeare Association. She has published on Shakespeare's language, Polish translations of Shakespeare, and the reception of Shakespeare in Poland. Her most recent book is *Polish Poets Read Shakespeare: A Refashioning of the Tradition* (2000).

GRAHAM KEITH GREGOR is Lecturer in English and Irish Literature at the University of Murcia, Spain. He is co-editor of *Teatro Clásico en Traducción*, and the author of numerous articles on Shakespeare and Renaissance culture. Is currently preparing a volume on the history of Shakespeare on the Spanish stage.

MARTIN HILSKÝ is Professor of English Literature at Charles University, Prague. His publications include a book on contemporary British fiction (1992), a book-length study of the modernists (1995), numerous articles, studies and essays on both British and American literature and translations of English fiction, poetry and drama. He has so far translated twenty-one plays by William Shakespeare. All his translations have been staged. He is currently general editor for two editions of Shakespeare in Czech. His dual language editions with book-length introductory studies and notes in English and Czech include *A Midsummer Night's Dream* (1996), *The Sonnets* (1997), *The Merchant of Venice* (1998) and *Hamlet* (2001). His Czech edition of Shakespeare's plays and poems should be finished by 2008 (twelve volumes have been published so far). He is a recipient of several literary awards and an honorary M.B.E.

TON HOENSELAARS is Associate Professor in the English Department of Utrecht University. He is the author of *Images of Englishmen and Foreigners in the Drama of Shakespeare and His Contemporaries* (1992). He has edited or co-edited *Shakespeare's Italy* (1993, revised edition 1997), *Denken over Dichten* (1993), *Reclamations of Shakespeare* (1994), *The Italian World of English Renaissance Drama* (1997),*Vreemd Volk* (1997), *Jeanne d'Arc entre les nations* (1997), *English Literature and the Other Languages* (1999), *The Author as Character* (1999), and *Traveling Theory* (1999). He has also written on Emily Brontë, James Joyce, T. E. Lawrence, and Joseph Conrad. He is the founding Chairman of the Shakespeare Society of the Low Countries, and managing editor of its journal, *Folio*. Currently writing a monograph on Shakespeare and Richard Wagner.

DENNIS KENNEDY is Samuel Beckett Professor of Drama and head of the School of Drama in Trinity College Dublin. His books include *Granville Barker and the Dream of Theatre* (1985), *Plays by Harley Granville Barker* (1987), *Looking at Shakespeare: A Visual History of Twentieth-century Performance* (1993; second edition, 2001), and *Foreign Shakespeare* (1993). He was an advisory editor for *The Oxford Companion to Shakespeare* (2001) and is the general editor of *The Oxford Encyclopedia of Theatre and Performance* (due in 2003). He is currently writing a book on *Shakespeare and the Director* and researching another on the condition of the spectator in theater, film, and sports.

FILOMENA MESQUITA is an assistant professor of English at the University of Coimbra (Portugal), and a researcher at the Centro de Estudos de Teatro of the University of Lisbon. She has published essays on Shakespeare and contemporary British women's writing.

MANFRED PFISTER is Professor of English at the Freie Universität Berlin (Germany). His main areas of research are the early modern period, the fin de siècle, and modern and contemporary literature. In terms of genre, his main interests are the theatre, poetry, and travel writing. He is co-editor of the *Jahrbuch der Deutschen Shakespeare-Gesellschaft* and *Poetica*, and author of *The Theory and Analysis of Drama* (1988). Recent books include *"The Fatal Gift of Beauty": The Italies of British Travellers* (1996), *Venetian Views, Venetian Blinds: English Fantasies of Venice* (1999), *Laurence Sterne* (2001), and *A History of Laughter* (2002).

RAFAEL PORTILLO is Professor of English at the Department of English Literature, University of Seville (Spain). He writes on theater and drama, and is also an amateur actor and director. He is co-author (with J. Casado) of an *English-Spanish, Spanish-English Dictionary of Theatre Terms* (1987), and of several books on Medieval and Renaissance English drama.

A. LUIS PUJANTE is Professor of English at the University of Murcia (Spain). He is the author of *Realismo y ciencia-ficción en la obra de John Wyndham* (1980) and *El manuscrito shakespeariano de Manuel Herrera Bustamante* (2001), and has edited, with Keith Gregor, *Teatro clásico en traducción* (1996) as well as *More European Shakespeares* (2001). He has published annotated Spanish translations of eighteen of Shakespeare's plays to date, and of Middleton's *A Game at Chess*. He has published critical essays on English Renaissance drama, and on literary translation. He is the head of a research project on Shakespeare's presence in Spain in the framework of European culture.

MERCEDES SALVADOR teaches English Literature at the University of Seville (Spain). She has published several articles on the Exeter Riddles and Shakespeare in Spanish translations. She is currently engaged in a research project on the reception of Shakespeare in the Iberian peninsula, and concentrates on Spanish and Portuguese parodies of the plays.

ISABELLE SCHWARTZ-GASTINE is Associate Professor of English Literature and Renaissance Drama at the University of Caen, Basse-Normandy (France). She is an associate researcher at the French

Centre National de Recherche Scientifique (CNRS). She is also a specialist on Renaissance theater in France and has recently completed a study of the "rude mechanicals" to be published in a volume on Amateur Theatre by the CNRS.

BOIKA SOKOLOVA has for many years taught Shakespeare and English Renaissance literature at the University of Sofia (Bulgaria), and is currently working at Royal Holloway, University of London. She has published many articles on Shakespeare and other early modern writers. She is the author of *Shakespeare's Romances as Interrogative Texts* (1992) and co-author (with Alexander Shurbanov) of *Painting Shakespeare Red: An East-European Appropriation* (UDP, 2001). Sokolova is also co-editor (with Derek Roper and Michael Hattaway) of *Shakespeare in the New Europe* (1994) and (with Evgenia Pancheva) of *Renaissance Refractions* (2001).

JOZEF DE VOS is Professor of English Literature and Theatre History at Ghent University (Belgium). He is vice-president of the Shakespeare Society of the Low Countries and editor of the Ghent-based theater journal *Documenta*. His publications include work on the reception of Shakespeare in the Low Countries and articles on modern English drama and on Shakespeare in performance in *Theatre Research International, Shakespeare Jahrbuch, Shakespeare Quarterly* and *Folio (Shakespeare Society of the Low Countries)*.

STANLEY WELLS is Emeritus Professor and Director of the Shakespeare Institute, University of Birmingham. He is general editor of the Oxford Shakespeare, editor of *The Cambridge Companion to Shakespeare Studies* (1986), co-author of *William Shakespeare: A Textual Companion* (1987), and author of books including *Shakespeare: A Dramatic Life* (1995) and *Shakespeare: For All Time* (2002).

G. D. WHITE is Senior Lecturer in Drama and Theatre Studies at Roehampton (University of Surrey, London). His research interests include postwar British drama and culture, radio drama, fascism and performance, and situationist theory and performance. He has also published on the theater of the English counterculture, and written for the stage, television, and radio, including an adaptation of Rex Warner's *The Aerodrome* for BBC Radio (2001).

SYLVIA ZYSSET is writing her doctoral dissertation at the University of Basel (Switzerland), a bilingual edition of *The Two Gentlemen of Verona* for the "English-Deutsche Studienausgabe der Dramen Shakespeares." As a founding member of the Sh:in:E (or Shakespeare in Europe) project (based at the University of Basel), she also conducts research in the fields of intercultural Shakespeare performance and reception, present-day Swiss Shakespeare production, and Shakespeare in Swiss-German dialects.

Index

Abuladze, Tengiz, 85–86
Addison, Joseph, 55
Adieux de Roméo et Juliette, Les (Eugène Delacroix, 227
Adventures in Dramatic Appreciation (A. K. Chesterton), 90
Age of Extremes (Eric Hobsbawm), 178 n. 9
All Quiet on the Western Front (Erich Maria Remarque), 92
Alternative Shakespeares (ed. John Drakakis), 127
Alternative Shakespeares 2 (ed. Terence Hawkes), 127
Amants de Vérone, Les (André Cayatte), 236
Amazing Monument (ed. Ivor Brown and George Fearon), 31
Amleto (Ermete Zacconi), 182
An Essay on Shakespeare's Sonnets (Stephen Booth), 72
Antoine, André, 231
Antony and Cleopatra (William Shakespeare), 74, 183, 228, 231, 232, 233, 237, 238
"Appel à toutes les nations de l'Europe" (Voltaire), 32
Appropriating Shakespeare (Brian Vickers), 36 n. 10
Ariost. Shakespeare. Corneille (Benedetto Croce), 86 n. 8
Aristotle (384–322 B.C.), 223
Arnold, Matthew, 44
Arouet, François-Marie. *See* Voltaire
Art of Shakespeare's Sonnets, The (Helen Vendler), 86 n. 5
Artaud, Antonin, 233, 236
Arte of Rhetoric, The (Thomas Wilson), 135
As You Like It (William Shakespeare), 165

Bab, Julius, 73
Bachmann, Stefan, 23, 196–208
Baker, David, 90, 92, 96
Bakhtin, Mikhail, 217
Balkan Sonnets (John Fuller), 108
Barrault, Jean-Louis, 232
Barthes, Roland, 44
Bate, Jonathan, 16, 18, 49
Bauer, Roger, 29
Béatrice et Bénédict (Hector Berlioz), 226
Beckett, Samuel, 175
Belén, Ana, 191, 192
Benoit, Jean-Louis, 233
Berlioz, Hector, 226
Bernhardt, Sarah, 188, 229–30
Beyer, Karin, 34
Beyle, Henri. *See* Stendhal
Biermann, Wolf, 79, 81–82
Bing, Rudolf, 164
Bisbetica domata, La. See *Taming of the Shrew, The*
Bloom, Harold, 33
Boccaccio, Giovanni, 9
Bodmer, Johann Jakob, 27, 29
Boguslawski, Wojciech, 20, 57, 61–63, 65, 66
Boileau, Nicolas, 68
Bonnefoy, Yves, 234, 238
Booth, Stephen, 72
Bordalo, Luís Maria, 155
Bordalo Pinheiro, Rafael. *See* Pinheiro, Rafael Bordalo
Borges, Jorge Luis, 22
Bourek, Zlatko, 191
Bradley, A. C., 33
Bradley, Omar, 167
Bragança, D. Luís de, 8, 22, 145–54
Branco, Camilo Castelo, 155
Braun, Volker, 79
Braunschweig, Stéphane, 235, 238

265

Brave Enterprise (A. K. Chesterton), 97 n. 18
Bravías, Las (Ruperto Chapí), 182
Brecht, Bertolt, 102, 104, 106, 107, 169–70, 171, 172, 176
Brezhnev, Leonid, 77
Briefe über Merkwürdigkeiten der Literatur (Heinrich Wilhelm Gerstenberg), 59
Bristol, Michael, 18, 168
Brook, Peter, 175–76, 236, 238
Brooks, Cleanth, 168
Brown, Ivor, 31
Buero Vallejo, Antonio, 189
Bulbena i Tosell, Antoni, 183
Burmann, Sigfrido, 188
Burns, Robert, 77, 78
Burt, Richard, 16
Bykowski, Ignacy, 58

Cacodémon-Roi (Bernard Chartreux), 237
Calderón de la Barca, Pedro, 50, 64
Calvario, Philippe, 238
Calle, Teodoro de la, 181
Calvo, Ricardo, 183–84, 192
Camões, Luís de, 149
Campoy, Ana María, 186
Camus, Albert, 164
Carnerero, José María, 45, 181
Carraro, Tino, 172
Carré, Jérôme, 225
Carreras, Luis, 46
Carrière, Jean-Claude, 236, 238
Castelo Branco, Camilo. *See* Branco, Camilo Castelo
Castorf, Frank, 197
Cayatte, André, 236
Ceaucescu, Elena, 83
Celenio, Inarco. *See* Fernández de Moratín, Leandro
Cernescu, Dinu, 21, 106
Cesare, Il (Antonio Conti), 27
Chambers, E. K., 44
Chapí, Ruperto, 182
Chartreux, Bernard, 237
Chaucer, Geoffrey, 168
Chéreau, Patrice, 23, 191, 234, 238
Chesterton, A. K., 21, 89–96
Christ and Nietzsche (G. Wilson Knight), 93

Churchill, Sir Winston, 98, 101
Cixous, Hélène, 235
Claus, Hugo, 83
Cléopâtre (Victorien Sardou), 229
Closas, Alberto, 191
Coello, Carlos, 183
Cold War Theatre (John Elsom), 178 n. 29
Coleridge, Samuel Taylor, 61
Colom, Carolina, 190
"Comin thro' the Rye, Poor Body" (Robert Burns), 78
Conti, Antonio, 27, 29
Copeau, Jacques, 232, 238
Coriolanus (William Shakespeare), 73, 171, 172, 211, 228, 231, 232, 233, 235
"Coriolanus" in Europe (David Daniell), 31
Corneille, Pierre, 29, 58
Craig, Hardin, 168
Croce, Benedetto, 73
Cruz, Ramón de la, 180
Current Shakespeare (ed. John Drakakis), 129
Custodio, Álvaro, 190
Cymbeline (William Shakespeare), 238
Czartoryska, Isabella, 57
Czartoryski, Prince, 57

D'hulst, Lieven, 15, 29
Dalí, Salvador, 165
Daniel, Leon, 105
Daniell, David, 31
Dante Alighieri, 30
Dasté, Jean, 233
Davenant, Sir William, 56
Dávidházi, Péter, 15, 18, 32
Decorte, Jan, 211
Delabastita, Dirk, 8, 15, 21, 29
Delacroix, Eugène, 227, 237, 238
Delporte, W. and Y., 237
Déprats, Jean-Michel, 238
Derrida, Jacques, 43
Desarthes, Gérard, 234
Desdémone et Emilia (Eugène Delacroix), 227
Desire and Anxiety (Valerie Traub), 222 n. 12
Després, Suzanne, 230

Deutsche Shakespeare-Rezeption seit 1945 (Ruth von Ledebur), 37n. 23
De Vos, Jozef, 23
Diario Mercantil de Cádiz, 45
Dickens, Charles, 44
Dillon, Arthur, 230
Discurso sobre Shakespeare y Calderón (J. F. Muntadas), 46
Dobson, Michael, 18
Doma de la bravía, La. See *Taming of the Shrew, The*
Dorn, Dieter, 202
Dos Hermanas, Marqués de, 149, 151
Drakakis, John, 127n. 17, 129
Drama nuevo, Un (Manuel Tamayo y Baus), 20, 47–50
Dresen, Adolf, 21, 103
Dubos, Jean Baptiste, 57
Ducis, Jean-François, 9, 23, 45, 54, 61, 63, 180, 181, 183, 185, 225
Dullin, Charles, 232, 234
Dumas, Alexandre, père, 227
Duncan-Jones, Katherine, 73
Dürrenmatt, Friedrich, 198
Duval, Alexandre, 44–45, 182, 226
Duval, Georges, 230

Edwaar the King (Tom Lanoye), 212, 215
Edward III (William Shakespeare), 228
Eisenstadt, Alfred, 207
Eisler, Hanns, 77, 78
Eliot, T. S., 167
Elsom, John, 174
Emmanuel, Giovanni, 182
Empson, William, 124
Encomium matrimonii (Desiderius Erasmus), 135
Encounter, 173
Endgame (Samuel Beckett), 175
Engel, Wolfgang, 80
Engler, Balz, 9, 19
En verlos ons van het kwade (Tom Lanoye), 212, 219
Epistle to Persuade a Young Gentleman. See *Encomium matrimonii*
Erasmus, Desiderius, 135
Erckenbrecht, Ulrich, 74, 77, 78
Espejo, José, 180
Espert, Nuria, 188, 192, 193

Essay on Shakespeare's Sonnets, An (Stephen Booth), 72
Essai sur l'histoire des sciences, des belles lettres et des arts (Félix Juvenel de Carlencas), 57
Esslin, Martin, 43
Esther (Jean Racine), 224
European Journal of English Studies, 129
European Shakespeares (ed. Dirk Delabastita and Lieven D'hulst), 15, 29, 150
Ewbank, Inga-Stina, 116, 150
Exile (Lion Feuchtwanger), 75–76

Farré, Maurici, 190
Fearon, George, 31
Fernández de Moratín, Leandro, 46, 180–81, 183, 184
Feuchtwanger, Lion, 75–76
Field of Drama, The (Martin Esslin), 43
Fierecilla domada, La. See *Taming of the Shrew, The*
Fischer, Joschka, 203
Fischer-Lichte, Erica, 204–5
"For a' that and a' that" (Robert Burns), 77
Foreign Shakespeare (ed. Dennis Kennedy), 17, 19, 31
Franco, Francisco, 20, 82
Freiligrath, Ferdinand, 77
Freud, Sigmund, 218
Frisch, Max, 198
Fujita, Minoru, 19
Fuller, John, 108

García de Villalta, José, 181
García, Ignacio, 190
García-Valdés, Ariel, 234
Garran, Gabriel, 233
Garrick, David, 25, 56
Gazeta Warszawska, 65
Gedichten, 1948–1993 (Hugo Claus), 88n. 41
Gémier, Firmin, 231
Genèse du mythe shakepearien, La. (Michèle Willems), 31
Genesis, 137
George, Stefan, 73, 76
Gerstenberg, Heinrich Wilhelm von, 59

268   INDEX

Geschichte der Shakespeare-Rezeption, Die (Klaus Peter Steiger), 29, 32
Gezelle, Guido, 220
Gibinska, Marta, 20
Gide, André, 232
Giovanni, Ser, 149
Gloucester Time (Matthias Langhoff), 234
Godard, Jean-Luc, 235
Goebbels, Joseph, 90, 203
Goethe, Johann Wolfgang von, 20, 60–61, 68, 100, 168
Gómez, José Luis, 191, 192
González Llana, Félix, 183
González Ruiz, Nicolás, 188
Gorbachev, Mikhail, 85
Got, Jerzy, 62
Gounod, Charles, 226
Grady, Hugh, 168
Graèan, Giga, 70
Granville-Barker, Harley, 33, 232
Greene, Robert, 47
Greg, W. W., 33
Gregor, Joseph, 74
Gregor, Keith, 20
Griffin, Roger, 93, 95
Groth, Ernst, 73
Grotowski, Jerzy, 21, 102
Grynäus, Simon, 26
Guerra, Ángel. *See* Soler, Father Gaietá
Guillermo Shakespeare (Enrique Zumel), 20, 46–47
Guizot, François, 149, 228
Gundolf, Friedrich, 73, 76
Günther, Matthias, 198, 200, 205
Gut Kirschenessen. DDR—ça ira!, 81

Habermas, Jürgen, 177
Habicht, Werner, 15
Halffter, Cristóbal, 189
Hall, Peter, 172
Hamburger, Maik, 21, 103, 171
Hamburgische Dramaturgie (Gotthold Ephraim Lessing), 58
Hamlet (ed. and trans. A. Luis Pujante), 195 n. 46
Hamlet (trans. Álvaro Custodio), 195 n. 42
Hamlet (trans. Ángel Guerra [Gaietá Soler]), 183
Hamlet (trans. Holger Klein), 132 n. 5
Hamlet (trans. José María Pemán), 194 n. 31
Hamlet (trans. Leandro Fernández de Moratín), 180
Hamlet (trans. Luis López-Ballesteros and Félix González Llana), 183–84
Hamlet (trans. Vicente Molina Foix), 195 n. 45
Hamlet (William Shakespeare), 21, 22–23, 35, 45, 46, 59, 62–65, 73, 101–7, 119–21, 145, 147, 154, 169, 171, 180–83, 224, 225, 228, 230, 233–38
Hamlet, Princep de Dinamarca (Antoni Bulbena i Tosell), 183
Hamleto, Rey de Dinamarca (Ramón de la Cruz), 180
Hattaway, Michael, 16, 29, 213
Hawkes, Terence, 16, 128, 129
Heilman, Robert, 168
Hendrik de Vijfden (Tom Lanoye), 212, 218
Hendrik Vier (Tom Lanoye), 212, 214, 220
Henry IV (William Shakespeare), 171, 218, 219, 235
Henry V (William Shakespeare), 84, 212, 219, 233
Henry VI (William Shakespeare), 212, 213, 214, 215, 219, 220
Henry VIII (William Shakespeare), 233
Hermans, Theo, 15
Hermlin, Stephan, 79, 81
Heufeld, Franz, 62
Hijos de Eduardo, Los. See *Richard III*
Hilský, Martin, 7, 8, 21
Histoire de l'influence de Shakspeare (Albert Lacroix), 125
History of Shakespeare Criticism, A (Augustus Ralli), 28
Hitler, Adolf, 74, 75, 77
Hobsbawm, Eric J., 166
Hobson, Harold, 165
Hodek, Břetislav, 134
Hodgdon, Barbara, 31
Hodler, Ferdinand, 201
Hoenselaars, Ton, 7
Holland, Peter, 16
Homar, Lluís, 192
Homer (ca. 800 B.C.), 9, 30
Hortmann, Wilhelm, 18, 31, 169, 202
Howard, Henry, Earl of Surrey, 136

Hron, Zdeněk, 134
Hübner, Hans, 79
Hugo, François-Victor, 149, 228
Hugo, Victor, 229

Ideology of Obsession (David Baker), 96 n. 1
In a Cold Crater (Wolfgang Schivelbusch) 178 n. 18
In de naam van de vader en de zoon (Tom Lanoye), 212, 217
Intérprete de Hamlet, El (Antoni Bulbena i Tosell), 183
Ionesco, Eugène, 237
Irving, Henry, 154

Jacquot, Jean, 165
Jakobson, Roman, 119
James, Henry, 44
Jardine, Lisa, 98
Jarry, Alfred, 237
Jean sans terre ou la mort d'Arthur. See *King John*
John, Saint, 73
Johnson, Samuel, 55
Johst, Hans, 90
Josué, Ito, 233
Jouvet, Louis, 232
Jowet, Benjamin, 135
Julius Caesar (William Shakespeare), 27, 35, 101, 228, 231
Jusic, Ibriça, 71
Juvenel de Carlencas, Félix, 57

Kaminski, Jan Nepomucen, 20, 63–65
Kavafis, Konstantin, 220
Kean ou désordre et génie (Alexandre Dumas, père), 227
Kellner, Leon, 74
Kemble, Charles, 226
Kennedy, Dennis, 8, 17, 22, 31
Kennedy, John, 167
King John (William Shakespeare), 226, 228, 233
King Lear (William Shakespeare), 33, 35, 60, 63, 64, 68, 73, 74, 175–76, 183, 211, 226, 228, 231, 234
Kirsch, Rainer, 79
Kláterský, Antonín, 134
Klein, Holger, 18, 119

Knight, G. Wilson, 44, 91, 92, 93, 94, 95, 96
Kohl, Helmut, 201
Kokkos, Yannis, 234
Kosintzev, Grigory, 104
Kossakowski, Józef, 62
Kott, Jan, 102, 104, 174–76, 215
Kotzebue, August von, 64
Kraus, Karl, 74

Lacroix, Albert, 125
La Harpe, Jean-François, 68
Lamb, Charles, 33
Lambert, José, 32
Landauer, Gustav, 73
Langhoff, Matthias, 234
Lanoye, Tom, 23, 84, 119, 212–220
La Place, Pierre-Antoine de, 180, 225, 233
Latorre, Carlos, 45
Lavaudant, Georges, 233, 234, 238
Lawlor, John, 126
Leal, Milagros, 186
Le Carré, John, 173
Ledebur, Ruth von, 30
Lee, Sir Sidney, 44
Lentino, Giacomo da, 136
Lessing, Gotthold Ephraim, 20, 58–59, 65, 169
Lester, Adrian, 236
Le Tourneur, Pierre, 225, 228
Lettres philosophiques (Voltaire), 58, 66
Letzten Tage der Menschheit, Die (Karl Kraus), 74
Levin, Yuri, 15
LeWinter, Oswald, 28–29
Liebe und Freiheit (Robert Burns), 87 n. 23
"Lili Marleen." 77
Loewen, Johann Friedrich, 58
Looking at Shakespeare (Dennis Kennedy), 31
Lope de Vega, Félix, 50
López-Ballesteros, Luis, 183
Loti, Pierre, 231
Lubimov, Yuy, 105
Lubomiv, Daniel, 21
Luca de Tena, Cayetano, 22, 186–88
Lugné-Poe, Aurélien, 230–31, 237, 238

Luís of Portugal, King. *See* Bragança, D. Luís de

Macbeth (William Shakespeare), 35, 47, 64, 68, 71, 181, 226–28, 233, 234, 237
Macbett (Eugène Ionesco), 237
Macek, Miroslav, 134
Mácha, Karel Hynek, 141
"Macpherson's Farewell" (Robert Burns), 78
Maeterlinck, Maurice, 230
Mahood, Molly, 124
Máiquez, Isidoro, 181
Máj (Karel Hynek Mácha), 141
Making of the National Poet, The (Michael Dobson), 18
Mallarmé, Stéphane, 228
Mao Tse-Tung, 167
Margaretha di Napoli (Tom Lanoye), 212, 214, 216, 219
Marín, Guillermo, 187
Marlowe, Christopher, 47
Marreca, António de Oliveira, 148
Marshall, George, 166
Marsillach, Adolfo, 186, 189, 192
Martínez, Salvador, 188
McCarthy, Joseph, 167
Measure for Measure (William Shakespeare), 228, 230, 233, 235, 236, 237
Meisel, Harry, 76
Memoirs (Wojciech Bogusławski), 62
Mendelssohn, Felix, 170
Mephisto ist müde (ed. Lothar Schöne), 204
Merchant of Venice, The (William Shakespeare), 22, 35, 146–57, 183, 231, 235
Mercier, Louis, 62
Merino, Vicente, 180
Merry Wives of Windsor, The (William Shakespeare), 233
Mesguich, Daniel, 234, 238
Mesquita, Filomena, 8, 22
Metamorphoses (Ovid), 135
Michaëlis de Vasconcelos, Carolina, 145, 149
Michelsen, Peter, 33
Mickiewicz, Adam, 67
Middleton, Thomas, 47
Midsummer Night's Dream, A (William Shakespeare), 34, 170, 183, 208, 230, 232, 233, 235–37
Milla, Fernando de la, 185
Milton, John, 26
Mnouchkine, Ariane, 176, 235, 238
Moix, Terenci, 190
Molière (Jean-Baptiste Poquelin), 64, 66, 169
Molina, Tirso de, 50
Molina Foix, Vicente, 191, 193
Monanieba (dir. Tengiz Abuladze), 85
Monitor, 55–58
"Monsieur de Voltaire *vs.* Billy the Kid" (Klaus Peter Steiger), 29
Monstres de Vérone ou Le Moine et la Nourrice, Les (Marie Ordinis), 237
Moratín, Leandro Fernández de. *See* Fernández de Moratín, Leandro
More de Venise, Le (Alfred de Vigny), 227
Moreno, Armando, 188
Morte de César, La (Voltaire), 224
Mosley, Oswald, 90–91, 95
Mounet-Sully, 228, 229
Much Ado about Nothing (William Shakespeare), 226
Muntadas, Juan Federico, 46
Musset, Alfred de, 229
Mussolini, Benito, 20

Nahon, Alice, 220
Nathan the Wise (Gotthold Ephraim Lessing), 169
Naturalisme au théâtre, Le" (Emile Zola), 231
Neue Drama, Das (*Un drama nuevo,* Manuel Tamayo y Baus), 53 n. 12
Neue Probstücke (Simon Grynäus), 26
New Accents, 127
New Companion to Shakespeare Studies, A (ed. Kenneth Muir and S. Schoenbaum), 125
New Drama, A (Un drama nuevo, Manuel Tamayo y Baus), 53 n. 12
New Unhappy Lords, The (A. K. Chesterton), 95
Niemcewicz, Jan Ursyn, 57
Nightingale, Benedict, 199
Nixon, Richard, 167
Nodier, Charles, 67

Nouvelle Revue, La (Aurélien Lugné-Poe), 230
Novelli, Ermete, 182
Nunn, Trevor, 202

"Oh wert thou in the cauld blast" (Robert Burns), 78
O Judeu (Luís Maria Bordalo), 155
O Judeu: Romance histórico (Camilo Castelo Branco), 155
O mercador de Veneza (D. Luís de Bragança), 150
O mercador de Veneza (Bulhão Pato), 150
Oliva, César, 186
Oliveira Marreca, António de. *See* Marreca, António de Oliveira
Olivier, Laurence, 188, 189, 192
"On the Illusion and the Imagination" (Samuel Johnson), 55
"On the Tragedies of Shakespeare" (Charles Lamb), 33
Oppenheimer, Robert, 167
Ordinis, Marie, 237
Ordnung im Spiegel (Rainer Kirsch), 79
Orduña, Luis, 186
Orff, Carl, 170
Osinski, Ludwik, 66, 67
Othello (William Shakespeare), 35, 46, 48, 65, 68, 181, 183, 224, 226, 228
Otro William, El (Jaime Salom), 20, 51
Ovid (Publius Ovidius Naso, 43 B.C.–A.D. 17), 9, 135, 136, 224

Painting Shakespeare Red (ed. Boika Sokolova and Alexander Shurbanov), 99
Panna na wydaniu (Prince Czartoryski), 57
Panova, Snezhina, 106
Par, Alfonso, 45, 183
Paradise Regained (John Milton), 26
Paris Gazette. See *Exile*
Partridge, Eric, 124
Pasternak, Boris, 77
Pato, Bulhão, 22, 145, 147–56
Pavis, Patrice, 200
Pechter, Edward, 30
Pecorone, Il (Ser Giovanni), 149
Peduzzi, Richard, 234

Pemán, José María, 186–88, 193
Perceval, Luk, 23, 84, 119, 212–20
Pericles (William Shakespeare), 233
Petrarch (Francesco Petrarca), 136
Pfister, Manfred, 8, 20
Phantome (Charles Nodier), 67
Piachaud, René-Louis, 232
Pinheiro, Rafael Bordalo, 146
Pixérécourt, René-Charles de, 64
Planchon, Roger, 171, 233, 238
Plato (?428–?348 B.C.), 135
Platter, Thomas, 27
Plaza, José Carlos, 23, 191
Plutarch (A.D. 46–?120), 224
Poel, William, 230
"Poet and Immortality, The" (G. Wilson Knight), 92
Poetics (Aristotle), 223
Poniatowski, Stanislaw August, 55
Portillo, Rafael, 22–23
Portugal, King D. Luís of. *See* Bragança, D. Luís de
Preface (Samuel Johnson), 55
Prefaces to Shakespeare (Harley Granville-Barker), 33
Prévert, Jacques, 236
Princesse Maleine, La (Maurice Maeterlinck), 230
Príncipe Hamlet, El (Carlos Coello), 183
Pronko, Leonard, 19
Pujante, A. Luis, 7, 182, 192, 193
Pushkin, Alexander, 100

Racine, Jean, 67–68, 224, 230
Racine et Shakespeare (Stendhal), 226
Ralegh, Sir Walter, 78
Ralli, Augustus, 28
Rassov, Gabor, 237
Réflections critiques (Jean-Baptiste Debos), 57
Reichert, Klaus, 84
Reinventing Shakespeare (Gary Taylor), 31
Remarque, Erich Maria, 92
Repentance. See *Monanieba*
Reservoir Dogs (dir. Quentin Tarantino), 220
Revelation (St. John), 73
Revue Indépendante, La (Stéphane Mallarmé), 228

Richaar Deuzième (Tom Lanoye), 212, 214, 217
Richard II (William Shakespeare), 22, 164–65, 182, 213, 214, 215, 219, 233, 234, 235
Richard III (William Shakespeare), 45, 182, 183, 212, 215, 228, 233, 234, 237
Risjaar Modderfokker den Derde (Tom Lanoye), 215
Ristori, Adelaida, 182
Rivas, Emilio, 190
Robbers, The (Friedrich von Schiller), 64
Robert, Clemence, 46
Robertson, J. G., 28, 29
Rochel, Polonia, 180
Rodin, Auguste, 187
Rojas, Agustín de, 190
Rollins, Hyder E., 73
Romantic Cult of Shakespeare, The (Péter Dávidházi), 18
Romea, Julián, 45
Romeo and Juliet (William Shakespeare), 26, 34, 35, 62, 63, 183, 226, 228, 235, 236
Romm, Mikhail, 100
Roper, Derek, 29
Rossi, Ernesto, 181, 182
Rossini, Giacomo, 182
Rouget de Lisle, Claude-Joseph, 227
Ryan, Kiernan, 104
Rylance, Mark, 101

Sainte-Croix, Camille de, 231
Salazar, António de Oliveira, 20
Sallent, Joan, 192
Salom, Jaime, 20, 50–51
Salvador, Mercedes, 22–23
Sánchez, Alberto, 49
Santacana, Juan, 22, 185
Sardou, Victorien, 229
Sartre, Jean-Paul, 164
Satires (Edward Young), 26
Saunders, Frances Stonor, 173
Schernikau, Ronald M., 80
Schiller, Friedrich von, 64, 68, 170
Schivelbusch, Wolfgang, 169
Schlachten! See *Ten Oorlog*
Schlegel, August Wilhelm von, 20, 62, 67–68, 149

Schoenbaum, Samuel, 34
School for Wives (Molière), 169
Schrijverke (Guido Gezelle), 220
Schröder, F. L., 54, 59, 60, 61, 62, 63, 64, 65
Schuenke, Christa, 79
Schwartz-Gastine, Isabelle, 23
Schwob, Marcel, 229
Seasons, The (James Thomson), 26
Seco, Carmen, 184
Seide, Stuart, 236, 238
Sellner, Gustav Rudolf, 170
Sémiramis (Voltaire), 224
Shaitanov, Igor, 85
Shakespeare (Julius Bab), 86 n. 10
Shakespeare (Kiernan Ryan), 108 n. 6
Shakespeare amoureux (Alexandre Duval), 44, 182, 226
Shakespeare-Bild in Europa, Das (Roger Bauer), 29
Shakespearean Constitutions (Jonathan Bate), 18
Shakespeare and Eastern Europe (Zdeněk Stříbrný), 18
Shakespeare and the Popular Tradition (Robert Weimann), 103, 171
Shakespearean Tragedy (A. C. Bradley), 33
Shakespeare Bulletin, 19
Shakespeare East and West (ed. Minoru Fujita and Leonard Pronko), 19
Shakespeare en España (Eduardo Juliá), 39 n. 43
Shakespeare en la literatura española (Alfonso Par), 45
Shakespeare enamorado (Ventura de la Vega), 20, 44–45, 182
Shakespeare First Folio, The (W. W. Greg), 33
Shakespeare in Europe (ed. Oswald LeWinter), 28
Shakespeare in Love, 34, 44, 70
Shakespeare in the New Europe (ed. Michael Hattaway, Boika Sokolova, and Derek Roper), 16, 29, 116
Shakespeare on the German Stage (Wilhelm Hortmann), 18, 31
Shakespeare Our Contemporary (Jan Kott), 102, 174
Shakespeare Review (ed. A. K. Chesterton), 21, 89, 90, 91, 92, 96

INDEX

Shakespeare's America / America's Shakespeare (Michael Bristol), 18
"Shakespeare sans décor" (Aurélien Lugné-Poe)
Shakespeare's Caliban: A Cultural History (Alden T. Vaughan and Virginia Mason Vaughan), 128
"Shakespeare's Detachment and Modern Progress" (A. K. Chesterton), 92
Shakespeare's Lives (Samuel Schoenbaum), 34
Shakespeares Sechsundsechzig (ed. Ulrich Erckenbrecht), 86n. 14
Shakespeare Survey, 116
Shakespeare: The Invention of the Human (Harold Bloom), 33
Shakespeare Trade, The (Barbara Hodgdon), 31
Shakespeare Translation (see also *Shakespeare Worldwide*), 125
Shakespeare und die Tradition des Volkstheaters (Robert Weimann), 103, 171
"Shakespeare und kein Ende" (Johann Wolfgang von Goethe), 60
Shakespeare Worldwide (see also *Shakespeare Translation)*, 125
Shakespeare Yearbook (ed. Holger Klein), 18
Shaw, George Bernard, 92
Shaw, Patricia, 30, 35
Shevardnadze, Edvard, 85
Shostakovich, Dmitri, 20, 77
Shurbanov, Alexander, 16, 99
Sidney, Sir Philip, 134
Sieffert, Peter, 202
Silva, Eric da, 238
Silva, António José da, 155, 238
Simply Fascism (Mikhail Romm), 100
Six Romances after Raleigh, Burns, and Shakespeare (Dmitri Shostakovich), 77
Slowacki, Juliusz, 67
Smidt, Kristian, 15
Smithson, Harriet, 226
Smoktunovskii, Innokentii, 104
Snoek, Paul, 220
Sobel, Bernard, 233
Sokolova, Boika, 16, 21, 29
Sokolyanski, Mark, 16
Soler, Father Gaietá, 183

Soler, Salvador, 186
Sonnets (William Shakespeare), 7, 22, 123
Sortilège des Gâtines, Le (W. and Y. Delporte), 237
Spectator, The, 32, 55
Staikova, Isabela, 82
Stalin, Joseph, 77, 167
Stanley, William, Earl of Derby, 51
Steiger, Klaus Peter, 29, 32
Stein, Stefan, 79
Stendhal (Henri Beyle), 226
Stone, Sharon, 207
Stoppard, Tom, 191
Stratford Herald, 21, 89, 90
Strehler, Giorgio, 165, 171, 172
Stříbrný, Zdeněk, 18
Sue, Eugène, 155
Suhamy, Henri, 238
Surrey, Earl of. *See* Howard, Henry
Svintilla, Vladimir, 82
Symposium (Plato), 135

Tabori, George, 207
Talma, François-Joseph, 181, 225–26
Tamayo, José (1800–73), 45
Tamayo, José (1920–), 186, 189
Tamayo y Baus, Manuel, 20, 22, 47–50, 51
Taming of the Shrew, The (William Shakespeare), 35, 182, 183, 232
Tarantino, Quentin, 214, 220
Tarlinskaja, Marina, 74
Tate, Nahum, 56
Taylor, Gary, 31
Taylor, John, 147
Taylor, Liz, 206
Tempera, Mariangela, 16
Tempest, The (William Shakespeare), 46, 94, 235, 236
Ten Oorlog (Tom Lanoye and Luc Perceval), 23, 84, 119, 211–21
That Was the Week that Was (Kenneth Tynan), 174
Théâtre anglois, Le (Pierre-Antoine de la Place), 225
Theatre of Cruelty, The (Antonin Artaud), 233
Thomas, Ambroise, 227
Thomas, Henri, 238
Thomson, James, 26

Tillyard, E. M. W., 44
Times, The (London), 98, 145, 199
Timon of Athens (William Shakespeare), 73, 74, 228, 236
Titus Andronicus (William Shakespeare), 235, 237
"To his Son" (Sir Walter Ralegh), 78
Tombs of Verona, The. See *Romeo and Juliet*
Tordesillas, Catalina, 180
Torquay Times, 90
Torres, Gloria, 188, 193
Traub, Valerie, 218–19
Troilus and Cressida (William Shakespeare), 23, 165, 196–208, 238
Trovatore, Il (Giuseppe Verdi), 85
Truman, Harry, 166
Tsankov, Vili, 21, 99, 106, 107
Twain, Mark, 44
Twelfth Night (William Shakespeare), 211, 232, 233, 235
Tynan, Kenneth, 174

Über dramatische Kunst und Literatur (August Wilhelm von Schlegel), 67
Ubu Roi (Alfred Jarry), 237
Ulloa, Alejandro, 186, 190
Unamuno, Miguel de, 50
Urbánková, Jarmila, 134

Valle-Inclán, Ramón María del, 50
Vanguardia Española, La, 189
Vega, Lope de. See Lope de Vega, Félix
Vega, Ventura de la, 44–45, 182
Vendler, Helen, 73
Venuti, Lawrence, 130
Verdad considerada como fuente de belleza, La (Manuel Tamayo y Baus), 50
Verdi, Giuseppe, 182
Vickers, Brian, 28
Vico, Antonio, 183
Vie criminelle de Richard III, La (Gabor Rassov), 237
Vigny, Alfred de, 227
Vilar, Jean, 163, 164, 170, 172, 233
Visconti, Luchino, 165
Visotsky, Vladimir, 105
Vitez, Antoine, 23, 233, 235
Vittoz, Michel, 234

Vladislav, Jan, 134, 140–41
Voltaire (François-Marie Arouet), 29, 32, 58, 65, 66, 224, 238

Waiting Room (Lion Feuchtwanger), 75
Wandering Jew, The (Eugène Sue), 155
Wangenheim, Gustav von, 169, 171
Warburton, William, 151
Wartesaal. See *Waiting Room*
Weimann, Robert, 103, 104, 171
Wells, Stanley, 98, 99
What Was Shakespeare (Edward Pechter), 30
White, Graham, 20
Who Paid the Piper? (Frances Stonor Saunders), 173
Wieland, Christoph Martin, 27, 59
Willems, Michèle, 31
William Shakespeare (Victor Hugo), 229
Wilson, John Dover, 124
Wilson, Richard, 44
Wilson, Thomas, 135
Windross, Michael, 29, 31
Winter's Tale, The (William Shakespeare), 232, 235
Witt, Hubert, 79, 80
Wójcicki, K. W., 68
Wordsworth, William, 30
Wyatt, Sir Thomas, 136

Xirgu, Margarita, 188, 193

Young, Edward, 26

Zacconi, Ermete, 182
Zaïre (Voltaire), 65, 224
Zeffirelli, Franco, 165
Zemin, Jiang, 100
Zie de dienstmaagd des Heren (Tom Lanoye), 212
Zola, Émile, 231
Zorrilla, José, 184
Zschokke, Heinrich, 64
Zuloaga, Ignacio, 188
Zumel, Enrique, 46, 51
"Zum Shakespears Tag" (Johann Wolfgang von Goethe), 60
Żurowski, Andrzej, 64
Zysset, Sylvia, 23